Lecture Notes in Business Information Processing   557

Series Editors

Wil van der Aalst ⓘ, *RWTH Aachen University, Aachen, Germany*
Sudha Ram ⓘ, *University of Arizona, Tucson, USA*
Michael Rosemann ⓘ, *Queensland University of Technology, Brisbane, Australia*
Clemens Szyperski, *Microsoft Research, Redmond, USA*
Giancarlo Guizzardi ⓘ, *University of Twente, Enschede, The Netherlands*

LNBIP reports state-of-the-art results in areas related to business information systems and industrial application software development – timely, at a high level, and in both printed and electronic form.

The type of material published includes

- Proceedings (published in time for the respective event)
- Postproceedings (consisting of thoroughly revised and/or extended final papers)
- Other edited monographs (such as, for example, project reports or invited volumes)
- Tutorials (coherently integrated collections of lectures given at advanced courses, seminars, schools, etc.)
- Award-winning or exceptional theses

LNBIP is abstracted/indexed in DBLP, EI and Scopus. LNBIP volumes are also submitted for the inclusion in ISI Proceedings.

Luise Pufahl · Kristina Rosenthal ·
Sergio España · Selmin Nurcan
Editors

Intelligent Information Systems

CAiSE 2025 Forum and Doctoral Consortium
Vienna, Austria, June 16–20, 2025
Proceedings

Editors
Luise Pufahl ⓘ
Technische Universität München
Heilbronn, Baden-Württemberg, Germany

Kristina Rosenthal ⓘ
Hochschule Niederrhein
Mönchengladbach, Germany

Sergio España ⓘ
Utrecht University
Utrecht, The Netherlands

Selmin Nurcan ⓘ
Université Paris 1, Panthéon - Sorbonne
Paris, France

ISSN 1865-1348   ISSN 1865-1356 (electronic)
Lecture Notes in Business Information Processing
ISBN 978-3-031-94589-2   ISBN 978-3-031-94590-8 (eBook)
https://doi.org/10.1007/978-3-031-94590-8

© The Editor(s) (if applicable) and The Author(s), under exclusive license
to Springer Nature Switzerland AG 2025, corrected publication 2025

This work is subject to copyright. All rights are solely and exclusively licensed by the Publisher, whether the whole or part of the material is concerned, specifically the rights of translation, reprinting, reuse of illustrations, recitation, broadcasting, reproduction on microfilms or in any other physical way, and transmission or information storage and retrieval, electronic adaptation, computer software, or by similar or dissimilar methodology now known or hereafter developed.
The use of general descriptive names, registered names, trademarks, service marks, etc. in this publication does not imply, even in the absence of a specific statement, that such names are exempt from the relevant protective laws and regulations and therefore free for general use.
The publisher, the authors and the editors are safe to assume that the advice and information in this book are believed to be true and accurate at the date of publication. Neither the publisher nor the authors or the editors give a warranty, expressed or implied, with respect to the material contained herein or for any errors or omissions that may have been made. The publisher remains neutral with regard to jurisdictional claims in published maps and institutional affiliations.

This Springer imprint is published by the registered company Springer Nature Switzerland AG
The registered company address is: Gewerbestrasse 11, 6330 Cham, Switzerland

If disposing of this product, please recycle the paper.

Preface

This volume of the Lecture Notes on Business Information Processing (LNBIP) series contains the accepted papers of both the Forum and the Doctoral Consortium of the 37th International Conference on Advanced Information Systems Engineering – CAiSE 2025, held in Vienna, Austria, during June 16–20, 2025.

The CAiSE conference series was started in Sweden, and its first two editions were organized in Stockholm (1989 and 1990). Since then, it has been held in 21 countries, mostly in Europe but also in locations on other continents (Canada, Australia, and Tunisia). Despite its roots in Europe, soon after its inception, CAiSE became the flagship international conference on information systems engineering, attracting some of the most original and scientifically rigorous articles in the field. Furthermore, it has always been an attractive event for early-career researchers as well as practitioners. After almost four decades of continuous organization, CAiSE continues to attract articles that address fundamental and timeless problems in the field.

As a conference attuned to new theoretical and societal challenges, each year a new focal topic is chosen as the theme of the conference. CAiSE 2025 was organized with a special emphasis on the theme of **Bridging Silos**. Engineering real-world information systems requires a coherent design, encompassing human, organizational, economic, societal, and technological aspects. Information systems are utilized in increasingly diverse contexts such as business process management, geographical information systems, and digital twins. At the same time, the discipline continually evolves with trends in data science, machine learning, process mining, blockchain, mobile computing, sustainability, new regulations, cyber warfare, and military conflicts all influencing its development. Each application context and emerging trend can lead to specializations within information systems engineering, necessitating various research traditions and needs. While beneficial, these specializations risk creating silos within the field of information systems engineering. The CAiSE conference series, the premier event for this discipline, aims to prevent such fragmentation.

April 2025

Gerti Kappel
Henderik A. Proper

Preface CAiSE 2025 Forum

The CAiSE conference series as a flagship international conference on information systems engineering provides a platform for exchanging experiences, research results, and ideas between academia and industry. The conference serves as the annual worldwide meeting point for the community of information system engineers. The 37th edition of the CAiSE conference was held in Vienna, Austria, June 16–20, 2025. This conference edition put a special emphasis on the theme "Bridging Silos", which means to consider information systems engineering as a cohesive design involving human, organizational, economic, societal, and technological aspects. The Forum session facilitates the interaction, discussion, and exchange of ideas among presenters and participants. Similarly to other recent Forum editions, two types of submissions were considered in 2025:

- Visionary papers that present innovative research projects which are still at a relatively early stage and do not necessarily include a full-scale validation.
- Demo papers that describe innovative tools and prototypes implementing the results of research efforts.

The Forum received 23 submissions. Additionally, 15 submissions were redirected to the Forum from the CAiSE main research track, and had already undergone the peer review process of the conference. The other submissions were reviewed by three Forum PC members in a single-blind review process. The submissions that achieved the highest consensus on novelty and rigor were accepted for presentation at the Forum. Out of the 23 regular submissions, 11 papers were accepted. Altogether, 26 papers were presented at the CAiSE 2025 Forum, which include 20 vision papers and six tool demonstrations.

We want to thank all the contributors to the success of the CAiSE 2025 Forum: We are grateful to the authors for submitting and presenting their research and to the reviewers for ensuring the quality of the research presented and discussed at the CAiSE Forum. We further thank the General Chairs, the Program Chairs of the main conference, the Organization Chair, and the Proceedings Chair for their support in coordinating the Forum organization.

June 2025

Luise Pufahl
Kristina Rosenthal

Organization

Chairs

Kristina Rosenthal — Niederrhein University of Applied Sciences, Germany
Luise Pufahl — Technical University of Munich, Germany

Program Committee

Sybren De Kinderen — Eindhoven University of Technology, The Netherlands
Agnes Koschmider — University of Bayreuth, Germany
Drazen Brdjanin — University of Banja Luka, Republic of Srpska
Jose Ignacio Panach Navarrete — Universitat de València, Spain
Cinzia Cappiello — Politecnico di Milano, Italy
Martin Henkel — Stockholm University, Sweden
Stefan Strecker — University of Hagen, Germany
Hans-Georg Fill — University of Fribourg, Switzerland
Jānis Grabis — Riga Technical University, Latvia
Abel Armas Cervantes — University of Melbourne, Australia
Yves Wautelet — KU Leuven, Belgium
Andrea Marrella — Sapienza University of Rome, Italy
Evangelia Kavakli — University of the Aegean, Greece
Michael Fellmann — University of Rostock, Germany
Mohamad Gharib — University of Tartu, Estonia
Irene Vanderfeesten — KU Leuven, Belgium
Oscar Pastor — Universidad Politécnica de Valencia, Spain
Manuel Wimmer — Johannes Kepler University Linz, Austria
Raimundas Matulevicius — University of Tartu, Estonia
Henrik Leopold — Kühne Logistics University, Germany
Tony Clark — Aston University, UK
Cristina Cabanillas — University of Seville, Spain
Manuel Resinas — University of Seville, Spain
Marite Kirikova — Riga Technical University, Latvia
Elena Kornyshova — Conservatoire National des Arts et Métiers, France
Patricia Martin-Rodilla — Spanish National Research Council, Spain

Simon Hacks   Stockholm University, Sweden
Sergio de Cesare   University of Westminster, UK
Jānis Kampars   Riga Technical University, Latvia
Hans Weigand   Tilburg University, The Netherlands
Chung Lawrence   University of Texas at Dallas, USA
Sérgio Guerreiro   INESC-ID/University of Lisbon, Portugal
Steven Alter   University of San Francisco, USA
Ben Roelens   Open Universiteit, Ghent University, Belgium
Janne J. Korhonen   Aalto University, Finland
Mattia Salnitri   University of Bergamo, Italy
Christophe Feltus   Luxembourg Institute of Science and Technology, Luxembourg
Maya Daneva   University of Twente, The Netherlands

Additional Reviewers

Thomas Ricardo Pathe
Marcel Bühlmann
Simon Curty
Bastian Kres
Philip Winkler
Dominik Janssen
Alberto Gaspar
Gkiorgki Georgiou
Moayad Almohaishi

Preface CAISE 2025 Doctoral Consortium

This volume contains the accepted papers presented at the Doctoral Consortium held in conjunction with the 37th International Conference on Advanced Information Systems Engineering (CAiSE 2025). The CAiSE 2025 conference took place in Vienna, Austria, from June 16 to 20, 2025, under the theme "Bridging Silos". In line with the tradition of the CAiSE conference series, the Doctoral Consortium aimed to attract PhD candidates working on foundations, techniques, tools, and applications in the Information Systems Engineering field. It provided a supportive environment for these candidates to present their research, receive constructive feedback from peers and senior faculty, and engage in discussions tailored to their needs and interests.

The CAiSE 2025 Doctoral Consortium received a total of 27 submissions, of which 12 were accepted for presentation and inclusion in these proceedings. The review process was single blind, with each submission being reviewed by at least two senior researchers from the Doctoral Consortium Mentoring Board. The main evaluation criteria included relevance, originality, significance, technical soundness, accuracy, clarity, and the expected benefits to the PhD candidate from participating in the Doctoral Consortium.

The accepted papers cover several topics within the scope of the conference and are structured in four sessions, having three papers each. Within the **Enterprise Architecture** session, Jan Schoonderbeek's research concerns the topic of managing the quality of Enterprise Architecture models, building upon ontology development. Sefanja Severin focuses on a method for designing consistent business capability models by aligning value streams, capabilities, and information concepts. Andrei Chiş proposes a modelling method and architectural proposition for operationalizing the Work Systems Framework using knowledge engineering and large language models. Within the **Digital Transformation** session, Xavier Portell presents an ongoing action-research project aimed at digitally enhancing occupational health and safety services for healthcare workers at a non-profit organisation using enterprise modelling, architecture, and information systems strategic planning. Mathis Wyffels examines the integration of real-time worker wellbeing in IoT-enhanced process orchestration within a manufacturing setting. Vjatšeslav Antipenko's research proposes a function-driven approach to security in automated manufacturing. Within the **LLM for Business Process Modelling** session, Angelo Casciani investigates the integration of LLMs and symbolic reasoning for framed autonomy in AI-augmented business process management. Luca Franziska Hörner's work explores a research approach and preliminary results towards an LLM-based conversational framework for business process modelling. Maximilian Möller's research aims to understand the comprehensibility of process models created manually, automatically by LLMs, or semi-automatically. Within the **Software Engineering** session, Susel María Matos Claro's work explores the generation of user interfaces for different contexts of use from conceptual models, potentially using model-driven engineering and low-code/no-code approaches. Robin D. Pesl analyses the adoption of

Large Language Models for automated system integration using service documentation. Yaimara Granada Hondares's research addresses the challenges and opportunities in bridging agile software development and modelling practices, discussing preliminary results from a survey on practitioners' perception. These papers highlight the diverse research being conducted within the Information Systems Engineering field, aligning with the CAiSE 2025 theme of "Bridging Silos".

Participation in the Doctoral Consortium offered PhD candidates the opportunity to receive constructive and personalised feedback from dedicated mentors, to interact with established researchers and practitioners, and to develop a supportive community of peer scholars. Furthermore, participants become eligible to apply for the "CAISE PhD Award" after their thesis has been defended.

We would like to express our gratitude to the CAiSE 2025 General Chairs, Gerti Kappe and Henderik A. Proper, and the Organization Chair, Dominik Bork, for their support. We are also grateful to the members of the Mentoring Board for their invaluable time and expertise in reviewing the submissions and providing guidance to the students. Finally, we thank all the PhD candidates for their contributions and active participation. We are confident that they have a successful career ahead of them.

April 2025

Selmin Nurcan
Sergio España

Organization

Chairs

Selmin Nurcan — Université Paris 1 Panthéon-Sorbonne, France
Sergio España — Universitat Politècnica de València, Spain

Doctoral Consortium Mentoring Board

Saïd Assar	Institut Mines-Télécom Business School, France
Fabiano Dalpiaz	Utrecht University, The Netherlands
Xavier Franch	Universitat Politècnica de Catalunya, Spain
Renata Guizzardi	University of Twente, The Netherlands
Sander J.J. Leemans	RWTH Aachen, Germany
Andrea Marrella	Sapienza University of Rome, Italy
Raimundas Matulevičius	University of Tartu, Estonia
Massimo Mecella	Sapienza University of Rome, Italy
Jan Mendling	Vienna University of Economics and Business, Austria
Giovanni Meroni	Technical University of Denmark, Denmark
Haralambos Mouratidis	University of Essex, UK
Óscar Pastor	Universitat Politècnica de València, Spain
Barbara Pernici	Politecnico di Milano, Italy
Pierluigi Plebani	Politecnico di Milano, Italy
Jolita Ralyte	University of Geneva, Switzerland
Manfred Reichert	University of Ulm, Germany
Hajo Reijers	Utrecht University, The Netherlands
Shazia Sadiq	University of Queensland, Australia
Kurt Sandkuhl	University of Rostock, Germany
Maribel Yasmina Santos	University of Minho, Portugal
Monique Snoeck	KU Leuven, Belgium
Pnina Soffer	University of Haifa, Israel
Janis Stirna	Stockholm University, Sweden
Arnon Sturm	Ben-Gurion University of the Negev, Israel
Dimitri Van Landuyt	KU Leuven, Belgium
Mathias Weske	University of Potsdam, Germany
Jelena Zdravkovic	Stockholm University, Sweden

Contents

CAiSE 2025 Forum – Vision Papers

Towards the Interoperability of Low-Code Platforms 3
    Iván Alfonso, Aaron Conrardy, and Jordi Cabot

The Work System Perspective as a Nexus Between Silos in IS Modeling
and Between Rigor and Broad Usability 12
    Steven Alter

Leveraging Profiling to Bridge Healthcare Silos for Federated Analyses 20
    Nelly Barret, Anna Bernasconi, Cinzia Cappiello, Giacomo Palu, and Pietro Pinoli

Lost in Models? Structuring Managerial Decision Support in Process
Mining with Multi-criteria Decision Making 29
    Rob H. Bemthuis

From Words to Workflows: Extracting Object-Centric Event Logs
from Textual Data 37
    Alina Buss, Christoph Kecht, Wolfgang Kratsch, Maximilian Röglinger, Sareh Sadeghianasl, and Moe T. Wynn

WSF4ADO: An ADOxx Deployment of the Work Systems Framework 45
    Andrei Chiş, Ana-Maria Ghiran, and Robert Andrei Buchmann

Robotic Datasets for Process Mining 53
    Flavio Corradini, Sara Pettinari, Barbara Re, Lorenzo Rossi, and Massimiliano Sampaolo

Automated Business Process Analysis: An LLM-Based Approach to Value
Assessment 62
    William De Michele, Abel Armas Cervantes, and Lea Frermann

Humidor: A Zero-Shot LLM Approach for Cumulative Knowledge
Building in Design Science Research 70
    Oscar Díaz, Xabier Garmendia, and Martin Horsfield

Trust Paradoxes in Machine Learning: An Ontological Approach 78
    Yuntian Ding, Nicolas Herbaut, and Camille Salinesi

Conceptualizing Business Process Dependencies That Propagate Cyber
Risk 86
    Gal Engelberg, Moshe Hadad, and Pnina Soffer

Towards a Data Satellite Architecture for Federated Digital Ecosystems:
Combating Data Pollution and Enhancing Trustworthiness 95
    Asif Qumer Gill and Anastasija Nikiforova

Towards an Ontology for Representing Time Series Knowledge:
Motivation, Requirements and Concept 103
    Alexander Graß, Rohit A. Deshmukh, Christian Beecks,
    and Stefan Decker

OLAP Operations for Object-Centric Process Mining 111
    Shahrzad Khayatbashi, Najmeh Miri, and Amin Jalali

Goal-Oriented Process Monitoring: An Artifact-Driven Monitoring
Extension 119
    Giovanni Meroni and Rik Eshuis

LLM4Model: Automated Requirements Specification Model Authoring 128
    Asha Rajbhoj, Akanksha Somase, Tanay Sant, Sushant Vale,
    and Vinay Kulkarni

A Pattern-Based Approach for Explaining Ontology-Driven Conceptual
Models 137
    Elena Romanenko, Diego Calvanese, and Giancarlo Guizzardi

Towards an AI-Agent-Based Framework for Agile Business Process
Management 145
    Lala Aïcha Sarr, Komlan Ayite, Anne-Marie Barthe-Delanoë,
    Dominik Bork, Guillaume Macé-Ramète, and Frédérick Bénaben

Studying Workarounds in Software Forms: An Experimental Protocol 153
    MohammadAmin Zaheri, Michalis Famelis, and Eugene Syriani

Pondering on Capability Brokering with LLM 161
    Jelena Zdravkovic, Janis Stirna, and Chen Hsi Tsai

CAiSE 2025 Forum – Tool Papers

MARTSIA: A Tool for Confidential Data Exchange via Public Blockchain 173
    Michele Kryston, Edoardo Marangone, Claudio Di Ciccio,
    Daniele Friolo, Eugenio Nerio Nemmi, Mattia Samory, Michele Spina,
    Daniele Venturi, and Ingo Weber

AOAME: An Enterprise Knowledge Graphs Editor for Domain Experts 181
  Emanuele Laurenzi

OpenBPT: An Extensible Platform for Conceptual Modeling and Analysis 189
  *Tom Lichtenstein, Maximilian König, Maximilian Körner, Anjo Seidel,
  Arsalan Ghasemi, and Mathias Weske*

SecBPMN2BC Online Editor: A Web-Based Tool for Designing Secure
Business Processes on Blockchains 197
  Giovanni Meroni, Anders Dalskov, and Alex Norta

A3S3 - Automated Android Audit of Safety and Security Signals 205
  Guillaume Nguyen and Xavier Devroey

FIREPRIME App: A Self-assessment Tool to Evaluate Home Risk
to Wildfires 213
  Marc Oriol, Lidia López, Huihui Xu, and Xavier Franch

Doctoral Consortium – Enterprise Architecture

Toward Improving the Quality of Enterprise Architecture Models 223
  Jan Schoonderbeek

Designing Consistent Business Capability Models: A Method for Aligning
Value Streams, Capabilities, and Information Concepts 231
  Sefanja Severin

A Modeling Method for Work Systems Knowledge Capture
and Traceability 239
  Andrei Chiş

CAiSE 2025 Doctoral Consortium – Digital Transformation

Enhancing Occupational Health and Safety for Healthcare Workers
Through Digital Innovation 249
  Xavier Portell

Integrating Real-Time Worker Wellbeing into IoT-Enhanced Business
Process Orchestration for Industry 5.0 257
  Mathis Wyffels

Security in Automated Manufacturing: A Function-Driven Approach 267
  Vjatšeslav Antipenko

CAiSE 2025 Doctoral Consortium – LLM for Business Process Modelling

Integrating LLMs and Symbolic Reasoning for Framed Autonomy in AI-Augmented Business Process Management 277
  Angelo Casciani

Towards an LLM-Based Conversational Framework for Business Process Modeling: Research Approach and Preliminary Results 286
  Luca Franziska Hörner

Towards the Comprehensibility of Manually, Automatically, and Semi-automatically Created Process Models: A Conceptual Framework ... 294
  Maximilian Möller

CAiSE 2025 Doctoral Consortium – Software Engineering

Generation of User Interfaces for Different Context of Use from Conceptual Models 305
  Susel María Matos Claro

Adopting Large Language Models to Automated System Integration 313
  Robin D. Pesl

Bridging Agile Software Development and Modeling 321
  Yaimara Granados Hondares

Correction to: Pondering on Capability Brokering with LLM C1
  Jelena Zdravkovic, Janis Stirna, and Chen Hsi Tsai

Author Index 329

CAiSE 2025 Forum – Vision Papers

Towards the Interoperability of Low-Code Platforms

Iván Alfonso[1]($\boxtimes$), Aaron Conrardy[1,2], and Jordi Cabot[1,2]

[1] Luxembourg Institute of Science and Technology, Esch-sur-Alzette, Luxembourg
{ivan.alfonso,aaron.conrardy,jordi.cabot}@list.lu
[2] University of Luxembourg, Esch-sur-Alzette, Luxembourg

Abstract. With the promise of accelerating software development, low-code platforms (LCPs) are becoming popular across various industries. Nevertheless, there are still barriers hindering their adoption. Among them, vendor lock-in is a major concern, especially considering the lack of interoperability between these platforms. Typically, after modeling an application in one LCP, migrating to another requires starting from scratch remodeling everything (the data model, the graphical user interface, workflows, etc.) in the new platform. To overcome this situation, this work proposes an approach to improve the interoperability of LCPs by (semi)automatically migrating models specified in one platform to another one. Migration is performed via a combination of rule-based and LLM-based strategies. The pipelines are built on the BESSER framework, serving as a pivot between the LCPs.

Keywords: Low-code · Interoperability · Data model · Vendor lock-in

1 Introduction

Model-driven approaches, such as model-driven engineering (MDE), aim to streamline and optimize the delivery of applications from design through development, deployment, and operation by leveraging models at different levels of abstraction [5]. Building on these concepts, the term low-code has become popular in the software industry. Low-code can be seen as a pragmatic style of model-based approaches, where a fixed and reduced number of model types are used together to model the system-to-be followed by a direct transformation of those models into the running system [8]. Low-code platforms (LCPs) usually provide three types of (mostly graphical) modeling sublanguages: a data modeling language, a user interface (UI) language and a behavioural language linking the two, i.e. stating what actions (e.g. CRUD operations) on the data model should be triggered based on a UI event.

Analyses of the current market, such as Gartner's Magic Quadrant [12], position LCPs as market leaders, such as Mendix, OutSystems, and PowerApps. Unfortunately, all major players are commercial products with limited import

---

I. Alfonso and A. Conrardy—These authors contributed equally to this work.

© The Author(s), under exclusive license to Springer Nature Switzerland AG 2025
L. Pufahl et al. (Eds.): CAiSE 2025, LNBIP 557, pp. 3–11, 2025.
https://doi.org/10.1007/978-3-031-94590-8_1

and export capabilities creating a vendor lock-in effect, which represents a significant risk for users and companies [3].

In this paper, we study the interoperability between the emergent market of low-code tools as it can have a significant impact in the adoption and long-term success of this new model-based style of software development.

We first analyze the current import/export options offered by major players in this market. Based on the identified limitations, we propose a model-based migration approach to enable interoperability among the leading LCPs. This model-based approach is enhanced with capabilities of visual large language models (LLMs) when needed.

The remainder of the paper is organized as follows. In Sect. 2, we perform the interoperability analysis of LCPs. Section 3 presents our model-based migration solution. Section 4 presents the tool support. Finally, Sect. 5 reviews related work and Sect. 6 concludes the paper.

2 Evaluation of the Interoperability Among Low-Code Tools

Vendor lock-in usually appears as one of the most common barriers in the adoption of low-code tools [7,13]. Indeed, due to lack of interoperability among LCPs, when an application is developed on a specific LCP, migrating to another provider often requires redevelopment on the new platform.

Interoperability between two LCPs could be defined at the model or runtime level. The latter would imply that applications generated by one LCP could be executed on another LCP. The former implies that the model created in one LCP can be imported in another LCP to enable the generation of the application in that LCP without starting from scratch. We are interested in this second option as we do not consider the first one feasible given the different runtime libraries and dependencies employed by each LCP.

There is currently no study that focuses on the model import/export capabilities of LCPs that would enable their interoperability. Therefore, we have evaluated the LCPs that are defined as Leaders or Challengers by Gartner's magic quadrant [12], as these are supposed to be the most popular and complete ones. For each tool, we have evaluated the import and export capabilities for the three major types of models provided by each LCP and the supported data formats. Proprietary or obfuscated file formats are not taken into account as they cannot be used in a migration pipeline. The collected data are summarized in Table 1. Note that some tools require the installation of third-party solutions to export the models and/or offer limited import capabilities that derive partial schemas from existing data sources but cannot import explicit models.

Particular emphasis was placed on analyzing the completeness of the data model during the export and import processes, given its central role in a low-code process. For instance, some tools only offer limited support where only classes (but no associations) can be exported. This is reflected in the data model column of Table 1, where models missing relationships are marked as "half."

Table 1. Interoperability Evaluation of Low Code Platforms ("✓/2" symbolizes partial support, "✓ *" symbolizes the need for a 3rd-party application)

Platform	Model Export				Model Import			
	Data	GUI	Behav.	Format	Data	GUI	Behav.	Format
Mendix	✓	✓	✓	JSON	✓/2			XLSX
OutSystems	✓*			XLSX	✓/2			XLSX
PowerApps	✓/2	✓	✓	CSV + JSON	✓/2	✓	✓	CSV + JSON
Appian	✓	✓	✓	XML	✓	✓	✓	XML
ServiceNow	✓*	✓*	✓*	XML	✓*	✓ *	✓ *	XML
Salesforce	✓ *			XLSX	✓/2			XLSX
Pegasystems	✓			XLSX	✓/2			XLSX
Zoho	✓	✓	✓	DS	✓	✓	✓	XLSX + DS
ReTool	✓/2	✓	✓	CSV + JSON	✓/2	✓	✓	CSV + JSON
Oracle Apex	✓	✓	✓	SQL	✓	✓	✓	SQL

We can draw several conclusions from the table, particularly regarding vendor lock-in. First, while some tools use the same format for storing their models (e.g. JSON) their internal schema is different therefore requiring a migration phase. Then, support for data models is (with limitations) common but there are many constraints for other model types (in terms of options, diversity and quality of the import/export). Finally, some tools do not offer a real model import feature, but they offer to initialize a project based on an existing data source (a database, a CSV or Excel file,...). So a pseudo path to import a model in those tools is, for instance, to create an Excel file that somehow represents the model we want to import. Obviously, there is an information loss (e.g. ambiguity in the definition of the data types, absence of explicit relationships among classes, no validation rules,...) as the model is not directly imported but has to be inferred from the CSV. For instance, Mendix, OutSystems, and PowerApps rely on this method.

3 Model-Based Migration Approach

Our model-driven solution for migrating models from an *LCP A* to an *LCP B* is summarized in Fig. 1 and discussed next.

3.1 Exporting the Model from LCP A

The first step consists of exporting the application model(s) from LCP A (input file in Fig. 1). If the LCP offers a formal model export feature, this file will contain the model expressed in a textual concrete syntax conforming to the LCP language (e.g. a JSON file conforming to a JSON schema mapping the language concepts). Otherwise, we use as an alternative an image file capturing the graphical model (i.e. a screenshot of the model displayed in the tool). This dual input format accommodates LCPs that lack complete export support.

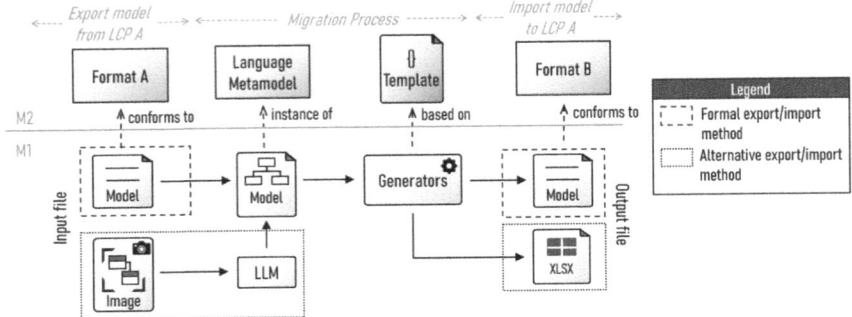

Fig. 1. Model-based migration solution for LCPs

In both cases (formal and alternative export method), the file is parsed and transformed into an intermediate model conform to the B-UML metamodel, the modeling language we used as pivot language. B-UML, part of the BESSER modeling framework [2], leverages and adapts well-known modeling standards, including UML for defining data models and IFML[1] for UI models.

Formal Export Method (Text to Model): When the LCP provides functionality to export the model in a readable text-based format, the model's information becomes accessible and can be extracted to prepare it for migration. This initial step in the migration pipeline is carried out through a Text-to-Model (T2M) transformation. The T2M transformation, guided by specific transformation rules, extracts information about the model elements such as classes, attributes, and relationships for data models; buttons, layouts, and styles for GUI models; and workflows and events for behavioral models. It then constructs a new LCP-independent model, conforming to the B-UML modeling language.

As an example, we have completely implemented the transformation rules for Mendix data models (exported as JSON files), although, the export process for other tools would be similar. Given this Mendix JSON, our T2M transformation, implemented in Python, reads the JSON object and constructs a data model instance of the B-UML metamodel following the mapping rules between Mendix and B-UML depicted in Fig. 2.

Note how several of these concepts are directly transformed without significant modifications, such as *DomainModel*, *Entity*, *Attribute*, and *Generalization*. For *Associations*, the ends are determined by the *child* and *parent* relationships, while the cardinality is defined by the *type* and *owner* attributes. Other concepts, such as *PrimitiveDataTypes* and *Enumerations*, are also transformed in a straightforward manner but are omitted from Fig. 2 for simplicity.

Alternative Export Method (Image to Model): In the case that an LCP does not provide an export functions, we leverage the power of visual LLMs to parse the model depicted in an image taken from the source LCP. Indeed, previous efforts have already highlighted the capabilities of visual LLMs to transform images of data models to actual models [9], especially when combining OpenAI's

---

[1] https://www.ifml.org/.

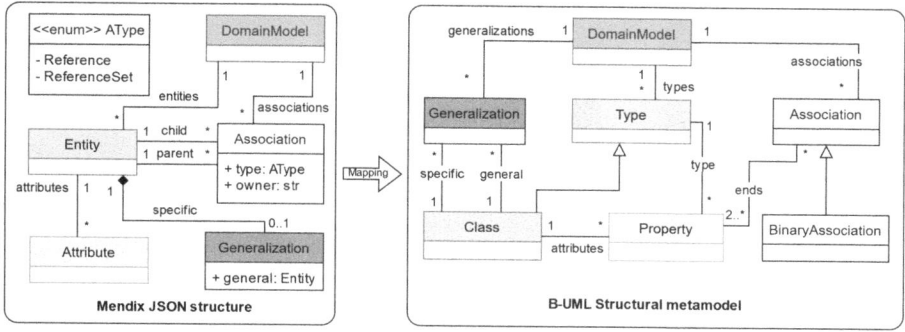

Fig. 2. Mapping of main concepts between Mendix and B-UML, highlighted by matching colors (e.g., a Mendix *Attribute* is mapped to a B-UML *Property*)

GPT as LLM, PlantUML[2] as the target metamodel and the prompt "Can you turn this hand-drawn UML class diagram into the corresponding class diagram in PlantUML notation?".

While the mentioned study focuses on data models defined as UML class diagrams, we believe the approach to still be viable, given that the LCP data modeling languages are heavily inspired by the UML (or ER) language. To improve the results, we first adapted the previously mentioned prompt to contain an LCP-specific description of the syntax of the graphical model.

When this alternative is used to complement a partial model export using the previously discussed T2M technique, we provide as well the partial model as additional resource and ask the LLM to respect the elements in that file and complement them with the missing ones (typically, associations that can be seen in the image but are missing in the export).

Figure 3 illustrates this alternative pipeline for PowerApps with the used prompt. PlantUML is used as the LLM's output language due to its compatibility [9] and the resulting PlantUML model is converted to a B-UML model. As the usage of an LLM does not guarantee the completeness and correctness of the transformation due to its nondeterministic nature, LCP users have the possibility to edit either the PlantUML or B-UML model to improve the results if necessary.

3.2 Generating and Importing the Model to LCP B

Once the *Model* is created, it can be refined or completed, if needed. Then, a template-based generator creates a textual representation of the model but now in terms of the concrete syntax expected by the target platform. We addressed generators for two scenarios: (1) generating the model for import into an LCP with a model importing functionality, and (2) producing, as an alternative, a spreadsheet for LCPs only able to infer models from structured data sources.

Formal Import Method: When an LCP provides a formal importer for models, the corresponding model file can be generated according to the LCP expected

---

[2] PlantUML is a popular textual syntax for UML models.

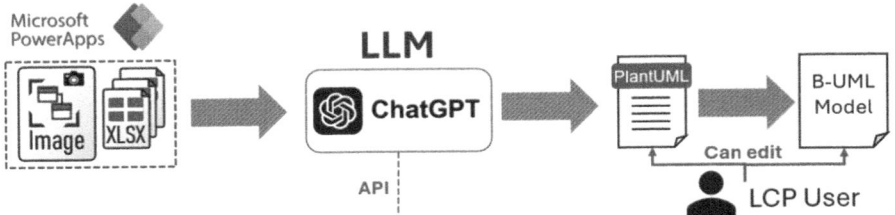

Prompt: "Can you turn this image of a data model into the corresponding class diagram in PlantUML notation? The image contains the graphical overview of the classes and a lot of redundant classes. The csv files contain the concrete attributes yet only copy the attributes unique to the classes. Add attributes using the notation 'attribute: type' and follow python type names."

Fig. 3. Overview of image to model pipeline with PowerApps data model

format via a Model-to-Text (M2T) transformation. This M2T transformation must map the B-UML concepts to the concepts of the LCP language and write them using the right concrete syntax. For example, Appian and Oracle Apex allow the import of the entire project, including the GUI, behavior, and data models definition from a set of XML and SQL files. As an example of an M2T transformation, we have developed a generator for Oracle Apex. This generator produces specific statements to define the data model in Oracle Apex, which stores data models as relational databases and UI and behavioral models as rows in a special set of predefined tables. The transformation rules for the data part of the M2T process were derived from [10], which defines the mapping of UML class diagrams to relational databases. An example of this generator is presented in our extended report [1].

Alternative Import Method: Most low-code platforms (LCPs) provide methods to import existing data in various formats, such as XLSX, JSON, and CSV as a way to initialize a new modeling project. From the ingested data, the LCPs infer a data model to be used to manage the imported data. For example, when importing data with a XLSX file, an LCP generates a data model where for each sheet the LCP creates a new class, for each column an attribute of that class, and the cells' format of the column is used as a data type. While this approach is not a formal or standardized method for importing data models (as it is primarily designed for data import), we propose using it as an alternative for platforms that lack a dedicated mechanism for data model import. Therefore, we have developed a generator that produces a structured spreadsheet file representing the input model's structure. Although this is an alternative for the data model, it is not a valid one for UI and behavioral models. Additionally, since a spreadsheet is not as semantically rich as models themselves, going via a spreadsheet representation may result in a model of lower quality that may need to be later refined.

4 Tool Support

As proof of concept, we have implemented some migration paths on top of the BESSER platform. Our prototype is open-source and available in the project repository[3]. The implemented paths exercise the different import/export combinations described in the previous sections. Our current tool support is restricted to data models and support for the interoperability of UI and behavioural models would follow the directives explained so far but it's left as future work. Examples of the tool are available in our extended paper version [1].

5 Related Work

Several secondary studies [7,13] have highlighted the concern of vendor lock-in in LCPs as a significant dependency risk for customers and only one of these [13] tackles the concept of interoperability in LCPs. Yet, the mentioned study fails to explore specific limitations and solutions regarding application migration.

Existing research has proposed technical solutions to ensure interoperability between modeling platforms using MDE, often referred to as bridges (e.g., [6] or [4] to name a few). However, these solutions assume that the models involved are accessible and serializable, an assumption that does not apply to all LCPs as seen in our analysis in Sect. 2. Furthermore, since LCPs are closed-source, it becomes challenging to develop extensions to support such functionality. Our solution is inspired by these previous ones but adapted (and extended, e.g. via LLMs) to deal with the specificities of the LCP ecosystem.

The idea of using a language as pivot representation has also been explored in the past [11,14]. For example, the unified metamodel KF proposed in [11] integrates the concepts of ER, ORM2, and UML, along with a set of transformation rules to map these models to KF. However, these solutions rely on source models that are built using standardized languages such as UML. In the case of LCPs, data models often do not adhere to any standard modeling language. In some cases, it is necessary to resort to more generic and flexible solutions, including as mentioned before, the need to deal with partial models.

To the best of our knowledge, ours is the first study to propose a solution to address the vendor lock-in problem of LCPs. Our solution not only proposes bridge transformations to enable model export and import between LCPs but also introduces alternative methods using an LLM to migrate data models from a screenshot of their graphical representation.

6 Conclusion

In this paper, we propose an approach to improve the interoperability of LCPs by (semi-)automatically migrating models from one platform to another.

As further work, we will extend our tool support, especially regarding the use of LLMs to export UI and behavioural models, to enable more interoperability bridges among the tools that cover not only the data model but also this behavioural and UI models. Moreover, we plan to develop a GUI to facilitate the use of our tool. LCP users will be able to indicate the source and target LCPs

---

[3] https://github.com/BESSER-PEARL/BESSER-Migration-Hub.

together and automatically obtain the ready-to-import files. Depending on the migration path, they may be prompted to answer a few questions to optimize the quality of the result (e.g. to validate the model inferred by a visual LLM).

Acknowledgments. This work is supported by the Luxembourg National Research Fund (FNR) PEARL program, grant agreement 16544475.

References

1. Alfonso, I., Conrardy, A., Cabot, J.: Towards the interoperability of low-code platforms. arXiv preprint arXiv:2412.05075 (2024)
2. Alfonso, I., et al.: Building Besser: an open-source low-code platform. In: van der Aa, H., Bork, D., Schmidt, R., Sturm, A. (eds.) Enterprise, Business-Process and Information Systems Modeling. BPMDS EMMSAD 2024 2024. LNBIP, vol. 511, pp. pp. 203–212. Springer, Cham (2024). https://doi.org/10.1007/978-3-031-61007-3_16
3. Bock, A.C., Frank, U.: Low-code platform. Bus. Inf. Syst. Eng. **63**, 733–740 (2021)
4. Bork, D., Anagnostou, K., Wimmer, M.: Towards interoperable metamodeling platforms: the case of bridging ADOxx and EMF. In: Franch, X., Poels, G., Gailly, F., Snoeck, M. (eds.) Advanced Information Systems Engineering. CAiSE 2022. LNCS, vol. 13295, pp. 479–497. Springer, Cham (2022). https://doi.org/10.1007/978-3-031-07472-1_28
5. Brambilla, M., Cabot, J., Wimmer, M.: Model-Driven Software Engineering in Practice, 2nd edn. Synthesis Lectures on Software Engineering, Morgan & Claypool Publishers (2017)
6. Brunelière, H., Cabot, J., Clasen, C., Jouault, F., Bézivin, J.: Towards model driven tool interoperability: bridging eclipse and Microsoft modeling tools. In: Kühne, T., Selic, B., Gervais, M.-P., Terrier, F. (eds.) ECMFA 2010. LNCS, vol. 6138, pp. 32–47. Springer, Heidelberg (2010). https://doi.org/10.1007/978-3-642-13595-8_5
7. Bucaioni, A., Cicchetti, A., Ciccozzi, F.: Modelling in low-code development: a multi-vocal systematic review. Softw. Syst. Model. **21**, 1–23 (2022). https://doi.org/10.1007/s10270-021-00964-0
8. Cabot, J.: The Low-code Handbook: Learn How to Unlock Faster And Better Software Development with Low-code Solutions. Jordi Cabot (2024). https://lowcode-book.com/
9. Conrardy, A.D., Cabot, J.: From image to UML: first results of image-based UML diagram generation using LLMs. In: STAF 2024 Workshops: AgileMDE, LLM4MDE, and MeSS. pp. 55–65. CEUR Workshop Proceedings, CEUR-WS.org (2024)
10. Daniel, G., Gómez, A., Cabot, J.: UmlTo [no] SQL: mapping conceptual schemas to heterogeneous datastores. In: 2019 13th International Conference on Research Challenges in Information Science (RCIS), pp. 1–13. IEEE (2019). https://doi.org/10.1109/RCIS.2019.8877094
11. Fahad, M.: ER2OWL: generating OWL ontology from ER diagram. In: Shi, Z., Mercier-Laurent, E., Leake, D. (eds.) IIP 2008. ITIFIP, vol. 288, pp. 28–37. Springer, Boston, MA (2008). https://doi.org/10.1007/978-0-387-87685-6_6
12. Oleksandr, M., Kyle, D., Akash, J.: Magic quadrant for enterprise low-code application platforms. Gartner report (2024)

13. Sahay, A., Indamutsa, A., Di Ruscio, D., Pierantonio, A.: Supporting the understanding and comparison of low-code development platforms. In: 2020 46th Euromicro Conference on Software Engineering and Advanced Applications (SEAA), pp. 171–178. IEEE (2020). https://doi.org/10.1109/SEAA51224.2020.00036
14. Vo, M., Hoang, Q.: Transformation of UML class diagram into owl ontology. J. Inf. Telecommun. **4**(1), 1–16 (2020). https://doi.org/10.1080/24751839.2019.1686681

The Work System Perspective as a Nexus Between Silos in IS Modeling and Between Rigor and Broad Usability

Steven Alter(✉)

University of San Francisco, 2130 Fulton Street, San Francisco 94117, USA
alter@usfca.edu

Abstract. This exploratory paper addresses challenges related to aspects of the theme of CAISE 2025, "bridging silos." That theme applies directly to low levels of synergy between entire academic disciplines and to similar issues involving different IS modeling traditions that encounter gaps between rigor and precision versus comprehension and usability by many IS stakeholders who lack advanced IT training. A work system perspective can address those issues by serving as an integrating nexus between disciplines and between IS modeling traditions while also bridging gaps between rigor and broad usability in IS modeling. The work system perspective provides a natural nexus at many areas of overlap between disciplines that focus on systems designed and operated to achieve goals. Other possibilities for bridging silos involving IS engineering traditions touch upon data, process, and software modeling.

Keywords: Bridging Silos · Work System Theory · Work System Perspective

1 A Nexus for Integrating Silos

The CAISE 2025 Call for Papers starts by saying "engineering real-world information systems requires a coherent design encompassing human, organizational, economic, societal, and technological aspects." That initial sentence points to many disconnects and gaps that IS engineering should take seriously but that are underplayed or invisible in most IS engineering research. Personal goals of employees often are not aligned with economic goals of firms, which often pay little attention to social and sustainability goals. Capabilities of human users are sometimes overwhelmed by methods and technical artifacts that seem complex, overwhelming, or indecipherable. Aspects of those issues appear frequently in discussions of the explainability and potential benefits and threats of AI. Related issues are relevant to IS engineering methods and practices whose abstractions and technical focus are useful for technical experts while often ignoring important realities in systems that are modeled. An especially important aspect of those

---

This paper is an 8-page reduction of a longer version that explains many points more fully. See: https://www.dropbox.com/scl/fi/73127n24sn8kgfrsc0val/CAISE-FORUM-2025-Using-WSP-to-Bridge-Silos-initial.pdf?rlkey=5ztj75ydyfkblfmdh2hl3b1o9&st=2gdcui1j&dl=0

© The Author(s), under exclusive license to Springer Nature Switzerland AG 2025
L. Pufahl et al. (Eds.): CAiSE 2025, LNBIP 557, pp. 12–19, 2025.
https://doi.org/10.1007/978-3-031-94590-8_2

realities applies to IT users in sociotechnical systems whose human participants exercise human agency and may or may not perform activities in a manner preferred or imagined by designers or managers.

Goal. This exploratory paper illustrates how the work system perspective (WSP) based on work system theory (WST) can serve as a nexus or conduit that addresses the CAISE 2025 theme of bridging silos. That issue applies in many fields covering domain-specific knowledge related to operational systems. The recent article "Quo Vadis Modeling" by Michael et al. [1] explains that it also applies to gaps between IS engineering subcommunities associated with three annual conferences (ER - data modeling, BPM - process modeling, MODELS - software modeling). This paper contributes by addressing concerns discussed in [1] and elsewhere while recognizing that many papers have focused on important issues within those subcommunities (e.g., [2, 3]).

Organization: Section 2 uses three recent articles as the impetus for five suggestions about bridging silos. Section 3 shows that WST and the broader WSP provide a core of ideas that apply to large overlaps between disciplines that study systems designed and managed to achieve goals. Section 4 summarizes how WST could contribute to bridging silos within IS engineering approaches such as data, process, and software modeling, if members of the IS engineering community are willing to relax some of their expectations regarding the form and content of models. Section 5 notes that the WSP applies to many topics identified in the CAISE 2025 Call for Papers. Section 6 identifies research areas that could help in bridging silos in IS engineering.

2 Suggestions Derived from Recent Articles Related to Silos

The following three articles provide impetus for this section's suggestions about bridging silos related to IS engineering.

An Article Reporting Divergences and Areas of Overlap between IS Engineering Subcommunities. A 2024 paper in *Software and Systems Modeling* [1] reports on a survey, bibliometric analysis, and interviews within IS engineering subcommunities. Three issues were important to subcommunities (data, process, and software modeling) associated with three separate conferences ER, BPM, and MODELS: (1) Modeling should be easier and should become more usable. (2) Modeling should be used by practitioners. (3) Modeling should enable and provide more automation. Issues of special interest in each community were also mentioned. "The responses from the ER community revealed a higher interest in showing benefits for other disciplines. BPM representatives see more importance in integrating modeling into the development life-cycle. MODELS representatives emphasize better tools and the need to provide tooling. ER and BPM representatives emphasize that modeling should be human-relevant and that we need to explicate benefits." (p. 18).

An Article about Democratizing Enterprise Engineering. A 2018 *BISE* research note co-authored by leaders in the enterprise modeling community [4] argued that EM "has yet to prove its benefits for the majority of business stakeholders and has not succeeded in being regarded mission-critical in most enterprises. EM is typically used by only few actors in the organization with an affinity to methods and modeling." (p. 70). The WSP provides lightweight approaches that would "support not only architects and corporate IT, but also organizational stakeholders that might benefit from improved models supporting their local analysis, design and/or decision problems."

An Article Proposing a Multilevel Modeling Method to Address Divergent Needs of Different Stakeholders. A 2020 *EMISAJ* paper [5] suggests relaxing common assumptions about the nature of modeling methods and related modeling languages and metamodels. It cites over 20 references concerning issues such as aptitudes, knowledge, purposes, cognitive load, and lack of flexibility. It identifies four requirements for more flexible modeling methods. Many tools based on the WSP support those requirements.

A Path Forward. The work system perspective can help in pursuing the following suggestions based directly or indirectly on those three articles:

- Recognize that rigorous methods, tools, and models are important for some stakeholders but neither helpful nor usable for other stakeholders.
- Provide methods, tools, and models that fit stakeholder purposes.
- Keep people in the loop where model-based automation is not the immediate goal.
- Rely on human attention and interpersonal communication to make sense of models that are not interoperable through automated techniques.
- Expect stakeholders to reject or misuse inscrutable methods, tools, and models.

3 The Work System Perspective as Conduit Between Disciplines that Study Operational Systems

Figure 1 shows the three components of work system theory. WST has been explained in detail many times and is the basis of the work system method (WSM) [6, 7]. The work system perspective (WSP) builds on WST and includes WST extensions such as service value chain framework, a theory of workarounds, a theory of system interactions, facets of work, IS usage theory, and other concepts, models, frameworks, and metamodels.

Figure 2 portrays a substantial area of overlap between multiple disciplines [6]. That area of overlap concerns operating and improving systems in and across organizations. Each discipline has its own areas of special concern (e.g., queuing theory in operations management and co-creation of value in service science), but the area of overlap between disciplines could be a nexus for bridging discipline-centric silos that inhibit exchange of ideas and possibilities for collaboration between disciplines.

The WSP is well suited for facilitating exchanges and collaboration between disciplines in Fig. 2 for two main reasons. First, the elements of the work system framework at its core (Fig. 1) are directly related to primary concerns of disciplines that study many types of systems. For example, sales, marketing, service science, and management are concerned with *customers, product/services, processes and activities*, and *environment*. Second, it outlines a practical, easily applied view of operational systems. Many hundreds of employed MBA and EMBA students have used versions of WSM (mentioned earlier) for writing and presenting management briefings about problematic systems of many types in their own organizations (e.g. [8]). Their ability to use many WSP ideas

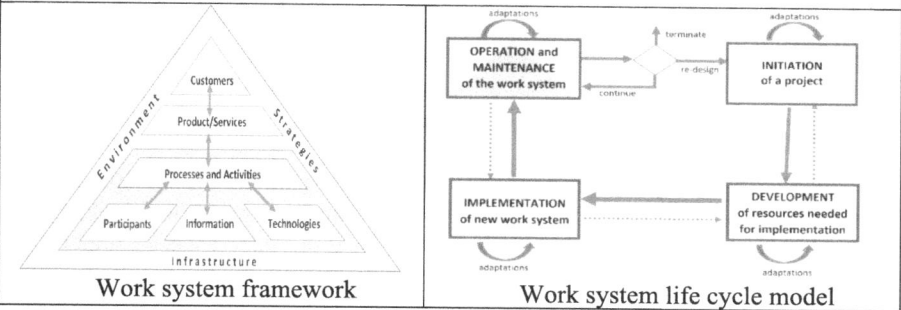

Fig. 1. Three Components of Work System Theory [6]

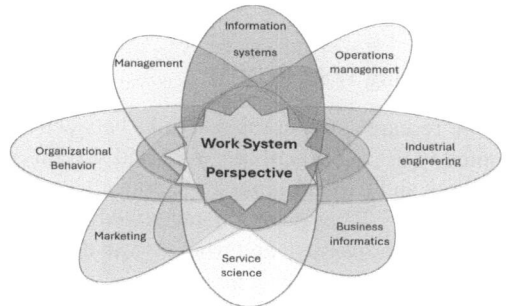

Fig. 2. The work system perspective as a major area of overlap between disciplines [6]

after brief explanations or illustrations implies that the WSP could be used for system-related analysis and communication both within and between the disciplines in Fig. 2. In effect, the WSP would serve as a set of shared concepts for interdisciplinary communication about system-related topics even as each discipline contains its own concepts for deeper and more specialized descriptions, analysis, and theory development.

4 Links Between the Work System Perspective and Data, Process, and Software Modeling

In addition to serving as a nexus between traditional disciplines, the WSP implies approaches for bridging three silos within the IS engineering community identified by [1], i.e., data modeling (viewed more broadly as conceptual modeling) vs. process modeling (e.g., uses of BPMN) vs. software modeling (e.g., uses of UML). In all cases, the nexus involves textual models of situations that identify situational elements identified by the work system framework. This can be done using work system snapshots, a type of informal model based on elements in Fig. 1 that is used in most applications of WST for summarizing the "as is" and "to be" work systems. Work system snapshots do not have required syntax but maintain rigor through definition-based internal consistency rules.

The next three subsections identify attempts to establish links from aspects of the WSP to conceptual modeling, process modeling, and software modeling, respectively.

4.1 Conceptual Modeling: Alternative Work System Metamodels

The work system framework is a terse diagrammatic representation of a conceptual model that links the elements shown in Fig. 1. Consistent with the suggestions in Sect. 2, the key point related to data modeling and conceptual modeling is that different stakeholders with different purposes (ranging from basic understanding to evaluating detailed designs or producing code) meet their responsibilities most effectively if they use metamodels that are appropriate for their purposes. Stakeholders who are fully engaged in relation to their own purposes should be able to rely on individual effort and interpersonal communication to make sense of models that are not interoperable through automated techniques.

4.2 Process Modeling: Linking WSP to BPM

Two papers from the WSP research stream suggest links between WSP and BPM [9]. A 2017 paper [10] attempted to use aspects of the WST and several extensions to expand the scope of BPM concepts and expand upon 20 technically oriented BPM use cases discussed by van der Aalst [11]. That paper characterized WST as focusing on work system analysis, design, and improvement and whereas van der Aalst's (2013) technical use cases emphasized process models and technical and computational issues. [10] discussed those 20 use cases and suggested 17 additional use cases related to work system elements and workarounds.

A more recent paper goes much further by presenting a new RAVC framework (Resources for Action, Value for Customers) that can be applied in different ways at six levels of granularity [12]. The levels are: (1) enterprise capabilities, (2) enterprise operation through intersecting work systems, (3) individual work system, (4) processes within a work system, (5) activities within a process, (6) services triggered by requests. The key point related to process modeling is that the RAVC metaphor can be applied to process-intensive situations across all six levels. Both the WSP and RAVC imply that process analysis or process mining can and should attend to how specific resources are used by specific activities and how that leads to value for customers. BPM researchers in process mining already explore related issues when inconsistent process sequence and variability in activity execution are important.

4.3 Software Modeling: Steps Toward Object-Oriented Analysis and Design Within the WSP

Preliminary efforts to produce a work system front end for object-oriented analysis and design (OOAD) found that work system snapshots lead directly to UML use case diagrams, class diagrams, and activity diagrams. Implications for other UML diagrams are less direct. A subsequent controlled experiment [13] involving 165 undergraduate software engineering students (inexperienced novices) allowed individual students in the control group 45 min to prepare user stories for a 454-word case example from a textbook. Students in the control group spent all 45 min producing user stories. Students in the treatment group spent 15 min producing a work system snapshot and 30 min producing user stories. The treatment group identified significantly more valid user stories and fewer invalid user stories.

A new "IS usage theory" provides a path toward a more complete object-oriented view of work systems that might be developed further by software modeling researchers. The new theory assumes that IS usage is performed within the context of work systems and that usage may involve human participants or automated entities such as robots, chatbots, automated machinery, and self-driving vehicles. That path treats work systems, information systems, and digital agents in a symmetrical way, somewhat consistent with proposals related to Bunge's systematist ontology [14]. OOAD use cases would focus on uses by sociotechnical or totally automated work systems. Initial class and activity diagrams could be derived from work system snapshots. Communication diagrams could describe message flow between a work system and an information system or digital agent that supports it.

5 Potential Applications of the Work System Perspective to IS Engineering Topics

In addition to its relevance as a nexus between IS modeling subcommunities, the work system perspective applies to many of the topics and types of modeling listed in the CAISE 2025 Call for Papers. Here are examples:

Applications of AI. The core of WST can be applied in understanding an application of AI in the practical context of a work system. It does not solve the mystery of how the AI-based algorithms operate but it does provide enough context that the application of those algorithms is not overwhelmed by the inscrutable nature of their operation.

Blockchain. The technology of blockchain is complex, but its application can be described clearly in work system terms. Blockchain applications always occur in a work system that performs activities to produce product/services in a business context. Use of blockchain to update a public ledger is a subsystem within the system for achieving the business purpose. Once again, a work system perspective helps in focusing on business rather than technical concerns.

Digital Twins. The use of digital twins involves two work systems. (1) the machine or production work system being monitored and controlled using the digital twin arrangement, (2) a larger, combined work system that includes the first work system and the operation of the digital twin arrangement that monitors and/or controls it. Different versions of the combined work system can be modeled or even simulated based on different interaction and control patterns, thus providing more complete descriptive and analytical power through the digital twin arrangement.

Big Data. Similar ideas apply to big data, whose use often encounters problems when it is not viewed as part or a work system. That work system often needs to include participation by stakeholders who are engaged enough to understand the results.

Process Automation (in general). The WSP provides many analysis and design tools for visualizing alternatives that involve different degrees of process automation. Initial understandings based on those tools can be augmented by BPMN diagrams, simulations, or other rigorous methods for evaluating relative advantages of alternatives.

Robotic Process Automation. The starting point for RPA is a work system containing highly repetitive steps that are performed manually. RPA involves the use of low-code or no code software to create a modified work system that automates repetitive steps but often does not automate everything. Work system snapshots and related tools can help in visualizing those situations and evaluating alternatives without using advanced modeling methods.

6 Conclusion: Steps Toward Greater Integration Across Modeling Traditions

The Challenge. This exploratory paper identified ways in which the work system perspective could serve as a nexus that supports integration across major modeling traditions within IS engineering. That integration would address the bridging silos theme of CAISE 2025. There is no suggestion of abandoning important IS engineering concepts and methods that have been applied successfully. Instead, this paper focused on paths toward creating and supporting bridges between existing knowledge and new approaches that might help in developing and implementing sociotechnical and automated systems in organizations. Related research would extend current concepts and tooling and would call for innovation in areas such as these:

Automatic or Semi-automatic Linkages between Modeling Levels. Section 4.2 identified six levels for applying the RAVC framework in modeling a work system. Description and analysis tools such as those identified in [12] could be extended substantially based on levels in the RAVC framework and other ideas in this paper.

Zooming between Different Focal Points and between Different Levels of Description and Analysis. Current tools focus on specific types of models such as class diagrams and activity diagrams. A WSP-based modeling suite would provide convenient links between textual models such as the work system snapshots and models based on formalisms such as BPMN or ERD. At least initially, those links could produce rough draft models that stakeholders would correct. The result would be greater stakeholder involvement and easier and more efficient modeling (as in [13]).

Modeling of Knowledge-Intensive Processes and Systems. BPMN and CMMN can be used together to model knowledge intensive processes [15], but they are inadequate for describing much of the variability and uncertainty in such situations. Ideas discussed in [7] but not mentioned here might be incorporated into new modeling methods that would treat knowledge intensive processes and systems more realistically.

Application of AI in Modeling. A textual version of the work system framework (Fig. 1) serves as a starting point for expressing knowledge about work systems in ongoing research that explores how a generative AI application could ingest knowledge in that form and could apply it to test cases or even real-world situations as a way to facilitate modeling just as AI has facilitated repetitive aspects of programming.

Caveat. Pursuing those challenges depends on the willingness of members of the different IS engineering communities to accept modeling methods that may not conform with their preferences. The new modeling methods might involve relaxed rigor and unfamiliar notation. Also, they might lack full interoperability with established methods that are limited by their own structure, format, and underlying assumptions.

References

1. Michael, J., Bork, D., Wimmer, M., Mayr, H.C.: Quo vadis modeling? Softw. Syst. Model. **23**, 7–28 (2024)
2. Delcambre, L.M., Liddle, S.W., Pastor, O., Storey, V.C.: A reference framework for conceptual modeling. In: Proceedings of ER 2018 (2018)
3. Panach, J.I., Pastor, Ó., Liddle, S.W., Storey, V.C., Mayr, H.C., Thalheim, B.: Evaluating a framework of conceptual modelling research. In: Proceedings of ER (2024)
4. Sandkuhl, K., et al.: From expert discipline to common practice: a vision and research agenda for extending the reach of enterprise modeling. Bus. Inform. Syst. Eng. **60**(1), 69–80 (2018)
5. Bork, D., Alter, S.: Satisfying four requirements for more flexible modeling methods: theory and test case. Enter. Model. Inform. Syst. Architect. **15**(3), 1–25 (2020)
6. Alter, S.: Work system theory as a platform: response to a research perspective article by Niederman and March. J. Assoc. Inf. Syst. **16**(6), 485–514 (2015)
7. Alter, S.: Making cyber-human systems smarter. Inf. Syst. **127**, 102428 (2025)
8. Truex, D., Alter, S., Long, C.: Systems analysis for everyone else: empowering business professionals through a systems analysis method that fits their needs. In: Proceedings of ECIS (2010)
9. Dumas, M., La Rosa, M., Mendling, J., Reijers, H.A.: Fundamentals of Business Process Management, 2nd edn. Springer, Berlin (2018)
10. Alter, S., Recker, J.: Using a work system perspective to expand BPM research use cases. J. Inform. Technol. Theory Appl. **18**, 47–71 (2017)
11. van der Aalst, W.M.P.: Business process management: a comprehensive survey. ISRN Softw. Eng. 1–37 (2013)
12. Alter, S.: Extending BPM by treating processes as components of work systems that produce product/services valued by their customers. In: Proceedings of ICIS (2024)
13. Bolloju, N., Alter, S., Gupta, A., Gupta, S., Jain, S.: Improving scrum user stories and product backlog using work system snapshots. In: Proceedings of AMCIS (2017)
14. Lukyanenko, R., Storey, V.C., Pastor, O.: Foundations of information technology based on Bunge's systemist philosophy of reality. Softw. Syst. Model. **20**(4), 921–938 (2021)
15. Berniak-Woźny, J., Szelągowski, M.: Towards the assessment of business process knowledge intensity–a systematic literature review. Bus. Process. Manag. J.Manag. J. **28**(1), 40–61 (2022)

Leveraging Profiling to Bridge Healthcare Silos for Federated Analyses

Nelly Barret, Anna Bernasconi, Cinzia Cappiello, Giacomo Palu, and Pietro Pinoli

Politecnico di Milano, Milan, Italy
{Nelly.Barret,Anna.Bernasconi,Cinzia.Cappiello,
Giacomo.Palu,Pietro.Pinoli}@polimi.it

Abstract. Healthcare is more and more relying on digital information, bringing new challenges for its management, exploration, and usage. Healthcare data represents a challenge for information systems because, for privacy regulations, it cannot exit the original silo in which it has been produced (typically owned by hospitals), and may be of various kinds (clinical reports, DNA sequences, MRI scans, etc.). To manage this complexity, it is natural to use Federated Learning to safely analyze the underlying silos' content. However, designing and running federated algorithms requires to know what the silos contain and how they can be joined (on which common attributes). Existing catalogs provide preliminary visualizations, which are hardly generalizable due to their underlying use-case-tailored data models. To overcome these limitations, we provide a general catalog conceptual model as well as profiling techniques to extract information of interest from silos. Our proposed catalog is general enough to be used in various healthcare scenarios with diverse kinds of data. It also facilitates experts' work in creating Federated Learning algorithms running in networks of interoperable healthcare silos.

Keywords: Conceptual model · Healthcare data · Federated learning

1 Introduction

The world's digitalization has led to unprecedented data creation rates in various industries, such as healthcare, transportation, social media, and education. To handle massive production and sharing, data often resides in more or less curated and interoperable silos maintained by data owners. Domain experts usually employ several silos simultaneously, e.g., to obtain more and/or finer information, whether this is with queries or federated learning (FL) algorithms. As an example, consider medical practitioners working on cancer: they seek to answer questions, such as "Which genes favor severe COVID-19 forms for kidney cancer patients?". For this task, they first need to identify silos of interest by inspecting stored data, then proceed with the design of federated analyses on the chosen datasets. Such course of actions allows to (*i*) combine several datasets (clinical reports, DNA analysis, scans, etc.) in a given silo; and (ii) enrich existing data in a silo with data present in other silos in terms of number of patients and/or number of features. In real-world scenarios, combining several datasets originating from a silo is a complex task; extending them with datasets from other silos is an even harder task. First, silos are created independently by actors, thus are not interoperable due to their high heterogeneity (inside and across silos). Second, they may contain sensitive data, which prevents the creation of a single curated silo according to current regulations, e.g., the GDPR. Third, users need to know which data is available in the silos and how it relates to other silos in order to formulate coherent federated analyses. These three reasons hinder the federated analyses of healthcare silos.

Toward bridging silos together and enabling cooperation between hospitals, we have initiated **I-ETL** [1], a framework to build healthcare networks with interoperability as a first-class citizen. In that work, we introduce a pipeline to make data (more) interoperable according to the metadata specified by experts as well as two novel general healthcare conceptual models for metadata and data. However, the I-ETL network cannot be used as such because, before formulating federated analyses, metadata and data of each silo require to be first discovered by means of a catalog. Therefore, we propose our twofold vision in this paper: (i) a **conceptual model** for cataloging silos' metadata and data in the I-ETL network; and (ii) a **pipeline to build a general catalog** implementing our conceptual model together with profiling techniques. Our paper is organized as follows. We first motivate our work with a real healthcare FL scenario (Sect. 2). Then, we present our approach (Sect. 3). We finally discuss related works (Sect. 4) before concluding (Sect. 5).

2 Motivating Example: FL for Cancer and COVID-19

We start with a motivating example featuring open data collected for ESKD (end-stage kidney disease) patients having COVID-19 [7,9]. ESKD is the last stage of chronic kidney disease, leading to slow kidney functioning and higher risks of severe COVID-19, thus necessitating extra care. In our example, we consider two hospitals. The former contains patient phenotypic data (age, ethnicity, life habits, etc.) and whether/how they were affected by COVID-19 (severity, nasal tests results, and MRI scans of their lungs). The latter contains genomic data collected during their ESKD analysis, i.e., RNA sequence counts for a panel of 60k genes. Having different kinds of data distributed across hospitals aligns with the typical situation where only a few large hospitals can run genetic analyses of their patients' DNA, due to the high monetary cost. In our scenario, experts seek to answer two questions: (i) *"How are COVID-19 symptoms amplified for ESKD patients?"*; and (ii) *"Which ESKD-related genes favor severe COVID-19 forms?"*. Keeping them in mind, we explain three tasks that healthcare experts will experience.

Task 1: Explore Silos Through the Catalog. Toward answering the above questions, healthcare experts first explore the datasets available in the two hospitals by browsing the general catalog. During this task, they can find out that 80% of patients are aged above 60yo, while the remaining ones are scattered between 50–59yo (10 patients) and 20–49yo (same). They can also see that males are prevalent (80%). Those observations will help them in interpreting the results of FL analyses and AI algorithms.

Task 2: Run a FL Analysis. A second task is to define a simple federated learning analysis, e.g., to compute the distribution of patients with severe COVID-19 symptoms based on the number of comorbidities they may have. This analysis requires to join the two silos based on patient identifiers, a task facilitated by the high interoperability in the network, guaranteed by applying I-ETL.

Task 3: Train a Federated AI Algorithm. A final task is to formulate complex federated AI algorithms, e.g., to predict whether a new ESKD patient will develop severe COVID-19 forms based on its phenotypic, biological, and genetic data. This can be done by training a binary classifier (decision trees, logistic regression, etc.) in a federated manner: individual models are trained locally in each silo and are subsequently aggregated in a general binary classifier. Afterwards, the model can be used for prediction or re-trained with different parameters and/or new data.

3 Modeling and Profiling Healthcare Silos

Figure 1 illustrates our approach, starting from the heterogeneous datasets residing in different hospitals' silos to the construction of the general catalog for exploring them and running federated analyses. Starting from the left, hospitals H_i have datasets $d_i^1..d_i^n$ to explore and use for further studies. Next, I-ETL [1] is run at each hospital on the set of datasets and produces an interoperable silo S_i containing all such data. Subsequently, we **profile** (Sect. 3.2) each silo to obtain an **individual catalog** C_i, an instance of our catalog conceptual model (Sect. 3.1). The set of individual catalogs is then merged into **a single general catalog** (Sect. 3.3). Lastly, experts can inspect the silos' content through the Web interface and design **federated learning (FL) analyses and algorithms**. To provide a secure and efficient architecture for that, we rely on the PHT [2] (Personal Health Train) and PADME [12]. Introduced in 2020, the **PHT** is a novel approach to enable FL between institutions that cannot centralize nor share their data without privacy risks. It follows a decentralized scheme where data always remains in the original silo, named a *station*. Next, FL tasks are encapsulated into *trains*, which collect intermediary results by going through all the stations. The train ends its road in the *central station* which takes care of aggregating the intermediate results and returns the final results to the expert. Released in 2022, **PADME** is an implementation of the PHT, widely adopted for its generality and applicability to several settings, including healthcare.

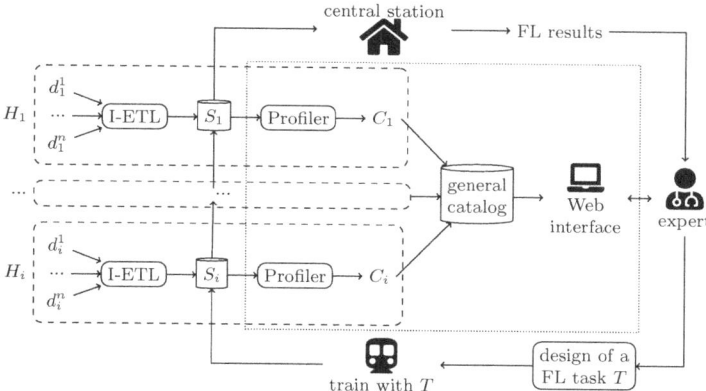

Fig. 1. Overview of our approach with processes (rounded boxes), data storage (cylinders), sequence flow (arrows). Dashed lines delimit hospitals' boundaries; dotted ones delimit our novel contributions.

3.1 The Catalog Conceptual Model

We seek a general catalog, flexible to various kinds of data and adapted to our silos. In turn, our conceptual model (i) builds on the I-ETL data model, promoting features (variable) and records (value for a given variable) for generality; (ii) profiles data (aggregates) and domain metadata (knowledge provided by experts about silos' data); (iii) allows for generic instantiation of charts for all features; and (iv) provides useful information to PADME to run FL tasks such as information on stations' capacities and data statistics. Figure 2 presents our catalog conceptual model. Rectangles are entities, rounded boxes are relationships and triangles are specializations. Primary keys are in **bold** and mandatory attributes are underlined. Our cardinalities adopt the notation of [4], e.g., a Dataset is composed of 1 to n Features, while it has exactly one DatasetProfile.

The central entity is the DATASET. Each dataset has an identifier *Did*, a *version* number (such as "2.1"), and an initial *releaseDate*. It may also have a *lastUpdate*, a text describing the last version's changes (*versionNotes*), and a *license* under which it can be used. The current version and the initial release date of each dataset are mandatory. Datasets are then analyzed in order to obtain a DATASETPROFILE composed of: a unique identifier $\overline{DPid}$, a short textual *description*, a *theme* (e.g., covid), the dataset's *fileTypes* (csv, xlsx, vcf, etc.), the dataset *size* in Mb, and the number of tuples (or the number of files if the data is not tabular) in *nbTuples*. The tuple completeness *tpCompl* is the ratio of patients with at least one record per feature while the tuple uniqueness *tpUniqueness* is the ratio of patients with no more than one record per feature.

Each dataset is composed of a set of FEATURES (variables), each defined by an identifier *Fid* and a *name* (both mandatory). Further, it may have a short text for *description*, an *ontology* to identify the represented concept in existing specialized ontologies (like SNOMED-CT, LOINC, or OrphaNet), and a *dataType* to

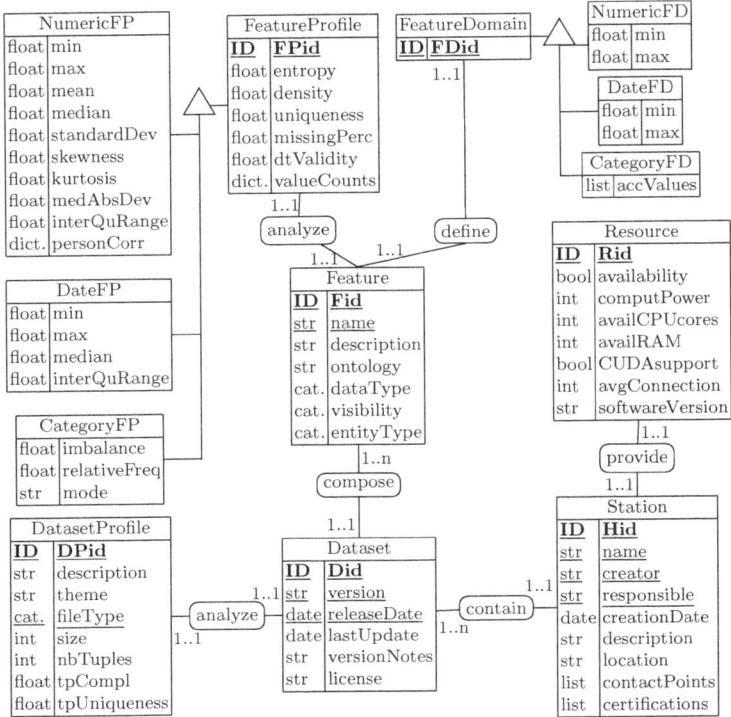

Fig. 2. The conceptual model we propose for individual and general catalogs.

specify the expected value type (integer, boolean, numeric, string, etc.). Next, the attribute *visibility* specifies whether data is shown with or without anonymization, e.g., dates are partially anonymized by removing the day while numeric values are not anonymized. The *entityType* is the type of data the feature represents (clinical, genomic, imaging, etc.). In our motivating example, feature examples are: patient age, ethnicity, smoking habits, visual artifacts in MRI lung scans, various DNA sequence counts, etc. The patient age feature would be instantiated with *description* = "Patient age in years", *ontology* = https://loinc.org/30525-0, *dataType* = "integer", *visibility* = "not anonymized", and *entityType* = "phenotypic".

Further, each feature is defined on a FEATUREDOMAIN, which is refined based on the feature *dataType*. For categorical features, their domain is limited to a list of values (*accValues* in CATEGORYFD). NUMERICFD and DATEFD limit values using *min* and *max* values. For instance, our patient age feature has a numeric feature domain, whose min and max values are 0 and 120.

Next, the feature is analyzed to obtain its FEATUREPROFILE. It holds 6 attributes, 5 for statistics and the latter for aggregated data. Precisely, statistics are: the *entropy* (disorder within the feature's values), the *density* (distance from the uniform distribution), the *uniqueness* (percentage of distinct values), the *missingPerc* (percentage of null values), the *dtValidity* (ratio of values conforming to the feature's *dataType*). In our motivating example, the patient age feature would have a feature profile with the following values: $entropy = 0.775$ (most values range between 60 and 90, but there are several younger patients, seen as "outliers"), $density = 0.01$ (the maximum frequency is 7, thus there are many different values with a low frequency), $uniqueness = 0.39$ (44 distinct values over 111 patients), $missingPerc = 0$ (every patient has an age in the dataset), $dtValidity = 1$ (all values could be cast to integers). Last, *valueCounts* associates each value with its frequency. This corresponds to the aggregated data that will be shown in the catalog; no individual data tuples can be shown.

Each feature's profile can be refined based on its type: numeric, date, or category, leading to the entities NUMERICFP, DATEFP, and CATEGORYFP. Their attributes are computed on non-null values, except if otherwise specified, and are exemplified on the feature age. For numeric feature profiles, a set of 10 statistics are computed, including the *skewness* (distribution asymmetry; -0.95 indicates a right-placed distribution, attested by the old age range), the *kurtosis* (distribution "tailness"; 1.22 indicates few outliers – recall the presence of few younger patients), the *medAbsDev* (outlier-robust version of the mean; 9.41 means that most patients are ± 9.4yo around the range 70–80yo), the *interQuRange* (difference between the 3rd and 1st quartiles; 14yo is the maximum age difference for half of patients). Finally, the attribute *pearsonCorr* stores the Pearson correlation coefficients for that feature with the 10 features having the highest number of values. This significantly lowers the heavy computation of Pearson coefficients, which may not be tractable if there are more than a few dozen of features (which is usually the case for healthcare datasets). For instance, the Pearson value of disease fatality with the age and the smoking habits is only 0.114 and -0.167, meaning that a more subtle and complex correlation exists. The date feature profile entity leverages a subset of the numeric FP entity's attributes. Last, the category feature profile exhibits the *imbalance* (ratio of the highest and lowest value frequencies), the *relativeFreq* (ratio of the highest value frequency and the number of values), and the *mode* (the most frequent value). All such statistics are precious to experts for designing FL tasks and interpreting results, but also to the FL algorithms themselves.

Finally, the STATION entity corresponds to a hospital and contains one or several datasets. It has a *name*, a *creator*, and a *responsible* (at a minimum). It may also have a *creationDate*, a short textual *description*, a *location*, a list of *contactPoints*, and a list of *certification* documents. Each station provides a computational RESOURCE environment, exhibiting its current state: its *availability*, the available computational power (*computPower*), the number of available CPU cores (*availCPUcores*), the available RAM (*availRAM*), whether it supports CUDA for GPU computations (*CUDAsupport*), the average speed connection (*avgConnection*), the currently deployed software version (*softwareVersion*; PADME version here, but this can be adapted to the project).

3.2 Profiling Silos for Individual Catalogs

Leveraging the conceptual model described in Sect. 3.1, we explain how to individually profile each silo in the network, leading to individual catalogs (C_1 to C_i in Fig. 1). Our profiler tool works as follows:

1. Identify the DATASETS in the silo;
2. Compute each DATASETPROFILE by gathering information previously provided by experts (including *description* and *theme* in Fig. 2) as well as statistics computed from the dataset itself (such as its *size*).
3. Enumerate all the FEATURES composing each DATASET and extract their metadata (*name, description, ontology*, etc.);
4. Extract the FEATUREDOMAIN, an information provided by experts in the metadata and based on the feature data type. Integer and float, respectively date and datetime, features lead to NUMERICFD, respectively DATEFD; boolean, string and category features lead to CATEGORYFD.
5. Analyze each FEATURE to obtain the according FEATUREPROFILE. Statistics (*entropy, density*, etc.) and aggregated data (*valueCounts* in Fig. 2) are computed directly in the silo using dedicated queries. The specializations are also made on the feature's data type.
6. Collect HOSPITAL information about their station and the computational resource they provide. This information is provided only once at the creation of the station in the hospital.

3.3 Building the Global Catalog

Finally, we build a global catalog intended for end users, e.g., healthcare or IT experts (recall Fig. 1). It results from the union of all the individual catalogs created at each hospital. When the underlying silos are updated, the individual catalogs are re-computed and the union is updated to obtain the new global catalog. Thanks to our general conceptual model, we are able to display all the data (datasets, features) and their associated profiles in a very simple way. It also eases the creation of visualization charts showing aggregated data. Numeric features can be plotted as histograms where the x-axis is for the values and the y-axis for their frequencies. Categorical features can be shown as pie charts where each slice is a value and its size is proportional to its frequency. Date features can be displayed as bar plots where the axes contain the dates (horizontal) and their frequencies (vertical). Remaining information can be shown as such in the Web interface.

4 Related Work

Many platforms have been proposed and developed toward facilitating the cooperation between healthcare centers. For instance, EHDEN [3,10] and OHDSI [8] are networks of healthcare databases, each mapped to the OMOP common data model [11], a conceptual model for representing observational data. Despite such models being convenient for specific use-cases, they fail at being general and require an (important) effort from experts to map their data to the model. Next, to create federated learning scenarios in a network of interoperable silos, users need catalogs to discover what silos contain (metadata, aggregated data, etc.). EHDEN exposes a Web interface providing a set of pre-defined statistics for each database (number of patients, gender and age distributions, etc.) while OHDSI proposes multiple interfaces, including statistics, ontology exploration and predictions. To generalize catalog modeling, several catalog models have been designed, including DCAT [6] (Data Catalog Vocabulary) and Data Cube Vocabulary [5], both W3C RDF vocabularies. Nevertheless, catalogs have to be (re)developed from scratch for every platform, thus limiting the set of visualizations. On the contrary, we adopt a more general approach based on I-ETL [1] and PADME [12]. Because I-ETL supplies a comprehensive data model not tailored to any specific use-case, we could design a general catalog, able to profile any silo without manual intervention and/or prior knowledge on the data.

5 Conclusion and Vision

In this vision paper, we presented our ongoing work toward enabling federated analyses and algorithms across healthcare silos. For this, we have proposed a holistic conceptual model for cataloging silos, as well as a pipeline to create a general catalog, necessary to experts for browsing and designing FL tasks. The main challenge was to design a catalog conceptual model carrying information and statistics both for data and metadata while remaining general. The system is under implementation and will raise many new challenges once finished, including the formulation of queries based on our global models, the query evaluation on aggregated data vs. real data, and the usage of LLMs to ask queries in natural language.

We believe that abstracting current conceptual models dedicated to tailored healthcare use-cases is a promising approach. This allows for their reuse and for the design of use case-agnostic pipelines, which can later be exploited in various settings (without the need to adapt models to the data). It also promotes easy exploration of large and complex silos.

Acknowledgments. This work is supported by the Horizon Europe project BETTER, Grant agreement n. 101136262. We thank all the partners involved in this project for their valuable contributions and feedback.

References

1. Barret, N., et al.: I-ETL: an interoperability-aware health (meta)data pipeline to enable federated analyses. Journal manuscript under revision (2025)
2. Beyan, O., et al.: Distributed analytics on sensitive medical data: the personal health train. Data Intell. **2**, 96–107 (2020)

3. Blacketer, C., et al.: Using the data quality dashboard to improve the EHDEN network. Appl. Sci. **11**, 11920 (2021)
4. Chen, P.P.S.: The entity-relationship model-toward a unified view of data. ACM Trans. Database Syst. (TODS) **1**, 9–36 (1976)
5. The Data Cube vocabulary. https://www.w3.org/TR/vocab-data-cube/
6. The DCAT vocabulary. https://www.w3.org/TR/vocab-dcat/
7. Gisby, J.S., et al.: Multi-omics identify falling LRRC15 as a COVID-19 severity marker and persistent pro-thrombotic signals in convalescence. Nat. Commun. **13**, 7775 (2022)
8. Hripcsak, G., et al.: Observational health data sciences and informatics (OHDSI): opportunities for observational researchers. In: MEDINFO 2015 (2015)
9. Dataset for multi-omics identify LRRC15 as a COVID-19 severity predictor and persistent pro-thrombotic signals in convalescence. https://zenodo.org/records/7410194
10. Puttmann, D., et al.: Assessing the FAIRness of databases on the EHDEN portal: a case study on two Dutch ICU databases. Int. J. Med. Inf. **175**, 105104 (2023)
11. Stang, P.E., et al.: Advancing the science for active surveillance: rationale and design for the observational medical outcomes partnership. Ann. Internal Med. **153**, 600–606 (2010)
12. Welten, S., et al.: A privacy-preserving distributed analytics platform for health care data. Methods Inf. Med. **61**, e1-1 (2022)

Lost in Models? Structuring Managerial Decision Support in Process Mining with Multi-criteria Decision Making

Rob H. Bemthuis[✉][iD]

University of Twente, Enschede, The Netherlands
r.h.bemthuis@utwente.nl

Abstract. Process mining is increasingly adopted in modern organizations, producing numerous process models that, while valuable, can lead to model overload and decision-making complexity. This paper explores a multi-criteria decision-making (MCDM) approach to evaluate and prioritize process models by incorporating both quantitative metrics (e.g., fitness, precision) and qualitative factors (e.g., cultural fit). An illustrative logistics example demonstrates how MCDM, specifically the Analytic Hierarchy Process (AHP), facilitates trade-off analysis and promotes alignment with managerial objectives. Initial insights suggest that the MCDM approach enhances context-sensitive decision-making, as selected models address both operational metrics and broader managerial needs. While this study is an early-stage exploration, it provides an initial foundation for deeper exploration of MCDM-driven strategies to enhance the role of process mining in complex organizational settings.

Keywords: Process Mining · Multi-criteria Decision Making · Managerial Decision Support · Analytical Hierarchy Process

1 Introduction

Recent advances in process mining have improved the ability to capture and analyze complex organizational workflows through event logs. However, this progress has led to an increasing abundance of process models, often overlapping in scope or providing divergent insights for different stakeholders (e.g., operational vs. managerial) [6,19,20]. This "model overload" phenomenon presents strategic challenges: rather than supporting decision-making, the sheer volume of (apparently) competing models can obscure key insights and hamper the alignment of process analytics with organizational objectives. As a result, managers may struggle to distinguish relevant models from irrelevant ones, making it difficult to focus on actionable insights (see e.g., [1,4,13,15]).

While process mining accelerates business process digitalization, its effectiveness depends on deeper integration with organizational goals, key performance indicators, and managerial expertise [21,26]. Achieving this integration across diverse processes and stakeholders necessitates a robust decision support mechanism that balances tacit knowledge with empirical findings. Traditional decision support systems often fall short in this regard, as they struggle to incorporate subjective managerial perspectives alongside quantitative process metrics. Consequently, decision-makers must navigate complex model repositories without structured guidance, increasing the risk of suboptimal or misaligned choices.

Multi-Criteria Decision-Making (MCDM) provides a structured framework for evaluating and prioritizing process models by combining quantitative performance metrics with qualitative managerial insights [18]. As a well-established decision analysis method, MCDM is particularly effective when no single optimal solution exists, enabling decision-makers to navigate trade-offs between competing criteria [3,23]. Applying MCDM to process mining extends beyond evaluating models based solely on fitness or precision, promoting alignment with both strategic and operational objectives.

This paper presents an approach for applying MCDM to address model overload in process mining. We propose an approach that synthesizes process mining outputs while integrating an organization's strategic priorities. By combining objective indicators (e.g., fitness, precision) with managerial assessments, MCDM provides a structured way for evaluating and prioritizing process models. This approach offers two key benefits: aligning model selection with strategic objectives and clarifying trade-offs in multi-stakeholder decision-making.

To illustrate the potential of this approach, we present an illustrative example in a logistics context, where the Analytic Hierarchy Process (AHP) is applied as an MCDM approach to filter and prioritize mined process models. Initial findings suggest that MCDM-based methods can reduce model selection complexity, guide resource allocation toward high-impact analyses, and improve communication between technical and managerial stakeholders. While full-scale validation remains an area for future research, we expect that this concept will generate valuable discussions on integrating decision-making theory, managerial insights, and process mining methods. This work proposes a structured approach for more strategic and context-aware use of process models.

The remainder of this paper is as follows. Section 2 discusses related work. Section 3 introduces the proposed MCDM approach. In Sect. 4, we present an illustrative example in the logistics domain, highlighting initial findings and challenges. Section 5 concludes the paper.

2 Related Work

The growing number of discovered process models often results in highly complex structures, commonly referred to as "spaghetti models", and an overwhelming number of variations. These models can obscure meaningful patterns, making it difficult to derive actionable insights [17]. While filtering and abstraction techniques help manage complexity, they frequently introduce redundant or conflicting perspectives, further complicating their alignment with organizational objectives [20]. Moreover, beyond the complexity of each individual model, the sheer volume of potentially overlapping or incompatible models can compound decision-making challenges. Research highlights that stakeholder needs contribute to model overload: highly detailed models, though technically accurate, may be too complex for managerial decision-making [2]. Analysts often struggle to determine which variant best represents the process in a given context, further complicating their evaluations.

Several techniques have been proposed to address complexity. Existing solutions focus on model filtering [11], abstraction [16,28], and domain-specific metrics [14]. Trace clustering [25] is a well-known method that groups similar traces and removes minor variations to enhance process comprehension. However, finding the right level of abstraction remains a challenge: excessive simplification may obscure critical details, while insufficient abstraction leaves models too complex. Process performance metrics, such as fitness, precision, and generalization [10], can assist in selecting promising process models. Furthermore, complexity measures-including control-flow complexity and node/edge counts-help detect overly complex models [4]. Nonetheless, these techniques primarily enhance structural clarity rather than directly supporting strategic decision-making.

Despite advancements in process mining, consolidating multiple discovered models into a coherent, decision-driven framework remains challenging. Most approaches emphasize structural refinement but often neglect managerial preferences, which favor simplicity and strategic relevance over purely technical model quality. Recent studies have explored MCDM techniques in process mining. For example, [24] applied MCDM to rank industrial machines for maintenance planning, integrating technical indicators with expert judgment. Similarly, [12] used AHP for process mining technology selection, incorporating uncertainty and sensitivity analysis to improve ranking robustness. While these studies demonstrate MCDM's potential for process-related decision-making, they focus on technology and asset selection rather than process model evaluation. Our work builds on that foundation by applying MCDM, specifically AHP, to structurally compare and prioritize discovered process models, thereby contributing to alignment with managerial objectives.

3 Proposed Approach

This section presents an MCDM approach to assist in selecting and prioritizing process models (typically obtained from large repositories). As illustrated in Fig. 1, the approach structures decision-making by ranking and selecting models based on multiple, potentially conflicting criteria:

1. **Problem definition**: define the selection objective, identifying the most relevant process model(s) from a set of discovered alternatives.
2. **Criteria identification**: evaluation relies on two broad categories. **Quantitative metrics**: process mining measures, such as fitness, precision, generalization, and simplicity. **Qualitative metrics**: managerial factors, such as decision-support value (e.g., the model's ability to highlight operational inefficiencies), stakeholder alignment (e.g., relevance to different stakeholder groups), and implementation feasibility (e.g., potential impact).

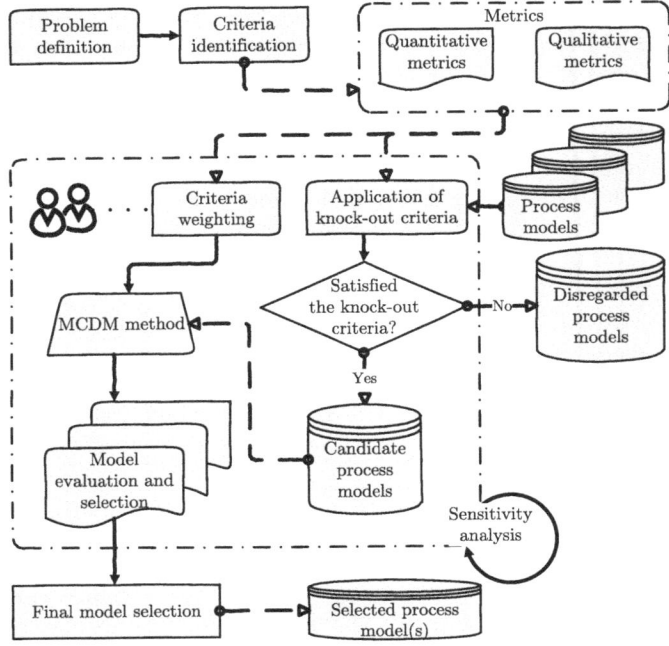

Fig. 1. Proposed MCDM approach for process model selection.

3. **Application of knock-out criteria**: models failing key constraints-such as structural completeness, data quality, or regulatory compliance-are eliminated early.
4. **Criteria weighting**: weights are determined using pairwise comparisons, entropy-based weighting, or expert input, to reflect each criterion's relative importance.
5. **Model evaluation and selection**: process models are ranked using an MCDM technique. The choice of method depends on the decision context, data availability, and stakeholder preferences (see [27] for an overview).
6. **Sensitivity analysis**: criteria weights are varied to assess ranking stability under different scenarios.

By structuring the selection process in these steps, this approach can mitigate bias, reduce reliance on purely technical measures, and better align process mining outputs with managerial decision-making.

4 Illustrative Example

To illustrate the feasibility of our proposed MCDM approach, we apply it to a logistics case study presented in [8], which focuses on selecting process models derived from event logs. The study includes a dataset comprising 270 event logs generated across 27 distinct system configurations [7], with each configuration yielding 20 log files. For this illustrative example, we concentrate on the first event log per experiment, thus evaluating one event log per configuration. Process models were extracted using the Inductive Miner, which is expected to produce sound, relatively simple models, and were subsequently evaluated.

4.1 Problem Definition

The objective of this illustrative study is to support decision-makers in selecting the most suitable *configuration for investment*, taking into account uncertainty in the decision-making process. Process models function as part of multiple evaluation criteria, alongside throughput time and implementation risk. A key challenge is to balance technical accuracy with practical feasibility, thereby contributing to a more informed and strategic investment decision.

4.2 Criteria Identification

To evaluate model quality, we consider quantitative metrics associated with key process mining quality dimensions: fitness, precision, and generalization. Simplicity is excluded due to its strong correlation with generalization [9]. Using the Inductive Miner, we obtained the scores for the scenarios detailed in [8], as illustrated in Fig. 2. As additional criteria, we include the throughput times specified in [8] and the implementation risk linked to business goal alignment.

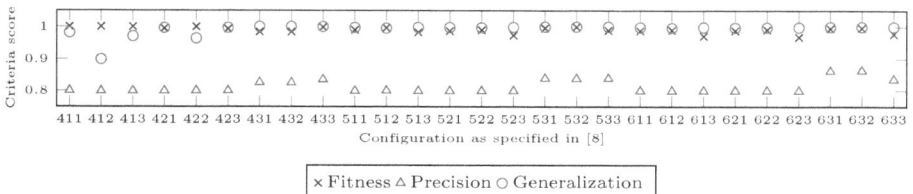

Fig. 2. Evaluation of process models extracted with the Inductive Miner.

4.3 Application of Knock-Out Criteria

To ensure high-quality model selection, we set a strict fitness threshold of 0.999. Out of the initial 27 process models, only 5 meet this criterion and are retained for further analysis.

4.4 Criteria Weighting

We use Saaty's AHP method [22], which is widely applied in decision-making [5], to determine the relative importance of *fitness* (F), *precision* (P), and *generalization* (G) via expert pairwise comparisons (Table 1). The resulting weights are $w_F = 0.57$, $w_P = 0.22$, and $w_G = 0.21$. *Throughput time* (T) is categorized into low (0-50 min, $C_2 = 1.0$), medium (50-100 min, $C_2 = 0.75$), and high (> 100 min, $C_2 = 0.50$). *Implementation risk* (IR), assessed externally, is classified as low ($C_3 = 1.0$), medium ($C_3 = 0.70$), or high ($C_3 = 0.50$). The *overall weight allocation* is $w_1 = 0.40$ (process model quality), $w_2 = 0.25$ (throughput time), and $w_3 = 0.35$ (implementation risk).

Table 1. Pairwise comparison results for F, P, and G.

Criteria	Stakeholder 1				Stakeholder 2				Stakeholder 3			
	F	P	G	Weight	F	P	G	Weight	F	P	G	Weight
F	-	6.00	7.00	0.76	-	5.00	5.00	0.71	-	1.00	0.33	0.23
P	0.17	-	1.00	0.12	0.20	-	1.00	0.14	1.00	-	2.00	0.40
G	0.14	1.00	-	0.12	0.20	1.00	-	0.14	3.00	0.50	-	0.37

4.5 Model Evaluation and Selection

The *final model score* is computed as: $C_{\text{total}} = \sum_{i=1}^{n} w_i C_i$, where C_1 (process model quality), C_2 (throughput time), and C_3 (implementation risk) contribute to the ranking (see Table 2). Although 532 leads in C_1 and C_2, 411 ranks best overall due to its balanced performance. This highlights the importance of multi-criteria evaluation integrating technical quality and practical feasibility.

Table 2. Performance comparison of different configurations.

Conf.	F	P	G	C_1	T (min)	C_2	C_3	C_{total}
411	1.000	0.800	0.981	0.952	73.3	0.70 (medium)	0.75 (medium)	**0.818**
412	1.000	0.799	0.899	0.934	211.9	0.50 (high)	0.75 (medium)	0.761
413	1.000	0.799	0.970	0.949	74.3	0.70 (medium)	0.75 (medium)	0.817
422	1.000	0.800	0.964	0.948	107.3	0.50 (high)	0.75 (medium)	0.767
532	1.000	0.825	1.000	0.964	33.13	1.0 (low)	0.50 (high)	0.811

Although we do not include a sensitivity analysis in this study, future work could explore its effect by adjusting criteria weights to assess ranking robustness. Further validation may involve expanding beyond traditional process mining dimensions (e.g., fitness, precision, generalization) to incorporate additional metrics, both quantitative and qualitative, as well as experimenting with alternative MCDM methods to enhance model selection stability.

5 Conclusions

This study highlights the potential of MCDM as a structured approach for mitigating model overload in process mining. By integrating quantitative metrics with managerial considerations, the proposed approach enables more context-sensitive selection and prioritization of process models. The logistics-based illustrative example demonstrates how MCDM facilitates trade-off analysis and promotes alignment between technical criteria and managerial objectives.

While the approach shows promise, further research is needed to evaluate alternative MCDM methods, incorporate additional decision criteria (e.g., risk, cost, compliance), and expand sensitivity analysis to assess ranking stability. Real-world adoption will also require addressing potential resistance to using the approach among stakeholders. Integration with existing process mining tools may further enhance practical applicability. Ultimately, empirical validation remains key to refining this approach into a broadly applicable decision-support solution.

Acknowledgments. This work was (financially) supported by the Dutch Ministry of Infrastructure and Water Management and TKI Dinalog (ECOLOGIC project; case no. 31192090).

References

1. Akhramovich, K., Serral, E., Cetina, C.: A systematic literature review on the application of process mining to Industry 4.0. Knowl. Inf. Syst. **66**(5), 2699–2746 (2024)
2. Ammann, J., Lohoff, L., Wurm, B., Hess, T.: How do process mining users act, think, and feel? An explorative study of process mining use patterns. Bus. Inf. Syst. Eng. 1–23 (2025)
3. Aruldoss, M., Lakshmi, T.M., Venkatesan, V.P.: A survey on multi criteria decision making methods and its applications. Am. J. Inf. Syst. **1**(1), 31–43 (2013)
4. Augusto, A., Mendling, J., Vidgof, M., Wurm, B.: The connection between process complexity of event sequences and models discovered by process mining. Inf. Sci. **598**, 196–215 (2022)
5. Aziz, N.F., Sorooshian, S., Mahmud, F.: MCDM-AHP method in decision makings. ARPN J. Eng. Appl. Sci. **11**(11), 7217–7220 (2016)
6. Batista, E., Solanas, A.: Process mining in healthcare: a systematic review. In: 2018 9th International Conference on Information, Intelligence, Systems and Applications (IISA), pp. 1–6. IEEE (2018)
7. Bemthuis, R., Koot, M., Mes, M., Bukhsh, F.A., Iacob, M.E., Meratnia, N.: Data underlying the paper: An agent-based process mining architecture for emergent behavior analysis (2019). https://doi.org/10.4121/12708839.v2
8. Bemthuis, R.H., Koot, M., Mes, M.R.K., Bukhsh, F.A., Iacob, M.E., Meratnia, N.: An agent-based process mining architecture for emergent behavior analysis. In: 2019 IEEE 23rd International Enterprise Distributed Object Computing Workshop (EDOCW), pp. 54–64. IEEE (2019)
9. Buijs, J., van Dongen, B.F., van der Aalst, W.: Quality dimensions in process discovery: the importance of fitness, precision, generalization and simplicity. Int. J. Cooper. Inf. Syst. **23**(01), 1440001 (2014)
10. Buijs, J., van Dongen, B.F., van der Aalst, W.: On the role of fitness, precision, generalization and simplicity in process discovery. In: Meersman, R., et al. (eds.) OTM 2012. LNCS, vol. 7565, pp. 305–322. Springer, Heidelberg (2012). https://doi.org/10.1007/978-3-642-33606-5_19
11. Conforti, R., La Rosa, M., Ter Hofstede, A.H.: Filtering out infrequent behavior from business process event logs. IEEE Trans. Knowl. Data Eng. **29**(2), 300–314 (2016)

12. Dogan, O.: Process mining technology selection with spherical fuzzy AHP and sensitivity analysis. Expert Syst. Appl. **178**, 114999 (2021)
13. Elkhovskaya, L.O., Kshenin, A.D., Balakhontceva, M.A., Ionov, M.V., Kovalchuk, S.V.: Extending process discovery with model complexity optimization and cyclic states identification: application to healthcare processes. Algorithms **16**(1), 57 (2023)
14. Hidalgo, L., Munoz-Gama, J.: Domain-driven event abstraction framework for learning dynamics in MOOCS sessions. In: Montali, M., Senderovich, A., Weidlich, M. (eds.) Process Mining Workshops. ICPM 2022. LNBIP, vol. 468, pp. 552–564. Springer, Cham (2022). https://doi.org/10.1007/978-3-031-27815-0_40
15. Imran, M., Ismail, M.A., Hamid, S., Nasir, M.: Complex process modeling in process mining: a systematic review. IEEE Access **10**, 101515–101536 (2022)
16. Jagadeesh Chandra Bose, R.P., van der Aalst, W.: Abstractions in process mining: a taxonomy of patterns. In: Dayal, U., Eder, J., Koehler, J., Reijers, H.A. (eds.) BPM 2009. LNCS, vol. 5701, pp. 159–175. Springer, Heidelberg (2009). https://doi.org/10.1007/978-3-642-03848-8_12
17. Klessascheck, F., et al.: Domain-specific event abstraction. In: Business Information Systems, pp. 117–126 (2021)
18. Köksalan, M.M., Wallenius, J., Zionts, S.: Multiple criteria decision making: from early history to the 21st century. World Scientific (2011)
19. Maneschijn, D.G., Bemthuis, R.H., Bukhsh, F.A., Iacob, M.E.: A methodology for aligning process model abstraction levels and stakeholder needs. In: 24th International Conference on Enterprise Information Systems, pp. 137–147. SCITEPRESS (2022)
20. Maneschijn, D.G., Bemthuis, R.H., Arachchige, J.J., Bukhsh, F.A., Iacob, M.E.: Balancing simplicity and complexity in modeling mined business processes: A user perspective. In: Filipe, J., Śmiałek, M., Brodsky, A., Hammoudi, S. (eds.) Enterprise Information Systems. ICEIS 2022. LNBIP, vol. 487, pp. 3–21. Springer, Cham (2022). https://doi.org/10.1007/978-3-031-39386-0_1
21. Reinkemeyer, L.: Process Mining in Action. Springer, Cham (2020). https://doi.org/10.1007/978-3-030-40172-6
22. Saaty, T.L.: Decision making with the analytic hierarchy process. Int. J. Serv. Sci. **1**(1), 83–98 (2008)
23. Sahoo, S.K., Goswami, S.S.: A comprehensive review of multiple criteria decision-making (MCDM) methods: advancements, applications, and future directions. Decis. Making Adv. **1**(1), 25–48 (2023)
24. dos Santos, C.F., Loures, E.d.F.R., Santos, E.A.P.: A smart framework to perform a criticality analysis in industrial maintenance using combined MCDM methods and process mining techniques. Int. J. Adv. Manuf. Technol. **136**(9), 3971–3987 (2025)
25. Song, M., Günther, C.W., van der Aalst, W.: Trace clustering in process mining. In: Ardagna, D., Mecella, M., Yang, J. (eds.) BPM 2008. LNBIP, vol. 17, pp. 109–120. Springer, Heidelberg (2009). https://doi.org/10.1007/978-3-642-00328-8_11
26. Vom Brocke, J., Jans, M., Mendling, J., Reijers, H.A.: A five-level framework for research on process mining (2021)
27. Zavadskas, E.K., Turskis, Z., Kildienė, S.: State of art surveys of overviews on MCDM/MADM methods. Technol. Econ. Dev. Econ. **20**(1), 165–179 (2014)
28. van Zelst, S.J., Mannhardt, F., de Leoni, M., Koschmider, A.: Event abstraction in process mining: literature review and taxonomy. Granul. Comput. **6**, 719–736 (2021)

From Words to Workflows: Extracting Object-Centric Event Logs from Textual Data

Alina Buss[1], Christoph Kecht[2,3,4(✉)], Wolfgang Kratsch[2,3,5], Maximilian Röglinger[2,3,4], Sareh Sadeghianasl[6], and Moe T. Wynn[6]

[1] TUM School of Management, Technical University of Munich, Munich, Germany
alina.buss@tum.de
[2] FIM Research Center for Information Management,
Augsburg & Bayreuth, Germany
{christoph.kecht,wolfgang.kratsch,maximilian.roeglinger}@fim-rc.de
[3] Branch Business & Information Systems Engineering of the Fraunhofer FIT,
Augsburg & Bayreuth, Germany
[4] University of Bayreuth, Bayreuth, Germany
[5] Technical University of Applied Sciences Augsburg, Augsburg, Germany
[6] Queensland University of Technology, Brisbane, Australia
{s.sadeghianasl,m.wynn}@qut.edu.au

Abstract. Organizations generate vast amounts of data in unstructured formats, such as textual descriptions, which remain largely untapped for process mining. This data is particularly valuable because it often captures critical exception cases and intricate dependencies that are absent in structured datasets, but crucial for understanding process deviations. Importantly, these unstructured sources frequently preserve the object-centric nature of real-world processes – information that is typically flattened or lost in traditional, case-centric event log formats. In this paper, we harness this potential and tackle the research gap by introducing a novel approach to extract Object-Centric Event Logs (OCELs) from unstructured textual descriptions using natural language processing techniques and large language models. Our approach consists of two subcomponents: a collector and a refiner. The collector aims to extract activities, timestamps, entities and their properties from textual descriptions, while the refiner integrates, cleans, and refines the extracted information from multiple descriptions. We implement both subcomponents in heuristic and generative forms, creating four distinct extractor variants that are compared against each other on synthetic textual descriptions derived from six publicly available OCEL datasets. Our results reveal that a generative collector combined with a heuristic refiner exhibits the strongest generalization capabilities on unseen textual descriptions.

Keywords: Object-Centric Event Logs · Process Mining · Natural Language Processing

1 Introduction

Process mining aims to analyze and optimize business processes by deriving insights from real-world event data. The starting point of all process mining activities are event logs, which are detailed records of process events that capture the sequence and context of activities taken within a process. Given their foundational role, the accurate and comprehensive extraction of these event logs is paramount for the success of subsequent process mining procedures [12,13]. Most existing approaches focus on extracting event logs from structured data within organizations' core information systems [7]. However, an increasing amount of process-related data is generated outside these systems in unstructured formats. This data often emerges as a result of deviations from the expected process behavior, such as manual interventions or exception handling, and, therefore, captures valuable information absent in structured data sources. Consequently, the targeted application of Natural Language Processing (NLP) to extract event logs from unstructured data sources, as successfully demonstrated in extant research [4,7], enables a more comprehensive representation of real-world processes.

Furthermore, real-world processes often exhibit object-centric characteristics that are typically reflected in textual descriptions. For example, a recruitment process may involve multiple entities such as different applicants, applications, and vacancies [14]. Traditional case-centric event log formats like the eXtensible Event Stream (XES) standard [6] are unsuitable for representing relationships between these entities due to simplifying assumptions. To overcome this limitation, advanced Object-Centric Event Log (OCEL) formats such as the Object Centric Event Data (OCED) meta-model [3] and the OCEL 2.0 format [2] have been proposed recently [14,15]. However, to the best of our knowledge, no existing approaches target the extraction of OCELs from unstructured textual data.

To address this research gap, we develop an approach that comprises two primary subcomponents: a **collector** that extracts activities, timestamps, entities and their properties from textual descriptions and a **refiner** that consolidates this information over multiple descriptions through data integration, cleaning, and refinement. Each subcomponent is implemented in both heuristic and generative forms, yielding four distinct combinations, referred to as extractor variants. We evaluate these variants on synthetic textual descriptions derived from six publicly available OCEL datasets, each containing 1,000 events. The results indicate that the most effective configuration combines a generative collector, which excels in semantic extraction, with a heuristic refiner that improves precision through clearly defined rules. On average, this hybrid extractor exhibits the strongest generalization capabilities on unseen data.

In summary, this paper makes two key contributions. First, it introduces a flexible approach for extracting OCELs from unstructured text. Second, it systematically compares four instantiations, highlighting the strengths and tradeoffs of NLP techniques and Large Language Models (LLMs). The implementation of the extractor variants and the evaluation data are available on GitHub[1].

---

[1] https://github.com/Alinabuss/OCEL-extractor.

2 Design and Development

Figure 1 illustrates our approach for extracting OCELs from unstructured textual descriptions. We aim to provide a generic and domain-independent solution by leveraging different NLP techniques, thus minimizing the need for human intervention and supporting automated extraction from large datasets. Our approach comprises two subcomponents: a **collector** and a **refiner**. Initially, the collector subcomponent iteratively processes textual descriptions of arbitrary length to extract relevant information and structure it into a preliminary OCEL format. Handling each description individually reduces overall execution time and supports the progressive addition of data. Next, the refiner subcomponent concatenates these preliminary snippets and aims to improve the overall coherence of the resulting OCEL by mitigating inconsistencies and redundancies arising from variations in data structures and terminologies that could lead to misinterpretations or an incomplete representation of the process.

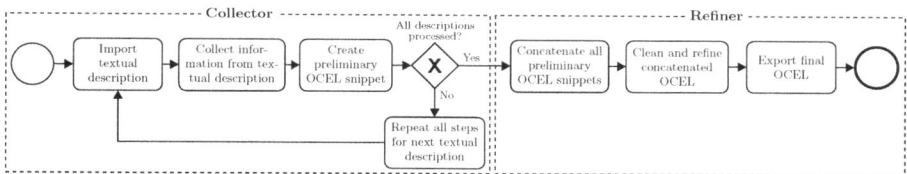

Fig. 1. Extraction approach

In the following, we instantiate the collector and refiner subcomponents in both heuristic and generative forms to extract event logs in the OCEL 2.0 format. The heuristic forms apply predefined rules, ensuring consistent outputs for the same input, while the generative forms utilize a LLM and thus allow for varying outputs for the same input. These subcomponents are combined into four distinct configurations, referred to as extractor variants: a HEU-HEU extractor (heuristic collector and refiner), a GEN-GEN extractor (generative collector and refiner), a GEN-HEU extractor (generative collector and heuristic refiner), and a HEU-GEN extractor (heuristic collector and generative refiner).

The **heuristic collector** gradually processes the provided textual descriptions using the Python NLP library SpaCy. A parsing pipeline tokenizes the text and extracts key token features, including dependency labels, Part-of-speech (PoS) tags, Named-entity recognition (NER) labels, and syntactic dependency relations such as children and ancestor tokens. Following a set of predefined rules, the collector evaluates the tokens, their dependencies, PoS tags, and NER labels to identify candidate values for the essential OCEL components: timestamps, activities, object labels, object types, attribute values, and attribute types. After refining the extracted values through lemmatization, analysis of their surroundings for reference values, and filtering redundant words extracted for multiple categories, these candidate values are assigned to OCEL components according to predefined rules. Furthermore, by evaluating the associated children and ancestor tokens of each candidate value, as well as its positional context within the text, the collector maps object labels to object types, attribute values to attribute types, object labels to other object labels to reveal Object-to-Object (O2O) relationships, activities to timestamps, attributes to timestamps, object labels to activity-timestamp combinations to extract Event-to-Object (E2O) relationships, and attribute values to object labels and activity-timestamp-combinations. Based on these mappings, the heuristic collector generates a preliminary OCEL snippet per textual description. For example, the sentence "On January 15, 2023, the employee John Doe attended a training session" results in the following snippet:

```
{"objectTypes": [{"name": "Employee", "attributes": []}],
"eventTypes": [{"name": "attend training session", "attributes": []}],
"objects": [{"id": "John Doe", "type": "Employee"}],
"events": [{
"id": "1", "type": "attend training session",
"time": "2023-01-15T00:00:00Z",
"relationships": [{"objectId": "John Doe", "qualifier": null}]}]}
```

The **generative collector** invokes OpenAI's `gpt-4o-mini-2024-07-18` LLM and utilizes its included file-search capabilities. The textual descriptions are gradually provided via a user prompt to the LLM, which is then requested to generate a preliminary OCELs snippet per textual descriptions. To guide the extraction process and ensure adherence to the OCEL 2.0 format, an example event log containing a single event in this format is stored in the LLM's knowledge base. The corresponding system prompt can be found in the GitHub repository.

Afterward, within the **heuristic refiner**, the preliminary OCEL snippets are concatenated to a unified version that then undergoes a series of cleaning and refinement steps, leveraging predefined rules and majority-based approaches. These steps are repeated until the log attains a final state, with a maximum of five iterations. Within these iterations, the refiner alleviates data quality issues by, for example, resolving name inconsistencies, merging synonyms, and enforcing alignment between the `objectTypes`, `eventTypes`, `objects`, and `events` components of the OCEL 2.0 format. For the aforementioned example, a follow-up message could be: "January 18, 2023: John completed the training". From this text entry, several data quality issues emerge at the collector level. First, `"John"` will not be assigned to the `object` label `"John Doe"` and second, his `objectType` `"Employee"` will be missing since it wasn't restated explicitly. However, given the semantic similarity of `"John"` and `"John Doe"`, and the previously identified `objectType`, the heuristic refiner is able to resolve both issues.

In contrast, the **generative refiner** relies on an LLM, in our implementation again OpenAI's `gpt-4o-mini-2024-07-18` model. To this end, the concatenated event log is loaded into the LLM's knowledge base and the LLM is prompted to refine the event log and represent it in the OCEL 2.0 format. The corresponding user prompt can again be found in the GitHub repository.

3 Evaluation

We evaluate the four extractor variants using ground-truth data derived from six publicly available OCEL, allowing performance comparisons across multiple domains. Figure 2 depicts our evaluation framework, which comprises a **generator** instance, an **extractor** instance, and a **comparison** instance.

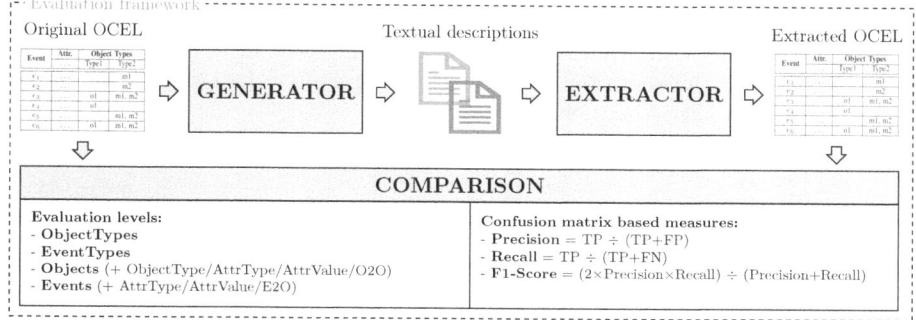

Fig. 2. Evaluation framework

Initially, we compile a dataset of six publicly available OCELs. Three of these logs – a recruitment log [1], logistics log [8], and Procure-to-Payment (P2P) log [11] – were previously employed in developing and validating the predefined rules in the heuristic collector and refiner. The remaining three logs – an order management log [9], a production log [5], and an Age of Empires log [10] – were not used during development, providing an opportunity to evaluate the generalization capabilities of each extractor variant. For each of the six event logs, we create a test subset of 1,000 events, ensuring there is no overlap between the test subsets and the subsets used during the development of the heuristic subcomponents.

The test subsets are then processed by the **generator instance**, tasked with converting the events into textual descriptions across three levels of complexity. One-third of the events is transformed into Complexity Level 1 descriptions – one textual description per event. Another third is converted into Complexity Level 2 descriptions – non-overlapping daily reports, with events grouped by day. The final third is transformed into Complexity Level 3 descriptions – overlapping reports, where events are grouped based on their related objects. To generate these textual descriptions, the generator instance utilizes OpenAI's `GPT-4o-mini-2024-07-18` model. The four extractor variants are then employed as the **extractor instance**, tasked with analyzing the provided textual descriptions to reconstruct the original OCEL. Each extractor variant leverages its respective heuristic or generative collector and refiner subcomponents to accomplish this task. As a result, one extracted OCEL in OCEL 2.0 format is created for each original OCEL.

Finally, the extracted OCELs are compared with their original counterparts using the **comparison instance**, which evaluates their alignment across various categories and levels of detail. The levels of detail – comprising parent and child levels – follow the structure of the OCEL 2.0 format. At the parent level, categories such as objectTypes, eventTypes, objects, and events are analyzed to ensure the existence of corresponding values in the extracted logs. Furthermore, at the child level, the comparison instance assesses whether specific child values are accurately mapped to their parent categories. For example, it verifies whether object types, attribute types, and attribute values are correctly linked to object labels, and whether the appropriate O2O and E2O relationships are identified. The overall score for each OCEL category is calculated by averaging the results across parent and child levels.

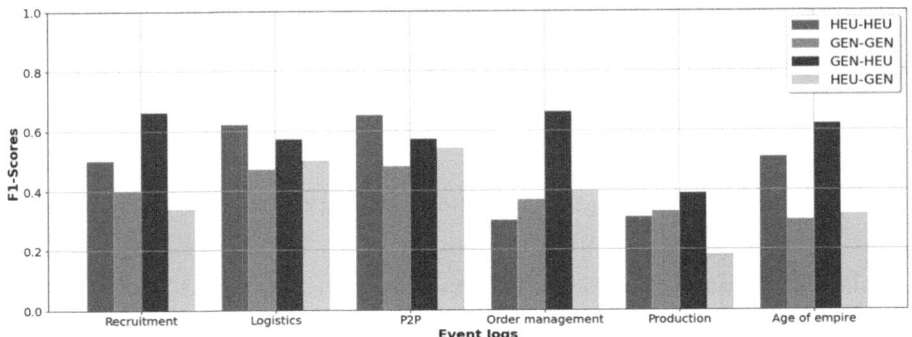

Fig. 3. Overall F1-score across all event logs

Figure 3 shows the overall F1-scores across all six event logs and all four extractor variants. The HEU-HEU extractor variant is particularly suitable for the three event logs used during the development of its heuristic subcomponents, surpassing all other variants on these three event logs, except for the GEN-HEU extractor variant on the Recruitment log. Although this finding suggests that the heuristic subcomponents were fine-tuned to the characteristics of the three event logs used during development, the HEU-HEU variant also shows promising generalization capabilities on the Age of Empires log, indicating that its performance is not strictly confined to the development data. In contrast, the GEN-GEN extractor variant achieves comparable, albeit more moderate results across all six event logs, which aligns with the fact that the LLM prompts were identical and not tailored to any specific log. However, the GEN-HEU extractor variant emerges as the overall best-performing approach, consistently outperforming both GEN-GEN and HEU-GEN variants on all six event logs, and exhibiting only minor performance differences between the development and test logs. Finally, the HEU-GEN extractor variant yields the lowest F1-scores on average, particularly struggling on the test event logs and remaining consistently behind the GEN-HEU variant.

In conclusion, we recommend using the GEN-HEU extractor variant, which combines the strengths of the generative collector and the heuristic refiner. This hybrid approach consistently achieves the best overall performance, delivering satisfactory F1-scores and robust generalization capabilities. Furthermore, its completely unsupervised nature eliminates the need for human intervention, enabling automatic application across a wide variety of topics and large datasets. The generative collector component can also be fine-tuned with minimal effort by adjusting the LLM prompt, allowing the extractor to easily adapt to domain-specific requirements. However, it is important to acknowledge that our results are based on synthetically generated textual descriptions, which may not fully reflect data quality issues present in real-world texts, such as missing timestamps or inconsistent terminology. Additionally, our heuristic components showed reduced effectiveness when processing datasets significantly differing from those used during their development. Addressing these limitations through evaluation with real-world datasets should be the focus of future research to further enhance the reliability and accuracy of the extraction process.

4 Conclusion

This paper presents a novel approach for extracting OCELs from unstructured textual descriptions, thereby tackling a critical gap in process mining by incorporating textual data that often captures edge cases overlooked in structured data sources. Our approach comprises two distinct subcomponents – a collector and a refiner – that systematically transform textual descriptions into OCELs. Each subcomponent was instantiated in both heuristic and generative forms, resulting in four combined extractor variants that we compared against each other in an artificial evaluation on synthetic textual descriptions derived from six publicly available OCEL datasets. Our results reveal that a generative collector combined with a heuristic refiner exhibits the highest average F1-score and the strongest generalization capabilities on unseen textual descriptions.

The key contribution of our research is a flexible approach that systematically leverages NLP techniques and LLMs to enable process mining on unstructured text data. Specifically, our approach addresses critical gaps by handling object-centric data embedded in textual descriptions, which often include valuable insights on process deviations and manual exception handling. Furthermore, we systematically compare heuristic and generative methods. The implementation of the extractor variants and the evaluation data are available on GitHub. Future work should apply our approach to real-world textual descriptions to demonstrate its viability in practice. In parallel, establishing robust benchmarks that assess how effectively the extracted OCELs support process mining in practical scenarios remains a promising avenue for future research.

Acknowledgments. This work was supported in part by the Bavarian Research Foundation (Bayerische Forschungsstiftung) [grant number AZ-1550-20].

References

1. Berti, A.: Collection of object-centric event logs (OCEL 2.0 format; JSON specification) (2023). https://doi.org/10.5281/ZENODO.8433706
2. Berti, A., et al.: OCEL (Object-Centric Event Log) 2.0 specification (2024). https://arxiv.org/abs/2403.01975
3. Fahland, D., et al.: Towards a simple and extensible standard for object-centric event data (OCED) – Core model, design space, and lessons learned (2024). https://arxiv.org/abs/2410.14495
4. Geeganage, D.T.K., Wynn, M.T., ter Hofstede, A.H.: Text2EL: exploiting unstructured text for event log enrichment. In: 2022 16th International Conference on Signal-Image Technology & Internet-Based Systems (SITIS), Dijon, France, pp. 1–8 (2022). https://doi.org/10.1109/SITIS57111.2022.00010
5. Heinisch, M., Graves, N., van der Aalst, W.M.P.: sOCEL 2.0: a sustainability-enriched OCEL of a hinge production process (2024). https://doi.org/10.5281/ZENODO.13638681
6. IEEE: IEEE standard for extensible event stream (XES) for achieving interoperability in event logs and event streams (2016). https://doi.org/10.1109/IEEESTD.2016.7740858
7. Kecht, C., Egger, A., Kratsch, W., Röglinger, M.: Event log construction from customer service conversations using natural language inference. In: 2021 3rd International Conference on Process Mining (ICPM), Eindhoven, Netherlands, pp. 144–151 (2021). https://doi.org/10.1109/icpm53251.2021.9576869
8. Knopp, B., Graves, N.: Container logistics object-centric event log (2023). https://doi.org/10.5281/ZENODO.8428084
9. Knopp, B., van der Aalst, W.M.P.: Order management object-centric event log in OCEL 2.0 standard (2023). https://doi.org/10.5281/ZENODO.8428112
10. Liss, L., Elbert, N., Flath, C.M., van der Aalst, W.: Object-centric event log for age of empires game interactions (2024). https://doi.org/10.5281/ZENODO.13365584
11. Park, G., Tacke genannt Unterberg, L.: Procure-to-payment (P2P) object-centric event log in OCEL 2.0 standard (2023). https://doi.org/10.5281/ZENODO.8412920
12. van der Aalst, W.: Process mining: overview and opportunities. ACM Trans. Manage. Inf. Syst. **3**(2), 1–7 (2012). https://doi.org/10.1145/2229156.2229157
13. van der Aalst, W.: Process Mining: Data Science in Action. Springer, Berlin, Heidelberg, 2 edn. (2016). https://doi.org/10.1007/978-3-662-49851-4
14. van der Aalst, W.M.P.: Object-centric process mining: an introduction. In: Cerone, A. (ed.) Formal Methods for an Informal World: ICTAC 2021 Summer School, Virtual Event, Astana, Kazakhstan, September 1–7, 2021, Tutorial Lectures, pp. 73–105 (2023). https://doi.org/10.1007/978-3-031-43678-9_3
15. Wynn, M.T., et al.: Rethinking the input for process mining: insights from the XES survey and workshop. In: Munoz-Gama, J., Lu, X. (eds.) Process Mining Workshops. ICPM 2021, Eindhoven, Netherlands, pp. 3–16 (2022). https://doi.org/10.1007/978-3-030-98581-3_1

WSF4ADO: An ADOxx Deployment of the Work Systems Framework

Andrei Chiș(✉) [iD], Ana-Maria Ghiran [iD], and Robert Andrei Buchmann [iD]

OMiLAB@Faculty of Economics and Business Administration, Babeș-Bolyai University, Cluj-Napoca, Romania
{andrei.chis,anamaria.ghiran,robert.buchmann}@econ.ubbcluj.ro

Abstract. The Work Systems Framework (WSF) gained recognition as a work-focused way to describe, decompose and drill-down enterprise systems. Several metamodels have emerged over the years to address a requirement for software tooling and machine interpretability as support for Work Systems analysis and design, i.e. alternatives to the traditional snapshot templates used in early adoption cases. The Work System conceptualization was itself gradually refined with taxonomies of its core notions, even formalized in a machine-readable knowledge graph to investigate possibilities of bridging to run-time operational data.

As a natural step forward, this paper presents WSF4ADO, an ADOxx deployment of the WSF conceptualization offering a diagrammatic DSML (domain-specific modeling language) that captures the core work system concepts and the intended drill-down navigation experience, with scripted mechanisms to ease the design experience and element typing, and the ability to run semantic queries over semantic networks of inter-related work systems. Methodologically, the research follows the Design Science research paradigm and Agile Modeling Method Engineering as a modeling tool deployment framework.

Keywords: Work Systems Framework · Domain-specific Modeling · Design Science · ADOxx · Knowledge Graphs

1 Introduction

The Work System Framework (WSF) [1] was introduced as a decomposable view of IT-reliant organizations and their systems of work - that generate products or services for internal or external beneficiaries (customers). Even though the theory was commonly applied to IT organizations, its core concepts can create snapshots of work systems on different levels of granularity, for any kind of modern organization.

WSF is lightweight, sacrificing the multi-view and layered approach of holistic frameworks such as Zachman Framework [2] for the benefit of reduced complexity and for maintaining focus on contextualized work activities. Instead of shifting viewpoints, it captures focused information for system design and analysis that encompasses an internal viewpoint and an external viewpoint, leverages conceptual economy and recursiveness across levels of granularity, avoiding architecture layers and conceptual overload. It

© The Author(s), under exclusive license to Springer Nature Switzerland AG 2025
L. Pufahl et al. (Eds.): CAiSE 2025, LNBIP 557, pp. 45–52, 2025.
https://doi.org/10.1007/978-3-031-94590-8_6

was successfully applied in many application cases [3] but there is still a shortage of diagrammatic languages to support it. It remains, as emphasized by [4], one of the few enterprise modeling methods that was mostly applied by non-diagrammatic means: Word document templates or Web front-ends, with some proposals of adopting established languages for certain aspects, e.g. BPMN for the process/activities elements [3, 5, 6]. In recent years the literature reported a growing interest in the refinement and ontological unpacking of WST concepts to a level of formalism that enables machine interpretation – e.g. through metamodels [7, 8] or knowledge graphs [9].

This work answers the artifact-building research agenda formulated in [5] and leverages the authors' experience with the engineering of DSMLs by means of metamodeling. The objective is to operationalize WSF in a tool realized on the ADOxx metamodeling platform [10], extended with the ability to run semantic queries over networks of interrelated work systems. Syntax and semantics are derived from WSF and its traditional design artifacts; the effort is also informed by previous efforts of unpacking the theory down to semantic constructs articulated in a knowledge graph [9]. Methodologically, the work is guided by the Design Science framework [11], where the phase of design & development was delegated to the AMME (Agile Modeling Method Engineering) framework [12] - a typical metamodeling approach for ADOxx deployments.

2 WSF Background

Although WSF was traditionally applied through tabular templates and front-end forms to capture work system snapshots and briefings, it conceptualizes a work system in semi-structured ontological terms (Fig. 1) that can be adopted for, or at least can inspire, the specification of first-class modeling constructs of a DSML.

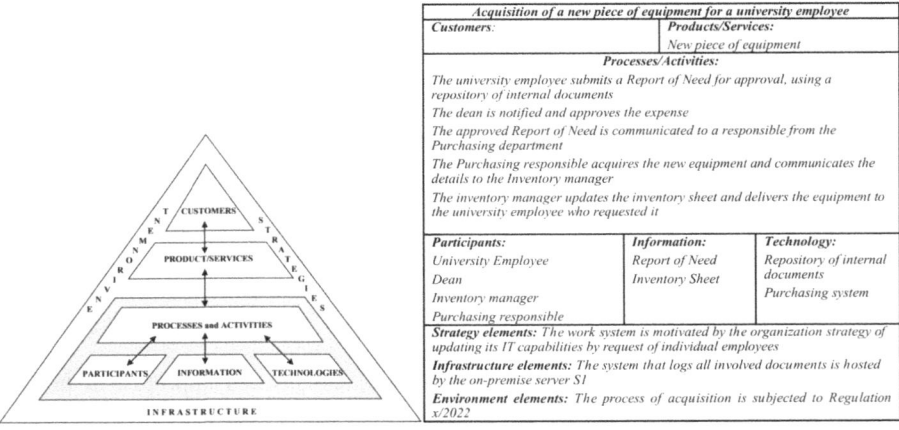

Fig. 1. The Work System Framework (left) [1] and an exemplar of WS snapshot (right) [9]

The WSF elements are: *customers, product/services, processes and activities, participants, information and technologies.* Apart from these internal elements, a work system is also shaped by external influences: *environment, strategies* and *infrastructure*. This knowledge structure is typically promoted as depicted in Fig. 1 (left) while its application in tabular or form-based templates is exemplified on the right side of Fig. 1.

In a work system, a product or service is made for a customer, which can be internal (participant in related work systems) or external. Someone can be a customer for a work system but participant in another one. To realize products/services, work processes/activities are executed, relying on information and technologies. Externally, each work system is subjected to elements of an environment, driven by explicit strategies and supported by specific infrastructure elements. To enable drill-down, each work system can be decomposed in sub-systems having a similar quasi-ontological structure [13].

3 Design Problem and Requirements

The modeling tool is iteratively developed along a Design Science research process [11]. The prospective user groups targeted by this include management staff, educators or business administration students that adopt WSF as a managerial lens/framework but find insufficient support in the traditional document templates or the fragmented recommendations reported by the past literature on WSF artifacts [5]. The design problem statement can be formulated according to the DSR template [14]:

> Enhance **work system design and analysis capabilities** *(problem context)* ... by treating them with a **modeling method derived from the WSF conceptualization** *(artifact)* ... to facilitate **visual design, traceability and query-based briefings on flexible levels of granularity** *(artifact service/requirements)* ... in order to support WSF practitioners **with a design space and semantic navigation approach that overcome limitations of traditional template-based toolkits** *(stakeholder goals)*

The design problem is decomposed in several tool requirements: (a) to enable the visual creation of WSF-based models, while separating the external and internal viewpoints to avoid visual cluttering; (b) to enable queries in WSF terms to retrieve relevant information for work systems briefings; (c) WSF concepts should be linkable/traceable to designs already familiar to enterprise modelers - BPMN, UML and others – thus acting as a semantic layer over related modeling standards, a recommendation derived from [7]; (d) to navigate or zoom over decomposed work systems, both by visual navigation and semantic queries across levels of decomposition.

4 Showcasing WSF4ADO for a Running Example

We start by showcasing the tool[1] to give a visual impression and an indication of semantic querying possibilities over interconnected models. The case is based on a real-world scenario from the university where the authors perform their research activities, referring to the admission of a new student (Fig. 2).

The *customer* of this work system is a high school graduate who wants to enroll as a student. *The service* resulted from the work system is the admission and the changing of

---
[1] https://github.com/andreichis97/WSTBPMN

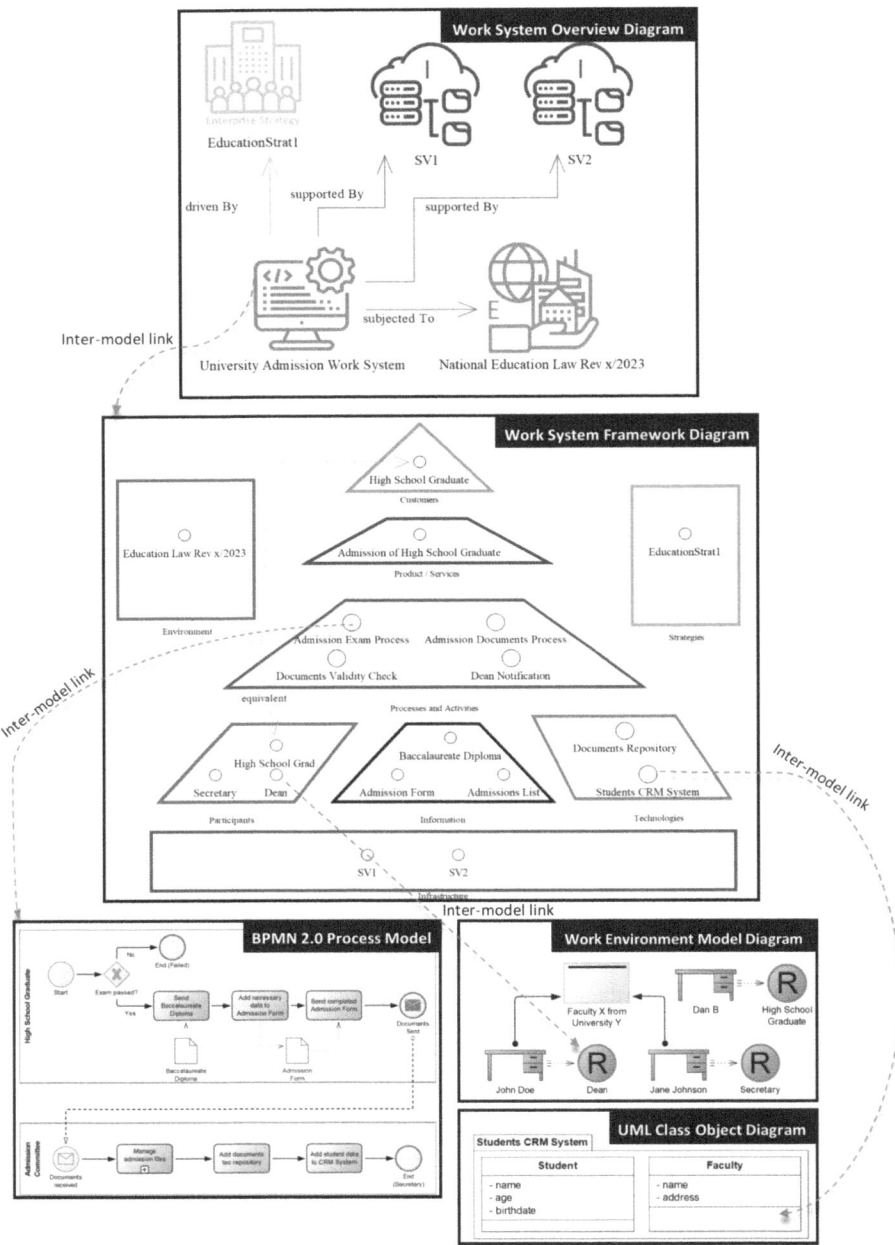

Fig. 2. Examples of WSF4ADO diagrams

their status from high school graduate to student. The main *activities* in the work system are *taking the admission exam, bringing the required documents (baccalaureate diploma, admission form) to the faculty if the exam is passed, checking of validity of documents by the secretary* and *notifying about the admission status of the candidate, sent to the dean of the given faculty*. The following *participants* are involved: *high school graduate* (dual role, both as customer and participant in some processes), *secretary, dean*. The *information* elements are *baccalaureate diploma, admission form* and a *list* of admitted students. Technologically, the work system is represented by a *repository of admission documents* and a *student CRM system*.

In the external viewpoint, the work system is motivated by the strategy element *EducationStrat1*, which states that admissions must be organized each year in order to increase the number of existing students. As *infrastructure elements* two servers, *SV1* and *SV2* are involved in storing documents and the CRM system. The legal environment is established by the National Education Law, Revision x / 2023, which sets the requirements for organizing admission exams.

In the upper part of Fig. 2, the Work System Overview captures the external viewpoint isolating the context given by Strategy, Environment and Infrastructure. The WorkSystemSnapshot element links to the internal viewpoint that resembles the WSF traditional depiction (left of Fig. 1) but provides containers for each WSF category where the elements of the work system are dropped – through a visual reasoning mechanism, the container where they are dropped decided their category and activates annotation properties according to the schema prescribed for each category. Furthermore, the WSF elements can be linked to model types of established conceptualizations – BPMN (for processes/activities), UML (for information or technological elements), Work environments (for participants). These "legacy model types" are inherited from the Bee-Up modeling tool[2], available for educational and experimentation purposes in the OMILAB Digital Innovation Environment [15]. This application of WSF as a semantic layer over models created according to traditional standards generates something similar to a "data fabric" but one applied over collections of diagrams instead of data sources, when the visual designs are exported to RDF graphs. In the same way that knowledge graphs act as data fabrics for master data management over legacy data sources, similar graphs are generated by the WSF models towards a flavor of "master model management", exploiting linking mechanisms to BPMN, UML etc. such as those available in Bee-Up (and in any ADOxx-based tool), as advocated under the label of "Linked Open Models", initially for domain-specific languages [16].

A notion of subsystem is applied as an additional kind of BPMN subprocess – similar to ad-hoc subprocesses but semantically contextualized as a WSF diagram, leading to the possibility of narrowing down, in an alternation manner, work systems to BPMN process descriptions, BPMN subprocesses into work subsystems and so on, to the desired level of granularity. This narrowing down is also navigable by semantic queries once a repository of RDF graphs is derived from the decomposed diagrams, while in the modeling tool it manifests as a hyperlink navigation experience.

Once turned into RDF graphs - according to patterns inspired by the ADOxx plug-in from [16], reimplemented here as a built-in WSF4ADO feature - these diagrams turn

---

[2] https://bee-up.omilab.org/activities/bee-up/.

into a semantic network accumulating graph patterns such as those isolated in Fig. 3. These are the basis for evaluating competency and traceability for debriefings.

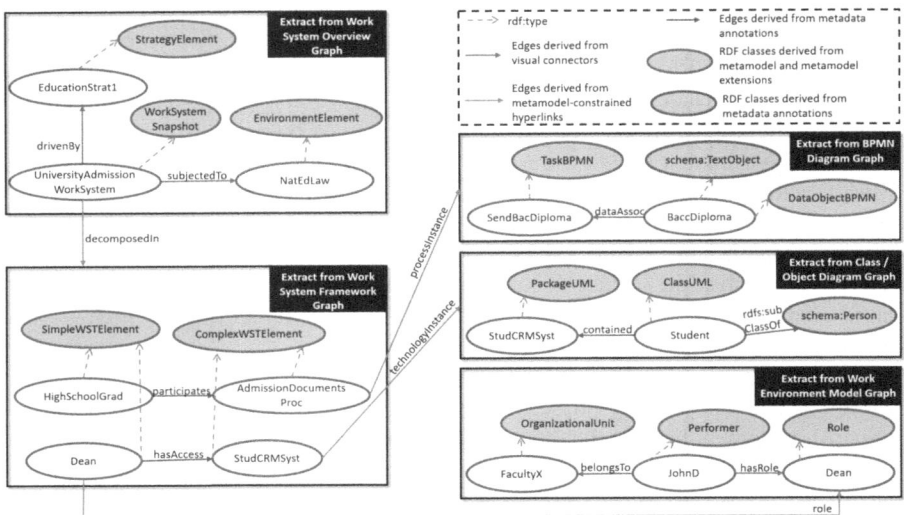

Fig. 3. RDF patterns derived from the diagrammatic WS designs

5 Competency and Traceability of WS Designs

In the current iteration, we focus evaluation on competency questions to be satisfied by semantic queries over a set of inter-related work systems. Such queries can be, to a limited degree, executed on the ADOxx query engine (AQL), directly in the tool, as shown in two examples in Fig. 4:

Fig. 4. AQL query examples (on the left) and results (on the right)

The more generalized query approach runs on the exported RDF graphs, with SPARQL providing more expressivity and features, necessary for recursive property chains, path finding (through GraphDB extensions) or drill-down, aggregating information about work systems' components, scope, involved technologies or participants, and customers served by them.

Query example: Which work systems are used to serve the High School Graduate? What technologies support these work systems and who are the participants performing work in these work systems? Which are the strategies motivating these work systems?

```
PREFIX : <http://www.example.org#>
PREFIX rdfs: <http://www.w3.org/2000/01/rdf-schema#>
SELECT
(GROUP_CONCAT(DISTINCT ?workSystemName; SEPARATOR=", ") AS ?workSystemNames)
(GROUP_CONCAT(DISTINCT ?strategyName; SEPARATOR=", ") AS ?strategyNames)
(GROUP_CONCAT(DISTINCT ?technologyName; SEPARATOR=", ") AS ?technologyNames)
(GROUP_CONCAT(DISTINCT ?participantName; SEPARATOR=", ") AS ?participantNames)
WHERE {
 { SELECT DISTINCT ?workSystemDecomposition WHERE { GRAPH ?workSystemDecomposition
    { ?s rdfs:label "High School Graduate";
         a :SimpleWSTElement; :ofWSTCategory :Customer. } } }
 { SELECT DISTINCT ?workSystem ?workSystemName WHERE
    { ?workSystem :decomposedIn ?workSystemDecomposition;
                  rdfs:label ?workSystemName. } }
 { SELECT DISTINCT ?strategyName ?technologyName WHERE
    { ?workSystem :drivenBy ?strategy; :supportedBy ?technology.
      ?strategy rdfs:label ?strategyName.
      ?technology rdfs:label ?technologyName. } }
 { SELECT DISTINCT ?participantName WHERE { GRAPH ?workSystemDecomposition
    { ?participant :ofWSTCategory :Participant; rdfs:label ?participantName. }}}}
```

Listing 1. Traceability of WSF elements through SPARQL

6 Outlook

In the reported iteration, WSF4ADO serves as a visual modeling tool tailored for capturing work system knowledge to facilitate semantic queries for analysis in WSF terms. WSF acts as knowledge schema that informs, at the same time, the metamodel of a DSML, and taxonomies in a derived knowledge graph, thus facilitating a semantic technology approach to work systems analysis. The development was driven by querying competencies, with some adjustments on the visual notation to apply lessons learned from the notational theory of Moody [17] – e.g. users are also allowed to upload preferred icons to bring the visual impression closer to their domain of activity. The RDF serialization of models is planned to be part of an interoperability set-up involving Large Language Models (LLMs) to achieve the targeted competency via natural language interaction between a WSF practitioner and an LLM using content accumulated from the model-based semantic network. As a platform for the diagram-RDF-LLM integration, we are exploring the GraphRAG patterns offered by Ontotext GraphDB [18].

References

1. Alter, S.: Work system theory: overview of core concepts, extensions, and challenges for the future. J. Assoc. Inf. Syst. 14(2), 72. AIS Journals (2013)
2. Zachman, J.A.: A framework for information systems architecture. IBM Syst. J. 26(3), 276–292 (1987)
3. Köhler, T., Alter, S., Cameron, B.H.: Enterprise modeling at the work system level: evidence from four cases at DHL express Europe. In: Buchmann, R., Karagiannis, D., Kirikova, M. (eds.) The Practice of Enterprise Modeling. PoEM 2018. Lecture Notes in Business Information Processing, vol. 335. Springer, Cham (2018). https://doi.org/10.1007/978-3-030-02302-7_19
4. Bock, A., Kaczmarek, M., Overbeek, S., Heß, M.: A comparative analysis of selected enterprise modeling approaches. In: Frank, U., Loucopoulos, P., Pastor, Ó., Petrounias, I. (eds.) The Practice of Enterprise Modeling. PoEM 2014. Lecture Notes in Business Information Processing, vol. 197. Springer, Heidelberg (2014). https://doi.org/10.1007/978-3-662-45501-2_11
5. Alter, S., Bork, D.: Systems analysis and design toolkit based on work system theory and its extensions. J. Database Manag. 31(3), 1–13. IGI Global (2020)
6. Alter, S., Bolloju, N.: A work system front end for object-oriented analysis and design. Int. J. Inform. Technol. Syst. App. 9(1), 1–18 (2016)
7. Bork, D., Alter, S.: Satisfying four requirements for more flexible modeling methods: theory and test case. Enterp. Modelling Info. Syst. Archit. 15 (2020). https://doi.org/10.18417/emisa.15.3
8. Alter, S., Recker, J.C.: Using a work system perspective to expand BPM research use cases. J. Inform. Technol. Theory Appl. 18(1), 47–71. AIS (2017)
9. Chiş, A., Ghiran, A.M., Alter, S.: Informing enterprise knowledge graphs with a work system perspective. Enterp. Modelling Info. Syst. Archit. 19 (2024). https://doi.org/10.18417/emisa.19.7
10. BOC GmbH, The ADOxx Metamodeling Platform. https://www.adoxx.org/live/home. Accessed 10 Mar 2025
11. Wieringa, R.J.: Design Science Methodology for Information Systems and Software Engineering. Springer, Heidelberg (2014)
12. Karagiannis, D.: Agile modeling method engineering. In: Proceedings of PCI 2015, pp. 5–10. ACM Press (2015)
13. Alter, S.: Encapsulation as a key concern in analysis and design for service systems. In: Proceedings of AMCIS 2016, vol. 4. AIS eLibrary (2016)
14. Wieringa, R.J.: Design Science Research Methods, https://wwwhome.ewi.ut-wente.nl/~roelw/DSM90minutes.pdf. Accessed 15 Mar 2025
15. Karagiannis, D., Buchmann, R.A., Utz, W.: The OMiLAB digital innovation environment: agile conceptual models to bridge business value with digital and physical twins for product-service systems development. Comput. Indust. 138, 103631. Elsevier (2022)
16. Karagiannis, D., Buchmann, R.A.: A proposal for deploying hybrid knowledge bases: the ADOxx-to-GraphDB interoperability case. In: Proceedings of HICSS 2018, 4055–4064 (2018). http://hdl.handle.net/10125/50399
17. Moody, D.: The "Physics" of notations: towards a scientific basis for constructing visual notations in software engineering. IEEE T. Software Eng. 35(5), 756–779. IEEE (2009)
18. Ontotext, What is Graph RAG. https://www.ontotext.com/knowledgehub/fundamentals/what-is-graph-rag/. Accessed 12 Mar 2025

Robotic Datasets for Process Mining

Flavio Corradini[1], Sara Pettinari[2], Barbara Re[1], Lorenzo Rossi[1], and Massimiliano Sampaolo[1(✉)]

[1] School of Science and Technology, University of Camerino, Camerino, Italy
{flavio.corradini,barbara.re,lorenzo.rossi,
massimilian.sampaolo}@unicam.it
[2] Gran Sasso Science Institute, L'Aquila, Italy
sara.pettinari@gssi.it

Abstract. As robotic systems become increasingly integrated into real-world applications, the need to better understand their operations continues to grow. Bridging the gap between process mining and robotics can enhance the transparency, accountability, and efficiency of these systems. However, applying process mining in this context is challenging due to the nature of robotic event data, which is mainly fine-grained and composed of multi-sensor readings rather than high-level activity events. In this exploratory paper, we present a collection of publicly available robotic datasets, providing a valuable resource for researchers and practitioners aiming to apply process mining to robotic systems. We identify 118 datasets and classify them based on application domain, type of robot involved, onboard sensors, collaborative behaviors, and their readiness for processing with process mining techniques.

Keywords: Robotic Systems · Process Mining · Robotic Datasets · Event Logs

1 Introduction

The increasing integration of robotic systems into everyday life has significantly transformed many real-world information systems, including those in smart industry, agriculture, warehouses, and healthcare [14]. These resulted in a growing need for techniques that provide insight into their operations [2,12]. Specifically, *analytical approaches* use mathematical models to describe system behavior and are suitable when the system is well understood and the uncertainty is minimal, such as detecting faults in a wheel motor controller. In contrast, *data-driven approaches* use sensor data or derived properties for monitoring and employ statistical methods, making them robust to uncertainty. For instance, they can effectively detect and isolate issues such as a low battery charge level that causes increased noise in sonar readings. Finally, *knowledge-based approaches* combine analytical and data-driven approaches into a hybrid monitoring system. For instance, a robot may infer that a motor anomaly is caused by carrying an object that is heavier than expected, by combining torque data with estimated object weight based on prior knowledge. Although these approaches are essential for the effective functioning of robots, restricting system analysis to fault detection and diagnosis is limiting.

In this regard, process mining can leverage the contextual perception of robotic systems to gain a holistic understanding of their operations, thereby enhancing transparency, accountability, and efficiency [3,11,13]. Exploring the potential of process mining in robotics requires understanding how robotic systems are structured and behave. These systems consist of sensors, actuators, and controllers, orchestrated to achieve specific goals, referred to as missions [10], by performing sequences of activities. During mission execution, robots operate in highly dynamic environments composed of people, objects, and potentially other robots. Process mining-based analysis can address the complexity of understanding how robots behave, interact, and verify the correctness of the system's execution as a whole. However, the ability of robotic systems to perform activities in their environment leads to the generation of vast amounts of data, typically recorded with fine granularity. This data primarily includes sensor readings and proprioceptive feedback, rather than high-level activity information. Despite this, some studies have applied process mining to analyze robotic systems. They use process discovery to reveal robot behaviors, understand decision-making [7], and capture multi-robot missions [15]. Conformance checking is used to verify execution correctness [11], while process enhancement helps analyze missions, area usage, execution time, and resource use [3,13]. These studies point to a common challenge in applying process mining to robotics: unlike traditional information systems with standardized event logs, robotic systems lack uniform data formats and detailed logging. Their large volumes of fine-grained data require significant preprocessing before process mining can be applied effectively.

In this paper, we explore robotic datasets to identify the features that make them suitable for process mining and to highlight the common characteristics they share. We scouted 118 publicly available robotic datasets and, after filtering out those that did not meet the identified features, obtained 102 datasets suitable for process mining. These were classified based on key characteristics such as application domain, type of involved robot, onboard sensors, collaborative behaviors, and readiness for process mining analysis. Of the 102 datasets, 90 contain only fine-grained data, while 12 include high-level activity annotations. Among these, 8 focus on human activity recognition and are thus outside the scope of this study, leaving 4 datasets ready for process mining.

The remainder of this paper is organized as follows. Section 2 describes the methodology for scouting and classifying the datasets. Section 3 presents the results. Finally, Sect. 4 concludes the paper and touches upon future directions.

2 Robotic Dataset Scouting and Classification

This section outlines the methodology used to identify robotic systems datasets. Notably, detailed outcomes from the dataset review are available online[1].

---

[1] https://bitbucket.org/proslabteam/robotic_datasets.

The scouting and classification of robotic datasets followed the methodology shown in Fig. 1, which includes dataset collection, filtering, and classification. We considered out of the scope of the study datasets related to Robotic Process Automation (RPA). While RPA logs are also fine-grained [1,9], they typically describe human behavior in software systems. In contrast, our focus is on physical robotic systems, where data is often multimodal, combining visual, auditory, tactile, or proprioceptive signals, and each modality offers complementary insights into robot behavior. Despite being a widely discussed topic in the process mining community [6], we also excluded IoT systems, even though some of the datasets may include robotic arms [4]. This is because these systems are typically designed to perform predefined actions in environments that change primarily due to external factors. In contrast, robotic systems can autonomously modify their environment based on the data they collect, leading to more dynamic and interactive behavior, as well as the generation of richer, multimodal data.

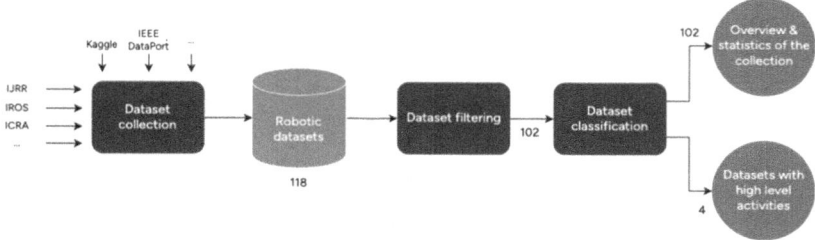

Fig. 1. Methodology adopted to conduct robotic dataset literature review

Dataset Collection. The initial step of the methodology involves searching for datasets provided as a contribution or a by-product of scientific articles. The collection has been done through a range of impactful journals and conferences in the robotics domain, such as the International Journal of Robotics Research (IJRR), the International Conference on Intelligent Robots and Systems (IROS), and the IEEE International Conference on Robotics and Automation (ICRA), among others. Additionally, we explored various specialized dataset repositories, including Kaggle and IEEE DataPort.

Dataset Filtering. The second step of the methodology consists of dataset filtering, which is used to keep only datasets that have characteristics suitable for the application of process mining techniques, with or without a preprocessing phase. We identified two main features, F1 and F2, that make a dataset a good candidate for being usable with process mining techniques.

F1. **Data involves (at least) one active participant**. This characteristic highlights the presence of an active participant within the dataset. This could range from data produced to control a robotic arm for assembly to more intricate data generated during robots autonomous navigation. The inclusion of an active participant implies an underlying process. For instance, datasets containing static images of mechanical components are not suitable for process mining-based analysis, as they lack activities or workflows, even with extensive preprocessing. However, if the dataset includes information about the robotic arm's movements during the assembly of those components, it would provide the necessary data for process mining techniques.

F2. **Data is in function of time**. The requirement for events to evolve over time is essential for making a process discoverable. Even with an active participant, process mining techniques can not be applied if we can not establish an ordering relationship between events. This does not necessarily mean that a dataset must contain explicitly defined timestamps or ordering indexes but rather that there must be a way to infer them. For instance, a video could serve as a valid dataset for process mining if we annotate activities and their corresponding timestamps.

It is important to notice that these two features are general requirements applicable across any dataset, not exclusively within the robotic systems domain.

Dataset Classification. The last step of the methodology serves multiple purposes: it helps create an index that allows researchers to efficiently search for datasets with specific attributes, and it can guide future research priorities by highlighting the most relevant characteristics. Considering the robotic systems domain, datasets were classified based on five characteristics, C1-C5.

C1. **Application** refers to the specific purpose or objective of the robotic system that generated the data.
C2. **Type of robot** classifies the robots that recorded the data.
C3. **Onboard sensors** describe which sensors the robot uses to perceive its surroundings.
C4. **Collaborative behaviors** defines whether the robots involved in the dataset collaborate with other participants during the activities execution.
C5. **Readiness** assesses the ease with which process mining techniques can be applied to the dataset, based on the data abstraction level. Datasets with high-level activities are more mature for process mining analysis, whereas datasets consisting only of fine-grained event data, such as position data or video captured by cameras, require a preprocessing step to abstract performed activities.

3 Resulting Datasets

Following the proposed methodology, we collected 118 datasets covering a wide range of robotic applications and filtered out those not compatible with features F1 and F2, resulting in 102 datasets.

Figure 2 presents a summary chart showing the interleaving of the most common application domains (C1), the different types of robots (C2) used in that domain, and the sensors used by that robot in that application (C3). The size of each segment corresponds to the frequency of the characteristic it represents. Considering the application (C1), most datasets focus on robots' spatial movement. Environment-sensing tasks are also quite common, ranging from odor perception to place categorization. Various grasping tasks have been studied, including tactile perception and common object manipulation, such as stacking objects. Assistive robotics is also well-represented. Throughout our research, we encountered various types of robots (C2), each suited for different environments, including ground vehicles such as cars and rovers, aerial drones, boats, and underwater robots. As shown in Fig. 2, rovers are highly adaptable across domains, while robotic arms are mainly used for grasping and assistive applications. The identified robotics applications make use of diverse sensors (C3), resulting in datasets with distinct signal sets. Robots capable of moving often rely on GPS, IMUs, and LiDARs. Cameras are especially common due to their versatility across robots and applications, and include types such as stereo, depth, and event cameras. Notably, we also identified more specialized applications and robots, such as those used in agriculture, along with specialized sensors like gas sensors, magnetometers, and sonar. Collaborative behavior among robots (C4) is rare in public datasets. We found only 4 that feature multi-robot scenarios involving either direct communication, such as message exchange, or indirect coordination, such as simultaneous localization and mapping. Finally, considering the readiness (C5), we identified 12 datasets enriched with high-level activity annotations. However, 8 out of the 12 datasets focus on human activity recognition and, therefore, do not provide any information about robot behavior. For this reason, they fall outside the scope of our research. As a result, we extracted 4 datasets D1-D4.

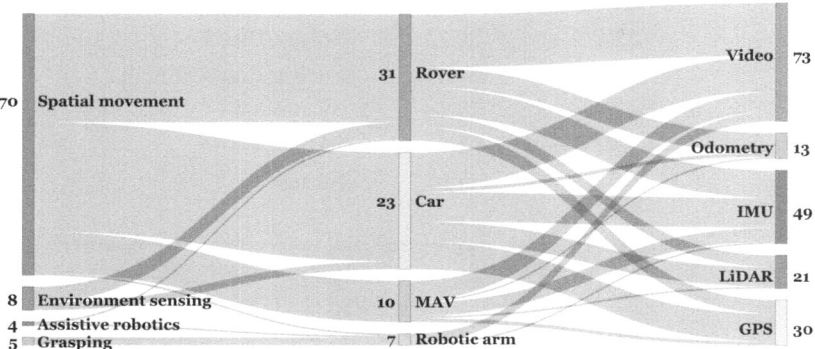

Fig. 2. Interleaving of applications, robots, and sensors in robotic datasets

D1. **ATLAS Dione** [16] is a dataset that provides video data of ten surgeons performing six different surgical tasks. The dataset has been enriched with annotations of robotic tools and the tasks performed per frame.

D2. **DORMADL** [5] is a dataset of human-operated robot arm motion in activities of daily living to be used within the context of assistive robotics. It contains both real and generated data and includes labels for the robot's pose, motion, and activity.

D3. **SCAND** [8] is a dataset collected from an autonomous mobile robot that can navigate within human crowds in a socially compliant manner by ensuring safe and comfortable human-robot coexistence.

D4. **TALE** [3] is a dataset collecting event logs extracted from the execution of a multi-robot system working in a smart agriculture environment. High-level robotic activities are produced by tags inserted in the robots' source code by the developer.

These 4 datasets are ready for process mining and require only standard preprocessing, such as fixing timestamps and merging events from multiple files. Figure 3 shows an excerpt from the ATLAS Dione dataset, with five video frames and timestamps illustrating two robotic arms tying sutures on a training support. Each frame marks the start of an activity listed in Table 1, which includes the activity name and its start and end times.

The remaining 90 datasets contain only fine-grained data without activity labels. However, since they meet the filtering criteria of our methodology, we include them as valuable input for applying novel preprocessing techniques. With suitable abstraction techniques, they can be effectively transformed for use in process mining.

Table 1. Excerpt of activity annotations on ATLAS Dione Dataset

Clip	Start Time (s)	End Time (s)	Action
1	12,91	22,73	Suture Pick Up
2	22,33	38,13	Suture Pull Through
3	38	77,7	Suture Tie
4	82,72	91,9	Suture Tie
5	118,17	141,37	Suture Tie

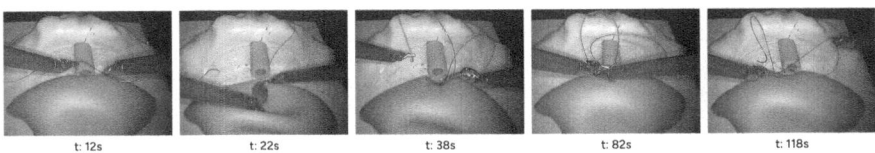

Fig. 3. Sequential video frames from the ATLAS Dione Dataset

4 Conclusions

The main goal of this paper is to provide the process mining community with a comprehensive selection of robotic datasets suitable for applying process mining techniques. To this end, we scouted 118 publicly available datasets, extracting their relevant features and characteristics. Among these, we identified 4 datasets structured in an activity-centric manner, requiring only standard preprocessing to be used with process mining techniques, while 90 others require additional effort to infer the performed activities. It is important to note that performing a systematic literature review to catalog all existing datasets was beyond the scope of this work.

Discussion. Creating robotic datasets containing both high-level and fine-grained data opens up new research lines critical for analyzing workflows that integrate robotic systems. Firstly, the heterogeneous nature of robotic data offers opportunities for developing advanced techniques to analyze robot behavior and context information, such as spatial positioning or battery levels. Secondly, the autonomy of robotic systems necessitates a focus on applying streaming process mining techniques. These techniques can capture and analyze robots' decision-making processes in real-time, enabling them to adapt and optimize their activities based on immediate insights. Lastly, process mining can play a key role in examining the social aspects of robotics. By analyzing human-robot or multi-robot interactions, we could analyze whether robots follow human safe practices or coordinate effectively with others.

On the Validity. The validity of this study is supported by the structured methodology used to scout and analyze 118 publicly available robotic datasets, highlighting their suitability for process mining applications. By extracting features and characteristics, we identified four datasets to which process mining techniques can be applied and outlined the preprocessing steps required for the remaining datasets. This approach ensures relevance and utility for the process mining community, aligning to foster integration between robotics and process mining. However, internal validity may be affected by the dataset selection process. The scope of this work was limited to publicly available datasets, which could exclude other valuable datasets from less accessible domains. We focused on clearly documenting our methodology and ensuring its reproducibility to mitigate this. Finally, the exploratory nature of the study constrains external validity. Specifically, the dataset classification may require additional characteristics or refinement to be fully generalized to all robotic system datasets beyond those analyzed in this work. However, this limitation does not invalidate the key findings of the proposed work. Rather, identifying new characteristics can be seen as additional information associated with the datasets.

Future Work. We aim to further advance the application of process mining in robotics by expanding the availability of suitable robotic datasets, similar to the initiatives undertaken with the BPI Challenge in the process mining community[2]. This includes providing access to robotic datasets that adhere to standards facilitating process mining analysis. In addition, we plan to deepen our investigation of the interaction between robotic systems and process mining to foster the development and application of techniques tailored to analyze and optimize the behavior and dynamics of robotic systems.

Acknowledgments. This work has been partially funded by (a) the PRIN project 2022JKA4SL - HALO: etHical-aware AdjustabLe autOnomous systems, and (b) the European Union - NextGenerationEU under the Italian Ministry of University and Research National Innovation Ecosystem grant ECS00000041 - VITALITY - CUP J13C22000430001.

References

1. Agostinelli, S., Marrella, A., Abb, L., Rehse, J.R.: Mastering robotic process automation with process mining. In: Di Ciccio, C., Dijkman, R., del Río Ortega, A., Rinderle-Ma, S. (eds.) Business Process Management. BPM 2022. LNCS, vol. 13420, pp. 47–53. Springer, Cham (2022). https://doi.org/10.1007/978-3-031-16103-2_6
2. Chiang, L.H., Russell, E.L., Braatz, R.D.: Fault Detection and Diagnosis in Industrial Systems. In: Baillieul, J., Samad, T. (eds.) Encyclopedia of Systems and Control. Springer, London (2000). https://doi.org/10.1007/978-1-4471-5102-9_223-1
3. Corradini, F., Pettinari, S., Re, B., Rossi, L., Tiezzi, F.: A methodology for the analysis of robotic systems via process mining. In: Proper, H.A., Pufahl, L., Karastoyanova, D., van Sinderen, M., Moreira, J. (eds.) Enterprise Design, Operations, and Computing. EDOC 2023. LNCS, vol. 14367, pp. 117–133. Springer, Cham (2023). https://doi.org/10.1007/978-3-031-46587-1_7
4. Ehrendorfer, M., Bertrand, Y., et al.: Internet of processes and things: a repository for iot-enriched event logs in smart environments. In: Business Process Management (Demos/Resources Forum), vol. 3469, pp. 92–96. CEUR-WS.org (2023)
5. Goldau, F., Shivashankar, Y., Baumeister, A., Drescher, L., Tolle, P., Frese, U.: Dormadl - dataset of human-operated robot arm motion in activities of daily living. In: Intelligent Robots and Systems, pp. 11396–11403. IEEE (2023)
6. Janiesch, C., et al.: The internet of things meets business process management: a manifesto. Syst. Man Cybern. Mag. **6**(4), 34–44 (2020)
7. Jimenez, J.F., Zambrano-Rey, G., Aguirre, S., Trentesaux, D.: Using process-mining for understating the emergence of self-organizing manufacturing systems. IFAC **51**(11), 1618–1623 (2018)
8. Karnan, H., Nair, A., et al.: Socially compliant navigation dataset (SCAND): a large-scale dataset of demonstrations for social navigation. Robot. Autom. Lett. **7**(4), 11807–11814 (2022)
9. Leno, V., Polyvyanyy, A., Dumas, M., La Rosa, M., Maggi, F.M.: Robotic process mining: vision and challenges. Bus. Inf. Syst. Eng. **63**, 301–314 (2021)
10. Menghi, C., Tsigkanos, C., Pelliccione, P., Ghezzi, C., Berger, T.: Specification patterns for robotic missions. IEEE Trans. Softw. Eng. **47**(10), 2208–2224 (2021)

---

[2] https://www.tf-pm.org/competitions-awards/bpi-challenge.

11. Nicoleta, T.C.: Process mining on a robotic mechanism. In: Software Testing, Verification and Validation Workshops, pp. 205–212. IEEE (2021)
12. Pettersson, O.: Execution monitoring in robotics: a survey. Robot. Auton. Syst. **53**(2), 73–88 (2005)
13. Roldán, J.J., Olivares-Méndez, M.A., del Cerro, J., Barrientos, A.: Analyzing and improving multi-robot missions by using process mining. Auton. Robot. **42**(6), 1187–1205 (2018)
14. Romeo, L., Petitti, A., Marani, R., Milella, A.: Internet of robotic things in smart domains: applications and challenges. Sensors **20**(12), 3355 (2020)
15. Rozinat, A., Zickler, S., Veloso, M., van der Aalst, W., McMillen, C.: Analyzing multi-agent activity logs using process mining techniques. In: Asama, H., Kurokawa, H., Ota, J., Sekiyama, K. (eds.) Distributed Autonomous Robotic Systems, vol. 8, pp. 251–260. Springer, Berlin, Heidelberg (2008). https://doi.org/10.1007/978-3-642-00644-9_22
16. Sarikaya, D., Corso, J.J., Guru, K.A.: Detection and localization of robotic tools in robot-assisted surgery videos using deep neural networks for region proposal and detection. IEEE Trans. Med. Imaging **36**(7), 1542–1549 (2017)

Automated Business Process Analysis: An LLM-Based Approach to Value Assessment

William De Michele, Abel Armas Cervantes[✉], and Lea Frermann

The University of Melbourne, Melbourne, Australia
wdemichele@student.unimelb.edu.au,
{abel.armas,lea.frermann}@unimelb.edu.au

Abstract. Business processes are fundamental to organizational operations, yet their improvement remains challenging due to the time-consuming nature of manual process analysis. Our paper harnesses Large Language Models to automate value-added analysis, which is mostly done manually, time-consuming, and subjective. Our method is more principled and operates in two phases: decomposing high-level activities into detailed steps to enable granular analysis; and performing a value-added analysis to classify each step according to Lean principles. Our approach was developed using 50 business process models, for which we collect and publish manual ground-truth labels. Our evaluation, comparing zero-shot baselines with structured prompts reveals (a) a consistent benefit of structured prompting and (b) promising performance for both tasks.

Keywords: BPM · Waste Identification · Value-Added Analysis · Natural Language Processing · Large Language Models

1 Introduction

Business Process Management (BPM) enables organisations to model, analyse, and improve their operational processes to reduce costs and enhance customer satisfaction [2]. A key phase in the BPM lifecycle is process analysis, where inefficiencies are identified in the as-is process to inform process redesign. Central to this analysis is the identification of waste – process steps that do not add value from the customer's perspective or are unnecessary for the business to operate [11]. Waste identification traditionally relied on manual expert analysis, which can be time-consuming, costly, and prone to subjectivity [15]. *Value-added analysis* (VAA) is a qualitative technique that identifies business steps that are of no value to the customer or the business. As organisations scale and processes become more complex, there is a growing need to automate techniques like VAA.

This paper introduces a novel approach that leverages Large Language Models (LLMs) to automate the identification of unnecessary steps in business processes (Fig. 1). Our approach operates in two phases: first, high-level activities are decomposed into fine-grained steps, and second, a value-added analysis [3] is performed over the steps to classify them based on Lean principles [22]. The approach is evaluated using a dataset of 50 business processes with BPMN models

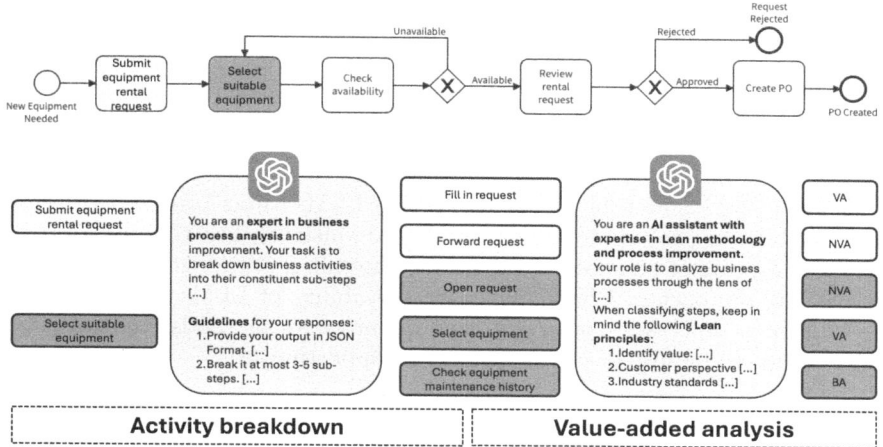

Fig. 1. Overview of our LLM-based VAA over an excerpt of a rental equipment process (top; [2]). Two activities (left) are broken down into steps (center) and labeled as value adding (VA), business value adding (BVA) or non-value adding (NVA) (right).

spanning diverse industries with manual annotation of activity-to-step breakdown, and step-level VAA. The extended version of this paper, code, data and prompts are available at https://github.com/wdemichele/WIPE.

2 Related Work

The language generation capabilities of recent LLMs offer new opportunities for automating complex tasks, including in the field of BPM [18]. LLMs combine transformer architectures with attention mechanisms [17] with self-supervised pre-training on massive text corpora followed by instruction tuning. This optimises the models' abilities to respond to natural language inputs (prompts).

The quality of LLM responses largely depends on prompt engineering [12] – designing input instructions that elicit desired model behaviors. Techniques range from simple prompting (zero-shot [23]); prompts with input-output examples (few-shot [19]); to chain-of-thought reasoning, which guides models through step-by-step reasoning processes [20]. Structured prompting techniques [5] incorporating role descriptions [6], task specifications, and output formats have proven effective for specialised tasks [24], often combined with systematic prompt optimization [25]. We use these advanced prompting techniques for VAA.

Waste Analysis with LLMs. Lashkevich et al. [8,9] use LLMs for the analysis and redesign of business processes to optimize waiting time, combining process mining outputs with structured prompting to generate both technical and strategic recommendations for process redesign. They find that different prompting approaches serve distinct purposes, with enhanced prompting generating specific, actionable recommendations for analysts, while baseline prompting produces strategic insights for management decision-making. While [8] address only one aspect of process waste, our work on Activity Breakdown and Value-added Analysis complements these efforts by focusing on qualitative waste identification through semantic understanding of activities.

While quantitative analysis has dominated much of the existing research of LLM applications in BPM (e.g., [1,4,8]), there is a lack of emphasis on qualitative aspects of processes. We address this gap by incorporating qualitative VAA approaches inspired by [3]. By leveraging LLMs to perform in-depth qualitative analysis of process activities, we provide insights into the semantic and contextual aspects of business processes that are often overlooked in traditional quantitative approaches. We demonstrate the ability of LLMs to qualitatively assess business processes, complementing quantitative methods, and providing a more complete picture of process efficiency opportunities.

3 Automated Value-Added Analysis

Our approach has two stages: **Activity Breakdown** divides activities into steps, and **Value-Added Analysis** categorizes each step with its perceived value.

Activity Breakdown. We develop a series of automated approaches to break down high-level activities into atomic "steps" (Fig. 1 (left)). Breaking an activity into steps can be subjective (see Sect. 4 for further discussion). A *zero-shot baseline* is used to assess the LLM's out-of-the-box capabilities without extensive guidance. To improve on the baseline, we (1) established standardised *Decomposition rules* to mitigate the inherent subjectivity and (2) designed *Structured Prompts* and systematically test the impact of different components on LLM performance. Our components cover (1) the role assigned to the LLM, (2) varying detail in the task description, (3) varying guidelines, (4) focus, (5) numbers and kinds of examples in the prompt [14], and (6) additional information (more details in our repository). The optimal combination of components are obtained through greedy grid-search over the combinatorial space [10,21]. Table 1 summarizes the components with optimal prompt values in bold.

Value-Added Analysis. Considering the contribution to the business process, in a value-added analysis each step is assigned one of the following three labels:

- **Value Adding (VA):** Steps that directly contribute to fulfilling customer needs and for which customers are willing to pay for;
- **Business Value Adding (BVA):** Steps that are necessary for business operations (e.g., compliance or quality control);
- **Non-Value Adding (NVA):** Steps that neither add value to the customer nor to the business (e.g., unnecessary or redundant activities).

Given a business process broken down into steps, we prompt the LLMs to (a) assign a value label to each step and (b) provide a justification for each label. Figure 1 (right) illustrates this with an example. To automate this process, we

Table 1. Structured Prompt Components for activity breakdown. The optimal choice for each component is highlighted in bold.

Component	Variations
Role Description	Neutral Analyst, Subject Matter Expert (SME), SME Detailed, **Business Process Expert**, Project Manager, Process Analyst, Operations Manager
Task Description	Breakdown Substeps, **Breakdown with Dependencies**, Breakdown Focusing on Outcomes
Guidelines	Standard Guidelines, **Detailed Guidelines**, Outcome-Focused Guidelines
Focus Shift	Action-Focused, Outcome-Focused, **Process-Focused**
Example Outputs	Zero-Shot (no examples), One-Shot (one example), **Few-Shot (multiple examples)**, Detailed One-Shot, Detailed Few-Shot
Context	**Include Business Context**, Emphasise Order and Dependencies

devise a *zero-shot baseline* that directly tasks the LLM to classify the steps without additional context. We then again devise a range of *Structured Prompts* specific to the VAA based on domain knowledge and best-practices in prompting. The components are summarized in Table 2. We identified the best-performing combination of component values (bold elements in the table) using grid-search.

4 Evaluation

Below we present the dataset, and the evaluation of the task breakdown and the value-added classification. See our repository for detailed results and prompts.

Dataset and Experimental Setup. To evaluate our framework, we curated a dataset of 50 publicly available business process models. These models were sourced from [2] and the SAP Signavio Academic Models (SAP-SAM) repository [16]. The processes span various domains, including banking, healthcare, and technology. Each process model was annotated with the activity breakdown and step-level value-added classification. The process models were randomly split into a development set (33 models) used for model and prompt engineering, and evaluation set (17 models). All experiments were conducted with GPT-3.5-Turbo-0125[1]. We set the model temperature to 0.1 to reduce randomness and ensure replicability [13] and the context window to 4096 tokens. All other model parameters were kept at their default values.

Activity Breakdown. Evaluation of activity breakdown is challenging because there is often not a single best solution. To quantify this inherent ambiguity, four annotators with basic background on BPM and VAA independently annotated a subset of models. The outcome revealed variation due to variation in the granularity, different customer value perception and paraphrases of equivalent steps.

---
[1] https://platform.openai.com/docs/models/gpt-3-5-turbo, 2024-10-25.

Table 2. Structured Prompt Components for Value-added Analysis. The optimal choice for each component is highlighted in bold.

Component	Variations
Role Description	Neutral Analyst (Baseline), **LEAN Analyst (Expert)**, Business Consultant, Process Engineer, Customer Advocate, SME (per sector), **SME (Detailed)**, Quality Assurance Specialist
Task Description	**Standard Classification**, Efficiency-Focused Classification, Waste Identification
Guidelines	Basic Guidelines, Context-Aware Guidelines, **Lean Principles Guidelines**
Classification Types	Basic, **Detailed**, Textbook, Contextualised
Example Outputs	**Simple Process Example**, Complex Process Example, Varied Process Examples
Context	Focus on Customer Value, Consider Regulatory Requirements, **Include Justifications**

To evaluate the model-generated activity breakdown, we developed a *Comparator LLM*, an LLM-based framework to evaluate step alignments mirroring human expert judgment. The comparator identifies matches between ground truth and the generated steps, considering four forms of alignment: *exact matches* (steps are identical), *semantic matches* (paraphrases of the same underlying action), *granularity variations* (steps at different levels of detail), and *no match* (steps with no pendant in the ground truth, indicating an error). The comparator was evaluated through manual validation on 20% of the dataset, where its classifications were found to be closely aligned with human expert judgment. We report the % of model-generated steps for each of the four alignment categories.

We evaluated the zero-shot baseline, and the best-performing structured prompts on the test set of 17 process models. Table 3 shows the results of the evaluation of the zero-shot baseline and the three best performing role descriptions (BPE, SME and PM (Detailed)) with the best performing remaining components (Table 1). For "Exact Match" and "Functional Equivalence" high scores are best, while for "No match" and "Granularity Difference" low scores are best. Most structured models outperform the baseline across the board. The Business Process Expert (BPE) role leads to best performance, overall, with almost 60% of steps being exactly or functionally equivalent, demonstrating the LLM's capability to decompose activities effectively. The 28.2% of steps with "No Match" highlight areas where the LLM diverges from expert interpretations. While these discrepancies may stem from contextual misinterpretations or insufficient domain-specific knowledge within the LLM, these are expected given the subjective nature of activity breakdowns.

Table 3. Activity breakdown performance (%) for the zero-shot baseline, and three versions of the structured prompt with different role types and other components (see bold values in Table 1). BPE=Business Process Expert, SME = Subject Matter Expert, PM = Project Manager. ↑ higher is better; ↓ lower is better.

	Exact Match ↑	Funct. Equiv. ↑	Granul. Diff. ↓	No Match ↓
Zero-shot Baseline	13.4	29.0	21.3	36.3
BPE	**20.8**	**38.9**	**10.1**	**28.2**
SME	11.6	37.4	19.8	31.0
PM (Detailed)	6.9	35.9	20.2	37.0

Value-Added Analysis Similarly to the activity breakdown, we asked the four human annotators to classify a given set of process steps. We assessed the inter-annotator agreement using Krippendorf's α [7], a widely used statistical measure of agreement across multiple items and annotators. The inter-annotator agreement was 0.53, indicating moderate agreement.

When using the LLMs to classify the steps in the test set, the results show 45% (N=929) steps were annotated as VA, 48% (N=992) were annotated as BVA and 6.3% (N=130) as NVA. The relatively even distribution between VA and BVA steps, coupled with the small proportion of NVA steps, aligns with expectations in real-world business processes that have undergone some degree of optimisation but may still contain hidden inefficiencies.

Table 4. VAA performance for the zero-shot baseline and four versions of the structured prompt with the best-performing role-types with optimal other components (bolded in Table 2). BC = Business Consultant; CA = Customer Advocate; SME = Subject Matter Expert.

	F1 (All)	F1 (NVA)
Zero-shot	0.53	0.23
BC	0.66	0.28
CA	0.60	0.49
SME (Detailed)	**0.72**	0.20
LEAN Analyst (Exp.)	0.61	**0.50**

The LLM predictions were directly compared against the human labels in our ground truth data. The overall performance is reported as *F1 Score (All)*. In practice, businesses are particularly interested in identifying NVA steps. For that reason, we separately report performance on this class only (*NVA F1-Score*).

The main results are shown in Table 4. All structured prompt models outperform the zero-shot baseline (except for SME on NVA). The SEM (Detailed) achieved the highest overall macro F1 score. However, the LEAN Analyst (Expert) demonstrated superior waste identification capabilities with the best F1 NVA score, while retaining an acceptable overall F1 score, which demonstrates its potential as a tool for waste identification when appropriately guided.

5 Discussion

The framework's ability to automate complex tasks, such as VAA, traditionally performed manually enables organisations to conduct more frequent and comprehensive process evaluations at scale. By leveraging standardised guidelines and prompt structures, our framework promotes consistency in analysis outputs – particularly valuable in large organisations where multiple analysts may be involved in process improvement efforts. LLMs' advanced language understanding capabilities can potentially uncover insights that might be overlooked by human analysts. Our framework may be most effectively implemented as a support tool rather than a replacement for human expertise. The framework excels at standardising routine analyses, but human oversight is crucial for contextualising results and making strategic improvement decisions.

Despite its strengths, our framework faces several limitations that warrant careful consideration. The moderate inter-annotator agreement among experts highlights the subjective nature of VAA, which extends to the LLM. Additionally, LLMs are well-known to be sensitive to prompt formulation. Taken together, this calls for careful validation of model consistency and reliability. Prompt optimization was based on 33 process models, which may not encompass all industry-specific terminology or practices. This can lead to misinterpretations or omissions in specialised and nuanced domains. Finally, while LLMs can provide justifications for their classifications, these explanations may lack the depth or clarity required for critical business decisions. Enhancing the explainability of the LLM's reasoning process is essential for building trust and facilitating acceptance among stakeholders.

6 Conclusion

We introduced the first LLM-based automated framework for VAA. We formalized the task as a two-step process that first divides activities into steps, and afterwards classifies each step regarding its value based on lean principles, enabling targeted waste identification. The experimental results shows robust performance of our best models on both tasks, particularly in the context of inherent ambiguity which leads to disagreement even between human.

In sum, our approach represents an advancement in the application of AI to business process management. It demonstrates the feasibility and benefits of integrating LLMs into process analysis and waste identification efforts. While the approach was presented as fully automated, we recognize that the integration of human expertise through a human-in-the-loop approach is necessary to obtain results that are more relevant for the analysed process.

References

1. Berti, A., Schuster, D., van der Aalst, W.: Abstractions, scenarios, and prompt definitions for process mining with llms: a case study. In: BPM, pp. 427–439. Springer (2023)
2. Dumas, M., Rosa, L.M., Mendling, J., Hajo Reijers, A.: Fundamentals of business process management. Springer (2018)
3. Eakin, J.M., Gladstone, B.: "Value-adding" analysis: doing more with qualitative data. IJQM 19, 1609406920949333 (2020)

4. Jessen, U., Sroka, M., Fahland, D.: Chit-chat or deep talk: Prompt engineering for process mining. In BPM Workshops, Springer, Cham (2023)
5. Jiang, W., Zhang, Y., Kwok, J.: Effective structured prompting by meta-learning and representative verbalizer. In: ICML, pp. 15186–15199 (2023)
6. Kong, A., et al.: Self-prompt tuning: enable autonomous role-playing in llms. arXiv preprint arXiv:2407.08995 (2024)
7. Krippendorff, K.: Computing krippendorff's alpha-reliability (2011)
8. Lashkevich, K., Milani, F., Avramenko, M., Dumas, M.: LLM-assisted optimization of waiting time in business processes: a prompting method. In: BPM, pp. 474–492. Springer (2024)
9. Lashkevich, K., Milani, F., Chapela-Campa, D., Suvorau, I., Dumas, M.: Unveiling the causes of waiting time in business processes from event logs. IS **126**, 102434 (2024)
10. Liashchynskyi, P., Liashchynskyi, P.: Grid search, random search, genetic algorithm: a big comparison for nas. arXiv preprint arXiv:1912.06059 (2019)
11. Mansar, S.L., Reijers, H.A.: Best practices in business process redesign: use and impact. BPMJ **13**(2), 193–213 (2007)
12. Marvin, G, Hellen, N., Jjingo, D., Nakatumba-Nabende, J.: Prompt engineering in large language models. In: ICDICI, pp. 387–402. Springer (2023)
13. Peeperkorn, M., Kouwenhoven, T., Brown, D., Jordanous, A.: Is temperature the creativity parameter of large language models? (2024)
14. Reynolds, L., McDonell, K.: Prompt programming for large language models: Beyond the few-shot paradigm. In: Extended abstracts of the 2021 CHI conference on human factors in computing systems, pp. 1–7 (2021)
15. Rudden, J.: Making the case for bpm: a benefits checklist. BPTrends 2007 (2007)
16. Sola, D., Warmuth, C., Schäfer, B., Badakhshan, P., Rehse, J.-R., Kampik, T.: SAP Signavio Academic Models: a large process model dataset. In: ICPM, pp. 453–465. Springer (2022)
17. Vaswani, A.: Attention is all you need. NeurIPS (2017)
18. Vidgof, M., Bachhofner, S., Mendling, J.: Large language models for business process management: Opportunities and challenges. In: BPM Forum, pp. 107–123. Springer, Cham (2023)
19. Wang, Y., Yao, Q., Kwok, J.T., Ni, L.M.: Generalizing from a few examples: a survey on few-shot learning. ACM CSUR **53**(3), 1–34 (2020)
20. Wei, J., et al.: Chain-of-thought prompting elicits reasoning in large language models. NeurIPS **35**, 24824–24837 (2022)
21. Wilt, C., Thayer, J., Ruml, W.: A comparison of greedy search algorithms. In: SoCS
22. Womack, J.P., Jones, D.T.: Lean thinking-banish waste and create wealth in your corporation. JORS **48**(11), 1148–1148 (1997)
23. Xian, Y., Schiele, B., Akata, Z.: Zero-shot learning-the good, the bad and the ugly. In: CVPR, pp. 4582–4591 (2017)
24. Zhang, S., et al.: Instruction tuning for large language models: a survey. arXiv preprint arXiv:2308.10792 (2023)
25. Zhu, B., Niu, Y., Han, Y., Wu, Y., Zhang, H.: Prompt-aligned gradient for prompt tuning. In: IEEE/CVF, pp. 15659–15669 (2023)

Humidor: A Zero-Shot LLM Approach for Cumulative Knowledge Building in Design Science Research

Oscar Díaz[iD], Xabier Garmendia[✉][iD], and Martin Horsfield[iD]

University of the Basque Country (UPV/EHU), San Sebastián, Spain
{oscar.diaz,xabier.garmendiad}@ehu.eus,
mhorsfield001@ikasle.ehu.eus

Abstract. Design Knowledge (DK) is the understanding of creating and improving artifacts to solve real-world problems. DK contributions often remain isolated, lacking integration and accumulation. This work explores using Large Language Models (LLMs) to build Knowledge Graphs for DK accumulation. We present *Humidor*, a zero-shot LLM framework that implements Wieringa's CGAR model (Context, Goals, Artifact, Requirements) for structured DK representation. The method involves extracting CGAR expressions from manuscripts into *localGraphs* and merging them into a *globalGraph* for cumulative knowledge building.

Keywords: Knowledge Graph · Design Science · Large Language Model · Design Knowledge

1 Introduction

Design Knowledge (DK) connects the problem and solution beyond mere artifact creation [3]. Knowledge accumulation refers to the systematic process of building upon existing DK to create new insights and solutions that can be used in future projects. However, DK faces limited reuse, hindering its accumulation and evolution [1]. This work explores the use of Large Language Models (LLMs) to create Knowledge Graphs aimed at DK accumulation.

LLMs have demonstrated significant potential in tasks like entity and relation extraction for the construction of Knowledge Graphs (KG) [6]. Our work aligns with these efforts but distinguishes itself by concentrating on design knowledge with a specific emphasis on facilitating knowledge accumulation across sources. Most existing KG construction methods predominantly adopt a localized perspective [2,9], extracting triplets at the sentence or paragraph level. While this approach is effective for shallow knowledge-such as (person, belongsTo, organization)-it falls short in scientific domains, where a global view is essential to capture complex, multi-layered relations between entities. While some Retrieval-Augmented Generation (RAG)-based methods for building KGs focus primarily on relation extraction from limited sources via retrieval, this often results in numerous disconnected KGs or sub-graphs where is difficult for the LLM to generate sensible relationships between entities coming from different documents. Recently, *Graphusion* incorporates a knowledge fusion step to integrate local knowledge into a global context directly, making it the first initiative we are aware to utilize LLMs for such a comprehensive merging process [14].

We follow the insights of *Graphusion*, considering the nuances introduced by DK. While *Graphusion* focuses on constructing KG for scientific purposes in general, we aim at constructing KGs for the accumulation of design knowledge, hereafter referred to as *'Design Graphs'*. This leads to our research question:

> **How to design** an LLM-assisted construction of Knowledge Graphs **that satisfies** the context-specificity, ephemerality, and malleable terminology of design knowledge **in order for** researchers to tap into existing instance-level design knowledge **in the context of** DSR knowledge accumulation?

2 Design Graphs

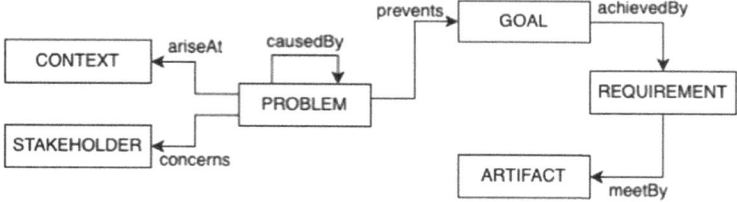

Fig. 1. The CGAR model for structuring Design Knowledge from research papers

We refer to a Design Graph (DG) as a graph that captures Design Knowledge (DK). Design Knowledge encompasses both practical and theoretical understanding of how to create and improve artifacts that address real-world problems [1]. Wieringa provides a template for capturing design questions [11]:

> How to <(re)design an **Artifact**> that satisfies <some **Requirements**> in order for <**Stakeholders** to achieve some **Goals**> in <a problem **Context**>?

Building upon the initials of these four concerns, Fig. 1 depicts the CGAR conceptual model. A design graph is a knowledge graph that conforms to the CGAR model.

3 Humidor: A Zero-Shot KG-Augmented LLM Framework for DG Construction

In prompt engineering, *zero-shot* refers to designing prompts for an LLM to perform a specific task without providing any examples or prior demonstrations of that task. The task at hand is DG construction:

$$DGconstruction = CGAR : globalDG \times Text : manuscript \longrightarrow CGAR : expandedDG$$

DGconstruction() takes a set of free text T (i.e., the manuscript) and generating a list of triplets (h, r, t) spanning an existing DG. Both the input graph and the output graph are to be compliant with the CGAR model. *DGconstruction()* comprises two main steps:

1. DG extraction, that obtains a DG out of a single manuscript (referred to as *localDG*).
2. DG merging, that merges a *localDG* into the *globalDG*, i.e., the DG that accumulates results from previously processed manuscripts.

3.1 Step 1: DG Extraction

```
RESEARCH_PAPER= {RESEARCH_PAPER}
-CONTEXT:
[... Context of DSR is provided here ...]
-GOAL:
[... state that the goal is to retrieve entities and relationships ...]
[... entity_types and definitions ...]
[... relationship_types and definitions ...]
[... guidelines ...]
[how1]  ... entities may be absent or multiple ...
[how2]  ... prioritize specific actions, ignore broader ones  ...
[how3]  ... focus on the most specific term ...
[how4]  ... split distinct notions in conjunctions/disjunctions ...
[how5]  ... avoid including 'context' in 'problem' names ...
[what1] ... name abstract categories, not instances ...
[what2] ... as artifactClass highlight functional principles, not tools ...
[what3] ... describe unmet objectives using negatives ...
[what4] ... reflect stakeholder intent, not utility ...
[what5] ... use specific research context ...
-STEPS:
[... ask for entity identification and its information ...]
[... ask for relationship identification and its information  ...]
[... ask for design question based on the template  ...]
-FINAL OUTPUT:
[... ask the output in JSON format   ...]
```

Fig. 2. The CGAR prompt

This step produces a CGAR-compliant DG out of a manuscript. Extracting domain-specific entities using LLMs in a zero-shot setting is challenging and may generate irrelevant entities. Typed entities help improving precision and contextual relevance, allowing the system to clarify each entity's role in the analysis. Typing also supports semantic structuring, facilitating entity alignment in the KG and reducing errors in linking related entities [7]. This turns the prompt's endeavour into a sort of deductive-coding effort. Here, the CGAR constructs act as the codes, and the prompt becomes the codebook. A codebook contains guidelines for assigning codes, often containing definitions of categories, instructions for assigning categories, and examples of coded data.

Figure 2 shows the CGAR prompt[1]. The prompt starts by describing each type (e.g. what a *Context* is, what a *Goal* is, etc.) and relationships (e.g. *arisesAt*). Definitions are adapted from [4,5,11]. Next, extraction guidelines are provided and identified through an ID (e.g., *how1*). This has proven extremely useful in debugging the prompt. The data to be collected includes the excerpts that ground the decision, which will be used for chunk linking [13]. Finally, we request the output in JSON format to ensure it can be readily consumed by *Neo4j*.

3.2 Step 2: DG Merging

The *localDG* extracted in the previous step is now to be considered for spamming the *globalDG*:

$$DGmerging : globalDG \times localDG \longrightarrow expandedDG$$

This process is not far from entity alignment, that is, the process of identifying and linking entities (such as people, places, organizations, etc.) from different manuscripts so that the LLM can recognize them as representing the same concept [12]. However, there exists main differences.

Topic-Based Alignment. Stakeholders, context, goals or requirements are often the case of nuisance variations in their description, hence, it is hardly the case of an exact match between the nodes being compared. We need to go beyond surface-level similarity (e.g., shared words) to focus on meaning, even if different words or phrases are used: topic matching. Topic matching involves comparing the conceptual or thematic content of two pieces of information to identify overlaps or connections in their underlying meaning [10]. Semantic similarity is based on *embedding*, numerical representations of data in a continuous vector space. By using metrics like cosine similarity on sentence-level embeddings (e.g., Sentence-BERT [8]), we can assess how similar two texts are. When it comes to topic matching, pairwise alignment is the most common approach. For instance, a *localDG* might describe a stakeholder as a "PhD student", while the *globalDG* might include "novel practitioner".We then hold that: **a *localDG*'s node is to be aligned insofar as it maintains some resemblance with the same-typed entities already in the *globalDG*.**

To this end, we introduce construct-based scores. More formally, let $globalDG_C$ and $localDG_C$ denote the set of nodes of type C in the *globalDG* and *localDG*, respectively. Construct-based scores are worked out as follows:

$$Score_C = \frac{\sum_{g \in globalDG_C} \sum_{l \in localDG_C} \text{sim}(g, l)}{|globalDG_C| \times |localDG_C|} \quad (1)$$

By averaging the similarity scores, the final score provides a comprehensive measure of the extent the *localDG* addresses a construct (e.g., stakeholder) that

---

[1] Full prompt available at: https://github.com/onekin/promptsHumidor/blob/main/paper2cgar.txt.

somehow is being covered in the *globalDG*. Yet, should $Score_{stakeholder}$ take hold above a certain threshold, the question arises about whether is this enough to proceed with the merging.

The localDG as the Unit of Merging. Entity alignment act upon a node basis. By contrast, we consider accumulation to handle the manuscript as an atomic unit: either the entire manuscript's *localDG* is merged, or none of its nodes are included. The understanding is that localDG describe a means-end relationship between the problem and the solution space that go in tandem. Adding only the problem nodes without the corresponding nodes, or vice versa, does not seem to make design sense. We then hold that: **a *localDG* is taken as an atomic unit for merging**.

The Merging Decision is Made on Either a Problem Basis or a Solution Basis. We hold that:

> for a *localDG* to be integrated into the *globalDG*, either the problem score *or* the solution score of the *localDG* should be above a certain similitude threshold.

$Score_{problem}$ is based on the similitude scores for *Context, Stakeholder, Goal* and *Problem*, while $Score_{solution}$ is based on the similitude scores for *Artifact* and *Requirement*. In addition, we consider that:

> CGAR constructs are equally important, and large discrepancies between CGAR constructs should lower the overall score.

Hence, *Humidor* combines the semantic similarities for different CGAR using the geometric mean to combine scores, emphasizing relative similarity. Specifically, for the solution realm:

$$Score_{solution} = (Score_{artifact} \cdot Score_{requirement})^{1/2} \qquad (2)$$

Using the geometric mean might imply that it is possible to take the decision to integrate a *localDG* into the *globalDG*, and yet none of its nodes be finally merged.

3.3 *Humidor* at Work

Humidor resorts to *gpt-4o* and *Neo4j* as the LLM and the graph DBMS, respectively. Figure 3 displays the design graph (partial) after merging 36 *localDG* obtained from primary studies in a literature review. Colours represent labels, *Neo4j*'s way to support construct types. On the right-side, the node collected properties: description (used for similarity comparison), embeddings, main excerpts, hypernyms, and paper IDs.

4 Evaluation

Goal. The CGAR prompt lays the groundwork for constructing the design graph. Therefore, it is crucial to evaluate the extent to which the CGAR prompt accurately identifies the CGAR constructs.

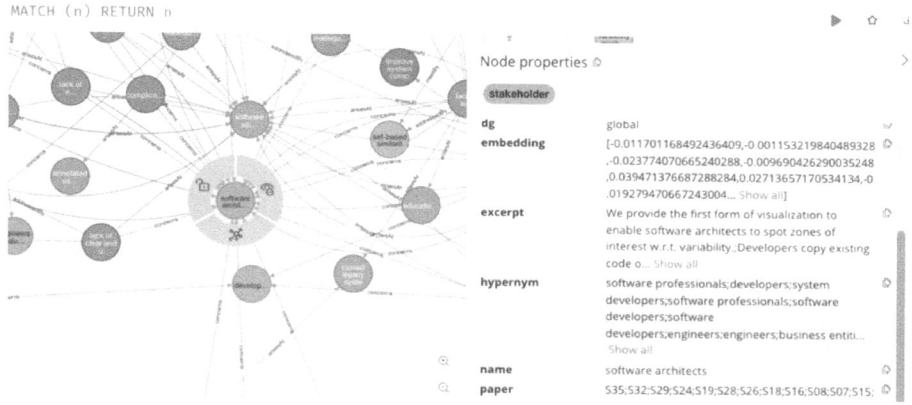

Fig. 3. Partial view of the graph with the node's attributes visualizer.

Design. As part of a postgraduate course on Design Science, we asked 10 PhD students to select three manuscripts within their area of expertise. For each manuscript, they were requested to manually characterize the paper as a CGAR expression: $CGAR_{human}$. Next, the student moved to $gpt4o$ to run the CGAR prompt tuned to return the result in terms of a CGAR expression: $CGAR_{AI}$. The students were then sent a questionnaire to compare $CGAR_{human}$ and $CGAR_{AI}$ in a construct basis. Comparison is set in terms of wording and meaning:

- Same wording: $CGAR_{AI}$ and $CGAR_{human}$ use the same words, though the word order might differ.
- Same meaning: $CGAR_{AI}$ and $CGAR_{human}$ convey the same meaning, even if the words are different.
- Different meaning, with $CGAR_{AI}$ being *more general* than $CGAR_{human}$: $CGAR_{AI}$ has a broader meaning or scope compared to $CGAR_{human}$.
- Different meaning, with $CGAR_{AI}$ being *more specific* than $CGAR_{human}$: $CGAR_{AI}$ has a narrower or more detailed meaning than $CGAR_{human}$.
- Different meanings: $CGAR_{human}$ and $CGAR_{AI}$ convey different meanings altogether.

Results. Figure 4 outlines the results. The constructs with the most coincidence between AI and human outputs are *Stakeholder* and *Artifact*, where high percentages of "Same Words" and "Same Meaning" (over 50% combined) demonstrate strong alignment. These results suggest that the AI is particularly adept at interpreting and replicating structured or well-defined concepts. For instance, the *"Stakeholder"* construct shows no instances of "Different Meaning", indicating a reliable understanding of roles or entities in context, while *"Artifact"* achieves the highest percentage of "Same Words" (30%), reflecting consistency in terminology. In contrast, the construct with the least coincidence is Requirement, where 10% of outputs fall under "Different Meaning", and a significant portion (over 40%) is divided between "More Specific" and "More General". We can conjecture that the alignment between LLM and human outputs is

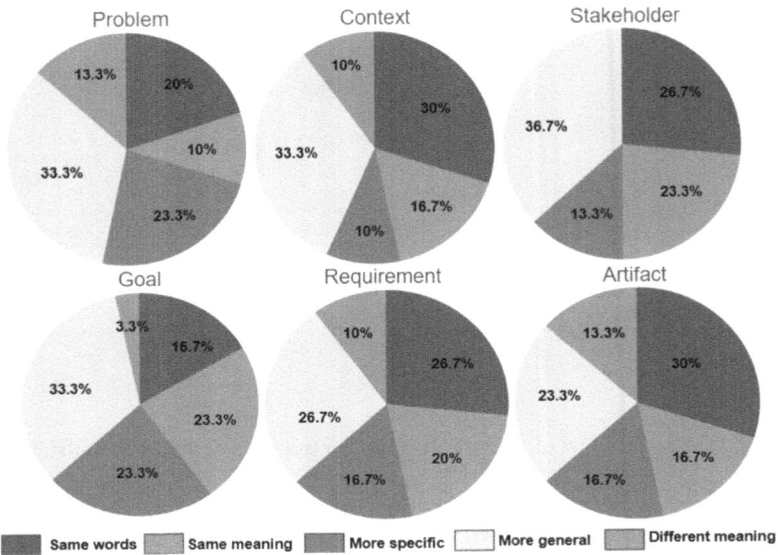

Fig. 4. $CGAR_{AI}$ vs. $CGAR_{human}$ based on 30 manuscript

closely tied to the degree of shared terminology within the community. Constructs with clear, standardized language (e.g., *Stakeholder*) benefit from this shared understanding, while those with more fluid or context-dependent terminology (e.g., *Requirement*) pose greater challenges for consistent interpretation. This suggests that the Humidor approach is better suited for domains with, to some extent, shared terminology. In addition, developing and embedding taxonomies specific to each construct (e.g., clear hierarchies for "*Requirement*" or "*Problem*") could help guide the LLM in organizing and interpreting information. These taxonomies would serve as reference points for consistent output generation.

5 Conclusion

This work presents *Humidor*, a KG-augmented LLM framework that tackles DSR accumulation. Using the CGAR model, the framework extracts, aligns, and integrates CGAR expressions from various manuscripts into a global graph, bringing about the vision of DG-augmented LLMs. Initial evaluations indicate the *Humidor*'s effectiveness in: extracting CGAR expressions from documents, as evaluated from a set of 30 documents with PhD students as ground truth providers.

Acknowledgement. Research supported by MCIN/AEI/10.13039/501100011033/ FEDER, UE and the "European Union NextGenerationEU/PRTR" under contract PID2021-125438OB-I00. Xabier Garmendia enjoys a grant from the University of the Basque Country - PIF20/236.

References

1. vom Brocke, J., Winter, R., Hevner, A., Maedche, A.: Special issue editorial - accumulation and evolution of design knowledge in design science research: A journey through time and space. J. Assoc. Inf. Syst. **21**(3), 520–544 (2020). https://doi.org/10.17705/1jais.00611, https://aisel.aisnet.org/jais/vol21/iss3/9/
2. Carta, S., Giuliani, A., Piano, L., Podda, A.S., Pompianu, L., Tiddia, S.G.: Iterative zero-shot llm prompting for knowledge graph construction. arXiv preprint arXiv:2307.01128 (2023)
3. Chandra, L., Seidel, S., Gregor, S.: Prescriptive knowledge in is research: Conceptualizing design principles in terms of materiality, action, and boundary conditions. In: 2015 48th hawaii international conference on system sciences, pp. 4039–4048. IEEE (2015)
4. Johannesson, P., Perjons, E.: An Introduction to Design Science. Springer, Cham, Switzerland (2014). https://doi.org/10.1007/978-3-319-10632-4
5. Maedche, A., Gregor, S., Morana, S., Feine, J.: Conceptualizing and communicating design knowledge in information systems research. J. Assoc. Inf. Syst. **20**(9), 1341–1366 (2019). https://doi.org/10.17705/1jais.00558
6. Pan, S., Luo, L., Wang, Y., Chen, C., Wang, J., Wu, X.: Unifying large language models and knowledge graphs: a roadmap. IEEE Trans. Knowl. Data Eng. **36**, 3580–3599 (2023). https://doi.org/10.1109/TKDE.2024.3352100
7. Paulheim, H.: Knowledge graph refinement: a survey of approaches and evaluation methods. Semantic web **8**(3), 489–508 (2017)
8. Reimers, N., Gurevych, I.: Sentence-bert: sentence embeddings using siamese bert-networks. In: Conference on Empirical Methods in Natural Language Processing (2019)
9. Sheng, J., Guo, S., Chen, Z., Yue, J., Wang, L., Liu, T.: Challenging the assumption of structure-based embeddings in few- and zero-shot knowledge graph completion. In: International Conference on Language Resources and Evaluation (2022). https://api.semanticscholar.org/CorpusID:252376765
10. Wang, Y., Xu, M., Yan, Y., Zhao, T., Chen, Y., Yang, J.: Exploring topic supervision with bert for text matching. In: 2022 International Joint Conference on Neural Networks (IJCNN), pp. 1–7. IEEE (2022)
11. Wieringa, R.J.: Design science methodology: For information systems and software engineering. Springer (2014). https://doi.org/10.1007/978-3-662-43839-8. https://link.springer.com/content/pdf/10.1007/978-3-662-43839-8.pdf
12. Xiang, E., Wang, J., et al.: Ontoea: Ontology-guided entity alignment via joint knowledge graph embedding. arXiv preprint arXiv:2105.07688 (2021)
13. Yang, C.: Why/How AI KG SDK Upgrade: Vector Chunk Linking with Graphs - Increasing Explainability & Accuracy. https://rebrand.ly/enterprise-rag/whyhow (2024). Accessed 29 Nov 2024
14. Yang, R., et al.: Graphusion: leveraging large language models for scientific knowledge graph fusion and construction in nlp education. arXiv preprint arXiv:2407.10794 (2024)

Trust Paradoxes in Machine Learning: An Ontological Approach

Yuntian Ding[(✉)], Nicolas Herbaut[(✉)], and Camille Salinesi

Centre de Recherche en Informatique, Univ. Paris 1 Panthéon-Sorbonne, Paris, France
{yuntian.ding,nicolas.herbaut,camille.salinesi}@univ-paris1.fr

Abstract. Despite significant advancements in the performance and capabilities of data-driven machine learning systems, establishing trust remains a profound challenge. Complex trust paradoxes, such as balancing transparency with performance, and personalization with privacy, complicate the establishment of trust. This paper builds on the main foundations of trust in technology from a systematically review of literature, focusing on the interplay between trust components and the tensions among competing favorable features and ethical principles. We then introduce a new trust ontology that captures the key elements of trust and their relationships. This ontology highlights the dynamics of trust, emphasizing the conflicting relationships between favorable features and how they influence trust between humans and machine learning systems.

Keywords: artificial intelligence · machine learning · trust · trust paradox

1 Introduction

The rapid development of artificial intelligence (AI) has led to widespread applications, raising discussions on trust and regulation. A recent incident involving David Mayer[1], who defended his rights against the use of his information by ChatGPT, highlighting persistent challenges in increasing user trust and ensuring that AI systems adhere to ethical and legal standards, even in areas where AI applications are relatively mature. While trust in AI encompasses a broad range of topics, including trust in machine learning, inference, and data management [16], this paper focuses on trust in data-driven machine learning (ML) systems.

Trust in AI systems is complex and riddled with paradoxes, shaped by factors such as performance, bias, transparency, privacy, and user expectations. For instance, personalization mechanisms can foster trust by generating outputs to users' contexts, but they also introduce subjectivity that challenges universal fairness. This tension reflects what is referred to as a "trust paradox". Neglecting trust paradoxes can lead to serious social issues and damage public trust in

---
[1] https://www.nytimes.com/2024/12/06/us/david-mayer-chatgpt-openai.html.

AI systems, as seen in AI biometric identification systems, where concerns over privacy, bias, and accuracy led to calls for regulations.

Regulatory frameworks, such as the AI Act, introduce basic requirements for ML system development, but trust paradoxes complicate the definition of trust and the establishment of trustworthy ML systems that align with ethical values. Addressing these paradoxes requires a nuanced understanding of how trust in ML systems is established and maintained.

To address this complexity, we pose the following research questions.

- **RQ1 :** What are the key components of trust in ML systems?
- **RQ2 :** How do trust paradoxes manifest when implementing trust-enhancing features in ML systems?

A systematic literature review offers a comprehensive overview of trust within the specific context of ML systems. We review the trust-building guidelines, from which we identify favourable features to enhance trust levels, and analyse trust paradoxes from existing literature, we briefly detail our research methodology. The main contribution is a new ontology of trust, focusing on its establishment in data-driven machine learning systems considering various trust paradoxes. It offers new insights for future regulatory and technical efforts in ML systems.

2 Background and Related Work

Trust is a fundamental social concept, but the literature presents different definitions of trust depending on the working context, including economic, sociological, and technological domains.

In 1979, Luhmann related trust to societal complexity, defining it as "confidence in one's expectation" and the willingness to act despite uncertainty. In this sense, trust is a "risky investment", but he also emphasized that trust is not blind; rather, it is an acceptance of certain vulnerabilities. The decision to trust can be based on human experiences, character, and social influences [11].

In 1998, Rousseau et al. explored the explored historical definitions of trust, highlighting how definitions and focal points vary across different disciplines. Despite these differences, they identified common characteristics of trust. They underlined the common understanding of trust as a psychological state in which individuals accept vulnerability by believing that others will act with good intentions and expected behavior [14].

Further research has explored the trust components across different fields. Trusting intentions refers to belief in other's capabilities and the willingness to accept the vulnerabilities; institutional trust represents belief in structural conditions; trust belief is cognitive, influenced by user's rational calculation; and dispositional trust reflects the user's natural intention to rely on general others [8,9].

In 2019, Amaral et al. proposed an ontology of trust using ontoUML, a modeling language grounded in the Unified Foundational Ontology (UFO), based on previously identified trust components and definitions [7]. They consider trust as a mental state of the trustor based on their intention to rely on the trustee, considering the trustee's capabilities, intentions, and vulnerabilities. Additionally, they introduce a quantity, "trust degree," which refers to the level of trust the trustor has toward the trustee [1]. While their ontology provides a useful framework for understanding trust, further specification and refinement are needed when applied to trust in ML systems.

This study specifies trustors as humans who rely on ML systems and trustees as ML systems perceived as trustworthy. Building trust in ML systems involves strategies to instill user confidence while aligning systems with societal and individual values. The key favorable features include performance, explainability, transparency, interaction quality, and privacy.

However, simply listing favorable attributes does not linearly increase trust in ML systems. For instance, the well-known tension between privacy and transparency illustrates this challenge. Another example is the paradox between explainability and system accuracy. Papenmeier et al. show that faithful explanations do not significantly increase trust ratings compared to systems without explanations, revealing a complex interplay between explanation quality, classifier accuracy, and user trust that requires further investigation [13]. These existing conflicts between favorable attributes—referred to as "trust paradoxes"—exacerbate the challenges in providing effective trust-building guidance for ML systems.

3 Methodology

To ensure the accuracy of our knowledge database, we followed Kitchenham's guidelines and extracted keywords from our research question: RQ2: how do trust paradoxes manifest when implementing trust-enhancing features in ML systems? The keywords were classified into three categories [10].

- **Population**: this includes artificial intelligence (AI), and machine learning (ML), as our study focuses on trust within this specific technological domain.
- **Intervention**: this includes concepts such as trust paradoxes, trust dilemmas, contradictions in trust, tension in trust, highlighting conflicts between trust factors.
- **Outcome**: the goal is to explore the manifestations of trust paradoxes.

Using these keywords, a Boolean search string was constructed: **(Artificial Intelligence OR Machine Learning) AND (Trust Paradoxes OR Trust Dilemmas OR Contradictions in Trust OR Tension in Trust)**. Applying this search string to **Scopus**, 220 articles published after 2019 were retrieved, of which 131 were available in English. During the primary selection process, we included papers that manifest trust paradoxes in ML systems. Papers focusing solely on challenges without addressing tensions between trustworthy principles were excluded. Additionally, as our research does not compare the trustworthiness of human trustees with machine learning trustees, papers focusing on human expertise versus ML systems were also excluded. After applying the inclusion and exclusion criteria, 40 papers were included in the final database.

A full-text review of these papers revealed 11 different trust paradoxes, including explainability vs. accuracy, explainability vs. performance, explainability vs. fairness, transparency vs. privacy (user sovereignty), transparency vs. performance, personalization vs. fairness, personalization vs. privacy, personalization vs. accuracy, performance vs. safety, performance vs. accuracy, performance vs. fairness. Identifying these paradoxes is essential, as tensions between these features influence the trust degree of trustees, and consequently impact user adoption of ML systems. In Sect. 4, these paradoxes are further illustrated through our ontology.

4 Trust Model: Trust Factors and Their Relations

A trust ontology is presented, built upon Amaral's work and extended by incorporating perceptions from our literature review.

Different from Amaral's work, we focus on the trust relationship between humans as trustors and ML systems as trustees. To visualize our contribution based on their work, the trust elements from Amaral's work are colored in orange.

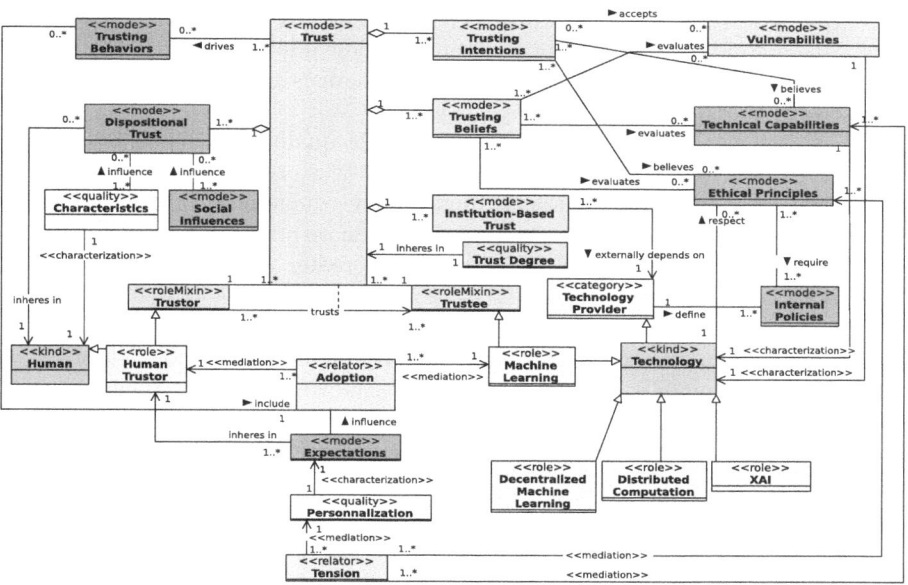

Fig. 1. Ontology of human trust in technology

4.1 Trust Components

This trust model, illustrated in Fig. 1, classifies trust components in the ML system into five principal categories.

- Trusting beliefs: this is a knowledge-based perception, referring to beliefs in technology's competence, influenced by various qualities like performance, explainability, and transparency. We categorized these qualities into *Ethical Principles* (legal and ethical requirements for the ML system) and *Technical Capabilities* (functional qualities of the ML system).
- Trusting intentions: this is the willingness to rely on technologies despite their vulnerabilities in the given context. Unlike trust between humans, machines do not have intentions, so this component reflects the willingness to trust the capabilities of technology. This is a subjective perception.
- Trusting behaviors: unlike trusting beliefs or intentions, it is observable in human behavior rather than their perceptions.
- Dispositional Trust: this component is shaped by personal characteristics and social influences. It represents the natural disposition to trust ML systems without any technical proof.
- Institution-based Trust: this refers to human belief in structural conditions, such as the reputation of the technology provider.

These five components evolve over time due to external influences as well as intrinsic changes. For instance, the results returned by an ML system meeting user expectations or the proof provided by technology providers on the ML system's capabilities are external influences, they impact *trusting beliefs* and *trusting intentions*. Intrinsic changes refer to changes in personal *dispositional trust* toward the ML system.

Trust degree is modeled as a non-perceivable quality that evolves as these components evolve. Two different stages of the trust relationship between the human trustor and the ML trustee illustrate its dynamics: *Expectations* and *Adoption*. There is an initial trust degree based on disposition trust, institution-based trust and trust intentions. If this degree is greater than a certain threshold, the human trustor trusts the ML trustee to this degree, a trusting behavior that can be observed as *Adoption*. At this stage, the human demonstrates the willingness to be exposed to the ML system's vulnerabilities by adopting it. Meanwhile, the human uses the ML system to achieve some goals, they naturally have *Expectations* about its outputs. The way the ML system satisfies their expectations will change their perception and adoption of the system, thereby affecting the overall trust relationship.

4.2 Trust Paradoxes

We identified 11 different trust paradoxes from our literature review and model tension as a **relator** between *Personalization*, *Ethical Principles* and *Technical Capabilities* in our ontology. These tensions were categorized into three main classes: (1) personalization-related tensions, (2) inner tensions within technical capabilities and in ethical principles, and (3) cross tensions between capabilities and ethical principles. To maintain clarity, typical examples of these tensions were illustrated rather than presenting a complete overview.

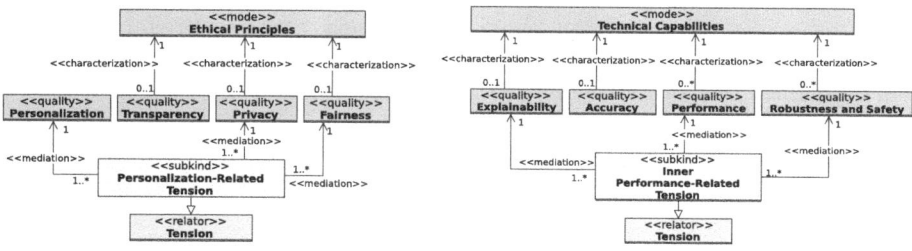

Fig. 2. Personalization-Related Tension   **Fig. 3.** Inner Tension

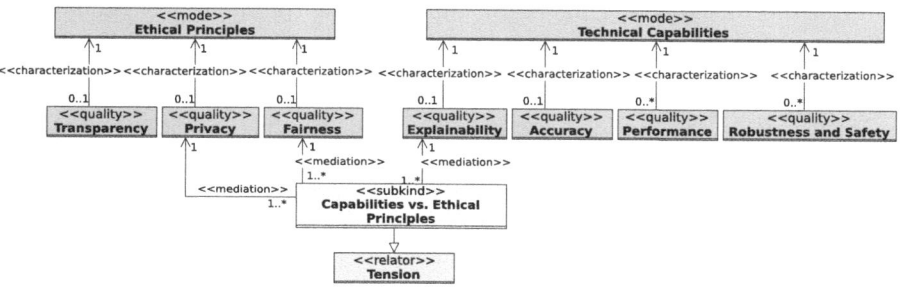

Fig. 4. Cross Tension

Personalization-Related Tension.
User satisfaction strongly depends on the ML system's ability to achieve their goals. One crucial factor is the quality of interaction between the system and the user, which was modeled as *personalization*. While strong personalization may better align with user expectations, an overemphasis on it causes strong biases, hence negatively impacting accuracy and fairness [3]. Additionally, excessive personalized output may not improve the satisfaction of users with strong privacy concerns; instead, it may reduce their trust level [5] (Fig. 2).

Inner Tension of Capabilities and Ethical Principles.
This category refers to tensions between different features within either *Technical Capabilities* or *Ethical Principles*. For example, while transparency is essential, excessive transparency can introduce new trust issues related to user rights, societal values, or legal compliance [15]. Similarly, tensions emerge between various capabilities, such as accuracy vs. explainability, performance vs. robustness and safety, and explainability vs. performance (Fig. 3).

Capabilities vs. Ethical Principles.
Conflicts often arise between an ML system's technical capabilities and ethical principles. There is a paradox between legal fairness requirements and the practical challenges of implementing effective audits, which causes great trust issues [12]. A well-known example is the "white-box", which refers to the tension between explainability as an important capability and privacy and fairness as

ethical principles. This paradox emerges from users' continued reliance on ML despite encountering errors, driven by the persuasive nature of explanations. Users' judgments of ML errors and explanation rationality influence their trust and willingness to adopt the system [4] (Fig. 4).

4.3 Synergy with Other Technologies

Technologies such as *Explainable AI (XAI)*, *decentralized machine learning*, and *distributed computation* have the potential to enhance both technical capabilities and ethical principles, addressing certain trust paradoxes. For instance, XAI addresses the "black-box" paradox by improving interpretability, explainability, and accountability, enhancing user understanding, mitigating biases, and fostering trust [2].

However, their integration does not necessarily increase trust. Users may still question their capabilities and ethical respects, similar to concerns with ML systems. Furthermore, these technologies face challenges; for example, Evans et al. highlight the tension between accuracy and performance in XAI, requiring complementary solutions. While simple and intuitive explanations improve usability, oversimplification risks misleading users or introducing biases [6].

5 Conclusion and Future Work

This study highlights the complex interplay of trust features that cause paradoxes in machine learning systems. Despite advancements in ethical frameworks, tensions between performance, transparency, fairness, privacy, and explainability persist. This impact is illustrated through our trust ontology. While technologies like explainable AI (XAI), distributed computation, and decentralized machine learning offer potential solutions, their limitations and human attitudes toward technologie may degrade the trust degree in ML systems.

To advance this field, future research must address the following key challenges: first, identifying unsolvable paradoxes, akin to the CAP theorem (consistency, availability, and partition tolerance), to provide clarity for regulation and their practical implications. Second, a lack of interdisciplinary dialogue between ethicists and legal experts, and machine learning engineers limits the integration of effective solutions regarding legal monitoring. Finally, evaluating to what extent ML systems respect ethical principles is difficult, as most principles are qualitative rather than quantitative, making it difficult to evaluate the exact nature of trustworthiness.

References

1. Amaral, G., Sales, T.P., Guizzardi, G., Porello, D.: Towards a reference ontology of trust. In: On the Move to Meaningful Internet Systems: OTM 2019 Conferences: Confederated International Conferences: CoopIS, ODBASE, C&TC 2019, Rhodes, Greece, October 21–25, 2019, Proceedings, pp. 3–21. Springer (2019)

2. Arrieta, A.B., et al.: Explainable artificial intelligence (xai): concepts, taxonomies, opportunities and challenges toward responsible ai. Inf. Fusion **58**, 82–115 (2020)
3. Burgess, E.R., et al.: Healthcare ai treatment decision support: Design principles to enhance clinician adoption and trust. In: Proceedings of the 2023 CHI Conference on Human Factors in Computing Systems, pp. 1–19 (2023)
4. Cabitza, F., Campagner, A., Natali, C., Parimbelli, E., Ronzio, L., Cameli, M.: Painting the black box white: experimental findings from applying xai to an ecg reading setting. Mach. Learn. Knowl. Extraction **5**(1), 269–286 (2023)
5. Cloarec, J., Meyer-Waarden, L., Munzel, A.: Transformative privacy calculus: Conceptualizing the personalization-privacy paradox on social media. Psychology & Marketing (2024)
6. Evans, T., et al.: The explainability paradox: challenges for xai in digital pathology. Futur. Gener. Comput. Syst. **133**, 281–296 (2022)
7. Guizzardi, G.: Ontological foundations for structural conceptual models (2005)
8. Harrison McKnight, D., Chervany, N.L.: Trust and distrust definitions: one bite at a time. In: Trust in Cyber-Societies: Integrating the Human and Artificial Perspectives, pp. 27–54. Springer (2001)
9. Israelsen, B.W., Ahmed, N.R.: "dave... i can assure you... that it's going to be all right..." a definition, case for, and survey of algorithmic assurances in human-autonomy trust relationships. ACM Computing Surveys (CSUR) **51**(6), 1–37 (2019)
10. Keele, S., et al.: Guidelines for performing systematic literature reviews in software engineering. Technical report, ver. 2.3 ebse technical report. ebse (2007)
11. Luhmann, N.: Trust and power. John Wiley & Sons (2018)
12. Mihaljević, H., Müller, I., Dill, K., Yollu-Tok, A., von Grafenstein, M.: More or less discrimination? practical feasibility of fairness auditing of technologies for personnel selection. AI Soc. **39**(5), 2507–2523 (2024)
13. Papenmeier, A., Kern, D., Englebienne, G., Seifert, C.: It's complicated: the relationship between user trust, model accuracy and explanations in ai. ACM Trans. Comput.-Hum. Interact. (TOCHI) **29**(4), 1–33 (2022)
14. Rousseau, D.M., Sitkin, S.B., Burt, R.S., Camerer, C.: Not so different after all: a cross-discipline view of trust. Acad. Manag. Rev. **23**(3), 393–404 (1998)
15. Schmitt, A., Wambsganss, T., Söllner, M., Janson, A.: Towards a trust reliance paradox? exploring the gap between perceived trust in and reliance on algorithmic advice. In: ICIS (2021)
16. Toreini, E., Aitken, M., Coopamootoo, K., Elliott, K., Zelaya, C.G., Van Moorsel, A.: The relationship between trust in ai and trustworthy machine learning technologies. In: Proceedings of the 2020 conference on fairness, accountability, and transparency, pp. 272–283 (2020)

Conceptualizing Business Process Dependencies That Propagate Cyber Risk

Gal Engelberg[(✉)][iD], Moshe Hadad[iD], and Pnina Soffer[iD]

University of Haifa, Abba Khoushy Ave 199, 3498838 Haifa, Israel
`gal.engelberg@gmail.com, spnina@is.haifa.ac.il`

Abstract. This paper explores the propagation of cyber risks within business processes, addressing the lack of process-awareness in existing research, especially regarding dependencies between process model elements. We propose a conceptualization that incorporates process model elements, dependencies, cyber risk events, and inference rules for capturing cascading effects. The conceptualization covers control flow, data flow, and resource-to-activity dependencies. A proof of concept, analyzing risk propagation in a credit evaluation process, demonstrates how confidentiality, integrity, and availability risks cascade across components. Our findings show how this approach uncovers cascading risks, providing insights for cyber risk assessment in interconnected environments.

Keywords: Risk Propagation · Secure Business Process · Risk Assessment

1 Introduction

The rise of IoT and cloud computing drives enterprises to migrate business processes to the cloud, exposing them to cyber-attacks [15]. Cybersecurity risks threaten business processes and objectives, underscoring the need to assess their resilience. This need is addressed via approaches using attack graphs to model adversary behavior [12], assess impacts on missions, services, and processes [3], and quantify risk propagation across abstraction layers [6]. Risk propagation refers to the cascading effect of risk events through a network of interconnected events and objects [7]. Business process model components are cyber-attack targets due to configurability and external interactions [9]. Elements governed by information systems are especially vulnerable, as attackers may alter routing or exploit insecure resources and data.

These threat events have a cascading effect on various business process components. For instance, consider a credit request evaluation process as presented in Fig. 1, where data elements as *Verification*, *Amount*, and *Final Decision* guide the flow, and human resources as *Assistants* and *Experts* manage activities as *Verification* and *Assessment*. Consider a scenario where an attack compromises the integrity and confidentiality of the *Amount* data in the credit evaluation process. Such an attack could lead to a loss of integrity in the *Decision* outcome, while simultaneously exposing sensitive financial data. Additionally, an attack on the personal computer of Sue for example, could compromise its availability, rendering the *Advanced Assessment* activity unavailable and disrupting the overall evaluation process. These examples illustrate how a single security event can initiate cascading effects across multiple entities, affecting not only data but also activities, events, gateways, and the entire process.

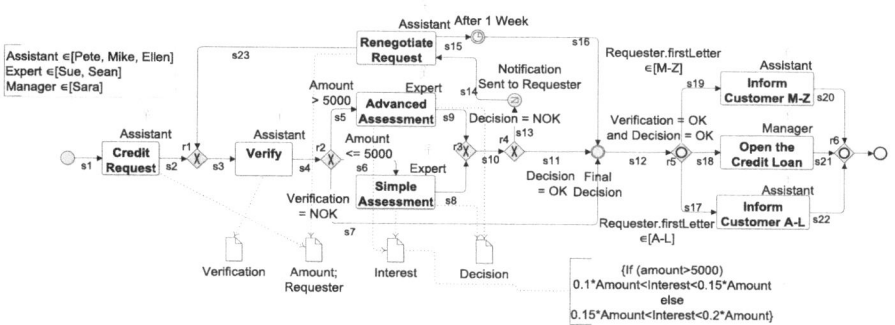

Fig. 1. A data-and-resource-aware credit evaluation process model, introduced in [5]

The existing literature models cyber risk propagation via resource and activity dependencies [3,6] but lacks full process-awareness. It overlooks dependencies critical to risk quantification, such as control flow beyond direct follows, data flow, and routing constraints. Overall, cyber risk propagation in business processes remains conceptually underexplored. This paper explores process dependencies that propagate cyber risk, addressing: *How is cyber risk propagated within a business process?* It presents a conceptualization integrating business process elements, dependencies, risk events, and inference rules to model risk propagation. The conceptualization defines how external events trigger and spread risk, with a proof-of-concept case study demonstrating its applicability.

The paper is structured as follows: Sect. 2 covers foundational concepts, Sect. 3 introduces the conceptualization, Sect. 4 details the proof-of-concept, and conclusions are provided.

2 Conceptualization Foundations

Ontological Foundations of Risk Assessment and Propagation. This work is inspired by the *Common Ontology of Value and Risk (COVER)* [14], which defines risk as a contextual, goal-oriented concept reflecting potential events that may affect goal achievement. Risk arises from uncertainties tied to anticipated events, requiring assessment of potential losses and their likelihood. Building on this, [7] conceptualized risk propagation as the spread of risk through interconnected system components. It involves event-event, object-event, and object-object relations, modeled as a graph, where nodes represent event or object types and edges capture dependencies such as precedence or participation. Event likelihoods are often modeled using Bayesian networks [13] or Markov chains [4], with overall risk quantified as a function of these likelihoods and their impact on goal achievement. This work focuses on modeling cyber risk propagation within business processes, emphasizing patterns of cascading effects across process components and dependencies.

Business Process Model and its Components. A business process model consists of activity models and execution constraints governing their interactions. Each process instance represents a specific operational case, made up of individual activity instances. The business process model serves as a blueprint for these instances, with each activity model providing the framework for corresponding activity instances [17]. This study focuses on the business process model level. A systematic review by [1] identified core components of business process meta-models, including *Activities* (units of work), *Events* (triggers or milestones), *Routing Constraints*, *Sequence Flow* (execution order), *Data Flow* (information transfer), and *Resources* such as humans, systems, or materials. This study adopts *Business Process Model Notation (BPMN)* [11], following its formal semantics in [2]. In BPMN, the main construct is the *flow element*, residing in a *flow element container* (a *process* or *subprocess*), and representing either a *flow Node* (i.e., *activity*, *event*, or *gateway*) or a *sequence flow*. Gateways act as decision points, with *expressions* evaluating flow conditions. While not explicitly defined in BPMN, *routing constraints* are modeled via a *gateway*, its incoming/outgoing *sequence flows*, and associated *expression*. Each *activity* specifies *input* and *output sets* through its *input output specification*, comprising *resource* instances (e.g., *software*, *material*, *human*, *data*). Though implicit, *data flow* can be inferred from the data resources associated with these sets.

Security Properties of Business Processes. A secure business process integrates security measures throughout its lifecycle, including design, implementation, execution, and monitoring, to protect sensitive information, maintain data integrity, ensure availability, and comply with regulations [10]. Central to this are the CIA properties: *Confidentiality* (protection from unauthorized access), *Integrity* (resistance to unauthorized modification), and *Availability* (ensuring access for authorized users) [15]. According to COVER [14], a threat event is a potential harmful occurrence enabled by a vulnerability and triggered by a threat agent, while a *Loss Event* is the realized damage. Threats exploit vulnerabilities to generate cascading *loss events*, which this work analyzes within business processes. An *object at risk*, either a *flow node* or *resource*, can initiate or be impacted by such events. For instance, a denial-of-service attack exploiting a server vulnerability degrades its availability, subsequently affecting dependent activities. This study focuses on understanding how such loss events propagate across process components.

3 Modeling Risk Propagation in Business Processes

3.1 Business Process Model Entities Participation in Loss Events

This work uses the semantics of a business process entity's participation in loss events, involving CIA properties. Even when a threat event jointly impacts all properties, we treat the cascading loss effects as disjoint. Loss of confidentiality propagates through threat agent exposure to process data, loss of integrity through data modification, and loss of availability through the sequence flow. Cascading effects between different loss types (e.g., from *LossOfAvailability* to *LossOfConfidentiality*) are outside this work's scope. According to COVER [14], risk participation refers to an object at risk. We model process components: objects, events, activities, and gateways, as at-risk entities since they are considered at the model (specification) level. We define *loss of availability* as the state where a business process entity becomes inaccessible for authorized parties, affecting resources, activities, events, and gateways. *Loss of confidentiality* refers to unauthorized disclosure, access, or theft of sensitive data associated with an entity, applicable to resources and activities but not events or gateways, as these do not directly manipulate data. *Loss of integrity* involves unauthorized modification of information, impacting resources, activities, events, and gateways.

3.2 Business Process Model Dependencies

We analyze how cyber loss events cascade across resources, activities, events, and gateways, focusing on three dependency types: *Resource-to-Activity*, where affected resources disrupt associated activities; *Control Flow*, where events impact subsequent process steps; and *Data Flow*, where compromised data resources influence other process entities. A formalization is available at (See footnote 2).

Resource-to-Activity Dependencies. Resources in business processes are either consumed or produced by activities [1]. Consumed resources, as data or materials, are used during execution, while produced ones, such as reports or components, serve as inputs for subsequent tasks. Activities depend on resources through OR or AND dependencies: the former allows an activity to proceed if any one of the resources is available, while the latter requires all specified resources to be present simultaneously [8]. In BPMN, these dependencies are modeled through input and output sets. Input sets include resources needed to start an activity; output sets contain those generated or modified by it. In Fig. 1, the *Advanced Assessment* activity requires two input sets: a human resource with the role *Expert*, and the data resource *Amount*. All *Experts* belong to one input set (OR dependency), while *Amount* is in another (AND across sets). Output resources, such as *Interest* and *Decision*, are defined by the activity's output. *Decision*, in turn, is used as input by later activities as *Renegotiate Request*.

Control Flow Dependencies. Control flow dependencies define the logical execution order in a business process. We focus on the core patterns from [17]:

Normal Sequence Flow, Exclusive, Inclusive, and Parallel. The *normal sequence flow* represents a direct progression from one activity or event to the next, without involving gateways. *Gateway* dependencies cover three types: The *exclusive* chooses one path based on conditions and continues without waiting for others. The *inclusive* activates multiple branches when conditions hold, synchronizing at the join once all selected paths complete. The *parallel* starts all branches concurrently and waits for all to finish before proceeding. These patterns involve input and output flow nodes connected to a gateway through input and output sequence flows. Output flows may include conditions that determine routing based on data values. For example, the *Verify* activity leads to an exclusive gateway with three branches: *Advanced Assessment*, *Simple Assessment*, and the event *Final Decision*. Routing is determined by expressions, e.g., if the amount exceeds 5,000, the process triggers *Advanced Assessment*.

Data Flow Dependencies. Data flow dependencies describe how data resources impact and are influenced by process components as activities, events, and routing constraints. [16] identified several types. *(1) Data on data.* This dependency occurs when data resources are interdependent, so modifying one updates the other. For example, the *Interest* value depends on the *Amount*. *(2) Data on activity & Activity on data.* The *data on activity* dependency arises when a data resource influences an activity's behavior or decisions, while *activity on data* occurs when an activity modifies a data resource. For example, *Amount* is an input for *Advanced Assessment* and *Simple Assessment*, which both create a *Decision* resource. *(3) Data on routing constraint.* This occurs when a data resource controls case routing, such as Gateway r2 directing flow based on *Amount ¿ 5000* or *Amount ¡= 5000*. *(4) Routing constraint on flow node.* Here, a flow node's activation depends on a gateway and a data-based condition, e.g., *Advanced Assessment* is triggered via r2 when *Amount ¿ 5000*.

3.3 Propagation of Security Property Loss in a Process Model

This section explains how the loss of CIA properties propagates between business process components via the dependencies described in the previous section. These explanations are formalized into inference rules available at (See footnote 2).

Availability. Loss of availability propagates between resources and activities, extending through flow nodes via control flow dependencies. We identified two main cases: *(1) Loss of availability propagation between resources and activities.* If a resource becomes unavailable as an input or output for an activity, the activity will also become unavailable. For example, if resources classified as *Assistants* become unavailable, all dependent activities will also be unavailable. If data resources are interdependent, meaning a modification of one impacts another, the unavailability of one leads to the unavailability of the other. For example, unavailability of the *Amount* data resource leads to unavailability of *Interest*. Furthermore, when an activity becomes unavailable, any data resources in its output set also become unavailable. For example, if *Advanced Assessment* becomes unavailable due to missing *Amount*, the *Decision* data resource also becomes unavailable. This unavailability propagates to activities relying on *Decision*, causing a cascading effect. *(2) Loss of availability propagation between flow nodes.* In a *normal sequence flow*, the unavailability of a flow node prevents the execution of the subsequent nodes. In a *gateway pattern*, loss of availability propagates between flow nodes based on the gateway type. For an *exclusive gateway*, unavailability of an input flow node causes the output nodes activated by a true expression to become unavailable, as the gateway cannot evaluate the expression correctly. For an *inclusive gateway*, all input nodes must be unavailable for the output nodes to become unavailable; if some inputs remain available, corresponding outputs can still be activated. For a *parallel gateway*, unavailability of at least one input node leads to the unavailability of the output nodes, as all input nodes are required for the activation of output nodes.

Confidentiality. Loss of confidentiality propagates when a process entity with access to a data resource compromises its confidentiality. A key scenario occurs when a non-data resource, as a personal computer, is compromised, allowing unauthorized data exposure. If such a resource is in the input set of an activity with data resources in its input or output sets, the confidentiality of these data resources is compromised. For example, if an *Expert*'s computer is compromised, it exposes the *Amount* data resource via the *Advanced Assessment* activity. Furthermore, if a data resource in an activity's input or output loses confidentiality, the activity is also compromised, since the compromised data directly impacts the activity.

Integrity. Loss of integrity propagates when a process entity can modify a data resource, affecting the integrity of other entities, such as activities, events, and gateways. A key scenario occurs when a compromised non-data resource, such as a personal computer, can alter data. If this compromised resource is part of an activity's input set and the activity produces data in its output set, the integrity of these output data resources may be compromised. For example, if an *Expert*'s personal computer is compromised, the integrity of the *Decision* data resource could be affected, leading to improper modifications of its value. If data resources are interdependent, a loss of integrity in one will propagate to others, for example, modifying *Amount* alters *Interest*. Another scenario occurs when an activity depends on a compromised data resource, its integrity will be affected. For example, if the *Amount* data resource is altered, the *Advanced Assessment* will also be compromised, as it relies on the modified value. Similarly, if an activity's integrity is compromised, its output data resource will also be affected. For example, an integrity loss of the *Advanced Assessment* activity will affect the *Decision* data resource. Finally, a loss of integrity of a data resource could impact gateway's integrity, as the gateway relies on data for routing decisions. If compromised, the gateway fails to ensure proper routing, causing incorrect process steps affecting the integrity of its output flow nodes.

4 Proof of Concept Implementation

We demonstrate the conceptualization's applicability through a proof-of-concept that evaluates its ability to explain CIA loss propagation in business processes. Using Neo4j[1] and an RDF-based OWL representation of BPMN [2], we modeled the credit evaluation process from Fig. 1. The inference queries represented cascading event as a node linked to its participants and triggering event. A Python script applied all inference rules recursively until no new nodes or edges were created[2]. Figure 2 illustrates this, with grey nodes for loss events and blue for participants. We simulated threat scenarios using *Amount* (data resource) and *Sue_PC* (non-data resource) as entry points. For *Amount*, an SQL Injection[3] triggered both integrity loss (value alteration) and confidentiality loss (data exposure). A phishing attack[4] on *Sue_PC* led to availability and confidentiality losses via separate paths.

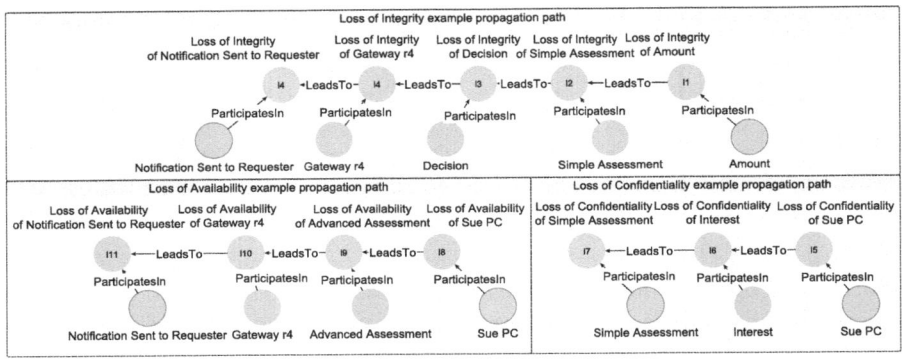

Fig. 2. Samples of risk propagation paths from the credit evaluation process.

We identified 61 cascading loss events: 18 availability, 29 integrity, and 14 confidentiality. Figure 2 illustrates three related propagation paths. The first begins with integrity loss of *Amount*, affecting *Simple Assessment*, skewing the *Decision* value, and causing misrouting by *gateway* r_4, leading to a flawed *Notification*. The second path starts with *Sue_PC*'s availability loss, disrupting *Advanced Assessment* and disabling the *Notification* via *Gateway* r_4. The third involves confidentiality loss of *Sue_PC*, exposing the *Interest* value and compromising both the data and *Simple Assessment*.

---

[1] https://neo4j.com.
[2] Implementation details: https://purl.archive.org/bp-risk-prop.
[3] https://owasp.org/www-community/attacks/SQL_Injection.
[4] https://attack.mitre.org/techniques/T1566/.

5 Conclusion

This paper addresses a gap in the literature by conceptualizing cyber risk propagation within business processes. It sets the foundation for analyzing cascading effects, focusing on control flow, data flow, and resource dependencies. A proof-of-concept in a credit evaluation process demonstrates its applicability. The work is limited by excluding inter-dependency risks beyond the modeled process components and not addressing cascading effects between security properties. Future research will extend this to include probabilistic aspects of loss event propagation and develop robust risk quantification methods.

References

1. Adamo, G., et al.: What is a process model composed of? A systematic literature review of meta-models in bpm. Softw. Syst. Model. **20**(4), 1215–1243 (2021)
2. Annane, A., et al.: BBO: BPMN 2.0 based ontology for business process representation. In: 20th ECKM, vol. 1, pp. 49–59 (2019)
3. Cao, C., Yuan, L.-P., Singhal, A., Liu, P., Sun, X., Zhu, S.: Assessing attack impact on business processes by interconnecting attack graphs and entity dependency graphs. In: Kerschbaum, F., Paraboschi, S. (eds.) DBSec 2018. LNCS, vol. 10980, pp. 330–348. Springer, Cham (2018). https://doi.org/10.1007/978-3-319-95729-6_21
4. Ching, W.K., Ng, M.K.: Markov chains. Models, algorithms and applications (2006)
5. De Leoni, M., et al.: Data-and resource-aware conformance checking of business processes. In: Business Information Systems: 15th Int. Conference, BIS 2012, Vilnius, Lithuania, May 21–23, 2012. Proceedings 15, pp. 48–59. Springer (2012)
6. Engelberg, G., et al.: An ontology-driven approach for process-aware risk propagation. In: Proceedings of the 38th ACM/SIGAPP Symposium on Applied Computing, pp. 1742–1745 (2023)
7. Fumagalli, M., et al.: On the semantics of risk propagation. In: International Conference on Research Challenges in Information Science, pp. 69–86. Springer (2023)
8. Goethals, F., et al.: Identifying dependencies in business processes. In: Communication and Coordination in Business Processes (LAP-CCBP) Workshop, Kiruna, Sweden, June. vol. 22 (2005)
9. Hacks, S., et al.: Towards automated attack simulations of BPMN-based processes. In: 2021 IEEE 25th International Enterprise Distributed Object Computing Conference (EDOC), pp. 182–191. IEEE (2021)
10. Neubauer, T., et al.: Secure business process management: a roadmap. In: 1st International Conference on Availability, Reliability and Security, pp. 8–pp. IEEE (2006)
11. Object Management Group: Business process model and notation (BPMN) specification, version 2.0. Technical report, Object Management Group (OMG) (2011). https://www.omg.org/spec/BPMN/2.0
12. Ou, X., et al.: A scalable approach to attack graph generation. In: Proceedings of the 13th ACM Conference on Computer and Communications Security, New York, NY, USA, pp. 336–345. Association for Computing Machinery (2006)
13. Pearl, J., Russell, S.: Bayesian networks (2000)

14. Sales, T.P., Baião, F., Guizzardi, G., Almeida, J., Guarino, N., Mylopoulos, J.: The Common ontology of value and risk. In: Trujillo, J.C., et al. (eds.) ER 2018. LNCS, vol. 11157, pp. 121–135. Springer, Cham (2018). https://doi.org/10.1007/978-3-030-00847-5_11
15. Soveizi, N., et al.: Security and privacy concerns in cloud-based scientific and business workflows: a systematic review. Future Generation Computer Systems (2023)
16. Tsoury, A., et al.: Data impact analysis in business processes: automatic support and practical implications. Bus. Inf. Syst. Eng. **62**, 41–60 (2020)
17. Weske, M.: Business Process Management: Concepts, Languages, Architectures. Springer, Cham (2012)

Towards a Data Satellite Architecture for Federated Digital Ecosystems: Combating Data Pollution and Enhancing Trustworthiness

Asif Qumer Gill[1](✉) and Anastasija Nikiforova[2]

[1] Faculty of Engineering and IT, School of Computer Science, University of Technology Sydney, Sydney, Australia
asif.gill@uts.edu.au
[2] Faculty of Science and Technology, Institute of Computer Science, University of Tartu, Tartu, Estonia
anastasija.nikiforova@ut.ee

Abstract. Data is fundamental to federated digital ecosystems yet managing it effectively across diverse agencies and jurisdictions remains a complex challenge. Among these challenges, data pollution—characterized by excessive, inconsistent, inaccessible, unusable toxic or dark data—significantly undermines data trustworthiness and utility. The critical question is: how can data pollution be detected and mitigated within the federated digital ecosystems? To tackle this, we propose a Data Satellite Architecture (DSA), a novel approach that integrates the disjoint data Governance, Quality assurance, Monitoring and Observability capabilities for combating data pollution and enhancing trustworthiness. The DSA is designed to combat data pollution, enhance trustworthiness, and ensure secure, reliable data flows across ecosystems. Using an echeloned Design Science Research methodology, we develop and evaluate the proposed DSA. This paper presents the initial alpha version (conceptual) of the DSA. This new concept of DSA is expected to spark new discussion and research areas in the context of data-intensive digital government ecosystems.

Keywords: Data ecosystem · Data governance · Data quality · Data observability · Data pollution · Federated digital ecosystem

1 Introduction

Data is core to federated digital ecosystem- a complex network of interconnected ecosystems and archetypes (subsystems)- yet its management and sharing across the overarching digital super-ecosystem present significant challenges [10, 17]. A critical issue within this context is data pollution, which refers to the collection, storage, retention, flow, or release of "harmful data" —excessive, inconsistent, inaccessible, irrelevant, poisoned, unsolicited, unusable toxic or dark data— within these federated digital ecosystems [4, 11]. Data pollution undermines trust in data, leading to disinformation or misinformation, and exacerbates existing complexities in managing Data Governance, Quality, Monitoring and Observability (GQMO) capabilities beyond local organisational boundaries and across various entities/agencies operating in the federated digital ecosystem [6]. This demands an integrated and overarching end-to-end approach to effectively address these challenges for the multi-agency federated digital ecosystem [11, 16]. To tackle this, the paper explores the research question: *How can data pollution be detected and mitigated in federated digital ecosystems?*

This paper proposes the Data Satellite Architecture (DSA) - framework designed to enable and facilitate integrated GQMO capabilities at different scales, ranging from sector-specific satellites (e.g., health data satellite, finance data satellite) to cross-sector and multi-level satellites, such as local, state, national and global data satellites [11]. This short paper introduces the initial alpha version of the DSA—conceptual model developed using the echeloned Design Science Research (DSR) method [19]. This paper is organized as follows: first, it presents the DSR methodology; second, it examines the problem analysis; finally, it discusses the proposed DSA and its conceptual framework.

2 Design Science Research Method

Given the complex nature of the problem at hand, this research adopts "five echelons" from the DSR method [19] and "five design principles" of (1) emergence, (2) connectivity & interdependence, (3) co-evolution, (4) historicity & time, (5) path-dependence from the complex adaptive systems (CAS) theory [18] to design the proposed DSA. As such, the research is organized into five iterative echelons or stages (Fig. 1), facilitating the design and development of the DSA through three planned increments: alpha, beta, and gamma.

This paper focuses on the first three DSR stages and initial alpha increment (version 1) of the DSA: (1) problem analysis, (2) objectives and requirements definition, and (3) design and development. Additionally, it outlines the plan for the remaining stages— (4) demonstration and (5) evaluation—within the practical context of Australian Government Data Ecosystem as an example by involving related stakeholders from the *Global Data and Digital Alliance*. As such, the proposed DSA is a domain-agnostic. The details of the DSR application are discussed in Sects. 3, 4, 5 and 6.

3 Problem Analysis

The problem analysis produces the *problem statement* (an intermediate artifact) based on the literature review on digital government data ecosystem and data architecture.

3.1 Digital Government Data Ecosystem

Digital government data ecosystem comprises several interconnected agencies or departments that collect, process, retain, and share data to facilitate effective digital service delivery [9]. Digital government data ecosystem forms the essential *data foundation* for evidence-based regulatory frameworks, policymaking and operational activities, including the support for trustworthy artificial intelligence and related initiatives [11]. Such

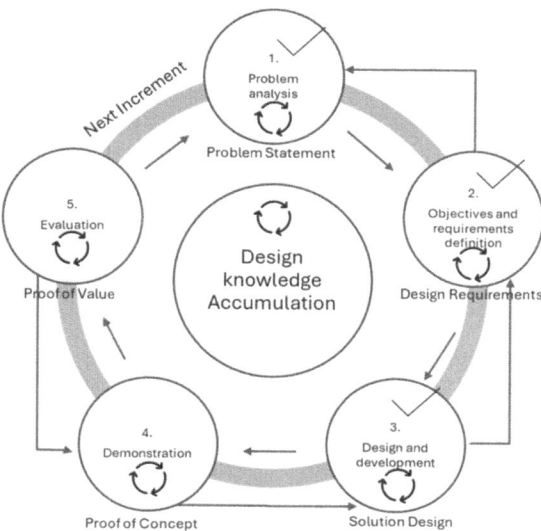

Fig. 1. Design science research method.

data foundation relies on various technological solutions (e.g., data warehouses, marts, lakes, lakehouses, exchanges, fabrics, factories, hubs, marketplaces, intelligence platforms, semantic graphs). While these solutions facilitate local data management and enable boundaryless data flows, they also introduce some pressing data management challenges, where disjoint data governance and quality mechanisms lead to *data pollution* problem in this complex federated digital government ecosystem(s).

3.2 Data Architecture

Before introducing the new class of DSA, it is important to first analyse existing data architectures to position and validate the *problem statement* and new data system/ architecture need within the existing landscape. Data architecture, a sub-discipline of enterprise architecture, deals with the design of data systems, sub-systems and components, their relationships and the principles guiding their design and evolution [12]. Over time, several data architecture patterns have emerged to address evolving data needs. Our review (summarised in Table 1) suggests that these include (1) single application database, (2) data warehouse, (3) data lake, (4) data lakehouse, (5) data mesh, (6) data fabric, and (7) data exchange patterns (e.g., [3, 5, 13, 15]). Based on this review, a new (8) DSA is proposed, which sits above these data architecture patterns to support GQMO capabilities by design. To support the GQMO capabilities, DSA uses the agents based semantic layer with federated enterprise knowledge graph to monitor and observe the critical data assets and their flows across the ecosystem. This paper aims to present this new DSA.

As data architecture patterns are broadly organized into data sourcing, integration and sharing patterns, we organize their description, respectively. Firstly, the **data sourcing**

Table 1. Data architecture patterns.

Pattern name	Description	Problem	Solutions	Description
Application database	A single application data store	Need to capture, manage, and report structured, semi-structured and unstructured operational data	- Relational database - NoSQL database - Document database - Graph database	- Easy to manage - Isolated data
Data warehouse	A unified repository for structured data from multiple sources	Need to integrate data from different sources into a centralized data store for historical reporting	- Inmon - Kimball - Data Vault	- Denormalized data - Duplicated data - ACID compliance
Data lake	A raw semi-structured and unstructured data store	Need for a centralized repository of raw datasets for advanced analytics and machine learning	- HDFS - Blob	- Duplicated datasets - Non-ACID compliance
Data lakehouse	A unified data store for structured, semi-structured and unstructured data	Need for a centralized repository for unified data for reporting, advanced analytics and machine learning	- Combines features of a data warehouse and a data lake	- Duplicate datasets - ACID compliance
Data mesh	A decentralized architecture enabling cross-domain data analysis	Need for a decentralized approach to manage and analyze data across domains	- Operational data products - Analytical data products	- Decentralized data - Decentralized governance
Data fabric	A data architecture to map and link disparate data sources	Need for a decentralized connected approach to manage data stored across repositories	- Data virtualization - Semantic layer with Enterprise Knowledge Graph	- Decentralized data - Decentralized governance - Avoids data duplication

(*continued*)

Table 1. (*continued*)

Pattern name	Description	Problem	Solutions	Description
Data exchange	A framework for sharing and exchanging data between providers and consumers	Need to enable controlled data sharing and exchange without duplication or central storage	- Data exchange catalog	- Controlled data sharing and exchange - Avoids data duplication
Data satellite (Proposed)	*A system to monitor and observe the critical data assets and their flows across the ecosystem*	*Need to monitor, manage and maintain data health, lineage, and flow integrity across the ecosystem*	- Agents based semantic layer with Federated Enterprise Knowledge Graph	- Controlled and trusted data flows

layer of data architecture consists of several standalone *single application databases* managed locally by agencies. These single application databases typically store data generated or captured by an independent application [5], with a range of application database types such relational and non-relational. Secondly, the **data integration layer** focuses on integrating data from disparate sources for analytics, reporting, and decision-making. This includes data warehouses [15], data lakes and data lakehouse [3], data mesh, data product, data fabric, and knowledge graph based semantic integrations [7]. Finally, **data sharing** led to the emergence of the data exchange architecture pattern [13] for enabling inter-agency collaboration and enhancing citizen experience [20]. However, data sharing introduces the risk of *data pollution,* particularly when data flows across national and international borders without integrated data governance, quality assurance, monitoring and observability. This matter is further complicated with the need to adhere to relevant local and international laws, ensuring that exchanged data meets regulatory, policy and quality requirements while avoiding harm to individuals or organisations operating within digital ecosystems.

3.3 Revised Problem Statement

The review of digital government data ecosystem and data architectures reveals a set of key challenges: (1) *data believability, consistency, and quality*; (2) *managing data governance, observability, and provenance*; (3) *toxic data* – data that are unusable, irrelevant, or *dark data* – data that remains unused, e.g., cannot be found or accessed by the users [8]; (4) *excessive, siloed and duplicate data* within local (internally) and global data ecosystems (externally) [2, 14]. These challenges collectively define the "*data pollution*" problem, eroding the trustworthiness and utility of data within federated digital government ecosystems. This calls for the establishment of a new class of data system "*data satellite*" and underpinning architecture (e.g. DSA). Thus, we designed a new DSA to integrate GQMO capabilities via agent based semantic federated enterprise knowledge graph approach, providing a framework to monitor, observe and mitigate data pollution and enhance data trust in digital government data ecosystems.

4 Design Objectives and Requirements Definition

The key DSA design requirements (based on [19]) are: (1) it must effectively address the identified problem; (2) it should encompass the requirements' perspective of relevant stakeholders; (3) it must be feasible from economic and technical implementation standpoints; (4) it should be operationally viable to address the data pollution problem. These requirements will be examined and implemented in the practical context of Australian Government Data Ecosystem through design and evaluation workshops and expert interviews with stakeholders from the Global Data and Digital Alliance. Additionally, a proof-of-concept prototype will be implemented for addressing the objectives 1,3–4 and logical reasoning to assess the DSA's value and its completeness.

5 Design and Development: Data Satellite Architecture

The alpha version of the DSA has been designed, based on the literature review, as a conceptual model to serve an overarching layer over the existing data architecture (Fig. 2). The DSA integrates four essential capabilities—governance, quality, monitoring, and observability (GQMO). *Data governance* capability [2] includes data accountability, responsibility, privacy, security, and decision-right management guarantees that data access, usage, and sharing do not contribute to data pollution across federated digital government ecosystems and comply with relevant laws and policies. *Data quality* capability [1] addresses the issues of data pollution by focusing on data accuracy, consistency, completeness, believability, reliability, and trustworthiness, preventing the contamination of data across systems. *Data monitoring* capability [11] supports the detection and reporting of data governance and quality incidents, such as data pollution, across federated digital government ecosystems. *Data observability* capability [11] focuses on analysing data pollution incidents reported by data monitoring, and determining data state, health, ownership, distribution, freshness, and flows across various digital government ecosystems.

The DSA is designed for implementing the data satellite systems for combating data pollution at various levels, tailored to specific scope and coverage, such as the sector-specific – health or finance data satellite, or cross-sector - local, state, national and global data satellite. These data satellites can be owned by a leading government agency within a specific sector or across sectors by a leading local, state, federal and global agency (e.g., local government area, state, national or UN's global data satellite). The primary function of a data satellite is to oversee the integrated governance, quality, monitoring and observability of critical data assets, enabling the proactive detection and mitigation of data pollution incidents. In contrast, the actual data sharing and data flows - from data production to data consumption - across digital government ecosystem are facilitated by the data exchange. In addition, data management sits beneath the data exchange layer. Similar to data satellite systems, data exchange systems can be established within a specific government sector (e.g., health data exchange) or across sectors (e.g., local area,

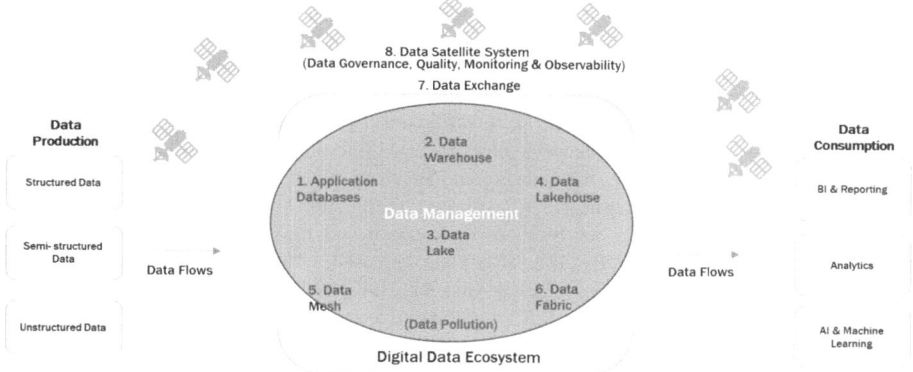

Fig. 2. Data satellite architecture (alpha version – conceptual model).

state, national or global data exchange). A hybrid approach combining sector specific and cross-sector exchanges can also be considered as per the specific data and digital government strategy.

6 Discussion and Conclusion

Data is the cornerstone of the digital ecosystem. However, not all data and associated activities hold equal importance. Therefore, it is crucial to establish a critical federated data asset catalogue, aligned with data governance and quality priorities of different agencies that identify and prioritize key data assets subject to data pollution monitoring and observability. This will inform the DSA design for the federated digital (government) data ecosystem. The proposed DSA builds upon existing architectural patterns, introducing an additional overarching and integrated layer of the data GQMO capabilities. The DSA has been designed and developed using the DSR method. This paper presents the alpha conceptual model of the DSA, laying a foundation for its iterative refinement and further development through the DSR approach.

The immediate next step involves conducting a design workshop with selected stakeholders from government agencies to demonstrate the applicability of the DSA and evaluate its utility in the practical context of the Australian government data ecosystem, including potential limitations or challenges of implementing DSA (e.g., costs, scalability). Feedback from this workshop will conclude the first alpha cycle or increment, and guide refinements to the problem statement, design objectives and requirements for the increment 2. Overall, this research aims to deliver the DSA through three increments, in line with the DSR methodology. Each increment will progressively enhance the architecture based on stakeholder feedback and practical evaluations, ensuring its alignment with the design objectives and dynamic needs of the federated digital government ecosystem.

Disclosure of Interests. The authors have no competing interests to declare that are relevant to the content of this article.

References

1. Altendeitering, M., Dübler, S., Guggenberger, T.M.: Data quality in data ecosystems: towards a design theory. In: AMCIS (2022)
2. Azeroual, O., Nikiforova, A., Sha, K.: Overlooked aspects of data governance: workflow framework for enterprise data deduplication. In: 2023 International Conference on Intelligent Computing, Communication, Networking and Services (ICCNS), pp. 65–73. IEEE (2023)
3. Begoli, E., Goethert, I., Knight, K.: A lakehouse architecture for the management and analysis of heterogeneous data for biomedical research and mega-biobanks. In: 2021 IEEE International Conference on Big Data (Big Data), pp. 4643–4651. IEEE, December 2021
4. Ben-Shahar, O.: Data pollution. J. Legal Anal. **11**, 104–159 (2019)
5. Batini, C., Lenzerini, M., Navathe, S.B.: A comparative analysis of methodologies for database schema integration. ACM Comput. Surv. (CSUR) **18**(4), 323–364 (1986)
6. Bernardo, B.M.V., São Mamede, H., Barroso, J.M.P., dos Santos, V.M.P.D.: Data governance & quality management—Innovation and breakthroughs across different fields. J. Innov. Knowl. **9**(4), 100598 (2024)
7. Blohm, I., Wortmann, F., Legner, C., Köbler, F.: Data products, data mesh, and data fabric: New paradigm (s) for data and analytics?. Bus. Inform. Syst. Eng. 1–10 (2024)
8. Cafarella, M., Ilyas, I.F., Kornacker, M., Kraska, T., Ré, C.: Dark data: are we solving the right problems?. In: 2016 IEEE 32nd International Conference on Data Engineering (ICDE), pp. 1444–1445. IEEE, May 2016
9. Department of Finance: Australian Government Data System (2024). https://www.finance.gov.au/government/public-data/public-data-policy/australian-government-data-system
10. Draheim, D., Krimmer, R., Tammet, T.: On state-level architecture of digital government ecosystems: from ICT-driven to data-centric. In: Hameurlain, A., Tjoa, A.M. (eds.) Transactions on Large-Scale Data- and Knowledge-Centered Systems XLVIII. Lecture Notes in Computer Science(), vol. 12670. Springer, Heidelberg (2021). https://doi.org/10.1007/978-3-662-63519-3_8
11. Gill, A.Q.: Data Satellite System for Observability and Navigation of Data in Digital Government Ecosystems. Public Sector Network (2024)
12. Gill, A.Q.: Adaptive enterprise architecture as information: architecting intelligent enterprises (2022)
13. Gill, A.Q.: A theory of information trilogy: digital ecosystem information exchange architecture. Information **2021**(12), 283 (2021)
14. Hasan, M.R., Legner, C.: Understanding data products: motivations, definition, and categories. In: ECIS (2023)
15. Inmon, W.H.: What is a data warehouse? Prism Tech Topic **1**(1), 1–5 (1995)
16. Leghemo, I.M., Segun-Falade, O.D., Odionu, C.S., Azubuike, C.: A collaborative model for data governance: enhancing integration across multi-line businesses. Gulf J. Adv. Bus. Res. **3**(1), 47–63 (2025)
17. Lnenicka, M., et al.: Understanding the development of public data ecosystems: from a conceptual model to a six-generation model of the evolution of public data ecosystems. Tele. Inform. 102190 (2024)
18. Mitleton-Kelly, E.: Ten principles of complexity and enabling infrastructures. complex systems and evolutionary perspectives on organisations: the application of complexity theory to organisations, 1, pp. 23–50 (2003)
19. Tuunanen, T., Winter, R., vom Brocke, J.: Dealing with complexity in design science research: a methodology using design echelons. MIS Q. **48**(2), 427–458 (2024)
20. van Donge, W., Bharosa, N., Janssen, M.F.W.H.A.: Data-driven government: cross-case comparison of data stewardship in data ecosystems. Govern. Inform. Q. **39**(2) (2022)

Towards an Ontology for Representing Time Series Knowledge: Motivation, Requirements and Concept

Alexander Graß[1,2(✉)], Rohit A. Deshmukh[1], Christian Beecks[1,3], and Stefan Decker[1,2]

[1] Fraunhofer Institute for Applied Information Technology FIT, Sankt Augustin, Germany
{alexander.grab,rohita.Deshmukh,christian.beecks, stefan.decker}@fit.fraunhofer.de
[2] RWTH Aachen University, Aachen, Germany
[3] University of Hagen, Hagen, Germany

Abstract. Time series analysis is an essential task in a variety of domains, where specialized ontologies can be leveraged to define data- and analysis-related specificities. However, the data management landscape lacks a comprehensive semantic data model for representing time series insights produced by data analysis operations. As these insights differ in format and interpretation, data reusability as well as the potential for synergy effects across various analysis methods are limited by the absence of such standardized data models.

In this paper, we introduce an ontology designed to systematically categorize insights inferred from time series analytics. By representing time series characteristics, such as anomalies, trends, or motifs as concrete knowledge entities, our approach facilitates the reuse and exploitation of knowledge across different levels of abstraction. To further enrich and combine this knowledge with prior information, it enables the integration and association of domain-specific facts provided by additional resources including human experts. In addition to introducing the ontology concept including requirements and limitations, we outline the applicability of our proposal with the help of an example.

Keywords: Ontology · Time Series · Data Analytics · Knowledge Graph

1 Introduction

Time series analysis has become an indispensable tool in many industries to identify and resolve process issues, uncover optimization opportunities and enable data-driven decision-making [10]. In 2024 alone, the global time series forecasting market was valued at USD 0.31 billion and is expected to reach USD 0.47

billion by 2033[1]. Especially, the continuous increase in the number of Internet-of-Things (IoT) devices[2] and the resulting accumulation of time series observations has led to a particular focus on time series analyses. In order to process these large amounts of data without intensive retraining of analytical models, it has become a common practice to preserve models for future reuse. However, in contrast to the maintenance of models, we observed a missing consideration of generated knowledge inferred from conducted analyses. This gap is problematic for two reasons for two reasons: First, in a company many data-related questions are asked repetitively by different individuals, and second, it potentially favors the isolated utilization of existing models. While the former fact leads to unnecessary and redundant inference processes, an independent utilization of task-specific models in the second case might further result in a neglection of synergy effects. As a result, previously generated insights are not being regarded in subsequent analysis. To consequently enable a systematic management and reuse of derived analytical time series knowledge, we see the need for a semantic data structure to efficiently classify time series related knowledge as well as associated specifics about processed data and knowledge generation methods.

In the context of data management and analysis, several ontologies and vocabularies have been developed that serve as foundational resources. Prominent contributions in the context of data interoperability and data management are the Data Catalog (DCAT) vocabulary [1] to standardize dataset information and the Data Cube Vocabulary [2] to structure multidimensional data to be consumed for analytical purposes. The development of more comprehensive solutions in the field of data analytics, including OntoDM [14], MEX [7] and Exposé, [19] enable a refined description of analytical processes and pipelines. Recent semantic frameworks such as ML-Schema [15] and MLSO [5] focus on the systematic integration of previous approaches while also extending some concepts with further details and corresponding vocabularies. Although these semantic structures enable a formalization of analytical processes, they lack a structured cataloging of analysis outcomes like cross-correlations and patterns. While SOSA [9] and IoT-Stream [6] present methods for the annotation of events or time series aspects, they fall short in classifying analytical knowledge or incorporating domain information. Approaches such as SemML [21,22] on the other hand, integrate domain knowledge into machine learning workflows, but focus more on contextually enriched analysis pipelines rather than on detailed insight classification.

Addressing these issues and building on the idea of hierarchically structured knowledge graphs for time series data [8], we present an initial version of an ontology to systematically preserve knowledge from time series analyses. We present the concept, discuss the requirements and limitations for representing and classifying insights derived from time series analyses and preexisting domain information. This facilitates advanced querying, inference, and reasoning capa-

---

[1] https://www.businessresearchinsights.com/market-reports/time-series-forecasting-market-114943, March 2025.
[2] https://iot-analytics.com/number-connected-iot-devices, Sep 2024.

bilities for the retrieval of data characteristics and facts. In the remainder of this paper, we refer to these information as knowledge, based on the information hierarchy model DIKW [12] and the associated idea of only considering condensed information valuable for informed decision-making.

The remainder of this paper is structured as follows: Sect. 2 presents our ontology for representing time series knowledge, including requirements, components, and limitations. Section 3 illustrates its applicability with an example. Section 4 concludes with maintenance plans and future work.

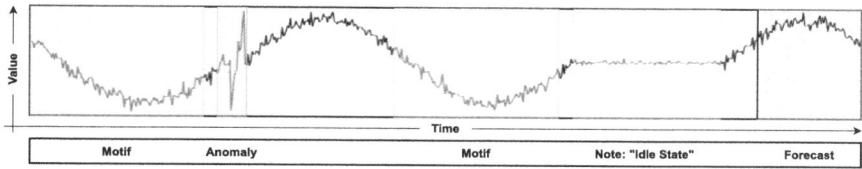

Fig. 1. A simplified illustration of segment-wise knowledge preservation.

2 Ontology for Time Series Knowledge

One of the main building blocks of the ontology facilitates the specification of informative data points or (potentially overlapping) intervals within time series data, further referred to as segments. A segment comprises characteristic knowledge associated with the covered time interval. Examples of such knowledge range from common time series features [4], and structural particularities such as anomalies [17] or motifs [20], to apriori information provided by domain experts.

Figure 1 exemplarily illustrates a selection of insights associated with time series data. Results from analyses such as detailed information of anomalies, motifs, or forecasts along with domain-specific information like event annotations are linked to individual segments. A classification and semantic representation of this knowledge enables organized reusability and effective propagation, leading to potential reductions of resources while enriching future analyses. To be able to support detailed definitions of specific settings, we make use of existing semantic approaches. For describing time series data, we use DCAT along with the OWL-Time [3] ontology. While the use of DCAT enables a reference to associated time series data, OWL-Time is employed to enable a rich set of options to define an index structure of time series data and individual segments. To extend the expressiveness of components as well as vocabularies in the scope of data analysis, our ontology reuses classes from ML-Schema including experimental settings and methodical specifications. Class specifics or hierarchical information are either enriched by vocabularies extending SKOS [13] concepts or inheritance.

2.1 Purpose and Requirements

Although the ontology can be considered agnostic with respect to application domains, we particularly see the need of its application in industrial settings [18]. In many companies, large volumes of stored data are analyzed independently, driven by data-related questions at various points in time. The potential of informed data analyses [16], combined with reusable knowledge, can help to minimize the risk of undesired effects and enable synergies. Additionally, sensor data and domain information are often not aligned, leading to further challenges in contextual integration. This lack of alignment typically originates from the use of heterogeneous database systems, each designed for a specific type of data. Another issue arises from the repeated application of analysis methods to address identical or similar questions over time, leading to unnecessary computational effort. Although process and analysis experts typically discuss and assess analysis outcomes, this semantically enriched knowledge is not always retained. The turnover of personnel and lack of documentation further amplify this issue. Requirements are therefore guided by the need to facilitate the preservation, classification, propagation, and integration of time series knowledge, and establishing connections and relationships among the given insights. In the following subsection, we present our vision and initial efforts in developing an ontology to address the identified problems.

2.2 Components

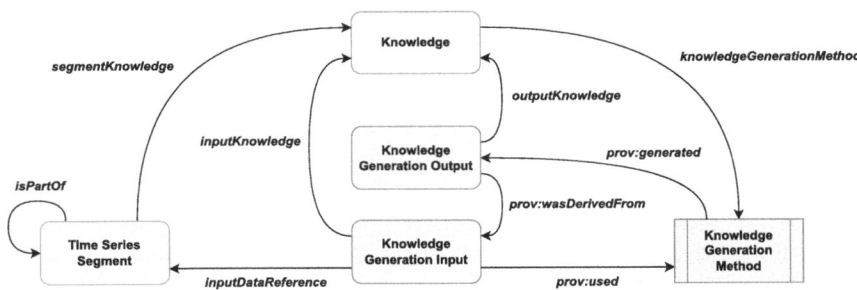

Fig. 2. Relationships between core ontology components. Green rectangles for data management classes, blue for knowledge representation, and red for knowledge generation. The knowledge generation method is highlighted as a process. (Color figure online)

While our ontology focuses on classifying time series knowledge into specific categories, another key design choice involves mapping knowledge to concrete intervals and dimensions of time series data. For this purpose, we model a class called *TimeSeriesSegment* to model time series segments. This class extends the DCAT *Dataset* class and is modeled such that a time series segment can be a part of another time series segment. This construct enables associating knowledge like the anomaly shown in Fig. 1 to a particular interval of reduced dimensionality or even a single data point. Index specifications are determined by *TimeIndex* extending classes from OWL-Time, whereas dimensional details are represented as *DataDimension*. In addition to a reference to the underlying raw data, the segment-wise consideration of knowledge indirectly serves as an index structure, linking meaningful time series data of varying complexity to categorized knowledge. At the highest level of abstraction, time series knowledge is categorized into three groups: (i) *DataKnowledge*, (ii) *ScenarioKnowledge*, and (iii) *MethodKnowledge*.

- *DataKnowledge* encompasses any information or insight which is either extracted directly from the underlying data or from the application of analytical methods. One example for this type of knowledge is a class membership derived from a conducted time series clustering.
- *ScenarioKnowledge* mainly describes verified context, such as data annotations or domain-specific process knowledge. This type commonly equals a priori information from domain experts, but can also be used to define facts associated with inferred knowledge.
- *MethodKnowledge* includes presets of analytical methods that have proven effective in previous analyses or correspond to mathematical and logical equivalents of known process information.

Furthermore, to develop hierarchies of individual knowledge instances, the ontology provides a class *KnowledgeGroup*, which is again recursively defined as knowledge. Figure 2 illustrates a selection of core classes from each of the groups together with their relationships. While the ontology can be used to make specific inquiries about analytical results and facts associated with time series data, its primary benefit lies in enabling interpretable knowledge dissemination. The reason is that classified data characteristics are not only induced information for knowledge retrieval, but are also serving as valuable input to subsequent analyses and semantic reasoning. It is important to note that knowledge propagation does not include dataset transformations, as these transformations are rather considered building blocks in data analysis pipelines. Instead, the aim is to maintain machine-readable insights at the end of these pipelines, ultimately facilitating the inference of new knowledge from existing information.

2.3 Challenges and Limitations

Time series analysis includes various approaches for specific tasks associated with methodical categories like clustering or classification. However, there generally is no standardized schema to automatically determine what information qualifies as knowledge. Moreover, individual knowledge might vary in type and structural complexity. A major challenge is therefore to find a generic representation, that matches all or at least most cases. However, a more generic representation contradicts with the representation of fine-grained details, as it abstracts from methodical particularities. In our solution, we thus combine inheritance and extendable concept vocabularies, such that details are defined in class-related concepts, while core structures such as *KnowledgeGroup* remain generic components to represent complicated or nested relationships. Another challenge is the previously mentioned complexity of information. While easily expressible knowledge such as the mean or variance of a multivariate time series can be directly stored as a single vector of floating point numbers, complex annotations - such as bounding box information in a video sequence - might demand for external storage solutions and the possibility to reference these information. In our ontology, we address this issue by introducing two subclasses of *Value* related to knowledge: *EmbeddedValue*, which represents the former scenario, and *ReferenceValue*, which facilitates the referencing of arbitrary data and extends the DCAT *Dataset* class, similar to the *TimeSeriesSegment*. The restriction to time series data and potentially sophisticated class instantiations due to implicit or latent knowledge are two limitations to be mentioned in the current version. However, an extension to further data types could be achieved by allowing for additional index structures.

3 Application Example

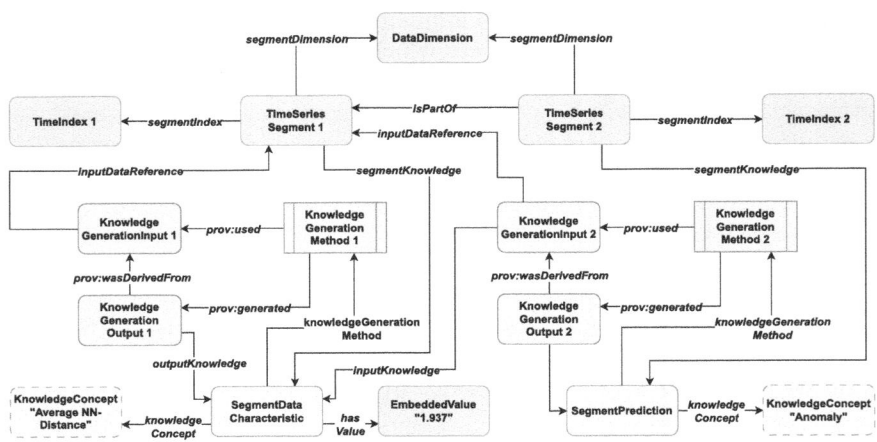

Fig. 3. Example for different knowledge classes and propagation. Dotted rectangles indicate concept classes.

To emphasize on the key aspects of the presented solution, Fig. 3 illustrates a simple scenario comprising univariate time series data. This scenario is used to demonstrate how explicit knowledge is classified, generated and reused via propagation. To not exceed the scope, we limit the amount of potential details where appropriate. In this example, we assume an earlier computation of the average nearest neighbor (NN) distance between adjacent data points in our time series, with the corresponding time series segment (*TimeSeriesSegment 1*) being defined based on inherent metadata, the associated index and dimension. In a subsequent analysis we perform an anomaly detection using the raw time series data and the previously derived knowledge of the NN distance average. By a comparison of raw data against this metric, we are able to identify an anomaly, which spawns a new segment (*TimeSeriesSegment 2*) that is assigned to the same dimension, yet described by another index only referencing the interval of the anomaly. Any generated knowledge is coarsely classified by the appropriate subclass of *Knowledge* and additionally defined through a *KnowledgeConcept*. While this example only provides a high-level view, it highlights the need of an ontology for representing time series knowledge for a concrete application scenario. A more comprehensive documentation of involved class entities and relations can be found under the reference listed in the following section.

4 Conclusion and Future Work

In this paper, we introduced an initial ontology version to systematically categorize knowledge derived from time series analytics and scenario-specific information. We outlined requirements and challenges that informed the selection of design decisions. We highlighted how our ontology reuses and extends widely used ontologies in accordance with the best practices for ontology development. Individual modules and components of the ontology were described and demonstrated in an example.

In the future, we plan to further detail and enrich the ontology with additional axioms and constraints to enhance validation and consistency. We aim to publish a comprehensive documentation and develop further vocabularies that define knowledge details including subtypes and hierarchies, akin to the taxonomy of learning methods from MLSO. Finally, we envision our solution for an automated retrieval and exploitation of time series knowledge in Large Language Models by means of Retrieval Augmented Generation [11]. The ontology as well as vocabularies are planned to be published, maintained and documented under the namespace "semts": https://w3id.org/semts, where "semts" stands for semantic time series.

Acknowledgments. This work was supported by a Fraunhofer ICON grant. The paper reflects only the authors views and the commission is not responsible for any use that may be made of the information it contains.

References

1. Data catalog vocabulary. https://www.w3.org/TR/vocab-dcat-3/. Accessed 17 Apr 2024
2. The RDF Data Cube Vocabulary. https://www.w3.org/TR/vocab-data-cube/. Accessed 17 Apr 2024

3. Time Ontology in OWL (2022). https://www.w3.org/TR/owl-time/
4. Christ, M., Braun, N., Neuffer, J., Kempa-Liehr, A.W.: Time series feature extraction on basis of scalable hypothesis tests (tsfresh-a python package). Neurocomputing **307**, 72–77 (2018)
5. Dasoulas, I., Yang, D., Dimou, A.: MLSEA: a semantic layer for discoverable machine learning. In: European Semantic Web Conference, pp. 178–198. Springer (2024)
6. Elsaleh, T., Enshaeifar, S., Rezvani, R., Acton, S.T., Janeiko, V., Bermudez-Edo, M.: IoT-stream: a lightweight ontology for internet of things data streams and its use with data analytics and event detection services. Sensors **20**(4), 953 (2020)
7. Esteves, D., et al.: Mex vocabulary: a lightweight interchange format for machine learning experiments. In: Proceedings of the 11th International Conference on Semantic Systems, pp. 169–176 (2015)
8. Graß, A., Beecks, C., Chala, S.A., Lange, C., Decker, S.: A knowledge graph for query-induced analyses of hierarchically structured time series information. In: European Conference on Advances in Databases and Information Systems, pp. 174–184. Springer (2023)
9. Janowicz, K., Haller, A., Cox, S.J., Le Phuoc, D., Lefrançois, M.: Sosa: a lightweight ontology for sensors, observations, samples, and actuators. J. Web Semant. **56**, 1–10 (2019)
10. Jensen, S.K., Pedersen, T.B., Thomsen, C.: Time series management systems: a survey. IEEE Trans. Knowl. Data Eng. **29**(11), 2581–2600 (2017)
11. Lewis, P., et al.: Retrieval-augmented generation for knowledge-intensive NLP tasks. Adv. Neural. Inf. Process. Syst. **33**, 9459–9474 (2020)
12. McDowell, K.: Storytelling wisdom: story, information, and DIKW. J. Am. Soc. Inf. Sci. **72**(10), 1223–1233 (2021)
13. Miles, A., Pérez-Agüera, J.R.: SKOS: simple knowledge organisation for the web. Catalog. Classif. Quart. **43**(3–4), 69–83 (2007)
14. Panov, P., Džeroski, S., Soldatova, L.: ONTODM: an ontology of data mining. In: 2008 IEEE International Conference on Data Mining Workshops, pp. 752–760. IEEE (2008)
15. Publio, G.C., et al.: ML-schema: an interchangeable format for description of machine learning experiments. Semantic Web 0.0 1–11 (2020)
16. von Rueden, L., Houben, S., Cvejoski, K., Bauckhage, C., Piatkowski, N.: Informed pre-training on prior knowledge. arXiv preprint arXiv:2205.11433 (2022)
17. Schmidl, S., Wenig, P., Papenbrock, T.: Anomaly detection in time series: a comprehensive evaluation. Proc. VLDB Endowment **15**(9), 1779–1797 (2022)
18. Soldatos, J.: Artificial Intelligence in Manufacturing: Enabling Intelligent. Flexible and Cost-Effective Production Through AI, Springer Nature (2024)
19. Vanschoren, J., Soldatova, L.: Exposé: an ontology for data mining experiments. In: International Workshop on Third Generation Data Mining: Towards Service-Oriented Knowledge Discovery (SoKD-2010), pp. 31–46 (2010)
20. Yeh, C.C.M., et al.: Matrix profile I: all pairs similarity joins for time series: a unifying view that includes motifs, discords and shapelets. In: 2016 IEEE 16th International Conference on Data Mining (ICDM), pp. 1317–1322. IEEE (2016)
21. Zhou, B., et al.: SEMML: facilitating development of ML models for condition monitoring with semantics. J. Web Semant. **71**, 100664 (2021)
22. Zhou, D., et al.: Ontology reshaping for knowledge graph construction: applied on bosch welding case. In: International Semantic Web Conference, pp. 770–790. Springer (2022)

OLAP Operations for Object-Centric Process Mining

Shahrzad Khayatbashi[1(✉)], Najmeh Miri[2], and Amin Jalali[2]

[1] Linköping University, Linköping, Sweden
shahrzad.khayatbashi@liu.se
[2] Stockholm University, Stockholm, Sweden
{najmeh.miri,aj}@dsv.su.se

Abstract. Analyzing process data at varying levels of granularity is important to derive actionable insights and support informed decision-making. Object-Centric Event Data (OCED) enhances process mining by capturing interactions among multiple objects within events, leading to the discovery of more detailed and realistic yet complex process models. The lack of methods to adjust the granularity of the analysis limits users in leveraging the full potential of Object-Centric Process Mining (OCPM). To address this gap, we propose four OnLine Analytical Processing (OLAP) operations: drill-down, roll-up, unfold, and fold, which enable changing the granularity of analysis when working with Object-Centric Event Log (OCEL). These operations allow analysts to seamlessly transition between detailed and aggregated process models, facilitating the discovery of insights that require varying levels of abstraction. We implemented these operations in an open-source Python library, making it available for researchers and practitioners to use in practice. This approach can empower analysts to perform more flexible and comprehensive process exploration, unlocking actionable insights through adaptable granularity adjustments.

Keywords: Object-Centric Process Mining · Object-Centric Event Log · Granularity Adjustment · OLAP

1 Introduction

The ability to analyze data at varying levels of granularity is crucial for organizations striving to identify bottlenecks and drive process improvements [25]. Adapting the level of detail allows users to seamlessly transition between granular views and high-level overviews of business processes. This flexibility enables the discovery of actionable insights that may remain hidden when confined to a single analytical perspective. In complex data environments, dynamic granularity adjustment based on specific analytical goals empowers stakeholders to tailor their analyses, resulting in more precise and effective decision-making.

Object-Centric Event Data (OCED) [9] offers a richer way to record process data by capturing interactions and dependencies between multiple objects within a single event. This capability surpasses traditional event logs [23], which often focus on single-case identifiers. Object-Centric Event Log (OCEL) [3], a widely adapted OCED log format [1,2,4,5,13–15,17], associates events with multiple objects. For example, in a hospital setting, the event 'register a test' may involve various objects, such as a patient,

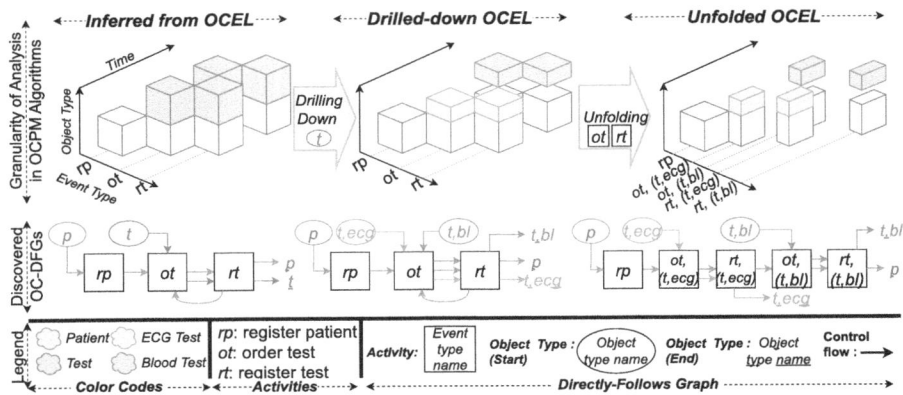

Fig. 1. The use of Drill-down and Unfold operations to enable identifying more detailed process patterns in OCPM.

caregiver, and different test types. Object-Centric Process Mining (OCPM) enables process analyses from each of these object types' perspectives.

Most OCPM algorithms operate at higher levels of abstraction, deriving process logic for Event Types based on the sequence of events that occurred for each Object Type over Time. This abstraction is illustrated in the upper left of Fig. 1, which serves as a running example throughout this paper. The inferred process logic enables discovering process models, e.g., PM4Py can discover an Object-Centric Directly-Follows Graph (OC-DFG) [5], which visualizes directly-follows relationships in the process, as shown in the lower left side of the figure.

Our running example is about the 'Chest Pain Evaluation' process in a hospital. The process begins with the registration of a patient (rp), followed by the ordering of an ECG test (ot), which is documented when the results are registered (rt). In practice, ordering different sorts of tests and registering their results produces events of the same type. This behavior arises because Electronic Health Record (EHR) systems are often designed to be generic, performing configurable tasks on various objects. In this example, if a caregiver finds the ECG result concerning, she will order a blood test (ot) as a standard care procedure, and the test result helps her to decide the next steps. However, such a procedure is not visible in OC-DFG due to the processing level of abstraction.

To address this challenge, this paper introduces four OnLine Analytical Processing (OLAP) operations, drill-down, roll-up, unfold, and fold, that enable users to dynamically adjust the level of detail in OCPM. These operations facilitate 'zooming in and zooming out', enabling the discovery of process models in different levels of abstractions using current OCPM algorithms. The OC-DFG discovered by transforming the running example log using these operations are demonstrated in the center and right sections of Fig. 1, showing how the standard care procedure can be revealed by setting the right level of abstraction. The proposed operations are implemented in an open-source Python library named *processmining*.

The remainder of this paper is organized as follows: Sect. 2 summarizes the related background and further elaborates on the problem using the running example. Section 3 introduces the approach informally. Finally, Sect. 4 concludes the paper.

2 Background

In data analysis, roll up and drill down of data is crucial so that useful insights can be extracted from large data sets [21]. It is particularly critical in multi-dimensional data analysis, where data is analyzed across various dimensions, increasing the complexity of the task. Microsoft Excel and Online Analytical Processing (OLAP) systems focus on the pragmatic utility and relevance of these techniques in real-world applications.

The need for drilling down and rolling up was identified early in process mining [21, 22]. van der Aalst introduced the concept of Process Cubes in 2013 with emphasis on OLAP operations such as slice, dice, drill-down, and roll-up for supporting data-driven process analysis [21]. Bolt and van der Aalst subsequently implemented Process Cubes [7,21] as a ProM plugin and as a standalone Java tool. These implementations allowed analysts to apply OLAP operations to process cubes and transform the results into a traditional event log by mapping one of the attributes to the case ID. However, this work did not support multi-dimensional process mining because object-centric process mining (OCPM) had not yet been defined.

Process cubes have then been applied in various domains. For example, Gupta and Sureka modeled a process cube with nine dimensions for defect resolution processes [10], demonstrating the application of OLAP operations. van der Aalst et al. [24] applied process cubes in education to compare the performance of student groups in a course. Bolt et al. proposed combining process mining with analytic workflows to facilitate comparative analysis at scale [6].

Jalali applied drill-down, roll-up, slice, and dice operations to investigate Dutch autonomous administrative authorities using process cubes, from control-flow as well as resource perspectives [11,12]. In healthcare, Weerdt et al. demonstrated that drill-up (another name for roll-up) and drill-down operators can reveal care flows to improve clinical procedures [8]. Further, Yeshchenko et al. emphasized the need for drill-down and roll-up operations when analyzing process drift, which is applying such methods to the discovery of concept drift beyond process discovery [26].

Despite the fact that slice-and-dice operations have been enabled by utilizing various filtering mechanisms in process mining tools, drill-down and roll-up are challenging to enact. Analysts often perform these operations manually, which not only increases the risk of implementation errors during data cleaning and reshaping but also increases the risk of biased interpretations [20].

The Object-Centric Event Log (OCEL) framework provides a systematic approach to describing such operations in the form of constructing relations among more than one object and event. This creates an organized, multi-dimensional space wherein levels of granularity can be established in different components.

In parallel with this paper, we explored how drill-down operations can uncover more patterns using Markov-based clustering [18]. In this work, drill-down, roll-up, fold, and unfold operations are properly defined while also providing tool support to apply them in practice.

Table 1. A simple example OCEL log for the running example.

Event ID	Event Type (Activity)	Timestamp	Related Objects
e1	register patient (rp)	2024-05-15 10:00:00 (t1)	[o1]
e2	order test (ot)	2024-05-15 11:00:00 (t2)	[o1,o2]
e3	register test (rt)	2024-05-15 12:00:00 (t3)	[o1,o2]
e4	order test (ot)	2024-05-15 12:20:00 (t4)	[o1,o3]
e5	register test (rt)	2024-05-15 13:00:00 (t5)	[o1,o3]

Object ID	Object Type	Current Attribute Values
o1	Patient	{"name": "Jessica"}
o2	Test	{"type": "ECG", result:"Suspicious"}
o3	Test	{"type": "Blood", result:"Normal"}

(a) A view over Events recorded with relation to multiple Objects in an OCEL

(b) A view over Objects with current object attribute values in an OCEL

3 Approach

This section elaborates on the problem and the proposed solution for drilling down, rolling up, unfolding, and folding OCELs. The section concludes with a discussion of the proof-of-concept implementation, which makes these operations accessible to researchers.

3.1 Problem Demonstration

To illustrate the problem and elaborate on our approach, we use the running example introduced in Fig. 1, which is derived from an OCEL log file summarized in Table 1. The table presents the data in two distinct views: *Events with connected objects* and *Objects with current attribute values*. It is important to emphasize that this running example is not intended to provide a detailed explanation of the OCEL 2.0 specification; for that, readers are referred to [3].

Each event in the log is characterized by an 'Event ID', 'Event Type', and 'Timestamp', and is associated with a list of related objects (qualifiers are abstracted in this example). The 'Related Objects' column contains object IDs that are detailed in a separate view. Each object is defined by an 'Object ID', 'Object Type', and its 'Current Attribute Values'. For simplicity, this example does not depict how attribute values evolve over time or how relationships between objects are captured.

A process discovery algorithm can analyze sequences of events for each object type and identify the relationships among activities. For instance, considering object o1, which represents a `patient`, the following relationships can be observed: $rp \xrightarrow{p} ot \underset{p}{\overset{p}{\rightleftarrows}} rt$, where p represents `Patient`. These relations can be observed by following blue cubes in the upper left side of Fig. 1, showing the sequence of event types in relation to Patient object type that happened over time. For objects o2 and o3, representing different Tests, the following relationships can be identified: $ot \xrightarrow{t} rt$, where t represents Test.

The overall Object-Centric Directly-Follows Graph (OC-DFG) is constructed as the union of all these relationships, as shown on the left side of Fig. 1. However, this abstraction fails to reveal direct relationships between ordering different tests. This limitation arises because the algorithm abstracts the log at the object type level, in this case, Test.

3.2 Proposed Solutions

To address the above challenges, this section introduces drill-down, roll-up, unfold, and fold operations for OCELs. These operations enable a more nuanced exploration of object-centric event log by allowing users to adjust the level of detail dynamically.

Drilling-Down and Rolling-Up: We propose altering object types by using a tuple consisting of the object type and a selected attribute value (e.g., the type attribute value) to distinguish between different tests in the running example. This transformation can also be applied in a nested manner. In the running example, this entails changing the object type from Test to a combination of Test and the type attribute value. This enables the discovery of OC-DFGs by distinguishing between different test types. This approach is applicable to other algorithms that rely on object types for discovery.

Applying this operation transforms the running example OCEL, resulting in object types (Test, ECG) and (Test, Blood). As illustrated in the upper centered part of Fig. 1, such transformation results in distinguishing different test types when the algorithm processes the log. Consequently, the OC-DFG algorithm identifies the following relations for each drilled-down object type: $ot \xrightarrow{(t, ECG)} rt$, and $ot \xrightarrow{(t, Blood)} rt$. This separation facilitates the discovery of an OC-DFG, as illustrated in the center of Fig. 1. Conversely, the roll-up operation aggregates data back to the original Test object type level.

Unfolding and Folding: Drilling down alone does not reveal the standard test procedure in the hospital (i.e., doctors ordering ECG tests before blood tests). This is because activity types remain undifferentiated. To address this limitation, we propose the unfolding operation. Unfolding involves projecting the event type to a combination of the event type and object type, segregating activities based on specific object types. For instance, unfolding the ot and rt activities with drilled-down object types in the running example changes the event type of e2 from ot to (ot, (Test, ECG)).

As illustrated in the upper right side of Fig. 1, such transformation enables the algorithm to distinguish between different test types when ordering the test or registering the test result. This transformation enables the identification of the following relationships within the OC-DFG:

- $\text{rp} \xrightarrow{\text{p}} (\text{ot}, (\text{t}, \text{ECG})) \xrightarrow{\text{p}} (\text{rt}, (\text{t}, \text{ECG})) \xrightarrow{\text{p}} (\text{ot}, (\text{t}, \text{Blood})) \xrightarrow{\text{p}} (\text{rt}, (\text{t}, \text{Blood}))$,
- $(\text{ot}, (\text{t}, \text{ECG})) \xrightarrow{(\text{t}, \text{ECG})} (\text{rt}, (\text{t}, \text{ECG}))$,
- $(\text{ot}, (\text{t}, \text{Blood})) \xrightarrow{(\text{t}, \text{Blood})} (\text{rt}, (\text{t}, \text{Blood}))$.

Such separation enables the discovery of an OC-DFG, as shown on the right side of Fig. 1, where the hidden relationships between the sequence of different tests can be identified. The reverse operation, which aggregates data back to the original event type level in our example, is called the fold operation.

Discussion on Nested Sequential Application: The proposed data operations are designed to support interactive and iterative process mining. However, when these operations are applied sequentially-especially in combination-their order can significantly affect both the resulting event log and the process models discovered from it. While nesting operations is possible, several important considerations must be kept in mind.

First, consider the case where an event type is unfolded based on a specific object type, and subsequently, a drill-down operation is performed on that same object type using one of its attributes. Implementation-wise, this results in event types that still refer to the object type at its original level of abstraction, while the actual object references in the event log have been refined into more detailed subtypes. Since event-to-object relationships are maintained through object identifiers (see the "Related Objects" column in Table 1), this does not break the structural integrity of the log. However, a semantic inconsistency is introduced: the activity names (event types) operate at a coarser level of abstraction than the object types they reference. This discrepancy can lead to confusion during process interpretation and should be considered when formally defining these operations and applying them in practice.

Second, the sequence in which operations are applied can influence how event types are defined and interpreted. For instance, if a caregiver orders both an ECG and a Blood test in the same event, unfolding the drilled-down log first based on the object type ECG and then on Blood yield different results than unfolding in the opposite order. This limitation should be taken into account when applying these operations, especially when multiple relevant object instances are associated with the same event. Resolving such overlaps or combined cases is a non-trivial challenge and represents a promising direction for future work.

3.3 Tools Support

We have implemented our approach as a proof of concept, providing the algorithms in an open-source Python library named *processmining*[1]. To facilitate reproducibility and broader application, the running example OCEL and the accompanying code demonstrating the application of these operations are made available on GitHub[2]. This allows readers to both replicate the results presented for the running example and apply the operations to their own object-centric event log.

---

[1] The library can be installed using !pip install processmining.
[2] https://github.com/shahrzadkhayatbashi/olap-operations4ocel.

Performance is a key aspect of any interactive tool as it can significantly influence its pragmatic acceptance. Our tool performed well when applied to real-life datasets in both the educational [19] and insurance [16] domains. As a means of additional testing for performance in a controlled and replicable setting, we aim to generate a synthetic event log as future work, which can be used to evaluate the scalability and computational efficiency of our approach.

4 Conclusion

In this work, we introduced and demonstrated the application of drill-down, roll-up, unfold, and fold operations for Object-Centric Process Mining (OCPM). By enabling these operations in the OCEL 2.0 framework, we supported precise and multi-dimensional business process analysis.

As OCPM continues to develop in the future, the combination of drill-down and roll-up operations will be essential in improving the depth and quality of knowledge gained from multi-dimensional process data. In conclusion, this research sets the stage for more extensive and dynamic process mining strategies, opening new pathways for organizational efficiency and innovation through data-driven process analysis.

References

1. Adams, J.N., Hastrup-Kiil, E., Park, G., van der Aalst, W.M.: Super variants. In: Business Process Management Conference, pp. 111–128. Springer (2024)
2. Adams, J.N., Park, G., van der Aalst, W.M.: OCPA: a python library for object-centric process analysis. Software Impacts **14**, 100438 (2022)
3. Berti, A., et al.: OCEL (Object-Centric Event Log) 2.0 specification (2023)
4. Berti, A., van der Aalst, W.M.: OC-PM: analyzing object-centric event logs and process models. Int. J. Softw. Tools Technol. Transfer **25**(1), 1–17 (2023)
5. Berti, A., van Zelst, S., Schuster, D.: PM4Py: a process mining library for python. Software Impacts **17**, 100556 (2023)
6. Bolt, A., De Leoni, M., Van Der Aalst, W.M., Gorissen, P.: Exploiting process cubes, analytic workflows and process mining for business process reporting: a case study in education. SIMPDA **1527**, 33–47 (2015)
7. Bolt, A., van der Aalst, W.M.: Multidimensional process mining using process cubes. In: Business Process Modeling, Development and Support Conference, pp. 102–116. Springer (2015)
8. De Weerdt, J., Caron, F., Vanthienen, J., Baesens, B.: Getting a grasp on clinical pathway data: an approach based on process mining. In: Emerging Trends in Knowledge Discovery and Data Mining: PAKDD 2012 International Workshops: DMHM, GeoDoc, 3Clust, and DSDM, Kuala Lumpur, Malaysia, May 29–June 1, 2012, Revised Selected Papers 16, pp. 22–35. Springer (2013)
9. Fahland, D., et al.: Towards a simple and extensible standard for object-centric event data (oced)–core model, design space, and lessons learned. arXiv preprint arXiv:2410.14495 (2024)
10. Gupta, M., Sureka, A.: Process cube for software defect resolution. In: 2014 21st Asia-Pacific Software Engineering Conference, vol. 1, pp. 239–246. IEEE (2014)

11. Jalali, A.: Exploring different aspects of users behaviours in the dutch autonomous administrative authority through process cubes. In: Business Process Intelligence (BPI) Challenge (2016)
12. Jalali, A.: Reflections on the use of chord diagrams in social network visualization in process mining. In: 2016 IEEE Tenth International Conference on Research Challenges in Information Science (RCIS), pp. 1–6. IEEE (2016)
13. Jalali, A.: Object type clustering using Markov directly-follow multigraph in object-centric process mining. IEEE Access **10**, 126569–126579 (2022)
14. Khayatbashi, S., Hartig, O., Jalali, A.: Transforming event knowledge graph to object-centric event logs: a comparative study for multi-dimensional process analysis. In: International Conference on Conceptual Modeling, pp. 220–238. Springer (2023)
15. Khayatbashi, S., Hartig, O., Jalali, A.: Transforming object-centric event logs to temporal event knowledge graphs. In: Accepted in BPM Workshop (2024)
16. Khayatbashi, S., Sjölind, V., Granåker, A., Jalali, A.: AI-enhanced business process improvements: a case study in the insurance domain using object-centric process mining (2025). submitted
17. Liss, L., Adams, J.N., van der Aalst, W.M.: Totem: temporal object type model for object-centric process mining. In: International Conference on Business Process Management, pp. 107–123. Springer (2024)
18. Miri, N., Jalali, A.: Uncovering patterns in object-centric process mining: an approach using drill-down and roll-up techniques. In: Delir Haghighi, P., Greguš, M., Kotsis, G., Khalil, I. (eds.) Information Integration and Web Intelligence, pp. 49–54. Springer, Cham (2025)
19. Miri, N., Khayatbashi, S., Zdravkovic, J., Jalali, A.: OCPM^2: extending the process mining methodology for object-centric event data extraction. arXiv preprint arXiv:2503.10735 (2025)
20. Van Der Aalst, W.: Spreadsheets for business process management: Using process mining to deal with "events" rather than "numbers"? Bus. Process. Manag. J. **24**(1), 105–127 (2018)
21. Van Der Aalst, W.M.,: Process cubes: slicing, dicing, rolling up and drilling down event data for process mining. In: Asia Pacific Business Process Management: First Asia Pacific Conference, AP-BPM 2013, Beijing, China, August 29–30, 2013. Selected Papers 1, pp. 1–22. Springer (2013)
22. Van der Aalst, W.M.: Process mining in the large: a tutorial. In: Business Intelligence: Third European Summer School, eBISS 2013, Dagstuhl Castle, Germany, July 7–12, 2013, Tutorial Lectures 3, pp. 33–76 (2014)
23. Aalst, W.: Object-centric process mining: dealing with divergence and convergence in event data. In: Ölveczky, P.C., Salaün, G. (eds.) SEFM 2019. LNCS, vol. 11724, pp. 3–25. Springer, Cham (2019). https://doi.org/10.1007/978-3-030-30446-1_1
24. van der Aalst, W.M., Guo, S., Gorissen, P.: Comparative process mining in education: an approach based on process cubes. In: Data-Driven Process Discovery and Analysis: Third IFIP WG 2.6, 2.12 International Symposium, SIMPDA 2013, Riva del Garda, Italy, August 30, 2013, Revised Selected Papers 3, pp. 110–134. Springer (2015)
25. van Zelst, S.J., Mannhardt, F., de Leoni, M., Koschmider, A.: Event abstraction in process mining: literature review and taxonomy. Granular Comput. **6**, 719–736 (2021)
26. Yeshchenko, A., Di Ciccio, C., Mendling, J., Polyvyanyy, A.: Visual drift detection for event sequence data of business processes. IEEE Trans. Visual Comput. Graphics **28**(8), 3050–3068 (2021)

Goal-Oriented Process Monitoring: An Artifact-Driven Monitoring Extension

Giovanni Meroni[1(✉)] and Rik Eshuis[2]

[1] Technical University of Denmark, Kgs. Lyngby, Denmark
giom@dtu.dk
[2] Eindhoven University of Technology, Eindhoven, Netherlands
h.eshuis@tue.nl

Abstract. Process monitoring is an approach for identifying how well running processes are performing with respect to performance measures and objectives. Artifact-driven process monitoring has been proposed as a specific technique to monitor business processes that are distributed among multiple stakeholders, each one controlling only a portion of the process. Artifact-driven process monitoring tracks the execution of tasks based on the changes in the conditions of the artifacts (physical or virtual objects) in the process. However, the monitoring information can be very detailed and difficult to relate to the process intents. In this paper, we propose an approach that uses goal models in combination with artifact-driven process monitoring to realize goal-oriented process monitoring.

Keywords: Process monitoring · Guard-Stage-Milestone · I-star

1 Introduction

Data-driven business processes are the backbone of modern enterprise. Many of these business processes are outsourced to external organizations. As a consequence, organizations no longer have control over these processes. Yet, these organizations specify business objectives that the processes should meet. Consequently, they should be able to check if the process executions meet the overall business objectives. Also, there could be regulatory stakeholders that need to check whether the processes comply with the relevant regulations.

To this aim, process monitoring has been proposed as a technique to observe the execution and performance of business processes and to check whether the execution complies with existing business rules and regulations and performance agreements [11]. However, most of the proposed approaches assume that a centralized execution log containing information on when each task in the process was executed is available. Getting such log is particularly difficult for multi-party processes, as it requires organizations to federate their information systems to share their data.

Artifact-driven process monitoring [15] is one of the few approaches that addresses this issue. By exploiting the Internet-of-Things paradigm, artifact-driven process monitoring collects information on the state of the artifacts -

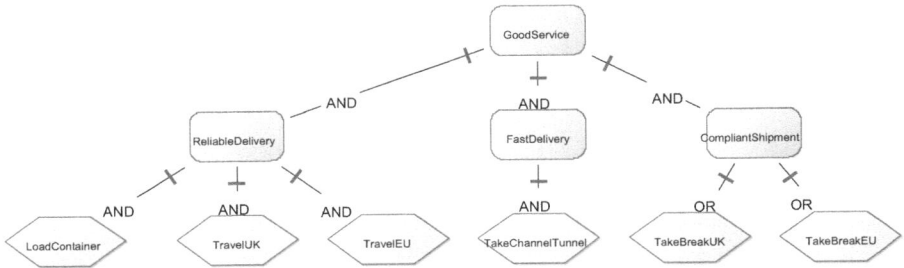

Fig. 1. I-star goal model for the shipment process.

physical or virtual objects - interacting with the process. It then infers from this information when tasks are executed, and if the dependencies between tasks are satisfied or violated.

However, artifact-driven monitoring offers a fine-grained view on process executions, in the form of E-GSM models. Such a view contains many execution details that can actually obscure the intended purpose of the process, especially for organizations who are not responsible for the execution of the process, but need to know if it is correctly executed.

In this paper, we propose to complement artifact-driven monitoring with a goal-oriented perspective. This makes it possible to identify which process portions satisfy or deny the main objectives of the process, which are expressed by *goals*. Goals capture the intent of business processes [10]. By focusing on goals rather than event sequences, clients of a process can view relevant information about the process, rather than very detailed info about event sequences that is not fully relevant for them.

The remainder of this paper is structured as follows. Section 2 provides motivating scenario for the approach. Section 3 discusses related work. Section 4 introduces the approach. Finally, Sec. 5 concludes this paper and outlines future work.

2 Motivation

To motivate the need for goal-oriented process monitoring, we consider the following motivating real-world example. A logistics company outsources the shipment of containers from London Heathrow to Amsterdam Schiphol airport to a truck driver. To meet the goal of providing a good service to its customer, the logistics company requires the shipment to be reliable, fast, and compliant with the EU regulations [6].

For the shipment to be reliable, the driver needs to load the container located in London Heathrow airport, then to travel in the United Kingdom, and finally to travel in mainland Europe until Amsterdam Schiphol airport is reached. For the shipment to be fast, the driver is expected to take the Channel tunnel that connects the United Kingdom with mainland Europe. Finally, for the shipment to comply with EU regulations, the driver is expected to take a break while traveling either in the United Kingdom or in mainland Europe.

Goal-Oriented Process Monitoring: An Artifact-Driven Monitoring Extension   121

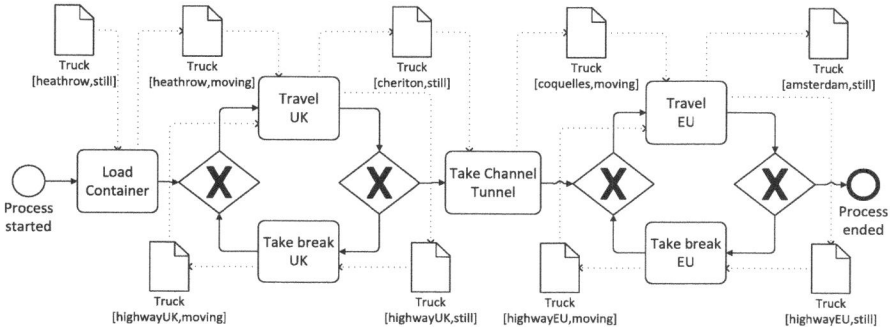

Fig. 2. BPMN model of the shipment process.

Figure 1 represents the main objectives that the delivery process should achieve, which are modeled using the I-star 2.0 goal modeling notation [4]. Rectangles represent goals, hexagons tasks. By performing tasks, goals are achieved. For instance, the task $TakeChannelTunnel$ helps to achieve goal $FastShipment$. A goal can be decomposed into other goals or into tasks that are required to achieve the goal. The overall goal $GoodService$ is decomposed into three subgoals that all need to be achieved in order to also achieve the overall goal (AND decomposition). The subgoal $CompliantShipment$ in turn is decomposed into two alternative ways (OR decomposition): either the subgoal is achieved by performing task $TakeBreakUK$ or by performing task $TakeBreakEU$.

Goals and Tasks can be marked with labels *satisfied*, *denied* or *unknown*, to indicate that, respectively, they were achieved, they were not achieved, and it is not known yet if they will be achieved or not. This allows to easily relate the effect of tasks on goals. In particular, it is possible to derive the label for a goal from the labels of its subgoals or tasks and from the type of decomposition (forward analysis). For example, if the truck driver does not take the Channel tunnel (i.e., task $TakeChannelTunnel$ is denied), the goal $FastShipment$ will be denied. In turn, denying $FastShipment$ will also cause $GoodService$ to be denied. Also, if the driver takes a break only in the United Kingdom (i.e., task $TakeBreakUK$ is satisfied and task $TakeBreakEU$ is denied), the goal $CompliantShipment$ will be satisfied.

Another advantage of this model is that it does not require the structure of the process to be specified. This could be useful to hide unnecessary details to stakeholders - such as the logistics company - who need to make sure that the goals are achieved, but does not need to know how the process is structured. Conversely, Fig. 2 represents the structure of the delivery process using the BPMN 2.0 notation [19], which is typically adopted for process monitoring. This model can effectively capture the tasks composing the process, as well as the control flow dependencies between them. Thus, it can detect if the execution deviates from the expected behavior (e.g., if the truck drives without loading the container). However, this model itself does not directly show the implications of a process deviation on the main goals of the process. For example, not taking the Channel tunnel would cause the execution to no longer conform with the

BPMN model. However, this information would need to be interpreted by a domain expert to determine the effect of this deviation on the goals for that process. Another example, if no breaks are taken (thus denying the well-being of the driver), the execution conforms to the BPMN model, but does not meet the business objectives outlined in Fig. 1.

3 Related Work

Process monitoring has been studied already for a long time [3,11,16]. In earlier work one of the authors developed an approach for artifact-driven process monitoring [14,15]. While that approach offers flexible monitoring of artifact-driven business processes, allowing processes to violate the prescribed control flow, it does not consider monitoring of goals.

There is limited related work that focuses on monitoring process executions for goal satisfaction. Jander et al. [8] propose a distributed approach for hierarchical event processing in goal-oriented workflows. They focus on establishing traceability of low-level events in relation to the achievement of high-level functional goals. Martinez et al. [13] propose the use of Tropos, a goal modeling approach that is based on i-Star, to monitor and control goals of workflows. Goals are quantified using metrics. Event logs are not considered for monitoring. Pourshahid et al. [17] introduce a framework for goal-oriented process monitoring, based on the User Requirements Notation (URN). The framework translates goal models and process models into performance models, which are used to monitor the achievement of KPIs. Event logs are not used in this approach. Koetter and Kochanowski [9] introduce an architecture for monitoring goals. They consider goals that are derived from KPIs, so goals are expressed as target values for KPI. They do not consider functional goals such as the ones in Fig. 1. Abualsaud et al. [1] propose a method to design an artifact-centric process model to monitor a given goal. The goal is in this case an process monitoring need, basically specifying which parts of the artifact-centric model that need to be visible. The method defines how to determine the appropriate level of detail of the artifact-centric process model in order to trace the status of the monitored goal.

Other works are less closely related. Akhigbe et al. [2] propose a method to check compliance of business data with regulatory goals, but they not consider business processes or process data in the form of event logs. Eshuis and Ghose [5] define an approach to check consistency of a goal model and an artifact-centric process, but they do not consider process monitoring. Goals have been proposed to guide the execution of knowledge-intensive processes by recommending the next activities to perform [20] However, these model-driven approaches do not consider goal monitoring.

A lot of research is currently exploring the field of Predictive Process Monitoring [12]. There, however, the focus is to predict properties of processes being executed. In our paper, we do not focus on predictions but on goal compliance.

As far as we know, no previous work considers the use of goal for flexible monitoring of fine-grained business processes whose behaviour is captured by event logs, which is the topic of this paper.

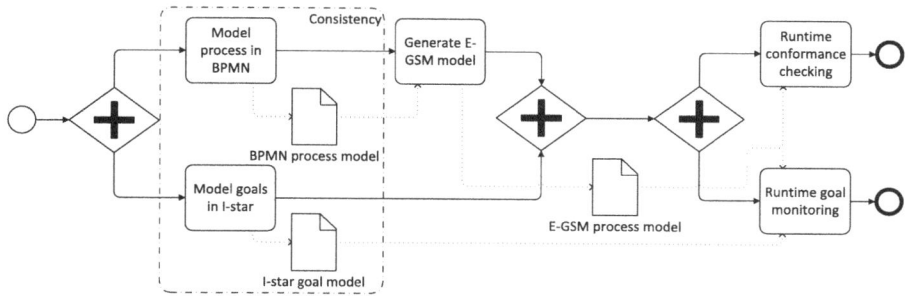

Fig. 3. Proposed approach.

4 Approach

The proposed approach, which is shown in Fig. 3, extends artifact-driven process monitoring by also including a goal-oriented perspective to the process to monitor. To this aim, besides modeling the process to monitor in BPMN, the designer is also expected to provide a goal model in I-star 2.0. The BPMN model can be refined from the I-star model following the goal-oriented requirements engineering principles [7], or the I-star model can be derived from an existing BPMN model [18]. Thus, we treat such modeling tasks independently, with the only assumption that the I-star model will contain a subset of the tasks in the BPMN model, in order to ensure that both models can be related to each other. It is worth noting that - with the exception of the tasks - the two models do not have any redundancy and are complementary.

Once the BPMN model has been produced, it is then converted into an E-GSM model for monitoring. To do so, the method discussed in [15] is adopted. With the exception of loop blocks, each process block is converted into one stage. Each process block is converted into two nested stages, representing the loop block itself and a single iteration of the loop. Figure 4 shows the E-GSM model for the shipping process, which is automatically derived from the BPMN model in Fig. 2.

The produced E-GSM model can be used alone to detect if the process execution deviates from the structure specified in the BPMN model (runtime conformance checking), or together with the I-star model to perform runtime goal monitoring. For the latter, E-GSM is extended to determine when tasks are satisfied or denied. This information is then projected to the I-star 2.0 model to determine the impact on goals. Section 4.1 explains the details on the extension.

4.1 Monitoring I-Star Models

E-GSM, thanks to the status and conformance attributes, is capable of monitoring when a task is executed and if it conforms to the control flow dependencies in the process. However, this information is not enough to determine whether

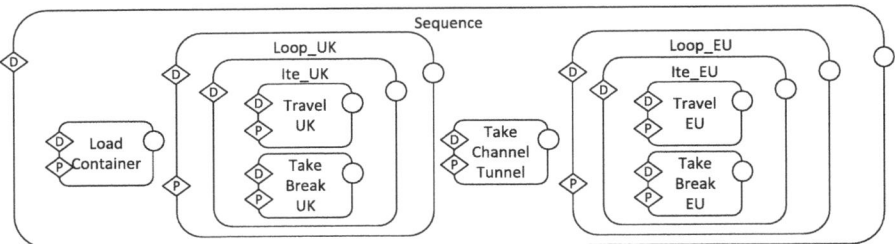

Fig. 4. E-GSM model of the shipment process.

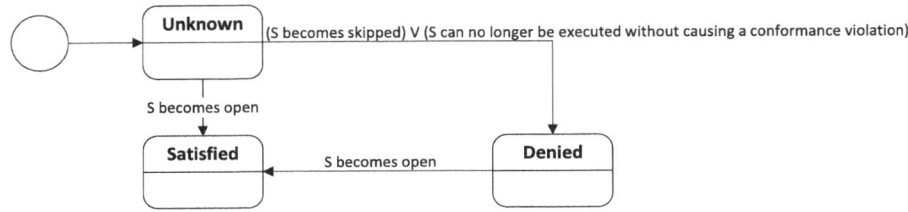

Fig. 5. Lifecycle of the fulfillment attribute for a stage S.

a task is satisfied or denied. In particular, if a stage is re-opened, the status and conformance of the child stages will reset to unopened and onTime. E-GSM does so to be able to monitor multiple executions of the same process portion, which, otherwise, would not be captured. However, we claim that, for a task to be satisfied in an I-star 2.0 model, it is sufficient to execute it only once. Also, the status and conformance attributes alone cannot tell if, from a certain point in the process execution, a stage is supposed to never be executed if that execution conforms to the model.

For example, given the E-GSM model in Fig. 4, once the container has left the Channel tunnel, if the driver did not take any rest in the UK, stage $TakeBreakUK$ should never occur. However, the values of the status and conformance attributes for that stage would be the same (unopened and onTime) both before and after the truck has left the UK. But in that case, the goal $TakeBreakUK$ should become denied (unachievable).

Thus, to determine if tasks can or cannot contribute to the achievement of a goal, an additional attribute named fulfillment is introduced for each stage in the E-GSM model. This attribute can assume the values *unknown*, *satisfied* or *denied*, and its meaning is the same as the one used for labels assigned to I-star 2.0 goals and tasks. Figure 5 shows the (simplified) lifecycle of the fulfillment of a stage S.

When the process starts, the fulfillment of all stages is unknown.

A stage S will become satisfied when it will be executed for the first time. More formally, if the status of S transitions from unopened to opened, S will become satisfied. Once S is satisfied, it will remain in that state throughout the execution of the process.

A stage S could also become denied during the execution of the process. Intuitively, this could happen if i) S is not executed when it should, or ii) it is no longer possible to execute S without causing a control flow violation in the process.

To detect i), it is sufficient to use the same condition as the one determining when the conformance of S becomes skipped. For example, if the stage $Loop\_EU$ becomes opened before $TakeChannelTunnel$ (i.e., $TakeChannelTunnel$ is skipped), the fulfillment of $TakeChannelTunnel$ becomes denied.

Detecting ii) is more complex, as it requires to evaluate the control flow dependencies that exist in the model. However, if the original BPMN process is block structured, and information on the type of the block (e.g., sequence, loop, etc.) has been propagated to the corresponding stages in the E-GSM model, reasoning over the status attribute and the nesting relationship of each stage is enough. For example, when stage Ite_UK - which represents a single iteration of the loop block - becomes closed, if stage $TakeBreakUK$ is unopened, the fulfillment of $TakeBreakUK$ remains unknown, since the loop may require more than one iteration. Conversely, when the stage $Loop\_UK$ - which represents the loop block - becomes closed, no iteration of that block can be executed anymore. Therefore, if stage $TakeBreakUK$ is unopened, the fulfillment of $TakeBreakUK$ becomes denied.

When the fulfillment attribute changes for one or more stages in the E-GSM model, the new value for that attribute can be then propagated to the corresponding tasks in the I-star model. From there, the following forward analysis rules are applied to compute the fulfillment for all the elements in the I-star model:

- Given an I-star element E decomposed into multiple child elements with an AND-decomposition, if at least one child element is denied, then is denied. If all child elements are satisfied, then is satisfied. In all other cases, E is unknown.
- Given an I-star element E decomposed into multiple child elements with an OR-decomposition, if at least one child element is satisfied, then E is satisfied. If all child elements are denied, then E is denied. In all other cases, E is unknown.
- Given an I-star element E decomposed into multiple child elements with an XOR-decomposition, if exactly one child element is satisfied and all the other child elements are denied, then E is satisfied. If all child elements are denied, or if two or more child elements are satisfied, then is denied. In all other cases, is unknown.

5 Conclusion

In this paper, we have presented goal-oriented process monitoring, a novel approach to provide high-level information on how a process is being executed. For this purpose, we have adopted the I-star 2.0 goal modeling language to capture which tasks are responsible for fulfilling which requirements, being modeled as goals and subgoals. We extended the artifact-driven process monitoring approach with an additional perspective, named fulfillment, to detect when tasks are executed, and to determine which process portions satisfy or deny application requirements.

Future work will focus on formalizing the rules to determine the fulfillment of a stage, and on supporting other intentional elements and patterns supported by i-Star 2.0 - such as qualities, resources and social dependencies - besides goal-task decomposition. Also, the proposed approach will be validated with real world models and logs from diverse domains, both quantitatively in terms of performance and scalability, and empirically by collecting feedback from potential users.

References

1. Abualsaud, R., Tran, H.N., Ober, I., Nguyen, M.K.: Toward a goal-oriented methodology for artifact-centric process modeling. In: ENASE 2023 Proceedings, pp. 656–663. SCITEPRESS (2023)
2. Akhigbe, O., Amyot, D., Richards, G., Lessard, L.: GoRIM: a model-driven method for enhancing regulatory intelligence. Softw. Syst. Model. **21**(4), 1613–1641 (2022)
3. Comuzzi, M., Angelov, S.: Patterns and tools for business process monitoring customization. Serv. Oriented Comput. Appl. **10**(3), 253–271 (2016)
4. Dalpiaz, F., Franch, X., Horkoff, J.: istar 2.0 language guide. CoRR abs/1605.07767 (2016)
5. Eshuis, R., Ghose, A.: Consistency checking of goal models and case management schemas. In: Polyvyanyy, A., Wynn, M.T., Van Looy, A., Reichert, M. (eds.) BPM 2021. LNBIP, vol. 427, pp. 54–70. Springer, Cham (2021). https://doi.org/10.1007/978-3-030-85440-9_4
6. European Union: Regulation (ec) no. 561/2006. Official Journal of the European Union, pp. L–102 (2006)
7. Horita, H., Honda, K., Sei, Y., Nakagawa, H., Tahara, Y., Ohsuga, A.: Transformation approach from KAOS goal models to BPMN models using refinement patterns. In: Proceedings of the SAC 2014, pp. 1023–1024 (2014)
8. Jander, K., Braubach, L., Lamersdorf, W.: Distributed monitoring and workflow management for goal-oriented workflows. Concurr. Comput. Pract. Exp. **28**(4), 1324–1335 (2016)
9. Koetter, F., Kochanowski, M.: A model-driven approach for event-based business process monitoring. Inf. Syst. E Bus. Manag. **13**(1), 5–36 (2015)
10. Kueng, P., Kawalek, P.: Goal-based business process models: creation and evaluation. Bus. Process. Manag. J. **3**(1), 17–38 (1997)
11. Ly, L.T., Maggi, F.M., Montali, M., Rinderle-Ma, S., van der Aalst, W.: Compliance monitoring in business processes: Functionalities, application, and tool-support. Inf. Syst. **54**, 209–234 (2015)
12. Márquez-Chamorro, A.E., Resinas, M., Ruiz-Cortés, A.: Predictive monitoring of business processes: a survey. IEEE Trans. Serv. Comput. **11**(6), 962–977 (2018)
13. Martinez, A., Gonzalez, N., Estrada, H.: A goal-oriented approach for workflow monitoring. In: istar'10 Workshop Proceedings. CEUR-WS, vol. 586, pp. 118–122 (2010)

14. Meroni, G.: Artifact-Driven Business Process Monitoring - A Novel Approach to Transparently Monitor Business Processes, Supported by Methods, Tools, and Real-World Applications, Lecture Notes in Business Information Processing, vol. 368. Springer (2019)
15. Meroni, G., Baresi, L., Montali, M., Plebani, P.: Multi-party business process compliance monitoring through IoT-enabled artifacts. Inf. Syst. **73**, 61–78 (2018)
16. Montali, M., Maggi, F.M., Chesani, F., Mello, P., van der Aalst, W.M.P.: Monitoring business constraints with the event calculus. ACM Trans. Intell. Syst. Technol. **5**(1), 17:1–17:30 (2013)
17. Pourshahid, A., et al.: Business process management with the user requirements notation. Electron. Commer. Res. **9**(4), 269–316 (2009)
18. de la Vara, J.L., Sánchez, J., Pastor, O.: On the use of goal models and business process models for elicitation of system requirements. In: Nurcan, S., et al. (eds.) BPMDS/EMMSAD -2013. LNBIP, vol. 147, pp. 168–183. Springer, Heidelberg (2013). https://doi.org/10.1007/978-3-642-38484-4_13
19. Weske, M.: Business Process Management - Concepts, Languages, Architectures, 3rd edn. Springer (2019)
20. Yurt, Z.O., Eshuis, R., Wilbik, A., Vanderfeesten, I.: Guiding knowledge workers under dynamic contexts. In: Proceedings of the CAiSE 2022. Lecture Notes in Computer Science, vol. 13295, pp. 218–234. Springer (2022)

LLM4Model: Automated Requirements Specification Model Authoring

Asha Rajbhoj[✉][iD], Akanksha Somase[iD], Tanay Sant[iD], Sushant Vale[iD], and Vinay Kulkarni[iD]

Tata Consultancy Services, TCS Research, Pune, India
{asha.rajbhoj,akanksha.somase,Tanay.sant,sushant.vale,
vinay.vkulkarni}@tcs.com

Abstract. Traditionally, early stages of the Software Development Life Cycle (SDLC), such as requirement elicitation and analysis are manual, require significant expertise. Creation of purposive machine-processable models is an intellect-intensive task requiring business domain as well as modeling expertise, which is in short supply. To address this, we propose the LLM4Model tool, a configurable, extensible, domain-agnostic solution for automating model authoring with Large Language Models (LLMs) to reduce cognitive load. We demonstrate its effectiveness with two real-world case studies, showing automated authoring of requirements specification model and sharing the results.

Keywords: LLM · GenAI · Model Authoring · AI in SDLC

1 Introduction

Requirements engineering is critical to the Software Development Life Cycle (SDLC) and directly influences project success. A well-executed requirements process ensures clear and accurate specifications, which serve as a blueprint for the entire development effort. However, errors in this phase, often due to ambiguous terminology or misinterpretations among stakeholders, can lead to costly and time-consuming issues later in the project. Particularly in new development projects, the quality of requirements specification plays a significant role in avoiding delays and additional expenses. These specifications are highly dependent on the expertise of subject matter experts (SMEs), making the process both skill-intensive and time-consuming.

To address these challenges, Model Driven Engineering (MDE) has emerged as a solution, shifting the focus from manual documentation to machine-processable models. These models not only provide traceability across SDLC stages but also facilitate automated transformations into other SDLC artifacts. However, creating these models is still a manual task that requires deep domain knowledge and familiarity with modeling languages, often not available to all involved parties. An effective solution must bridge the gap between domain experts, who may struggle with technical modeling languages, and IT professionals, who may lack business domain knowledge.

Trained on vast datasets, LLMs have the potential to handle complex, domain-specific knowledge and can assist in requirements engineering [1, 2]. However, their application in this field is still underexplored. The meta-model guided prompting approach for interacting with LLMs has shown promising results in our prior work [3, 4]. LLM4Model builds on this foundation by further automating the process. It integrates LLMs with Model-Driven Engineering (MDE), allowing Subject Matter Experts (SMEs) to easily generate models through intuitive interactions with LLMs. By leveraging meta-models and a pattern-based approach, LLM4Model reduces the cognitive load and manual effort required in model authoring, allowing SMEs to create models more efficiently and with higher quality. In this paper we present our approach and share the findings of its application through real-world use cases.

2 Background and Related Work

There is increasing interest in the application of LLMs for requirements engineering [1, 2, 5]. White et al. proposed prompt design techniques for software engineering in the form of patterns for improving requirements elicitation, rapid prototyping [6]. Arvidsson et al. explored prompt engineering guidelines for generative AI models [7]. Jianzhang et al. conducted an empirical evaluation of ChatGPT on retrieving requirements information, specifically non-functional requirements (NFR), features [8]. ChatGPT has been proposed for improving requirements elicitation, and software design [9]. Deepika et al. explored the usefulness of Bidirectional Encoder Representations from Transformers (BERT) language models for detecting incompleteness in natural-language requirements [10]. Xianchang et al. proposed an approach of prompt learning for requirement classification using BERT [11]. Lola et al. discussed how MDE can be enhanced using Artificial Intelligence (AI) [12]. Fill et al. explored the generation of conceptual models such as E-R diagrams, Business process diagrams, UML class diagrams [13]. Ruan et al. presented an automated framework for generating requirements models from requirements written in natural language using ChatGPT [14]. Overall, there has been an increasing trend for the use of LLMs for model creation. Nevertheless, the unexplored synergy between LLMs and MDE approaches holds great potential. We propose a solution that enables the use of LLM for domain knowledge, and the use of MDE for LLM prompt generation for model authoring.

3 Overall Approach

Figure 1 outlines LLM4Model high-level architecture. It is configured by defining a purposive meta-model and patterns over meta-model. LLM4Model provides a Pattern mapping language to specify how model elements should be authored through LLM-based information elicitation. It has Pattern Interpreter, Prompt Generator and Model Populator. The **Pattern Interpreter** checks the mapping syntax of input Patterns for grammatical errors and interprets the specified syntax for Pattern elements. Pattern mapping may use "*GENPROMPT*" function that generates prompt based on meta-model, or "*PROMPT*" function that help specifying custom prompt. **Prompt Generator** generates the necessary prompts that encompass text related to instructions, context, and the desired format for the response output. Instructions are derived using meta-model elements, and model authored so far is used for context setting. The generated prompt is executed on LLM and response from LLM is used by **Model populator** for model creation. The model authoring process allows SMEs to review responses through a human-in-loop interface. If a response is unsatisfactory, SMEs can manually edit it or instruct the LLM to make corrections.

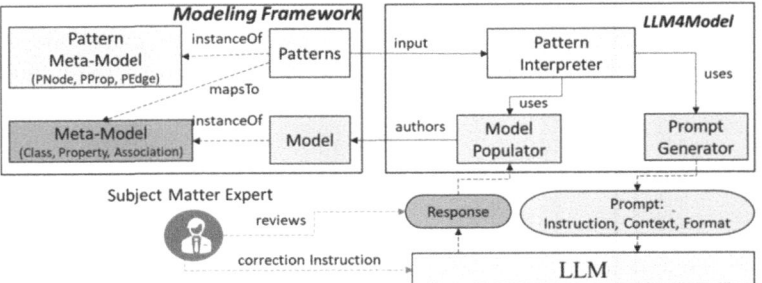

Fig. 1. LLM4Model Approach

To efficiently instantiate large models, a divide-and-compose approach is most effective. This requires a mechanism to define subsets of the meta-model. For model authoring, a relevant subset of the meta-model and the mapping of model construction tasks to meta-model elements are specified using Patterns. Purposive Patterns can be defined based on the size of model to be created, combining closely related meta-model elements in a pattern and mapping of LLM response text with meta-model elements.

A subset of a meta-model of interest is defined using a pattern model [15]. A Pattern is a tree of PNodes, where each PNode maps to a meta-model Class, each PProp maps to a Property, and each PEdge maps to an Association of the Class. The Pattern has a root PNode. Mappings for PNodes, PProps, and PEdges are specified using pattern mapping language. Section 4 provides examples of how patterns are defined. The pattern mapping language supports various types of statements such as prompt specification using model elements, invoking of functions, setting default values for model elements, conditional statements, etc. Pattern interpreter takes mapping specification as parameters, processes these statements and returns the JSON response. Model populator authors model using JSON responses.

4 Configuring LLM4Model for Requirements Specification Model Authoring

LLM4Model can be easily configured for any meta-model and has been used to author models for various meta-models. This paper illustrates the generation of a Requirements Specification Model. To generate this model, LLM4Model is configured with appropriate patterns tailored to the requirements specification meta-model. This section provides an overview of the requirements specification meta-model and the associated patterns.

4.1 Requirements Specification Meta-Model

Figure 2 outlines the key elements in the Requirements Specification meta-model [16]. Business functionality decomposition for a product/application is specified as a subFeature association. Each *Feature* is implemented through a *Process*. *Process* may have multiple *subprocess*. *Process* is described with multiple *Activity*. Process may have multiple RuleSet. A *RuleSet* depicts the logical grouping of multiple *Rule*. Activity takes multiple input-output (IO) *Parameter* logically grouped by a *ParamSet*. All Classes have *Name* and *Description* properties. Process has additional properties- *entryCriteria*, *exitCriteria*. Rule has *ruleType* property. Parameter has *dataFormat* properties.

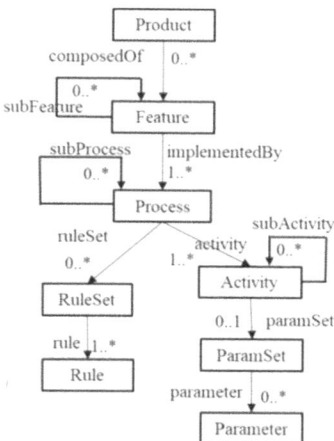

Fig. 2. Meta-Model

4.2 Patterns Definition

For instantiating requirements specification models two patterns are defined – (i) Feature Pattern, (ii) Feature Specification Pattern as shown in Figs. 3 and 4 respectively. For readability purpose model reference statements are marked with blue color. The Feature Pattern is used for instantiation of feature hierarchy. The Feature Specification Pattern is used to instantiate the specification model (Process, Activity, ParamSet, Parameter, RuleSet, Rule along with associations) for each subfeature. We briefly illustrate interpretation of the feature pattern in the case study section.

5 Case Study

We validated LLM4Model using ChatGPT for generating requirements specification models for two products - i) Employee Pension System (Case 1): manages employee pension funds and ii) Depository System (Case 2): handles the electronic storage, transfer, and settlement of securities for efficient and secure trading.

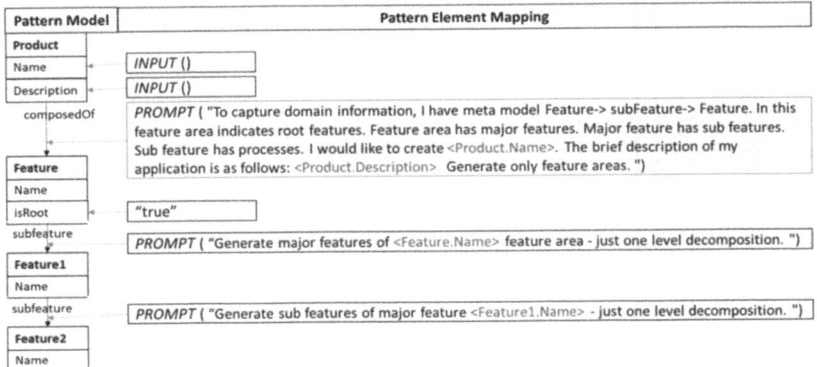

Fig. 3. Feature Pattern

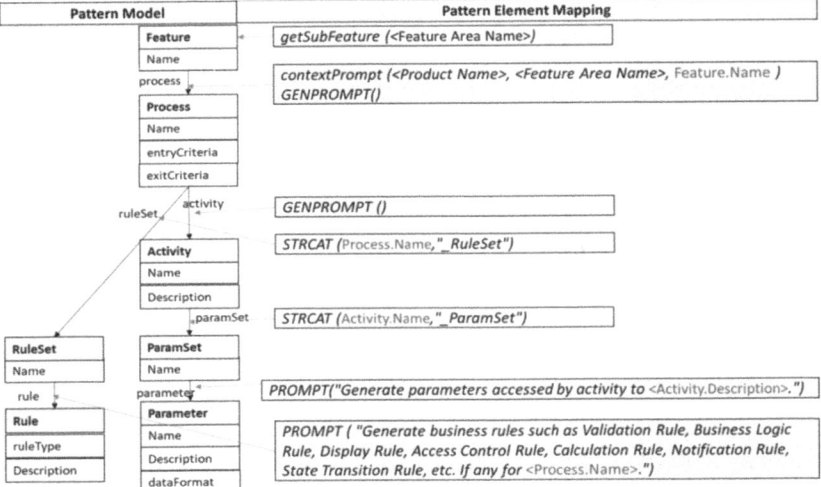

Fig. 4. Feature Specification Pattern

5.1 Pattern Interpretation Illustration

This section presents a partial **Feature Pattern** interpretation for the Employee Pension System using LLM4Model. Pattern mapping is shown for pattern elements along with description of pattern interpretation. Responses from LLM are shown with violet color.

Pattern interpretation begins with the interpretation of the mapping of root PNode followed by its associated PNodes through PEdge interpretation.

PProp: Product.Name:

`INPUT ()` Input given *"Employee Pension System"*

PProp: Product.Description:

`INPUT ()` Input given *"The application context is INDIA Geography."*

"Outlined below are the application business requirements: On-board new employees to the pension plan and capture employee information, Enable employees to allocate their funds to available asset types, Allow administrator and employee to view their current and past fund balances, and their contribution allocation on a monthly basis, Record month-end returns for the various asset types and incorporate these returns into the employee balances, Provide employee-specific and overall dashboards of fund-wise balances."

PEdge: Product.composedOf:

> PROMPT ("To capture domain information, I have meta model Feature-> subFeature-> Feature. In this feature area indicates root features. Feature area has major features. Major feature has sub features. Sub feature has processes. I would like to create <Product.Name>. The brief description of my application is as follows: <Product.Description>. Generate only feature areas. ")

Prompt is generated by replacing Product.Name and Product.Description and executed. Received a JSON response as - {"Feature Areas": [{"Name": "Employee Management"}, "Name": "Fund Allocation"}, {"Name": "Balance Tracking"}, ...]}. Using the JSON data Feature objects are created and "isRoot" default property is set to "true".

PEdge: Feature.subfeature:

> PROMPT ("Generate major features of <Feature.Name> feature area - just one level decomposition. ")

Prompt is generated for each feature area to elicit major features by replacing Feature.Name with feature area name. For instance, for the first feature area *"Employee Management"* following prompt is generated: *"Generate major features of Employee Management feature area - just one level decomposition. Generate output in below format: {Feature:[{Name}, {Name},..., {Name}]}"*. The generated prompt is executed, and the response received in JSON format as - {"Feature": [{"Name": "Employee Onboarding"}, {"Name": "Employee Information Capture"}]}.

PEdge: Feature1.subfeature:

> PROMPT ("Generate sub features of major feature <Feature1.Name> - just one level decomposition. ")

Prompt is generated for each of major feature to elicit sub features by replacing Feature1.Name with major feature name. For instance, for the major feature *"Employee Onboarding"* following prompt is generated: *"Generate subfeatures of major feature Employee Onboarding - just one level decomposition. Generate output in below format: {Feature: [{Name}, {Name}, ..., {Name}]}"*. The generated prompt is executed, and the response received in JSON format as - {"Feature": [{"Name": "New Employee Registration"}, {"Name": "Pension Plan Enrollment"}]}.

Similarly, prompts are prepared and executed for all major features in each feature area to get feature hierarchy.

5.2 Requirement Specification Model Authoring and Validation

Table 1 shows the summary of automatically authored through LLM4Model. Authored models are validated against well-formedness constraints and sanity. Generated models are further analyzed manually for relevance, accuracy, and completeness. For manual validation, a model sheet is generated. Each model element is given a score "1" for meeting all the criteria and "0" was given for lack of relevance, partial accuracy, or complete inaccuracy. Processes are validated against the input business requirements and coverage of the necessary details such as "create", "delete", or "update" related functionality, rules are validated against predefined rule types, parameters are validated for data types and so on. It was observed that a few process names were not meaningful. For instance, generated process names were, "*Reporting*", "*Data Acquisition*" and "*Market Indices*". The rest of the process names were appropriate and started with verb words such as "create", "update", "delete", "provide", etc. A few activities, rules, and parameters were inaccurate. There was a lack of clarity in the generated description of rules and activities. Many rules had only high-level information about data validation and did not include validation criteria. Data formats for a few parameters were incorrect. For instance, the data format generated for the parameter "*current credit rating*" of an activity was "*Categorical Rating or Score*" instead of "*Integer*". The scores are provided considering these factors and accuracy is computed. For both the case studies feature hierarchy generated was satisfactory. In Case1, the F1 scores were approximately 100% for features, 90% for processes, 86% for activities, and 89% for rules. In Case 2, the F1 scores were approximately 100% for features, 87% for processes, 89% for activities, and 90% for rules. For both cases, the F1 score for parameters was about 93%.

Table 1. Generated Model Summary

Pattern	Meta-Model Element	Case1 Count	Case2 Count
Feature Pattern	Feature Area	5	2
	Major Feature	10	12
	Feature	20	50
Feature Specification Pattern	Process	40	250
	Activity	70	715
	RuleSet	20	200
	Rule	85	1355
	Param Set	70	715
	Parameter	231	3442

6 Discussion and Conclusion

Traditional manual model creation requires substantial skill, time, and effort. LLM4Model automates the model generation process. Several challenges and insights emerged during the evaluation of LLM4Model on two industry-strength use cases for requirements specification model generation. Structured interaction with LLMs was essential for optimal results, and the meta-model played a crucial role in guiding this process. However, automatic prompt generation from the meta-model was not always possible. Complex meta-model concepts, such as inheritance, associations, and composition relationships, required specific prompt descriptions. This is addressed using user-defined prompt text along with model for context setting. Patterns and mappings helped in generating the LLM prompts to yield the desired outputs consistently. Patterns are made generic and parameterized to work for any domain. An initial product description was critical in defining the scope and setting the context for generating specifications.

To avoid errors due to the probabilistic nature of LLMs, LLM4Model provides a human in-loop user interface for SME review. Occasionally, context forgetting is observed for authoring. This issue was addressed through divide and composing strategy by authoring models by feature area. Based on our experience, the creation of these specifications would have taken ~ **4 months** SME effort. Whereas, using LLM4Model, for Case1 it took us ~ **7 person days** and for Case2 it took us ~ **14 person days**. A large amount of effort saving is observed. Multiple large-scale use cases validation gives us confidence that it can be widely used across multiple applications and domains.

References

1. Arora, C., Grundy, J., Abdelrazek, M.: Advancing requirements engineering through generative AI: assessing the role of LLMs. In: Nguyen-Duc, A., Abrahamsson, P., Khomh, F. (eds.) Generative AI for Effective Software Development. Springer, Cham (2024). https://doi.org/10.1007/978-3-031-55642-5_6
2. Luitel, D., Hassani, S., Sabetzadeh, M.: Using language models for enhancing the completeness of natural-language requirements. In: Ferrari, A., Penzenstadler, B. (eds.) Requirements Engineering: Foundation for Software Quality. REFSQ 2023. Lecture Notes in Computer Science, vol. 13975. Springer, Cham (2023). https://doi.org/10.1007/978-3-031-29786-1_7
3. Kulkarni, V., Reddy, S., Barat, S., Dutta, J.: Toward a symbiotic approach leveraging generative AI for model driven engineering. In: 2023 ACM/IEEE 26th International Conference on Model Driven Engineering Languages and Systems (MODELS), pp. 184–193. IEEE (2023)
4. A Rajbhoj, A., Somase, A., Kulkarni, P., Kulkarni, V.: Accelerating software development using generative AI: ChatGPT case study. In: Proceedings of the 17th Innovations in Software Engineering Conference, pp. 1–11 (2024)
5. Hou, X., et al.: Large language models for software engineering: a systematic literature review. ACM Trans. Softw. Eng. Methodol. (2023)
6. White, J.: A prompt pattern catalog to enhance prompt engineering with chatgpt. arXiv preprint arXiv:230211382 (2023)
7. Arvidsson, S., Axell, J.: Prompt engineering guidelines for LLMs in Requirements Engineering (2023)

8. Zhang, J., Chen, Y., Niu, N., Liu, C.: Evaluation of chatgpt on requirements information retrieval under zero-shot setting. Available at SSRN 4450322 (2023)
9. White, J., Hays, S., Fu, Q., Spencer-Smith, J., Schmidt, D.C.: ChatGPT prompt patterns for improving code quality, refactoring, requirements elicitation, and software design. In: Nguyen-Duc, A., Abrahamsson, P., Khomh, F. (eds.) Generative AI for Effective Software Development. Springer, Cham (2024). https://doi.org/10.1007/978-3-031-55642-5_4
10. Luitel, D., Hassani, S., Sabetzadeh, M.: Improving requirements completeness: automated assistance through large language models. Requirements Eng. **29**, 73–95 (2024)
11. Luo, X., Xue, Y., Xing, Z., Sun, J.: PRCBERT: prompt learning for requirement classification using bert-based pretrained language models. In: Proceedings of the 37th IEEE/ACM International Conference on Automated Software Engineering, pp. 1–13 (2022)
12. Burgueño, L., Cabot, J., Wimmer, M., Zschaler, S.: Guest editorial to the theme section on AI-enhanced model-driven engineering. Softw. Syst. Model. **21**, 963–965 (2022)
13. Fill, H.-G., Fettke, P., Köpke, J.: Conceptual modeling and large language models: impressions from first experiments with ChatGPT. Enterprise Model. Inform. Syst. Arch. (EMISAJ) **18**, 1–15 (2023)
14. Ruan, K., Chen, X., Jin, Z.: Requirements modeling aided by chatGPT: an experience in embedded systems. In: 2023 IEEE 31st International Requirements Engineering Conference Workshops (REW), pp. 170–177. IEEE (2023)
15. Rajbhoj, A., Reddy, S.: A graph-pattern based approach for meta-model specific conflict detection in a general-purpose model versioning system. In: Moreira, A., Schätz, B., Gray, J., Vallecillo, A., Clarke, P. (eds.) Model-Driven Engineering Languages and Systems. MODELS 2013. Lecture Notes in Computer Science, vol. 8107. Springer, Heidelberg (2013). https://doi.org/10.1007/978-3-642-41533-3_26
16. Rajbhoj, A., Nistala, P., Kulkarni, V., Soni, S., Pathan, A.: DizSpec: digitalization of requirements specification documents to automate traceability and impact analysis. In: 2022 IEEE 30th International Requirements Engineering Conference (RE), pp. 243–254. IEEE (2022)

A Pattern-Based Approach for Explaining Ontology-Driven Conceptual Models

Elena Romanenko[1](✉), Diego Calvanese[1], and Giancarlo Guizzardi[2]

[1] Free University of Bozen-Bolzano, Bolzano, Italy
{eromanenko,diego.calvanese}@unibz.it
[2] University of Twente, Enschede, The Netherlands
g.guizzardi@utwente.nl

Abstract. Conceptual models—designed as means for knowledge sharing—are expected to be extensively reused within their respective domains. However, studies reveal that people often struggle to understand already existing models. Assuming that specific conceptual model views can serve as explanations for particular exploratory questions, we demonstrate how these views and questions can be systematically constructed for OntoUML models. This paper presents the results of a preliminary evaluation of the approach conducted through a questionnaire. The findings highlight that our pattern-based approach enables the construction of model views that contain fewer elements than the original model while remaining sufficient to answer the targeted questions.

Keywords: Ontology-Driven Conceptual Models · Conceptual model explanations · OntoUML · User studies

1 Introduction

Conceptual modeling, defined as "the activity of formally describing some aspects of the physical and social world around us for purposes of understanding and communication" [13], is usually employed during the early stages of information system analysis and design. The ultimate output of this process—a *conceptual model* (CM) or an *ontology-driven conceptual model* (ODCM)—is intended to facilitate effective communication during the later stages among users with different backgrounds.

However, a model can only be utilized effectively if it is understood by its users [15]. Given that the number of modeling elements can often be overwhelming, proper comprehension of the model might require suitable explanations. Although the literature presents different types of explanations [2], this paper focuses on a *pragmatic approach*: explaining the original model by constructing a reduced version that still addresses the user's request.

In this paper, we refer to an ontology as what is commonly termed a *foundational ontology* and utilize *Unified Foundational Ontology* (UFO) [8] for our goals. By an ODCM we understand a concrete artifact that represents *conceptualization of a specific domain*, whose development was guided by the ontology. We address the problem of explaining ODCMs by answering the following research question: *How can we systematically construct model views in response to user requests for an explanation?*

The remainder of the paper is organized as follows: Sect. 2 provides definitions and represents the semantics of the explanation process; Sect. 3 shows how the views can be generated in request for an explanation for the OntoUML models; Sect. 4 discusses the results of the preliminary experiment; Sect. 5 elaborates on final considerations and future work. The list of patterns and their corresponding exploratory questions, as well as the complete version of the questionnaire with anonymized results are available on the project's GitHub page: https://w3id.org/ExpO/github/CAiSE25.

2 A Pattern-Based Approach to ODCM Explanations

If we agree that an explanation is an answer to a *request-for-explanation* (typically, a *why-question*) as suggested in [9, p.334], and consider a CM as our explanation of the domain, then the model should be able to answer a number of corresponding questions.

The idea of having a list of questions that should be answered is quite popular in ontology engineering, for example. Grüninger & Fox suggested considering user queries that an ontology should answer as informal *competency questions* (CQs) [5]. Although, in theory, CQs should guide the modeling process, in practice ontology engineers face difficulties when writing, using, and managing CQs [18], and, as a result, the final list of questions is rarely shared.

In a domain of (logic-based) eXplainable AI, there is a notion of *prime implicant* or *abductive explanations*—a minimal set of features sufficient for ensuring the prediction of the classifier [12]. If we consider elements of the model (e.g., concepts, relations, generalization sets, etc.) as model features, then the following definitions can be suggested.

Definition 1. *An* explanation of the ODCM with respect for a given question *is an ODCM view sufficient to answer that question.*

Definition 2. *An* ODCM view *is a model obtained from a given reference model by applying one or more explanation transformations that is consistency-preserving.*

These definitions are based on the ideas of the model's *consistency* and its *sufficiency* for answering questions. According to [1], a class is consistent if the model admits an instantiation in which this class has a non-empty set of instances. In the case of ODCMs, the inconsistency may happen due to design errors and violations of the rules of the underlying ontology.

Unlike the definition of a 'view' for ontologies (see [14]), we are not solely focused on a 'portion' of the original ODCM. In general, any transformation that maintains the model's consistency is permitted.

Still, this approach—where CQs are treated as questions of interest and the model is regarded as an explanation for these questions—has at least two drawbacks. First, in contrast to classification systems, the judgment of whether the given model sufficiently answers a question can sometimes be subjective. Second, given that CQs are rarely given, this suggests the hypothesis that the user (who is assumed to be unfamiliar with the model) must first be able to formulate a question and then apply the necessary transformation(s) to find the answer in the model.

Reoccurring ontology modeling situations can be addressed using *ontology design patterns* [4]. Thus, in the case of ODCMs, we may use the incorporated semantics and suggest that *each modeling pattern corresponds to a set of exploratory question templates*. Therefore, we may help our users by generating questions that the model can answer where the sufficiency of the resulting ODCM view is guaranteed by the pattern.

The idea of having a particular model view that is sufficient to answer a question correlates with the concept of pragmatic explanation for domain ontologies [16] and complexity management of CMs (see [3,11]).

3 OntoUML Models and Their Explanation

In principle, ODCMs are not bound to any specific ontology, but we chose UFO [8] because of the existence of an associated ontology-driven conceptual modeling language, named OntoUML. *OntoUML* is a language that extends UML class diagrams by defining a set of stereotypes. These stereotypes expand the UML's meta-model so that classes and associations decorated with them bring precise (real-world) semantics grounded in the underlying UFO [7]. For a detailed discussion and formal characterization of UFO and OntoUML, we refer the reader to works by Guizzardi *et al.* [7,8], while in this paper we focus on explaining the approach through an illustrative example.

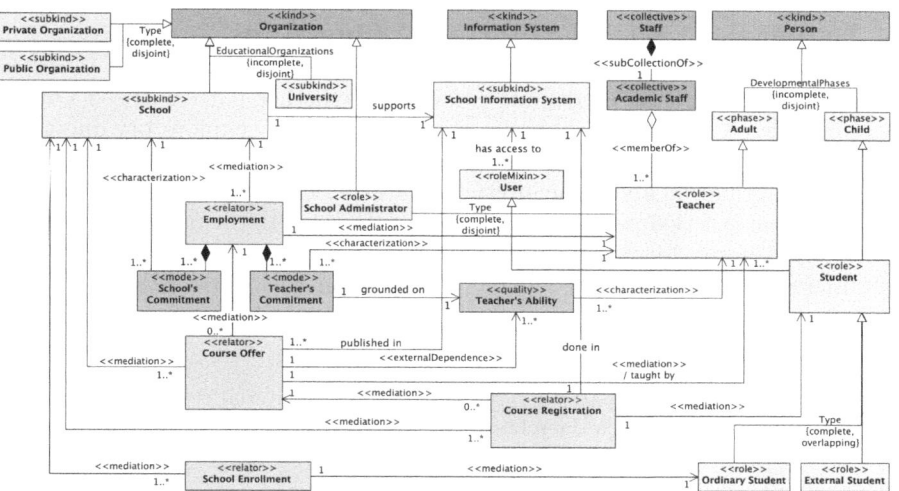

Fig. 1. Student enrollment and course management in OntoUML model.

The OntoUML model shown in Fig. 1 was developed based on the following description of the domain of student enrollment and course management within a school:

Children are enrolled in the school and can register for various courses offered by the school through an information system. Each course has an assigned teacher, and part of their responsibility under their employment contract is to conduct these courses. In addition, students from other schools, referred to as external students, are also allowed to participate in these courses. The school information system records enrollment details and the controlling organization has the ability to monitor this information, including which students are enrolled in which courses.

In the model: *(1)* the coloring schema follows the color convention of the OntoUML plugin for Visual Paradigm[1]; and *(2)* material relations derived from relator types are omitted[2]. Here we are not considering *events* and *situations*. All concepts in the example are *endurants* (object-like entities) [7].

As mentioned, OntoUML is an ontology pattern language [19], where the patterns are formulated in terms of possible stereotypes (for details, see [6,17]). Table 1 shows *Subkind* and *Relator* patterns and how they are exemplified in our model. Table 2 presents templates for exploratory questions aligned with these two patterns. It also includes how these questions are realized for our example and text answers. A complete list of all templates is available on the project's GitHub page.

We recognize that users may would like to have the flexibility to pose arbitrary questions of interest: Can the 'Teacher' of one 'Course' be a 'Student' in another 'Course'?[3] For such questions, we hypothesize that a *combination of patterns* could serve as an explanation. To evaluate whether this approach improves user perception of the generated views, we used a questionnaire.

4 Experiment with Exploratory Questions

The primary goal of the study was to evaluate whether pattern-based ODCM views are perceived as effective explanations for arbitrary exploratory questions.

The questionnaire consisted of three sections. The first section focused on gathering information about the interviewees' experience with conceptual modeling. The second section presented a complete ODCM with the narrative and then several views derived from this ODCM, along with the corresponding questions. The final section assessed participants' satisfaction with the views, specifically

---

[1] https://github.com/OntoUML/ontouml-vp-plugin.
[2] According to the relator pattern [17], there can be a material relation between the mediated concepts to which the relator refers. In the case of 'Employment', this could be the 'works for' relation from 'Teacher' to 'School'. These relations are ommitted here due to space limitations.
[3] In the example any course is always conducted by an adult and followed by children, so the answer is 'No'.

Table 1. Patterns in OntoUML and their exemplifications.

Name and idea	Template	Example in Fig. 1
Subkind pattern is used when there is a need to distinguish rigid (static) specializations of a kind. This can be applied to kinds whose instances are objects, quantities, collectives, qualities, modes and relators.	Subkind → Rigid Sortal OR Subkind →{disjoint, [complete]} 2..* Rigid Sortal	'Organization' with 'Private Organization' and 'Public Organization', 'School' and 'University' subkinds (these two sets are orthogonal, see [6]); 'School Information System' as subkind for 'Information System'.
Relator pattern is a pattern which objectifies a material relation and aggregates all these externally dependent modes that the involved relata acquire in the scope of that relation.	Relator —mediation→ Substantial; Relator —mediation→ Substantial; Mode Pattern	'Employment' with 'School's Commitment' and 'Teacher's Commitment'; 'Course Offer'; 'School Enrollment'; 'Course Registration'.

Table 2. Some templates for generating exploratory questions.

Pattern	Question template	Generated question	Text answer
Subkind	Can a <$Subkind_1$> become a <$Subkind_2$>?	Can a 'Private Organization' become a 'Public Organization'?	No, that would be a new 'Organization'.
Subkind	Can a <$Subkind_1$> be a <$Subkind_2$> at the same time?	Can a 'Private Organization' be a 'Public Organization' at the same time?	No, because the corresponding generalization set is disjoint.
Relator	What is in the nature of a <RelatorType>? What are the aspects that the relata acquire when mediated by a <RelatorType>?	What is in the nature of an 'Employment'? What are the aspects that 'Teacher' and 'School' acquire when mediated by an 'Employment'?	Both 'Teacher' and 'School' acquire a number of commitments in the scope of an 'Employment'.
Relator	When is a particular <$Relatum_1$> related to a particular <$Relatum_2$>?	When is a particular 'Student' related to a particular 'School'?	A 'Student' is related to a particular 'School' iff there is a 'Course Registration' that connects them.

142   E. Romanenko et al.

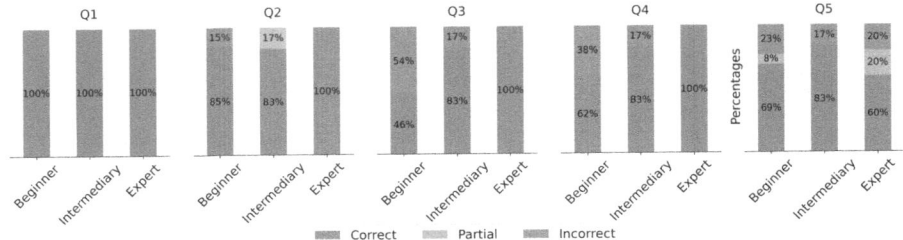

Fig. 2. Correctness of answering questions.

considering their *sufficiency as explanations for the questions*. The questions in the final section were adapted from the System Causability Scale (see Fig. 3) [10].

To reduce the internal validity threat of our evaluation, we grounded the main section of the questionnaire on two different models and randomized our interviewees among them. Both models did not require special knowledge. The first one was our example from Fig. 1 (but without OntoUML stereotypes), while the second one described the relations between Customers and Fitness Studio.

The number of elements in each model was not very high but still demanding some time for an exploration. First, we asked three simple preliminary True / False questions to make sure the respondent can understand the model. For example, one of the questions for the model on Fig. 1 was "According to the model every Child has to be a Student" (False). After the preliminary questions, the interviewee received five multiple-choice questions (Q1–Q5). Our goal was to check whether the questions could be correctly answered based on the views. Finally, the respondent received five exploratory questions with the already given text answers and views (SQ1–SQ5), where our question to the interviewees was "Does the model contain sufficient information to answer this question?".

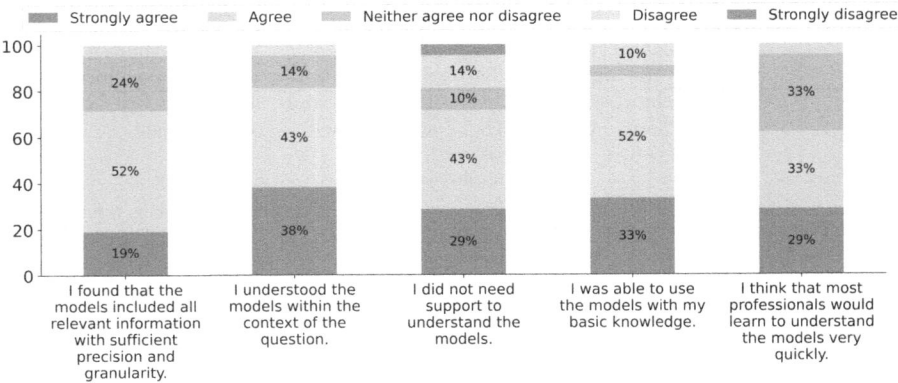

Fig. 3. Results for the adapted System Causability Scale.

In total we received 30 responses. However, the answers of 6 interviewees were disqualified as they made mistakes while answering our preliminary questions. In general, about half of our interviewees were beginners in conceptual modeling and—from the second part of the questionnaire—we can see that the correctness of the responses correlates with the expertise (see Fig. 2). On average, the respondents have spent about 20 min answering the questionnaire.

Most of the time our questions were answered correctly (Fig. 2). Moreover, the confidence in answers was also quite high. Furthermore, respondents reported that the given ODCM view is complete enough with respect to the question to which it is supposed to answer: 78% in average for one model and 83% for another one. The results of the adapted System Causability Scale are presented in Fig. 3 and are also positive (details are available on the project's GitHub page).

5 Conclusions

The paper presents a pattern-based approach for constructing pragmatic explanations of ontology-driven conceptual models. We suggested that specific model views—consistent and sufficient to answer the question of interest—are perceived as explanations of the original model.

In order to guarantee sufficiency, we used model patterns as building blocks for constructing the final views. Since each pattern corresponds to a set of questions, we can also generate by template some exploratory questions to help our users familiarize themselves with the model.

In the conducted questionnaire, we extracted only 'portions' of the models as explanations. In general, the approach we suggest does not limit us in model transformations as soon as consistency with the original model is kept. Thus, we can also apply abstraction in order to reduce the number of modeling elements.

Acknowledgements.. This research has been partially supported by the Province of Bolzano and DFG through the project D2G2 (DFG grant n. 500249124), by the Wallenberg AI, Autonomous Systems and Software Program (WASP) funded by the Knut and Alice Wallenberg Foundation, by the HEU project CyclOps (under GA n. 101135513), by PNRR MUR project PE0000013-FAIR, by project EFRE-FESR 1047 AI-Lab, by project EFRE-FESR 1078 CRIMA, and by the Province of Bolzano and FWF through the project OnTeGra (FWF grant n. 10.55776/PIN8884924).

References

1. Berardi, D., Calvanese, D., De Giacomo, G.: Reasoning on UML class diagrams. Artif. Intell. **168**(1–2), 70–118 (2005). https://doi.org/10.1016/j.artint.2005.05.003
2. Chari, S., et al.: Explanation ontology: a general-purpose, semantic representation for supporting user-centered explanations. Semant. Web **15**(4), 959–989 (2024). https://doi.org/10.3233/sw-233282
3. Figueiredo, G., et al.: Breaking into pieces: an ontological approach to conceptual model complexity management. In: Proceedings of RCIS 2018, pp. 1–10 (2018). https://doi.org/10.1109/RCIS.2018.8406642

4. Gangemi, A., Presutti, V.: Ontology design patterns. In: Handbook on Ontologies, pp. 221–243 (2009). https://doi.org/10.1007/978-3-540-92673-3_10
5. Grüninger, M., Fox, M.S.: Methodology for the design and evaluation of ontologies. In: Proceedings of the IJCAI 1995 Workshop on Basic Ontological Issues in Knowledge Sharing (1995). http://www.eil.utoronto.ca/wp-content/uploads/enterprise-modelling/papers/gruninger-ijcai95.pdf
6. Guizzardi, G., Almeida, J.P.A.: Stability patterns in ontology-driven conceptual modeling. In: Proceedings of ONTOBRAS 2020. CEUR, vol. 2728, pp. 148–160 (2020). https://ceur-ws.org/Vol-2728/paper11.pdf
7. Guizzardi, G., et al.: Types and taxonomic structures in conceptual modeling: a novel ontological theory and engineering support. Data Knowl. Eng. **134**, 101891 (2021). https://doi.org/10.1016/j.datak.2021.101891
8. Guizzardi, G., et al.: UFO: unified foundational ontology. Appl. Ontol. **17**(1), 167–210 (2022). https://doi.org/10.3233/AO-210256
9. Hempel, C.G.: Aspects of scientific explanation. In: Aspects of Scientific Explanation and Other Essays in the Philosophy of Science, pp. 331–496 (1966)
10. Holzinger, A., Carrington, A., Müller, H.: Measuring the quality of explanations: the system causability scale (SCS). KI - Künstliche Intelligenz **34**(2), 193–198 (2020). https://doi.org/10.1007/s13218-020-00636-z
11. Lozano, J., et al.: Ontology view extraction: an approach based on ontological meta-properties. In: Proceedings of ICTAI 2014, pp. 122–129 (2014). https://doi.org/10.1109/ICTAI.2014.28
12. Marques-Silva, J., Ignatiev, A.: No silver bullet: interpretable ML models must be explained. Front. Artif. Intell. **6** (2023). https://doi.org/10.3389/frai.2023.1128212
13. Mylopoulos, J.: Conceptual modeling and Telos. In: Conceptual Modelling, Databases and CASE: An Integrated View of Information Systems Development, pp. 49–68 (1992)
14. Noy, N.F., Musen, M.A.: Traversing ontologies to extract views. In: Modular Ontologies: Concepts, Theories and Techniques for Knowledge Modularization, vol. 5445, pp. 245–260 (2009). https://doi.org/10.1007/978-3-642-01907-4_11
15. Parush, A.: Conceptual Design for Interactive Systems: Designing for Performance and User Experience (2015). https://doi.org/10.1016/c2013-0-06903-4
16. Romanenko, E., Calvanese, D., Guizzardi, G.: Towards pragmatic explanations for domain ontologies. In: Proceedings of EKAW 2022, vol. 13514, pp. 201–208 (2022). https://doi.org/10.1007/978-3-031-17105-5_15
17. Ruy, F.B., et al.: From reference ontologies to ontology patterns and back. Data Knowl. Eng. **109**, 41–69 (2017). https://doi.org/10.1016/j.datak.2017.03.004
18. da Silva Quirino, G.K., Salamon, J.S., Barcellos, M.P.: Use of competency questions in ontology engineering: a survey. In: Conceptual Modeling, vol. 14320, pp. 45–64 (2023). https://doi.org/10.1007/978-3-031-47262-6_3
19. Zambon, E., Guizzardi, G.: Formal definition of a general ontology pattern language using a graph grammar. In: Proceedings of FedCSIS 2017, vol. 11, pp. 1–10 (2017). https://annals-csis.org/Volume_11/drp/pdf/001.pdf

Towards an AI-Agent-Based Framework for Agile Business Process Management

Lala Aïcha Sarr[1(✉)], Komlan Ayite[1], Anne-Marie Barthe-Delanoë[1], Dominik Bork[2], Guillaume Macé-Ramète[3], and Frédéric Bénaben[1,4]

[1] Centre Génie Industriel, IMT Mines Albi, Université de Toulouse, Albi, France
{Lala.Sarr,Komlan.Ayite,Anne-Marie.Barthe,
Frederick.Benaben}@mines-albi.fr
[2] Business Informatics Group, TU Wien, Wien, Austria
dominik.bork@tuwien.ac.at
[3] ITEROP, Colomiers, France
guillaume@iterop.com
[4] ISyE, Georgia Institute of Technology, Atlanta, USA

Abstract. The traditional approaches in dynamic and collaborative environments that use Business Process Management (BPM) methodologies usually lack the ability to adapt to real-time changes in case of heavy human involvement in repetitive processes. The agility of social BPM is, however, still limited because of a lack of context-sensitive tool support. This paper proposes a mapping framework that leverages conversational AI agents on a social media platform to enhance BPM agility. AI-driven conversational agents are mapped to the respective phases of the BPM lifecycle to provide real-time guidance, recommendations, and context-sensitive feedback. The agents' collaborative features enable inclusive co-construction, interactive task execution, and continuous monitoring of the processes. That allows dynamic adaptation of the processes in case of changes so that tasks remain aligned with the users' needs and contextual demands. This framework is developed through an exploratory approach that integrates literature review, deductive design, and use case-based evaluation. This framework could bridge gaps in the current BPM practices by integrating BPM, AI, and social media, thereby offering a new model for agile and collaborative business process management.

Keywords: Business Process Management · Agility · Conversational Agents · LLM · Social media

1 Introduction

Before the formalization of Business Process Management (BPM), organizations operated without proper processes or structured workflows. As businesses became increasingly complex, leaders saw the need to review former organizations in order to gain better control over different operations. This led to the introduction of pre-established processes: business processes (BPs). They designate a series of interdependent actions or procedures carried out coherently to achieve a specific objective [12].

However, traditional BPM is often notorious for its inability to handle changing environments requiring flexible, evolving real-time processes [4]. In a Volatile, Uncertain, Complex, and Ambiguous (VUCA) world, businesses are all too prone to rapid, unpredictable change, requiring flexibility and context awareness. Our research addresses this issue by proposing a framework that relies on generative AI, here, conversational agents (CAs), that will evolve in a social media environment to enable genuine agile BPM. The latter can provide real-time support for the process and feedback to adapt the process to real-time constraints.

The aim of this research is to support process agility, where processes can adapt in real-time to real-world situations, with a convergence of design-time and run-time of BPs. From the perspective of this paper, our research question is: **How can BPM be more flexible and context-aware to bring the required adaptation and real-time support to an organization's BPs?** Based on this, the present paper develops a theory underpinning BPM from social media platforms. The work will be presented as follows: we will start with a background check on BPM, agility, and CAs in Sect. 2. Next, we will present the framework in Sect. 3 and show its feasibility in an illustrative use case in Sect. 4. Finally, we will conclude (Sect. 5) by highlighting the different challenges and benefits presented by BPM combined with CAs.

2 Background and Related Work

BPM initially focused on the detailed design of processes, which were then executed in a linear, predefined way with standardized tasks. The BPM lifecycle can generally be broken down into two main phases. First, we have the "**design time**," which is the phase when the process is identified, defined, and ratified. Then there's the "**run time**" when the process is actually executed.

2.1 Agile and Social BPM

Agile BPM has emerged as a response to the limitations of traditional BPM, emphasizing iterative, user-centric approaches that allow processes to evolve in line with changing needs. Agility, in the context of BPM, is about observing the need for change, choosing an effective response, and implementing that response efficiently [11]. To this end, a framework for integrating and improving agility in BPM has been defined [8]. Using this framework could bring greater responsiveness to change, making processes more responsive, adaptable, and efficient, while supporting better decision-making. However, although agile BPM offers greater adaptability, it often lacks real-time assistance tools that help users react proactively during the process.

Our framework envisages Social BPM as a means of overcoming the shortcomings identified above. Social BPM is an approach that integrates social media technologies into BPM practices to improve communication, transparency, and stakeholder involvement [10]. Unlike traditional BPM, which focuses on automation and technical efficiency, Social BPM integrates users' ideas, feedback, and contributions in real-time. It avoids response delays and back-and-forth exchanges when several parties are involved. Stakeholders become active players in the design, execution, and improvement of processes.

2.2 LLMs and Conversational Agents

Today, one of the most significant technological advances in AI is the introduction of Large Language Models (LLMs): "These transformative models, using statistical methods like n-gram models, can predict the likelihood of word sequences and create novel text based on given prompts." [1, p. 5050]. Furthermore, an innovative approach is Retrieval-Augmented Generation (RAG), which is a combination of information retrieval from a database or external system, and text generation. RAGs improve the accuracy of LLMs by using only concrete retrieved information, reducing hallucinations. They are useful for question-answer systems, document retrieval, and chatbots [7].

CAs or chatbots are the interfaces through which these LLMs are presented to interact with users. They can act as collaborators, support decision-making, and automate routine tasks [2]. One of the main assets of CAs is their ability to adapt to user needs. Being highly context-aware and able to learn from previous interactions, these agents can understand users' preferences, adapt their responses accordingly, and provide relevant information at the right time.

In BPM, generative AI is already being explored for its ability to help with specific tasks, such as data mining for process models from text [3]. Also, a proposal of "Large Process Models" has been made recently by Kampik et al. [5], which would be a system integrating BPM knowledge to generate recommendations for the execution of a BP.

3 Framework Concept

Social media are now part of our professional lives with Teams, Slack, or Discord. Its features, such as comments, group discussions, or notifications, encourage engagement. Social media could offer those involved in a BP (distinguished by its significant repeatability and human involvement) the possibility of communicating via this platform to co-construct the process from A to Z but also to put it into execution at the same time.

What if CAs were integrated into a BPM-style social media platform with co-constructed processes, acting as participants? It would enhance the agility of BPM by automating repetitive tasks. What's more, unlike static BPM systems, CAs could leverage NLP capabilities to interact with users in a natural, conversational way, thereby improving communication and understanding between stakeholders, and encouraging greater stakeholder participation. In addition, these agents, which can analyze process data and user interactions, would be able to make informed recommendations, automate routine tasks, and anticipate potential risks, thereby improving efficiency. In the context of BPM, this could be extremely valuable not only to help teams stay agile but also to enable data-driven decision-making. Instead of relying on assumptions, teams could base their adjustments on clear information, improving effectiveness and efficiency throughout the entire BPM lifecycle.

To accomplish this best suited to the concrete needs of stakeholders, it is necessary to define CAs that would be responsible for overseeing the design and execution of the BP, assessing its goals and expectations, and offering suggestions in the form of feedback and suggestions for tasks.

3.1 Framework Design and Key Components

We define our framework aimed to enable these features along two dimensions, as shown in Fig. 1. The first dimension is the phase of the BPM lifecycle. The second dimension is the strategic BPM/operational BPM. Strategic BPM concerns contextual elements such as strategic alignment and governance, without a technical foundation. Operational BPM, on the other hand, involves activities related to specific processes, with business knowledge of the process, and often with a view to their continuous improvement [6]. To achieve agility, it is important to combine these two complementary levels: strategic BPM lays the foundations and defines orientations, while operational BPM executes and improves processes. The proposed framework involves four main types of CAs (summarized in Table 1), each playing a specific role across different BPM stages and introduced in the following.

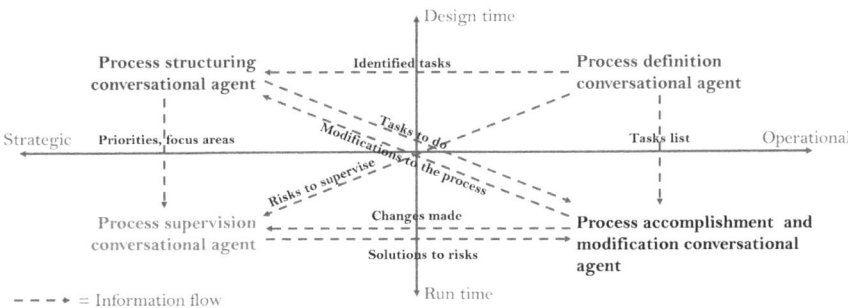

Fig. 1. Characterization of the different CAs planned for the BPM platform [9]. (Color figure online)

The Fig. 1, resumed in Table 1, is intended to be explanatory, but does not show a notion of temporality. Indeed, these CAs will not evolve sequentially but will communicate with each other at the same time according to a choreography. The result is an AI ecosystem supported by social media, where users and CAs interact with a whole chain of interventions.

Design Time. During the BP design phase, the first CA to intervene is a **process definition agent** (yellow in Fig. 1). It all starts when a user posts an activity that corresponds to a BP. In this post, they give a very precise description of their objective and identify the first users concerned. Our process definition CA will intervene at this point in the first instance, to identify and present the tasks required to execute the process. With subsequent comments from others involved, it continues its role of listing tasks until the users have a clear and detailed list of tasks with the users who are to carry them out. This implies a certain familiarity with the domain side of the BP. On the other hand, this agent plays a crucial role in risk prevention and management. It provides a combination of responses like "if this happens, then do that" scenarios. These combinations are known in advance, on the basis of tasks carried out in previous related processes, or on the basis of the CA knowledge.

As soon as the latter provides the to-do list of identified tasks, another CA comes into play during project planning. This is a **process structuring agent** (pink in Fig. 1), whose main task is to help define sub-tasks, set priorities, and manage dependencies between tasks. As some process tasks are wide-ranging, they need to be segmented to make them easier to understand. The agent also rearranges tasks to maximize efficiency and workflow. It achieves this with knowledge of BPs, risk management, and planning skills, but no business knowledge of the process.

Run Time. When entering the execution phase of the BP, a **process supervision CA** (blue in Fig. 1) is responsible for overseeing the process execution. This CA is designed to monitor task progress in real-time, enabling users to concentrate on their tasks without having to think about deadlines. It will track these deadlines and notify users of any delays. This CA is able to identify anomalies, such as delays, unexpected results, missed milestones, or priorities left behind, and propose solutions on a case-by-case basis for smooth, efficient resolutions. However, it does not carry out the deduced solutions.

The process supervision CA passes on these solutions to users and to the **process accomplishment and modification CA** (orange in Fig. 1) which will assist throughout the execution of the BP. It explains each step of an activity, answers questions, and proposes real-time modifications to tasks according to the user's needs. This requires in-depth knowledge of the tools and mechanisms needed to execute the task, and the ability to make the process adjustments that are necessary.

4 Illustrative Scenario

To demonstrate feasibility, we use a fictional illustrative scenario. In other words, we don't carry out a real call for tenders, from start to finish, but we make a storyboard of what we want from our agents. It relies on public documents such as public procurement regulations (available online to the public) and private documents issued by a public organization (RAG performance). What justifies the

Table 1. Roles and Characteristics of Conversational Agents in Business Processes.

Conversational Agent	Role	Process Lifecycle step
Process definition CA	• Enumerates and presents the tasks required • Gathers inputs to create a structured tasks list • Identifies, assigns, and sequences tasks • Prevents risks & identifies corrective methods	Design time; During task identification
Process structuring CA	• Organizes and structures tasks • Assists in defining subtasks, setting priorities • Optimizes the arrangement of tasks	Design time; After task listing
Process supervision CA	• Monitors the progress of tasks and BPs • Identifies potential bottlenecks and solutions • Tracks deadlines and schedules	Run time; During task execution
Process accomplishment and modification CA	• Assists with the completion of specific tasks • Provides detailed instructions and answers • Facilitates real-time adjustments of tasks • Takes proactive action for risks and priorities	Run time; During modifications

use of these agents is the complexity of public procedures, with strict regulatory requirements and a big need for efficient task execution.

There are three project participants (Employee1-3) who belong to the same public organization, and the CA named Virtual Assistant. It is a multi-faceted entity assuring both roles such as definition and structuring process.@Employee1 needs to buy a server to run some code. To do so, she has to issue a call for tender which leads to a BP.

She will start by logging into her account on the social media platform, and she will create a dedicated channel named after the objective (buying a server, here). She will then post, stating her needs as follows.

```
Employee1: Good morning. I hope you're all right. For our lab project, I have code to run.
I would like to buy a server to run it. I've looked at https://www.lci-albi.biz/,
and the server's budget is 20k€. @employee2 @employee3 @virtual_assistant Could
you advise us of the detailed procedure to follow and distribute the tasks among us?
```

Virtual_assistant steps in rapidly to suggest the right way to achieve employee1's request by gathering Employee1's input and converting the needs into a task list. It makes sure that her needs align with local legal requirements and identifies key tasks such as defining specifications. We can see here that it acts as the process definition and structuring CA.

```
Hello !
From the sources provided, the process of call for tender for a server for public projects
would generally follow the following steps:
1. Defining the need : Define your server requirements (size, specifications, etc.)
and identify the resources needed for your project.
2. Search for tenders: Look for server tenders from various suppliers, especially those
who have already worked on projects similar to yours.
3. Evaluate bids: Evaluate each option in terms of your needs and priorities.
4. Rendering of work: Rendering of work to validate the server specifications and
conditions of agreement.
As far as regulatory provisions are concerned, it's important to note that the process
```

of finding a server must comply with current rules and regulations. This may include considerations such as confidentiality, security and ethics.

To refine the list, we ask the *@virtual_assistant* to split the tasks between @employee1, who is a research engineer, @employee2, who is in charge of the finance department, and @employee3, who will be the main user of the server.

```
Here is a proposed work plan to divide the tasks between the three employees:
- Task 1: Defining the need : @employee1 (research engineer)
- Task 2: Search for tenders : @employee1 (research engineer):
- Task 3 and task 4: Evaluate bids and render work, and validation of specifications :
@employee3 (main server user)
- Coordinate work between the three employees : @employee1 (research engineer)
```

This agent would continue to work with the users and provide effective support by offering services to identify tasks, ensure compliance with public regulations regarding the budget, and align employee needs with legal and procedural requirements. In addition, for the process structuring service part, it could help organize the sequence of tasks at a basic level. Throughout the process, the process supervision CA would monitor deadlines, adherence to priorities, and performance. It would send alerts for upcoming milestones, such as the tender publication deadline and the proposal evaluation schedule. The process accomplishment and modification CA would provide real-time assistance, helping the employees adjust specifications if suppliers request clarification.

5 Conclusion

This paper proposes a conceptual framework for integrating CAs into a social media-based BPM platform, aiming to improve process agility, collaboration, and real-time adaptability. The framework leverages intuitive interactions to address long-standing BPM challenges. In our paper, we proposed a framework that shows the mapping of CAs to BPM steps that enables agility in the design time and run time of business processes. We have demonstrated the practical application of the framework in an illustrative scenario that shows the potential impact of CAs in real-world, agile BPM scenarios.

Integrating CAs into BPM has implications that go beyond improving individual processes. Indeed, the combination of generative AI, social media platforms, and agile methodologies would represent a paradigm shift towards more dynamic, user-centric BPM systems. Enhanced collaboration tools facilitated by CAs would help bridge the gaps between departments, fostering a more cohesive organizational culture. This research also paves the way for exploring other AI-based technologies, such as predictive analytics in BPM contexts.

The proposed framework lays the foundations for further research and development. Future work should implement the agents, either opting for one CA per role or a CA performing part of or all the identified roles. The framework should also be tested in complex processes to validate its scalability and robustness. We would also like to assess the level of prior knowledge required from agents for qualitative responses by playing with different given prompts.

References

1. Bharathi Mohan, G., et al.: An analysis of large language models: their impact and potential applications. Knowl. Inf. Syst. 1–24 (2024)
2. Casheekar, A., Lahiri, A., Rath, K., Prabhakar, K.S., Srinivasan, K.: A contemporary review on chatbots, AI-powered virtual conversational agents, ChatGPT: applications, open challenges and future research directions. Comput. Sci. Rev. **52**, 100632 (2024). https://doi.org/10.1016/j.cosrev.2024.100632
3. Grohs, M., Abb, L., Elsayed, N., Rehse, J.R.: Large language models can accomplish business process management tasks. In: De Weerdt, J., Pufahl, L. (eds.) Business Process Management Workshops, pp. 453–465. Springer (2024)
4. Imgrund, F., Janiesch, C.: Understanding the need for new perspectives on BPM in the digital age: an empirical analysis. In: Di Francescomarino, C., Dijkman, R., Zdun, U. (eds.) BPM 2019. LNBIP, vol. 362, pp. 288–300. Springer, Cham (2019). https://doi.org/10.1007/978-3-030-37453-2_24
5. Kampik, T., et al.: Large process models: a vision for business process management in the age of generative AI. KI-Künstliche Intelligenz 1–15 (2024)
6. Kourani, H., Berti, A., Schuster, D., Van der Aalst, W.M.: Evaluating large language models on business process modeling: Framework, benchmark, and self-improvement analysis (2024). https://doi.org/10.13140/RG.2.2.11821.70880
7. Liu, J., Lin, J., Liu, Y.: How much can rag help the reasoning of LLM? (2024). https://arxiv.org/abs/2410.02338
8. Majidian-Eidgahi, M., et al.: Integrating social media and business process management: Exploring the role of AI agents and the benefits for agility. In: Business Process Management Workshops - BPM 2023, pp. 205–216. Springer (2023). https://doi.org/10.1007/978-3-031-50974-2_16
9. Sarr, L.A., Ayite, P.K., Barthe-Delanoë, A.M., Bork, D., Macé-Ramète, G., Bénaben, F.: Towards the integration of conversational agents through a social media platform to enhance the agility of BPM. In: 25th IFIP WG 5.5 Working Conference on Virtual Enterprises, PRO-VE 2024, pp. 36–48. Springer (2024). https://doi.org/10.1007/978-3-031-71739-0_3
10. Schmidt, R., Zimmermann, A., Möhring, M., Jugel, D., Bär, F., Schweda, C.M.: Social-software-based support for enterprise architecture management processes. In: BPM 2014 International Workshops, pp. 452–462. Springer (2015)
11. Triaa, W., Gzara, L., Verjus, H.: Organizational agility key factors for dynamic business process management. In: 18th IEEE Conference on Business Informatics, CBI 2016, pp. 64–73. IEEE (2016). https://doi.org/10.1109/CBI.2016.16
12. Zairi, M.: Business process management: a boundaryless approach to modern competitiveness. Bus. Process. Manag. J. **3**(1), 64–80 (1997)

Studying Workarounds in Software Forms: An Experimental Protocol

MohammadAmin Zaheri[✉], Michalis Famelis[✉], and Eugene Syriani[✉]

DIRO, Université de Montréal, Montreal, Canada
{zaherimo,famelis,syriani}@iro.umontreal.ca

Abstract. Workarounds enable users to achieve goals despite system limitations but expose design flaws, reduce productivity, risk compromising data quality, and cause inconsistencies. We propose an experimental method to investigate how users employ workarounds when the data they want to enter does not align with the constraints of software forms. By conducting user studies based on this method, we can analyze how workarounds originate and impact system design and data integrity. Understanding workarounds is essential for software designers to identify unmet user needs.

Keywords: Workarounds · Experimental Protocol · User Study

1 Introduction

Software applications often require users to enter data for subsequent processing. Examples include a citizen applying for benefits, a banking assistant recording transaction details in a financial system, a sales representative reporting customer visits in a CRM platform, a physician documenting patient symptoms and diagnostics in a medical application, a customer filing an insurance claim, or a photographer inputting parameters to optimize image rendering in a photo editor. In most cases, such tasks are accomplished through forms, which serve as the primary interface for data entry.

In Information Systems, software applications often misalign with user needs and goals [17], leading them to improvise solutions. These improvised *workarounds* are deliberate deviations from intended software usage that emerge when application forms and workflows fail to accommodate user needs [2]. Sometimes, developers recognize workarounds as useful system features and integrate them in their designs. Workarounds can have positive and negative consequences [3]. They can reveal missing features, overlooked design flaws, or inefficient workflows. For example, users might develop complex external processes to generate a report, unaware of an existing built-in functionality for the task. While workarounds can be beneficial by enabling users to overcome system limitations, they also pose risks. Deliberate deviations may lead to unintended consequences, such as data loss, system inconsistencies, or compromised data quality.

For instance, a user entering irrelevant data to bypass a required field might unintentionally affect the accuracy of downstream reports, resulting in semantic inconsistencies where the system operates technically correctly but the data becomes unreliable [29]. Understanding the implications of workarounds is thus critical for improving software design and usability.

In this paper, we propose an experimental method for investigating how users develop workarounds when their goals do not align with software constraints. This method enables descriptive analysis of workaround origins and their effects on system design and data integrity. Our approach provides insights into user behaviour during misalignments, advancing research in workaround detection and user-centered design. Analysis of these workarounds can inform automated detection mechanisms and recommendation systems for stakeholders in software design and usage.

2 Background and Related Work

Gasser defines workarounds in computing as follows [10]: *"working around means intentionally using computing in ways for which it was not designed or avoiding its use and relying on an alternative means of accomplishing work."* They emerge for various reasons, such as limitations in computing systems, challenges in existing workflows, or the need for quick solutions [2]. Users often improvise when encountering technology misfits or data misalignments to complete their regular tasks. In our context, a *technology misfit* is a mismatch between the technology in use and the practical needs or contingencies of everyday work. *Data misalignment* occurs when application processes or forms do not align with real-world data. Workarounds are often seen as examples of bricolage and/or improvisation: *Bricolage* "involves making do with available resources, occurring over short or long periods" [12]; *Improvisation* "refers to bricolage in a short timeframe" [15].

Some workarounds are executed and disappear once the obstacle is overcome; others become informally embedded into organizational routines [25]. Often, institutionalized workarounds become stepping stones for planned changes to processes and software [2]. Researchers have thus attempted to systematize and understand them. A workaround ontology was developed by Röder et al. [19], while Zainuddin et al. proposed a taxonomy [31].

The data generated during the operation of information systems has been extensively leveraged to detect workarounds, e.g., by mining logs using deep learning methods [24], or for process mining [4,22]. A common approach is to track the sequence of actions and keystrokes users take when interacting with software systems. Workarounds can then be identified by comparing intended processes to actual user behaviour. Other studies focus on understanding the impact of workarounds, noting that users are often unaware of the potential consequences when they engage in these behaviours [8,18]. Additionally, Schou et al. highlighted how unnoticed workarounds can have negative effects on organizational processes [20].

Detecting workarounds in workflows often relies on interviews and case studies. Soffer et al. investigate the motivations for workarounds in processes and find that they arise from misalignments between user goals and official processes or conflicts among the goals themselves [21]. Van der Waal et al. investigated how workarounds evolve over time and whether they are adopted by individuals or groups, emphasizing the need for continuous monitoring [23]. Davidson et al. explored the reasons behind workarounds, such as inadequacies in information systems, where users bypass formal processes simply to get their work done [6]. Wibisono studied how workarounds affect data quality, noting that users may interpret data in ways that introduce subjectivity and result in pseudo-data quality [26]. Davidson et al. examined the role of no-code/low-code [7] tools in enabling workarounds that deviate from established organizational processes [5]. Mubarkoot et al., taking the perspective of software compliance, highlighted that while end-user workarounds have been studied, there is a lack of research on workarounds for software engineers [16].

3 Studying Workarounds

We aim to analyze the workarounds users perform when interacting with forms in the context of misalignment between the data they entered and the components of the software form. We want to characterize their impact on user effort and data quality, with respect to frequency, and systematic behavior.

Designing experimental studies [28] using our proposed experimental method, researchers can investigate workarounds by examining their types, frequency, and relationships with each other and various types of misalignments. Another important aspect to explore is the association between form widgets and the workarounds users attempt with them. This helps characterize the different workaround strategies based on the available widgets users interact with when navigating software forms or workflows. Additionally, researchers can analyze recurring patterns and systematic approaches users adopt when implementing workarounds. Another possible investigation is whether the frequency of misalignments affects the effort users invest in finding workarounds.

Experimental Instruments. When investigating workarounds, researchers must clarify three key factors before conducting experiments: the creation of forms used in the study, the input data, and the assignment of users. Another critical instrument in workaround studies is a logger integrated into forms and workflows to capture user interactions, including widget usage, timing information, keystrokes, and mouse clicks. These logs are essential for analyzing interactions with form widgets and application navigation during workarounds.

For controlled or pilot experiments, researchers can use synthetic forms, data, and scenarios. They are responsible for recruiting and assigning users while designing various types of data misalignment, where input data does not fit the provided forms and workflows. Each form dataset should include both easily enterable records (where data format and content match expectations) and misaligned records.

There are multiple form widget categorizations, such as *action/data/static* [13] or *navigation/input/control/presentation* [14]. We propose a categorization based on a widget's affordance for user workarounds, i.e., the degree of freedom it offers for data manipulation. **Open widgets** allow users to freely modify input data, such as text boxes and text areas with minimal or no validation rules. **Predetermined widgets** contain preset data, requiring users to select from existing options, such as dropdown lists, combo boxes, radio buttons, checkboxes, and colour pickers. **Controlled widgets** accept data within a constrained (but potentially large) range, such as sliders, number spinners, file uploads, and date pickers. When designing forms, researchers should balance the distribution of widgets from these three categories to fit their controlled experiment.

Although the results of such experiments may not be fully generalizable, they provide valuable insights and build confidence in conducting further empirical studies, such as case studies or natural experiments [9,11]. Since these types of studies require access to real data, applications, and users, a lot depends on the degree of implication with an industrial partner. In a case study, researchers do not create the forms but advise the case study partner on software form and workflow design. There is no synthetic data, but researchers may provide guidance on user assignment. In a natural experiment, researchers do not influence form design or user assignment. Their role is limited to integrating the logger, which captures user interactions within the software forms and workflows.

These studies can contribute to understanding workarounds and improving their detection. They can be useful to help to identify missing requirements, validate software forms and workflows, and even automate pull request generation for missing features.

Experiment Process. In controlled experiments and case studies, each participant requires an individual session to enter their data into the system. Sessions consist of three parts: introduction, tasks, and exit survey. During the introduction, researchers present experimental tasks and provide documentation about the software forms or workflows, including screenshots of completed forms to familiarize participants with the interface and key features. Participants should remain unaware of the experiment's focus on workarounds and receive instructions only to enter data through the forms and workflows. While loggers capture quantitative data, they may miss certain behavior, necessitating the exit survey. After completing data entry tasks, participants must complete this survey about their experience. The survey can include questions about the participant's occupation or field of study, self-assessment of difficulty entering misaligned data, self-reporting of workaround usage, and open-ended questions explaining employed workarounds or suggesting improvements to handle misalignments.

Metrics. In experiments where misalignments and widget forms are known, researchers must label records that expose a misalignment (i.e., for which a workaround is expected) according to the workaround *type* and *quality*. They also collect the widget involved and its widget category (open, predetermined, or controlled).

Workaround type reflects how users adapt to misalignments. Examples include "Data Adjustment", which entails modifying the original data so that they can be aligned with the constraints of the form; "Functional Adjustment", i.e., using the elements of form in surprising, unintended ways; and "Fallback", that depends on some open ended form field to explain the misalignment [31].

Workaround quality assesses data integrity and semantic consistency between original and entered data [29]. We propose a four-valued score for workaround quality, reflecting the degree to which the workaround helps user succeed in entering their data: 1. significant data loss; 2. partial data loss; 3. indirect data retention (entered elsewhere or reported differently while preserving intent); 4. prominent input of misaligned data. We assign no score when the user completely discarded the misaligned data, i.e., they did not employ any workaround.

From record save times captured in the logger, researchers can deduce the workaround implementation time. Since participants have unique data entry paces, we propose to compute a normalized save time taking into account the save time each participant takes for normal records as baseline. As this baseline is sensitive to the time distribution, we propose the following statistics to capture it. For a normal distribution of time to complete the records, they can use the mean; for left/right-skewed distributions, use the $30^{th}/70^{th}$ percentile, respectively; for heavy-tailed distributions, use the trimmed mean (excluding the lowest/highest 10%); and for other cases, use the median. The suggested metric is, thus, the *relative workaround effort* which represents time to complete a workaround adjusted to baseline, computed as the ratio of workaround save time to participant's baseline.

Finally, a *systematicity score* indicates how consistently participants apply the same workaround type for the same misalignment type, calculated as the proportion of instances where the most common workaround was used, averaged across misalignment types.

4 Pilot Experiment

We conducted a sample pilot experiment [30] to instantiate our proposed method for studying user workarounds in software applications by analyzing interactions with forms for entering misaligned data. We used convenience sampling, sending invitations to research groups and communities within our network. No prior knowledge of any specific software was required, and 15 participants completed the experiment. They were tasked with entering prepared datasets into instrumented software applications we developed. Across the 3 tasks, each participant encountered at least 4 misalignment types for a total 45 misaligned data.

This pilot experiment allowed us to assess both the feasibility of our experimental method and the concepts we proposed for investigating workarounds. While our findings are not generalizable due to the small sample size, they provided valuable insights.

For users encountering misalignments, we observed when they resorted to workarounds, how these workarounds affected data quality, and how users prioritized their strategies based on the quality of the final data they could enter. We also gained experience with our widget categorization: Open widgets provided flexibility, enabling users to enter unstructured or misaligned data; Predetermined widgets were more prone to data loss due to their rigidity; and how Controlled widgets influenced workaround strategies and data quality. Additionally, we explored whether users developed systematic strategies after repeatedly encountering the same type of misalignment.

Our results indicate that applying this experimental method, along with our proposed research concepts, metrics, and recommendations on instruments and process, can yield valuable insights into workarounds. Conducting larger experiments with more participants, case studies, or natural experiments based on our experimental method would be a worthwhile next step.

Threats to Validity. Our workaround quality measurement, though based on data retention to reduce subjectivity, may not fully reflect true quality. The systematicity score assumes that repeated use of the same workaround type indicates intentional behaviour, potentially overlooking factors like user background or problem interpretation. Participants might attempt more workarounds than usual due to the Hawthorne effect [1]. To mitigate this, we carefully worded experiment instructions to focus on data entry and software interaction without mentioning workarounds.

Despite task and misalignment randomization, earlier tasks may unintentionally improve performance in later ones. The tasks and application domains in our pilot experiment cannot fully represent real-world scenarios or capture the complexity of real-world misalignments, limiting the generalizability of our findings. While forms provide a suitable focus for this research stage given their pervasiveness in software, this scope may limit findings' applicability to systems where workarounds differ.

Our participants' engineering and computer science backgrounds may have influenced their approach despite being assigned non-technical tasks. For instance, computational thinking [27] might affect workaround types employed. Future experiments should include more diverse participants. Researchers adopting our experimental method should consider participant background diversity.

Finally, our interpretations of participants' workaround choices may involve subjective judgment. We mitigated this by interpreting results and then cross-referencing participants' exit survey responses to corroborate findings.

5 Summary and Discussion

We proposed an experimental method to study how users employ workarounds when software forms do not align with their data or goals. A pilot experiment validated its feasibility and research questions. Applying this method provides insights that support future research and help designers better address user needs. Future work could extend this approach to non-form-based systems and explore automated workaround detection to improve user-centred software.

Experiments based on this method can reveal patterns in how users handle form data misalignments. Researchers can determine whether users choose workarounds over abandonment, prioritize data integrity in their workaround strategies, or combine multiple workarounds. Another key aspect is whether users become more efficient after repeatedly encountering misalignments. Additionally, our widget categorization provides a framework for examining the relationship between workaround quality and widget affordances.

Workarounds highlight design flaws but also pose risks to data integrity. Software designers must proactively understand workarounds to identify unmet user needs and mitigate risks. The survey results from these experiments can further help researchers assess whether detecting workarounds uncovers design problems or confirms that misaligned designs push users toward *shadow systems* or *complete bypasses* [10].

References

1. Adair, J.G.: The hawthorne effect: a reconsideration of the methodological artifact. J. Appl. Psychol. **69**(2), 334 (1984)
2. Alter, S.: Theory of workarounds (2014)
3. Alter, S.: Beneficial noncompliance and detrimental compliance: expected paths to unintended consequences (2015)
4. Beerepoot, I.M.: Workarounds: The Path From Detection to Improvement. Ph.D. thesis, Utrecht University (2022)
5. Davison, R.M., Wong, L.H., Alter, S.: Combining low-code/no-code with noncompliant workarounds to overcome a corporate system's limitations. MIS Q. Exec. **23**(3), 5 (2024)
6. Davison, R.M., Wong, L.H., Ou, C.X., Alter, S.: The coordination of workarounds: insights from responses to misfits between local realities and a mandated global enterprise system. Inf. Manag. **58**(8), 103530 (2021)
7. Di Ruscio, D., Kolovos, D., de Lara, J., Pierantonio, A., Tisi, M., Wimmer, M.: Low-code development and model-driven engineering: two sides of the same coin? Softw. Syst. Model. **21**(2), 437–446 (2022). https://doi.org/10.1007/s10270-021-00970-2
8. Drum, D., Pernsteiner, A., Revak, A.: Workarounds in an sap environment: impacts on accounting information quality. J. Account. Organ. Change **13**(1), 44–64 (2017)
9. Easterbrook, S., Singer, J., Storey, M.A., Damian, D.: Selecting empirical methods for software engineering research. In: Guide to Advanced Empirical Software Engineering, pp. 285–311 (2008)
10. Gasser, L.: The integration of computing and routine work. ACM Trans. Inf. Syst. (TOIS) **4**(3), 205–225 (1986)
11. Leatherdale, S.T.: Natural experiment methodology for research: a review of how different methods can support real-world research. Int. J. Soc. Res. Methodol. **22**(1), 19–35 (2019)
12. Levi-Strauss, C.: The savage mind. Nature of Human Society, University of Chicago Press, Chicago (1968)

13. Lo, R., Webby, R., Jeffery, R.: Sizing and estimating the coding and unit testing effort for gui systems. In: Proceedings of the 3rd International Software Metrics Symposium, pp. 166–173. IEEE (1996)
14. Meneses Viveros, A., Hernández Rubio, E., Vázquez Ceballos, D.E.: Equivalence of navigation widgets for mobile platforms. In: Marcus, A. (ed.) DUXU 2014. LNCS, vol. 8518, pp. 269–278. Springer, Cham (2014). https://doi.org/10.1007/978-3-319-07626-3_25
15. Miner, A.S., Bassof, P., Moorman, C.: Organizational improvisation and learning: a field study. Adm. Sci. Q. **46**(2), 304–337 (2001)
16. Mubarkoot, M., Altmann, J., Rasti-Barzoki, M., Egger, B., Lee, H.: Software compliance requirements, factors, and policies: a systematic literature review. Comput. Secur. **124**, 102985 (2023)
17. Outmazgin, N., Soffer, P., Hadar, I.: Workarounds in business processes: a goal-based analysis. In: Dustdar, S., Yu, E., Salinesi, C., Rieu, D., Pant, V. (eds.) CAiSE 2020. LNCS, vol. 12127, pp. 368–383. Springer, Cham (2020). https://doi.org/10.1007/978-3-030-49435-3_23
18. Pernsteiner, A., Drum, D., Revak, A.: Control or chaos: impact of workarounds on internal controls. Int. J. Account. Inf. Manag. **26**(2), 230–244 (2018)
19. Röder, N., Wiesche, M., Schermann, M., Krcmar, H.: Toward an ontology of workarounds: a literature review on existing concepts. In: 2016 49th Hawaii International Conference on System Sciences (HICSS), pp. 5177–5186. IEEE (2016)
20. Schou, P.K., Nesheim, T.: What we do in the shadows: how expert workers reclaim control in digitalized and centralized organizations through 'stealth work'. Organ. Stud. **45**(5), 719–744 (2024)
21. Soffer, P., Outmazgin, N., Hadar, I., Tzafrir, S.: Why work around the process? Analyzing workarounds through the lens of the theory of planned behavior. Bus. Inf. Syst. Eng. **65**(4), 369–389 (2023)
22. van der Waal, W., Beerepoot, I., van de Weerd, I., Reijers, H.A.: The sword is mightier than the interview: a framework for semi-automatic workaround detection. In: International Conference on Business Process Management, pp. 91–106. Springer, Heidelberg (2022). https://doi.org/10.1007/978-3-031-16103-2_9
23. van der Waal, W., van de Weerd, I., Beerepoot, I., Reijers, H.A.: The emergence and evolution of workarounds: a study of stability and change (2024)
24. Weinzierl, S., Wolf, V., Pauli, T., Beverungen, D., Matzner, M.: Detecting temporal workarounds in business processes-a deep-learning-based method for analysing event log data. J. Bus. Anal. **5**(1), 76–100 (2022)
25. White, M.S.: Workarounds and shadow it-balancing innovation and risk. Bus. Inf. Rev. **40**(3), 114–122 (2023)
26. Wibisono, A.: Workarounds produce pseudo-data quality: insights from case studies. Procedia Comput. Sci. **234**, 725–732 (2024)
27. Wing, J.M.: Computational thinking. Commun. ACM **49**(3), 33–35 (2006)
28. Wohlin, C., Runeson, P., Höst, M., Ohlsson, M.C., Regnell, B., Wesslén, A., et al.: Experimentation in Software Engineering, vol. 236. Springer, Heidelberg (2012)
29. Zaheri, M., Famelis, M., Syriani, E.: Catch me if you can: detecting model-data inconsistencies in low-code applications. J. Obj. Technol. **23**(1), 1–20 (2024)
30. Zaheri, M., Famelis, M., Syriani, E.: How users employ workarounds in software forms (2025). https://arxiv.org/abs/2503.17624
31. Zainuddin, E., Staples, S.: Developing a shared taxonomy of workaround behaviors for the information systems field. In: 2016 49th Hawaii International Conference on System Sciences (HICSS), pp. 5278–5287. IEEE (2016)

Pondering on Capability Brokering with LLM

Jelena Zdravkovic(✉) ⬤, Janis Stirna ⬤, and Chen Hsi Tsai ⬤

Department of Computer and Systems Sciences, Stockholm University, 7003, SE-16407 Kista, Sweden
{jelenaz,js,chenhsi.tsai}@dsv.su.se

Abstract. Capabilities provide a structured and stable business-centric view of what an organization does. By enabling the organization's architecture of what it is able to do, as modular functional building blocks, capability has become a standard design element of enterprise architecture frameworks such as TOGAF, Archimate, OMG Business Architecture, and many others. Despite clear modularity and purpose of the capability notion, for many companies becoming capability-aware and being able to continuously and efficiently manage a large portfolio of capabilities is a very tedious task. To address this challenge, this study sets a foundation to leverage capability management by the means of a capability middleware broker and LLM support. The envisioned theoretical solution is exemplified by a real business case from the HE domain.

Keywords: Capability-driven design · Capability Map · LLM · Enterprise Modeling

1 Introduction

The idea of business capabilities emerged as organizations sought a business-focused way to define what an organization does, independent of its structure, technologies, or processes. They provide a clear enterprise framework that helps organizations to improve agility, and as such are becoming recognized as fundamental components to describe core business functionalities that fulfil business goals [1–3]; Capabilities support configurability according to changes in business context, with a focus on continuous result delivery by fulfilling goals and established KPIs [4]. E.g., capability "Energy Consumption Control" can be offered by various providers in different ways - as remote or local, and with different KPIs in relation to accuracy of control, or its pace.

Capabilities form the functional portfolio of a single organization or of a group of organizations collaborating in a business ecosystem; such a portfolio is called *capability map* [1]. Today, many organizations strive to organize their business to such a map. However, this effort is tedious, because it requires defining and modeling each capability

---

The original version of the chapter has been revised. The last name of the first author has been corrected. A correction to this chapter can be found at https://doi.org/10.1007/978-3-031-94590-8_39

and its related indicators (context and KPI), as well as relating it with similar capabilities, and finally placing it into the capability map. As a consequence, many companies do not manage to create the map, or if they do, the map often becomes static and underspecified in terms of supporting goals, KPIs and context of use.

With the proliferation of Generative AI [5] there is an emerging number of studies doing research on how LLMs can support system engineering. For example, the study [6] shows how an LLM can be used to increase quality and efficiency in model-driven enterprise engineering. Some recent studies focus to *semantic-driven system engineering*, and while emphasizing some deficiencies of LLM related to knowledge capture based on statistical instead of conceptual models, they also acknowledge the potential of their use for this purpose [7]. A recent study exercises this LLM role for unifying the knowledge on capability maps, i.e. their content building [8].

Our study aims for leveraging the entire cycle of capability management by the means of a LLM enabled middleware, i.e. *capability broker*. The main motivation for the study lies in the fact that organizational capabilities are typically underspecified; or they are specified in an unstructured, non-uniform or non-processable way that hinders organization's ability for their efficient management in terms of discovery, specification, deployment, and monitoring. To this end the purpose of the broker is to increase efficiency in the management of capabilities by augmenting human-based effort with automation and generative AI (i.e. LLM).

The rest of the paper is organized as follows. Section 2 gives a brief background to capability-driven design and capability maps. Section 3 presents the proposal for the architecture of the capability broker, and the way of its use. Section 4 elaborates the proposal on a business case. Concluding remarks are presented in Sect. 5.

2 Capability Driven Design and Capability Maps

Capability is the ability and capacity that enable an enterprise to achieve a business goal in a certain context [2]. A common practice for capability-aware organizations is to collect capabilities into a map, to represent a complete view of what the business does [1]. Capability maps are hierarchical i.e. they include several levels of capabilities (e.g. level 1, level 2, level 3…), where each level is a refinement of the previous one. At the top level, capabilities are typically highly stable. Lower levels capabilities are more operational and related with the IT applications supporting them. Each capability presented in the map has its internal design – it has specified how the capability will be delivered by processes, resources, and services to meet a goal and in which situation (context) is capability suitable to apply. These are the common aspects that capability design description covers and what is addressed by capability meta-models [9].

3 Capability Broker - Architecture and Use

3.1 Architecture

Figure 1 presents a high-level architecture of the capability broker with the focus on its main components - *assets* and *frontend*. The architecture is a centralized point for registering, discovering, executing and monitoring the capabilities in an organization, or an organization' unit context. The asset components of the capability broker include:

Capability Map: The component contains the hierarchical structure of the designed capabilities to give to the business unit a clear view of the available business functions. Following the theory of the map as presented in Sect. 2, we consider a practical way of working with capabilities. We assume that the majority of capabilities on the top (1) level are *known* and steady i.e. remain the same as long as the business model of the organization does not extend or shrink with respect to the domain. Differently, capabilities on the lower levels (2, 3,…) are more operational as they represent organization-specific ways of delivering the top-level capabilities, depending on the business context. These capabilities differentiate quality and performance related alternative, as well as organization's capabilities (internal) and capabilities that are supplied by external partners (outsourced). The capability map concept helps having an easy overview of capabilities; we extend it with context indicators and KPIs [2].

LLM Component: It is used (i) as the interactive assistance to the business analyst (i.e. expert) and (ii) for automated searching and managing capabilities for increasing the quality of capability management in any of the other components. The component links to the broker selected generic LLMs, as well as it can use an internal LLM, domain-specific and / or fine-tuned trained with organization-specific data; the Retrieval-Augmented Generation (RAG) can be used for optimizing the output of a LLM, by referencing a desired knowledge base such as *Capability Map*, or even some given external relevant capability sources, thus increasing the semantic quality of the search.

Capability Recommender (with Candidate Repository): This algorithmic component is used for finding the best-fit capability based on the requirements given by the expert (or a system) to the *Matching* component. The search is done from (i) *Capability Map*; or, (ii) LLM is, with the given input requirements, asked for proposals which are then placed in Candidate Repository for consideration to be designed and a status is set and followed (such as "for-design", "in-design", "dormant", "moved-to-map", etc.)

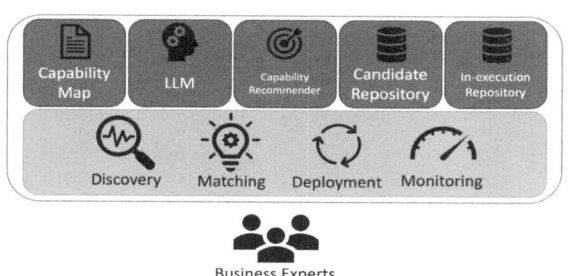

Fig.1. High-level architecture of the Capability Broker

The frontend components in Fig. 1 are to be used by the experts or external systems:

Matching. When the business unit needs to deliver a capability, it looks for its own capabilities or for the capabilities of the company's suppliers – in *Capability Map*. The expert is giving the requirements that may include: capability name, description of tasks, related context indicators, KPIs and business goals, for matching against the capabilities that are available in the map. This involves automated searching within the map for getting candidate capabilities where *Capability Recommender* calculates the fitness score showing how well a candidate supports the needed capability.

Discovery. When there is a need for a capability not existing in *Capability Map*, the expert seeks for candidate capabilities by: (i) searching in the *Candidate Repository* using the *Capability Recommender*, or by (ii) invoking the LLM component to generate or refine capability descriptions from raw business inputs: (a) document-based descriptions of capabilities (provided by suppliers, in Word, Excel, etc.) and b) online non-structured descriptions of offered functionalities from service-type websites.

Deployment (with *In-execution Repository*): After matching a capability in *Capability Map*, the capability will be (i) selected for the use, and (ii) registered as *in-execution* in the repository including all its resources (infrastructure, humans) that are described in the design model of the capability, and related KPIs and context indicators.

Monitoring (with In-execution Repository): This is the function that is: (i) scanning for new capabilities from the environment external to the broker, and (ii) tracing the conditions, performance, and the extent of use of the existing capabilities: for example, the "health" of the capabilities in execution and availability of the related resources. The component also provides the information on capabilities based on their status, such as "internal", "outsourced", "in-design", "deployed" etc.

3.2 Process of Use

The process of the capability broker's use for capability management is envisioned as Fig. 2 depicts it on a high-level - the use of the process steps depends on which state of advancement of the capability use the organization finds itself.

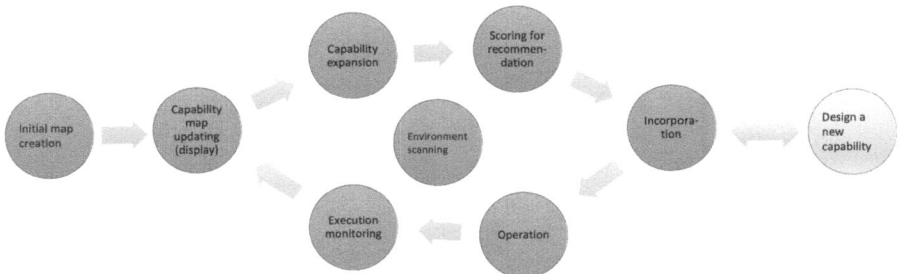

Fig. 2. Overview of the work process supported by the Capability Broker

Initial Map Creation: This task requires entering the organization's capability map into the broker. This can be done in two ways. If the organization does not have an explicit capability map, this task involves building an initial *Capability Map* in the broker. This starts with the business experts describing the abilities and capacities of their business units. The organization can also use the LLM component and enter its business descriptions as prompts to get suggestions for possible capabilities (and its indicators), i.e. the prompting could start already at level 1. Subsequent prompting can then be used to refine the level 1 capabilities at level 2 and into more detailed lower-level capabilities. If the organization has a capability map, then it needs to be entered into the broker i.e. for obtaining the machine-readable format, also unified from the perspective of use. Once completed, the described step does not need to be repeated, except when the structure or content of the map would require some major changes.

The rest of the steps are envisioned for frequent use:

Capability Map Display: This task provides the view of the existing capabilities to the expert for looking for a needed capability by browsing from higher to lower levels or by giving the input requirements to *Matching* that are processed by *Capability Recommender*; if the capability is found and its KPI and context indicators are satisfying to the expert, then the *Operation* step is initiated by *Deployment.*

Capability Expansion: The task enables identification of new capabilities when the capability is not found in the map. A request to find a capability that supports a needed business activity is given to *Discovery* by providing a brief description of the needed functionality (i.e. "study program management at university"), with or without the specification of the context indicators and KPIs (i.e. the study program level, max number of students, etc.) - providing these parameters contribute to increasing the relevance of the suggestions. *Capability Recommender* scans *Candidate Repository* for finding a match; if it is not found, prompting in the *LLM* component is initiated; if the human expert is satisfied with the proposal, the process moves to the next step.

Scoring for Recommendation: The expert defines capability needs in terms of KPIs and then asks for recommendations of capabilities that deliver the same KPIs from *Capability Recommender.* Each matching gets a fitness score [10] calculated; based on a satisfying score the capability candidate status changes to "for-design" or it discards.

Incorporation: The candidate capability needs to be designed in detail, i.e. its underlying process and needed resources (skills, infrastructure, etc.); the design is done outside of the broker, i.e. using model-based tools in the first place. Once designed, the capability is placed in *Capability Map* below the level of its parent capability.

Operation: Once the capability is moved to this process step, the *Deployment* component is activated and the capability starts executing. C.f. [4] for design of components for capability deployment and execution monitoring.

Execution monitoring: Using a dashboard, this step is showing the condition of the capabilities in execution using the *Monitoring* component for pooling the status of KPI and context indicators from the *In-execution Repository* (for example, for a study program a KPI is the targeted number of applicants while a context indicator may be percentage of an applicant segment, such as national); these values may be stored in the repository manually or automatically (if the indicator source is a sensor such as in manufacturing, or a computer log, such as of study administration). In case a KPI status drops below the defined value, or a context indicator is not satisfying, the dashboard indicates this and suggests that some additional capability should be activated.

Environment scanning: This task is envisioned for discovering new candidate capabilities by scanning the external environment - the *LLM* component searching in real time or on schedule for emerging or relevant business capabilities, that could potentially extend or enrich the organisation's current *Capability Map*. Specfically, the LLM component assists for (i) source scanning, classification, and relevance analysis (such as trend reports or academic sources), (ii) identify in the sources nouns and verbs indicating potential new capabilities, (iii) structure the findings according to capability attributes (name, description, etc.), and (iv) matching further to Candidate Repository.

4 Example Case

The example case concerns the management of study programs at a department of an international university. The authors consider themselves business experts for this case - they have more than 15 years of experience in leading several study programs as well as leading a large computer science department. The example focuses on a use of the LLM component in the broker: expert's design-thinking is mirrored by iterative prompting with GPT-4 as a dialog-based process where the expert provides a base prompt and asks an initial question, evaluates responses, and then refines results through follow-up prompts to complete the task:

> Prompt: *Capability is the ability and capacity that enable an enterprise to achieve a business goal in a certain context. Suggest capabilities for university study program management.*

It returned the following suggestions of capabilities on level 0: 1. Program Design & Development; 2. Student Enrollment & Admissions; 3. Course & Class Scheduling; 4. Student Performance & Assessment; 5. Faculty & Staff Management; 6. Student Support & Experience; 7. Digital Learning & Technology Integration; 8. Industry & Alumni Engagement; 9. Quality Assurance & Continuous Improvement; 10. Financial & Resource Management. Majority of the suggestions were relevant and corresponded to how the department operates. After detailed analysis, we decided that some of the suggested capabilities, such as capability 5 Faculty & Staff Management and capability 10. Financial & Resource Management are general to the whole department and are not to be included on this level. The resulting capability map is available in Fig. 3.

Then, the broker assisted the experts to expand the map by providing suggestions on more refined capabilities based on the level 0 capabilities. Due to the lack of space, we chose to elaborate only one capability - 2. Student Enrollment & Admissions. The broker was requested to provide more sub-capabilities of *"Application processing"* with related context indicators and business goals with the following prompt:

> Prompt: *One of the sub-capabilities of Student Enrollment & Admissions is "Application processing". Elaborate this sub-capability in more sub-capabilities. For each sub-capability specify context indicators and the business goals it supports.*

The output is visible in Table 1. One suggestion was not included, namely Data Management & Compliance Reporting, because it is considered an overarching capability of the university. Our assessment of the suggested context indicators is that they are reasonable and possible to implement.

To address a specific problem of admission of MSc students, we wanted to explore other options of additional selection criteria with the following prompt.

1. Program Design & Development	2. Student Enrollment & Admissions	3. Course & Class Scheduling	4. Student Performance & Assessment
Curriculum development & revision. Learning outcomes definition. Accreditation and compliance. Course catalog management.	Application processing. Admission criteria management. Enrollment tracking. Scholarship & financial aid processing. Tuition fee & payment processing.	Timetable planning. Faculty assignment. Classroom & resource allocation. Online & hybrid course integration.	Exam & grading management. Continuous assessment & feedback. Academic progress tracking. Learning analytics & reporting.
6. Student Support & Experience	7. Digital Learning & Technology Integration	8. Industry & Alumni Engagement	9. Quality Assurance & Continuous Improvement
Academic advising & mentoring. Career services & internships. Mental health & counseling services. Student feedback & grievance management.	Learning management system (LMS). Online & blended learning support. AI & adaptive learning technologies. Digital credentialing & e-transcripts.	Internship & industry collaboration. Alumni networking & events. Corporate research partnerships. Continuing education programs.	Program performance monitoring. Institutional benchmarking. Accreditation & compliance audits. Student & faculty satisfaction analysis.

Fig. 3. Initial capability map on level 0

Table 1. Sub-capabilities of Student Enrollment & Admission capability

Sub-Capability	Context Indicators	Business Goals Supported
2.1 Application Collection & Submission	Application volume trends, digital maturity, geographical diversity, accessibility	Increase application volume, enhance applicant experience, ensure accessibility
2.2 Application Eligibility Pre-Screening	Admission criteria complexity, automation capacity, data quality	Improve processing efficiency, maintain academic standards, reduce admin overhead
2.3 Application Review & Evaluation	Faculty availability, evaluation consistency, applicant quality trends	Select high-quality candidates, ensure fairness
2.4 Communication & Follow-Up	Applicant engagement, communication channel effectiveness, application cycle timeline	Enhance applicant satisfaction, increase completion rates, strengthen brand
2.5 Final Admission Decision & Offer	Admission quota, applicant pool competitiveness, offer acceptance trends	Optimize enrollment, select best-fit candidates, improve yield rates

Prompt: *Considering the sub-capabilities above, a key challenge of this department is that for the master program the admission office needs to review about 5000 applications coming from all over the world in a short time. Many of the applications are similarly competitive and selection based on grades is not sufficient. A suggestion would be to use university rank in Times Higher Education ranking as a criterion Please suggest sub-capability for this purpose and suggest context indicators and the business goals it supports.*

The suggestion was to introduce a new sub-capability: Application Prioritization Based on Institutional Reputation (Rank-Aware Screening). It provided a list of goals, context indicators, as well as process steps and criteria to use. These outputs were analyzed and used to generate the capability description in Table 2.

Table 2. Description of capability Application Prioritization Based on Institutional Reputation.

Context indicators	Business goals
Application volume Competitive applicant pool Global diversity Ranking data availability Time constraints Fairness policies Data integration readiness	Improve processing efficiency Enhance fairness & transparency Increase student quality Support internationalization Reduce administrative burden
Overview of the process: Fetch University Rank (e.g., from Times Higher Education API) Score application based on: Source university ranking band, GPA (normalized to university system if possible), Bonus points for outstanding motivation letters, work experience (optional automated scoring) Output: Ranked application list, categorized as: Tier 1 (High priority): High-ranked university + high GPA; Tier 2 (Medium priority): Mid-ranked university + good GPA. Tier 3 (Low priority): Lower-ranked university or lower GPA	
Decision Matrix for Application Scoring and Prioritization	

Criterion	Weight (%)	Scoring Explanation
Academic Performance	40%	Normalized GPA considering country/university system
University Rank (THE/Equivalent)	30%	Points assigned based on ranking band (e.g., Top 100 = 30 pts, 101–300 = 20 pts)
Motivation Letter / Statement of Purpose	15%	Quality of fit, career goals, and alignment with program focus
Work/Research Experience	10%	Relevant professional or academic projects, publications
Recommendation Letters	5%	Strength and credibility of recommendations

5 Conclusions

We have presented a novel information system, namely Capability Broker, the purpose of which is to support organizations in their work with business capabilities. We have discussed the system architecture components, key functionality areas and the way of working with such a capability broker. The proposed vision was exemplified by discussing an example of capability development for study program management. ChatGPT 4o was used to create examples of the interaction steps with the Capability Broker where support from a LLM is expected.

Concerning limitations of this study, except for LLM, we have not elaborated some other technologies envisioned for use in the broker, such as those used for storing the capabilities (i.e. architectural metadata repositories, vector databases, or other knowledge structures). Furthermore, the focus of this paper was not on evaluating LLM by different prompting strategies, rather using it to, by iterative prompting reflecting iterative design-thinking, assess its potential to support the business expert for working with capabilities and receiving suggestions for new ones. We believe more precise recommendations for capabilities and the components in their descriptions could be achieved by adding the capability meta-model and definitions through service prompts, which we, in parallel with developing an initial prototype for the broker, consider for near future work.

References

1. Ulrich, W., Rosen, M.: The business capability map: the 'Rosetta stone' of business/IT alignment. Enterprise Arch. **14/2** (2014)
2. Bērziša, S., et al.: Capability driven development: an approach to designing digital enterprises. Bus. Inf. Syst. Eng. **57**(1), 15–25 (2015). https://doi.org/10.1007/s12599-014-0362-0
3. Loucopoulos, P., Kavakli, E.: Capability oriented enterprise knowledge modeling: the CODEK approach. In: Karagiannis, D., Mayr, H., Mylopoulos, J. (eds.) Domain-Specific Conceptual Modeling. Springer, Cham (2016). https://doi.org/10.1007/978-3-319-39417-6_9
4. Sandkuhl, K., Stirna, J.: Capability Management in Digital Enterprises. Springer (2018)
5. Vaswani A., et al.: Attention is all you need. In: Advances in Neural Information Processing Systems, vol. 30 (2017)
6. Kolev, P.A., Pruss, H.H., Wilken, J.R., Sandkuhl, K.: Grass-root enterprise modelling: how large language models can help. In: Paja, E., Zdravkovic, J., Kavakli, E., Stirna, J. (eds.) The Practice of Enterprise Modeling. PoEM 2024. Lecture Notes in Business Information Processing, vol. 538. Springer, Cham (2025). https://doi.org/10.1007/978-3-031-77908-4_8
7. Buchmann, R., et al.: Large language models: expectations for semantics-driven systems engineering. Data Knowl. Eng. **152/6** (2024)
8. Samarasekara, I., Bandara, M., Rabhi, F., Benatallah, B., Meymandpour, R.: LLM driven approach for capability modelling with context-enriched prompt engineering. In: The Proceedings of ACIS Conference, AIS Electronic Library (2024)
9. Koutsopoulos, G., Henkel, M., Stirna, J.: An analysis of capability meta-models for expressing dynamic business transformation. Softw. Syst. Model. **20**(1), 147–174 (2021)
10. Chan, A., et al.: Towards a new method for designing manufacturing capabilities. In: Lupeikienė, A., Ralyté, J., Dzemyda, G. (eds.) Digital Business and Intelligent Systems. DB&IS 2024. Communications in Computer and Information Science, vol. 2157. Springer, Cham (2024). https://doi.org/10.1007/978-3-031-63543-4_3

CAiSE 2025 Forum – Tool Papers

MARTSIA: A Tool for Confidential Data Exchange via Public Blockchain

Michele Kryston[1,2](✉), Edoardo Marangone[1], Claudio Di Ciccio[2], Daniele Friolo[1], Eugenio Nerio Nemmi[1], Mattia Samory[1], Michele Spina[1], Daniele Venturi[1], and Ingo Weber[3]

[1] Sapienza University of Rome, Rome, Italy
kryston.1844733@studenti.uniroma1.it, edoardo.marangone@uniroma1.it
[2] Utrecht University, Utrecht, The Netherlands
{m.kryston,c.diciccio}@uu.nl
[3] School of CIT, Technical University of Munich and Fraunhofer Gesellschaft, Munich, Germany
ingo.weber@tum.de

Abstract. Blockchain technology streamlines multi-party collaborations in decentralized settings, especially when trust is limited or difficult to establish. While public blockchains enhance transparency and reliability by replicating data across all network nodes, they also conflict with confidentiality. Here, we introduce Multi-Authority Approach to Transaction Systems for Interoperating Applications (MARTSIA) to address this challenge. MARTSIA provides fine-grained read-access control at the message-part level by combining user-defined policies with certifier-declared attributes. The approach guarantees that even though data is replicated across the network to maintain consistency, fault tolerance, and availability, its confidentiality is securely preserved through encryption. To this end, MARTSIA integrates blockchain technologies, Multi-Authority Attribute-Based Encryption, and distributed hash-table file storages. This architecture effectively balances the transparency inherent in public blockchains with the privacy required for sensitive applications. We present the tool and its applicability in a business scenario.

Keywords: Business Process Management · Blockchain Technology · Multi-Authority Attribute Based Encryption · InterPlanetary File System · Ciphertext Policy

1 Introduction

The emergence of blockchain technology has reshaped secure and transparent interactions among untrusted parties [10]. This technology provides security, ensured by cryptography; resilience, achieved through the decentralization of network nodes; and transparency, as anyone can verify past transactions recorded in the ledger. Public blockchain protocols strengthen these guarantees at scale, as they resort to an open peer-to-peer network, where data is replicated across all nodes, improving its availability and integrity. In modern business environments, these blockchain properties offer significant advantages over traditional e-business models, which for decades have relied on centralized databases and intermediaries to safeguard trust and enforce processes. Centralized systems excel in effectiveness although they suffer in several aspects such as single points of failure, susceptibility to data breaches and inefficiencies in data reconciliation between multiple parties. Public blockchains typically entail non-negligible operational costs and additional processing times due to their decentralized nature, but these aspects are often compensated by the security and transparency they guarantee. As a result, blockchain technology has experienced increasing adoption in information systems within enterprise domains over the last few years [9]. Nevertheless, full data transparency may pose a problem in multi-party business settings wherein sensitive information needs to be kept confidential between involved participants [4,13].

To overcome this issue, we bridge the silos of blockchain technologies and encryption with information systems engineering. In this paper, we present the tool implementation of Multi-Authority Approach to Transaction Systems for Interoperating Applications (MARTSIA) [6], a fully decentralized framework providing confidential information sharing through public blockchain technologies, Multi-Authority Attribute-Based Encryption (MA-ABE), and distributed hash-table file storages. Inspired by the Control Access via Key Encryption (CAKE) approach [7], MARTSIA enhances decentralization by removing CAKE's central nodes needed for data encryption and decryption.

The paper proceeds as follows. In Sect. 2, we discuss the underlying technologies of the framework, while Sect. 3 introduces a running example. In Sect. 4, we present its features by depicting the application of MARTSIA in the running example. Section 5 evaluates the maturity of the framework, assessing its versions and readiness for deployment. In Sect. 6, we review related work in the literature, placing MARTSIA in the context of existing solutions. Finally, Sect. 7 concludes the paper and proposes directions for future research and development.

2 Background

Before delving into our approach, in this section we discuss its building blocks.

A **blockchain** is a decentralized and distributed ledger that stores transactions securely and tamper-resistantly. Transactions are stored in blocks linked to the previous one, forming a chain. This structure ensures transparency, security, and immutability of recorded information. Most blockchains, such as Ethereum,[1] are additionally featured with the ability to execute code, namely **smart contracts**, in a decentralized manner through virtual machines, thus allowing complex protocols to be built at an application layer.

The cost of performing a transaction primarily depends on the amount of information being stored and, in the case of a smart contract, on the computational effort required for execution. For this reason, users often leverage additional technologies, such as distributed hash-table file storages, to store large

---
[1] https://ethereum.org/, accessed: 2025-03-12.

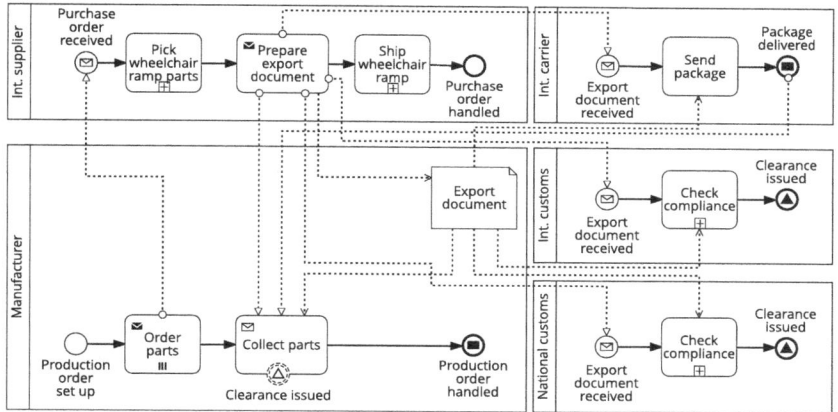

Fig. 1. A segment of the collaboration diagram illustrating the control and data flow of the process

amounts of data. An example is **InterPlanetary File System (IPFS)**. As on public blockchains, data stored on IPFS are decentralized and transparent, making them accessible to anyone. IPFS allows data retrieval via content-addressed locators, e.g., the hash of the stored data. In this way, a single-byte difference between two data generates a completely different locator. These locators can then be stored on the blockchain to benefit from its properties.

Access to data stored on IPFS can be restricted to specific users through the application of **Attribute-Based Encryption (ABE)**. ABE, a public-key encryption scheme, links encrypted data with corresponding decryption keys via attributes. One type of ABE is Ciphertext-Policy Attribute-Based Encryption (CP-ABE), where each user is associated with attributes and data are encrypted using policies, e.g., logical formulas built upon user attributes. However, CP-ABE relies on a single authority to generate user decryption keys. MA-ABE [1] overcomes this limitation by improving decentralization. In MA-ABE, multiple authorities generate partial decryption keys. The user who requests the partial keys can merge them, obtaining a complete key to decrypt the data.

3 Running Example

In this section, we introduce a running example that we will use throughout the paper to provide a clearer explanation of MARTSIA.

Figure 1 depicts a Business Process Model and Notation (BPMN) collaboration diagram illustrating a fragment of a supply-chain process in the automotive sector: the production of a custom car for an individual with paraplegia. In this fragment of the process, the Manufacturer proceeds to acquire the necessary ramp components for the cars if they are unavailable; in this situation, the Manufacturer orders them from an International supplier. International customs supervises the international transit of goods, while National customs supervises

Table 1. The Export document in clear, sent by the International supplier

Slice	Recipients	Data	Policy

1	Manufacturer
	Nat. customs
	Int. customs
	Int. carrier
		Manufacturer:Beta
		Delivery: 8, B Lane
		E-mail: b@mail.com
		Ramp run: 3
		Kickplate: 12
		Amount_paid: $5000
			Customs@A or
			((Supplier@C and
			  International@B) or
			Manufacturer@A or
			(Carrier@B and
			  International@C))

2	Nat. customs Int. customs	Workers_rights: Ok Human_rights: Ok Ecosys_protection: Ok	Customs@A or (Supplier@D and International@B)
3	Manufacturer	Manufacturer:Beta Address: 8, B Lane Reference: 26487	(Supplier@2+ and International@B) or Manufacturer@A
4	Manufacturer Nat. customs Int. customs	Invoice_ID: 101711 Billing: 5, G Lane Gross_total: $5000 Company_VAT: U12345678 Issue_date: 2022-05-12	Customs@A or ((Supplier@C and International@B) or Manufacturer@A)

the national transit. Both dispense Customs clearance. Thereafter, the International carrier ships the goods to the Manufacturer. We will focus on the Export document in Fig. 1, which comprises multiple records, presented in Table 1 as four distinct slices. Given a single sender, the International supplier, we have different recipients for each slice: the Manufacturer, the National customs, the International customs, and the International carrier.

4 Innovations and Features

In this section, we explain the components and operations of MARTSIA considering the example described in Sect. 3.

Figure 2 outlines the general architecture of MARTSIA. Our solution provides three main functionalities: *(i)* **Store actor metadata**, assigning attributes to users. Considering our example, the chosen attributes designated to match the actors' names are: Supplier, Manufacturer, Customs, and Carrier. Furthermore, we introduce the International attribute. The International supplier, the International customs, and the International carrier are thus characterized by the conjunction of the International attribute with Supplier, Customs, and Carrier, respectively; *(ii)* **Store encrypted data**, applying a policy expressed as a propositional formula built upon users' attributes, thereby restricting access only to authorized actors. Table 1 outlines the policies governing read access to the Export document; *(iii)* **Read encrypted data**, accessing and decrypting data if the requester's attributes satisfy the access policy. In the example, column *Data* in Table 1 shows the decrypted data. These three functionalities include the support of other tasks (depicted in grey in the figure) we explain next.

Our solution employs three fundamental components: *(ii)* the **Certification Manager** records the attributes the users hold in a collaborative process; *(ii)* the **Data Manager** encrypts and stores data; and the *(iii)* **Key Manager** generates partial decryption keys derived from the user's attributes. The user merges these partial decryption keys into a single key to read encrypted data.

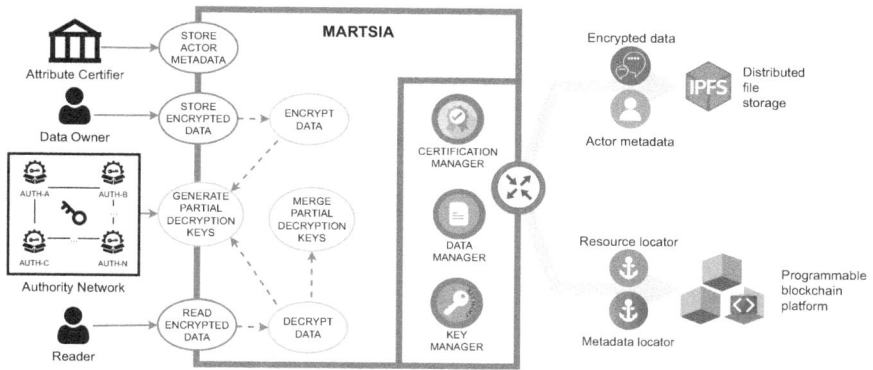

Fig. 2. An overview of the MARTSIA architecture

Four main classes of actors are involved in the interaction: *(i)* the **Attribute Certifier** deploys the smart contracts, and assigns and stores the actors' metadata; *(ii)* the **Data Owner** encrypts, determines reading access to the data, and stores it for sharing. In our example, this role is played by the International supplier, who encrypts the Export document; *(iii)* the **Reader** interested in reading the shared data. In the example, this role is fulfilled by the International supplier and the Recipients in Table 1; *(iv)* the **Authority Network** generates partial decryption keys tailored to the Reader's attributes. Henceforth, we assume that the network consists of four Authorities: A, B, C, and D.

Due to the costs associated with storing data directly on the blockchain, MARTSIA stores on InterPlanetary File System (IPFS)[2] the encrypted data and the actors' metadata, along with additional information. Smart contracts on the blockchain are employed to record IPFS locators, ensuring data integrity. Consequently, although anyone can access the public ledger, it cannot discern information about the encrypted data, the Data Owners, or the Readers. Confidentiality with recipients is preserved by uniquely denoting each process instance with an identifier. This identifier, automatically added to the policies by MARTSIA, is used to characterize the actors involved, thereby limiting the range of potential Readers. The Data Owner must specify the Authorities responsible for validating each policy. Considering the running example in Sect. 3, the complete access policy of the third slice in Table 1 reads as follows: (43175279@4+ and ((Supplier@2+ and International@B) or Manufacturer@A)). In this case: the process instance 43175279 needs to be verified by all the Authorities, the attribute Supplier by at least two, attribute International by Authority B, and attribute Manufacturer by Authority A. This policy specifies that the International supplier (the sender) and the Manufacturer involved in process instance 43175279 can access this slice. A detailed explanation of the policies and their grammar can be found in [5].

---

[2] https://ipfs.tech/, accessed: 2025-03-12.

Following the encryption phase, the International supplier uploads the document to IPFS through MARTSIA. The corresponding IPFS resource locator (e.g., `Qmb4Hz[...]CAd8iG`) is then stored on the blockchain and associated with a unique *message ID*. Since the Export document includes multiple slices for various recipients, each record has also a unique *slice ID*. To obtain the decryption key, a Reader must request all the partial decryption keys to the Authorities. The Authorities generate these partial keys using the Reader's metadata retrieved from the blockchain. Then, the Reader assembles the key parts, obtaining the final key necessary to read the encrypted data. To retrieve them, we have implemented secure channels resorting to TLS (direct) and RSA (via blockchain). In our example, if the Manufacturer intends to read the third slice of the Export document (Table 1), they must request the decryption keys to all the Authorities. If the Manufacturer is involved in the process instance 43175279 and possesses the correct `Manufacturer` attribute, they meet the policy requirements for decryption. In contrast, the National customs, which only holds the `Customs` attribute, does not meet the access policy and is consequently unable to decrypt the content. An actor lacking authorization from all the Authorities cannot decrypt the data. Although different Authorities collaborate in validating the policy's formulae, the record can be decrypted only by the requesting actor.

Here, we can derive a core feature of MARTSIA. Multiple Readers read distinct slices out of a single encrypted data object. Therefore, one message can be generated for multiple Readers interested in separate parts of it, rather than sending a copy for each such part, at the risk of potential inconsistency and communication overhead. In our example, we have one Export document sliced into four parts, accessible by four, two, one, and three participants, respectively. However, the message remains one, rather than being spread across ten replicas.

5 Maturity

In this section, we describe the current state of the MARTSIA tool.

We implemented MARTSIA in two different variants, to show its platform-independence. Its smart contracts run on the Ethereum Virtual Machine (EVM) and the Algorand Virtual Machine (AVM). Smart contracts are written in Solidity v. 0.8.20 for EVM and PyTeal v. 0.20.0 for AVM. All other scripts are encoded in Python, including the integration with IPFS. The source code and documentation with implementation details are available at github.com/apwbs/MARTSIA. Among other things, the tool also includes additional features such as the possibility to use multiple Attribute Certifiers employing multi-signature operations, and the customizability of the communication means to exchange partial decryption keys (either direct, via TLS channels, or indirect, via blockchain). Furthermore, we include the input data, launching scripts, and experimental results of performance tests run on different EVM blockchains to verify transaction costs and latency, and a Wiki offering a step-by-step tutorial on system setup and operation. To demonstrate MARTSIA's versatility across key domains, we integrated and tested our prototype with three publicly available DApps from different domains: NFT trading, supply-chain management, and retail [5].

The scripts and Wiki to reproduce this demo for the EVM version are available at github.com/apwbs/MARTSIA-Demo. For a brief video showcase, visit youtube.com/watch?v=RAcifWw1_B0.

6 Related Work

In recent years, blockchain technology has experienced significant developments due to its distinctive properties, sparking growing interest in solutions to ensure data confidentiality. Zou et al. [14] propose SPChain, a system built upon blockchain to guarantee privacy and effortless sharing of medical data. This is achieved through a proxy re-encryption scheme and local databases of medical institutions. Gan et al. [3] present a search method for encrypted medical data stored on a blockchain, resorting to an access control mechanism. Their architecture relies on: a consortium blockchain built on Ethereum for experimental analysis; several encryption methods such as probabilistic encryption and order-preserving encryption; and a non-relational database to store data. Remaining in the medical field, Miyachi and Mackey [8] introduce a framework for data privacy based on both on-chain and off-chain systems. They leverage consortium blockchains and asymmetric cryptography, while storing data off-chain. Unlike [3,8,14], MARTSIA operates on public blockchains to store IPFS locators, encrypts sensitive information with MA-ABE, and stores data on IPFS.

Yan et al. [12] illustrate a scheme providing fine access control with low computational consumption. Their work leverages blockchain to store metadata, IPFS to store data, and proxies for encryption and decryption. In addition, their scheme provides policy hiding and attribute revocation. However, two centralized entities are employed: the Proxy encryption server (ES) and the Proxy decryption server (DS). Wu et al. [11] in their work present an efficient attribute-based encryption scheme to ensure privacy. Their method leverages the blockchain for non-repudiation and data integrity. Feng et al. [2] introduce a scheme utilizing blockchain for data storage; and identity-based encryption (IBE) and attribute-based encryption (ABE) for sharing and verifying the correctness of data. In their scheme, there is a centralized entity called Private Key Generator that takes care of the setup phase and attribute key generation. In contrast to [2,11,12], our solution utilizes a decentralized attribute-based encryption scheme.

7 Conclusion and Future Work

In this paper, we introduced MARTSIA, a framework leveraging blockchain and MA-ABE to control data access in multi-party business scenarios. Our approach resorts to IPFS to store encrypted data and actors' metadata, and to smart contracts to link IPFS resource locators to the blockchain. MARTSIA guarantees access control, data reliability, immutability, and auditability in a decentralized manner. Areas for future development include data access revocation through InterPlanetary Name System (IPNS), automatic policy validation, conducting robustness field tests, and expanding the policy language to open the door to secure data calculations using TEEs.

Acknowledgments. This work was partly funded by projects SERICS (PE00000014) under the NRRP MUR program funded by the EU-NGEU, PINPOINT (B87G22000450001) under the PRIN MUR program, and Healt-e-Data, funded by the EU-NGEU under the Cyber 4.0 NRRP MIMIT programme.

References

1. Chase, M.: Multi-authority attribute based encryption. In: Vadhan, S.P. (ed.) TCC 2007. LNCS, vol. 4392, pp. 515–534. Springer, Heidelberg (2007). https://doi.org/10.1007/978-3-540-70936-7_28
2. Feng, T., Wang, D., Gong, R.: A blockchain-based efficient and verifiable attribute-based proxy re-encryption cloud sharing scheme. Information **14**(5), 281 (2023)
3. Gan, C., Yang, H., Zhu, Q., Zhang, Y., Saini, A.: An encrypted medical blockchain data search method with access control mechanism. Inf. Process. Manag. **60**(6), 103499 (2023)
4. Köpke, J., Necemer, M.: Measuring the effects of confidants on privacy in smart contracts. In: BPM (Blockchain and RPA Forum), vol. 459, pp. 84–99 (2022)
5. Marangone, E., Di Ciccio, C., Friolo, D., Nemmi, E.N., Venturi, D., Weber, I.: Enabling data confidentiality with public blockchains. CoRR arxiv:2308.03791 (2023)
6. Marangone, E., Di Ciccio, C., Friolo, D., Nemmi, E.N., Venturi, D., Weber, I.: MARTSIA: enabling data confidentiality for blockchain-based process execution. In: EDOC. vol. 14367, pp. 58–76 (2023)
7. Marangone, E., Di Ciccio, C., Weber, I.: Fine-grained data access control for collaborative process execution on blockchain. In: BPM (Blockchain and RPA Forum), vol. 459, pp. 51–67 (2022)
8. Miyachi, K., Mackey, T.: hOCBS: a privacy-preserving blockchain framework for healthcare data leveraging an on-chain and off-chain system design. Inf. Process. Manag. **58**(3), 102535 (2021)
9. Stiehle, F., Weber, I.: Blockchain for business process enactment: a taxonomy and systematic literature review. In: BPM (Blockchain and RPA Forum), vol. 459, pp. 5–20 (2022)
10. Weber, I., Xu, X., Riveret, R., Governatori, G., Ponomarev, A., Mendling, J.: Untrusted business process monitoring and execution using blockchain. In: La Rosa, M., Loos, P., Pastor, O. (eds.) BPM 2016. LNCS, vol. 9850, pp. 329–347. Springer, Cham (2016). https://doi.org/10.1007/978-3-319-45348-4_19
11. Wu, A., Zhang, Y., Zheng, X., Guo, R., Zhao, Q., Zheng, D.: Efficient and privacy-preserving traceable attribute-based encryption in blockchain. Ann. Telecommun., 401–411 (2019). https://doi.org/10.1007/s12243-018-00699-y
12. Yan, L., Ge, L., Wang, Z., Zhang, G., Xu, J., Hu, Z.: Access control scheme based on blockchain and attribute-based searchable encryption in cloud environment. J. Cloud Comput. **12**(1), 61 (2023)
13. Zhang, R., Xue, R., Liu, L.: Security and privacy on blockchain. ACM Comput. Surv. **52**(3), 51:1–51:34 (2019)
14. Zou, R., Lv, X., Zhao, J.: SPChain: blockchain-based medical data sharing and privacy-preserving ehealth system. Inf. Process. Manag. **58**(4), 102604 (2021)

AOAME: An Enterprise Knowledge Graphs Editor for Domain Experts

Emanuele Laurenzi(✉)

FHNW University of Applied Sciences and Arts Northwestern Switzerland,
Riggenbachstr. 16, 4600 Olten, Switzerland
emanuele.laurenzi@fhnw.ch

Abstract. The creation and maintenance of Enterprise Knowledge Graphs (EKGs) are knowledge-intensive tasks that require both ontology and domain expertise. AOAME is a modeling tool that supports these tasks by enabling domain experts to create and maintain EKGs through meta-modeling and modeling. This paper describes the foundational approach and mechanisms underlying AOAME for creating and maintaining knowledge graphs from graphical models. AOAME has enabled the development of applications that support the creation of ontology-based models across various domains and is also used for teaching purposes at universities. Unlike other knowledge graph editors, AOAME does not require ontology expertise and ensures consistency between domain-specific graphical models and knowledge graphs, even when changes are made to either.

Keywords: Knowledge graph editor · Ontology-based models · AOAME

1 Introduction

Enterprise models contain relevant knowledge of a specific enterprise reality. Their graphical notation allows the human interpretation of the knowledge [1]. A business process model, for example, enables stakeholders to achieve a shared understanding of a particular business process. It can be used as a basis for discussions to understand and analyze a situation, to compare it with alternatives, and to find potential improvements. Models can also be processed by machines. For example, workflow engines parse BPMN process models to assign tasks to humans or machines. Taking this a step further, when models are represented using an ontology formalism [2], they can support automatic reasoning.

Enterprise Knowledge Graphs (EKGs) are lightweight ontologies that describe enterprise-relevant concepts, typically represented using W3C standards such as RDF(S)[1]. Recent developments in AI-particularly the rise of Large Language Models (LLMs)-have further increased the relevance of EKGs, which are now increasingly used to supplement LLMs with structured domain knowledge [3].

---
[1] https://www.w3.org/TR/rdf-schema/.

However, the creation of EKGs is highly challenging, as it requires both domain and ontology expertise. To address this issue, this paper presents an ontology-based modelling environment (AOAME) that transforms enterprise models into knowledge graphs during their design and adaptation. The proposed tool instantiates the agile and ontology-based meta-modeling approach introduced in [4]. It supports several modeling languages, including BPMN, ArchiMate, and various domain-specific modeling languages developed over the years through research projects.

The remainder of the paper is structured as follows. Section 2 presents the problem description and related work. Section 3 illustrates the proposed approach, detailing the architecture of the artefact, the set of ontologies, and their relationships. Section 4 describes the operators and mechanisms used to transform graphical models into corresponding knowledge graphs. Finally, Sect. 5 concludes the paper.

2 Problem Description and Related Work

The combination of enterprise graphical models and ontologies is discussed in literature and can be grouped into two main approaches: *semantic lifting* [5–7] and *ontology-based modeling* [8,9].

Semantic lifting adds ontological annotations to existing enterprise models or meta-models. For example, Fill [10] adds ontological annotations to business process models. In [11] an ontology is used to detect early warning signals in the procurement risk management. Semantic lifting keeps the graphical and ontological representations separate, thus potentially causing inconsistencies between the two if either representation is modified. The alignment of both is a knowledge-intensive manual task that may be prone to errors and may require considerable effort [4]. In real-world scenarios this problem is amplified as enterprises are subject to frequent changes which require changes of the enterprise models and the corresponding ontology.

Mechanisms for the automatic transformation of models into ontologies strive to relieve this effort. Buchmann et al. [12] focus on legacy data sources containing domain-specific graphical models and export them into ontologies to make them queryable in a Linked Data environment. Gailly et al. [13] automatically annotate models using enterprise ontologies. Although the automatic transformation relieves the manual annotation issue, the consistency problem remains because of the two separate knowledge representations. In fact, the class structure of the ontology must be aligned with the meta-model of the graphical modeling language before model transformation.

The ontology-based meta-modeling paradigm resolves the consistency problem by integrating the two representations. Specifically, it replaces the meta-model with an ontology, where ontology concepts in the meta-level are supplemented with graphical notations and then instantiated in a model [8]. In [4] the ontology-based meta-modeling is further expanded to be used in domain-specific modeling adaptation. As an implementation of this approach, the AOAME tool ensures consistency between the graphical and the machine-interpretable knowledge, even when the modeling language is extended or adapted.

The work presented in this paper builds on the ontology-based meta-modeling paradigm to ensure consistency between graphical enterprise models and their corresponding ontologies. To support this, the AOAME model editor has been extended with CRUD (Create, Read, Update, Delete) operations and semantic mechanisms. As a result, modelers are empowered to create or adapt ontologies through enterprise models, while knowledge and data engineers can use these ontologies as a foundation for building an enterprise knowledge base that can, in turn, be visualized as graphical models. The semantic mechanisms also ensure that any changes made to the ontology models are automatically reflected in the graphical models.

3 Software Architecture of AOAME and Ontologies

The software architecture of AOAME follows a three-tier architecture:

(1) Apache Jena Fuseki is a triplestore with which we retain ontologies expressed in Resource Description Framework Schema RDF(S), thereby enabling the use of the 13 RDF(S) entailments for reasoning purposes. These entailments are particularly useful for two reasons: (a) model instances inherit the properties of the language constructs, and (b) class-instance mappings are made explicit not only for the defined classes but also for their superclasses, thereby enriching the semantic representation. For example, an instance of the class BPMN Service Task is also recognized as an instance of the classes Task, Activity and Flow Object. Additional reasoning services we use in AOAME consist of validating RDF(S)-based graphical models against SHACL[2] constraints; however, this approach is not detailed in the current paper.

(2) The graphical user interface displays modeling languages and enables the creation of models. It is an Angular application that integrates the canvas library written in JavaScript, goJS (gojs.net).

(3) The web service is a JEE application which implements the logic to fetch the ontologies and to propagate changes in the modeling languages and models from the user interface to the triple store.

A video showcasing the use of AOAME can be found in[3]. An online version of AOAME is available on GitHub[4] and can be deployed locally following the instructions reported at[5].

3.1 AOAME Ontologies

The definition of modeling languages proposed by [14] serves as the foundational theory for the structuring of notation, abstract syntax, and semantics.

---

[2] https://www.w3.org/TR/shacl/.
[3] https://tube.switch.ch/videos/mNnKBxJb8s.
[4] https://aoame.herokuapp.com.
[5] https://shorturl.at/5Ok4Q.

The tool AOAME instantiates this theoretical specification by distinguishing between three types of ontologies: the Palette Ontology for graphical notation, the Meta-Model Ontology for abstract syntax, and the Domain Ontology for specifying additional semantics.

The Model Ontology is introduced with the prefix "mod" to complement the existing ontologies. Its purpose is to describe the concepts and relations associated with the instantiated model and its elements. Instances from the Model Ontology inherit properties from concepts of the aforementioned three ontologies.

The main concepts in the Model Ontology are the following three:

(a) Conceptual elements instantiate concepts from the Meta-Model Ontology.
(b) Shape elements instantiate concepts from the Palette Ontology; Shape elements are mapped to conceptual elements because they associate a graphical notation to an element.
(c) The Model concept serves as a container for model elements and is linked with shape elements because a model shall display graphical elements.

Consistent with the argumentation of [15], the visual aspect of the model element should be separated from its conceptual counterpart. The visualizations, or shapes, encapsulate model-specific information such as the displayed image, positioning, scaling, and labels. Following this concept, a model element is represented as two instances in the Model Ontology, each referencing the other. To instantiate a Shape, it is typed as *mod:Shape* and is related to the Palette Ontology through *mod:shape-Instantiates-Palette-Construct*. The property *mod:shape-Visualises-Conceptual-Element* references the Conceptual Element. To describe visual information, a Shape instance has presentation properties (coordinates, height and width of the displayed symbol, and the label) and the property *mod:shapeRepresents-Model* that allows relating the Shape to another model. The second part of the model element, the instance known as the Conceptual Element, serves as the source subject for this relation. This relation is established via *rdf:type*, indicating that the model element is an instance of a class. To instantiate a conceptual element, it is typed as *mod:Conceptual-Element*. The use of the type relation allows the model element to inherit properties defined in the concepts of the meta-model. Consistent with [4], the constructs in the abstract syntax ontology have a mapping to the constructs in the domain ontology describing the semantics. In AOAME, this relation is implemented by the object property *lo:element Is Mapped With DO Concept* with a concept of the Meta-Model Ontology as its domain and a concept of the Domain Ontology as its range [4].

4 From Graphical Models to Knowledge Graphs

The visual and ontology knowledge representations are kept consistent by operators and subsequent semantic mechanisms. The creation and implementation of the operators in AOAME followed the methodological approach described in [16].

4.1 Operators

The following operators have been derived from common conceptual modeling activities and then implemented as APIs within AOAMEs Java WebService component.

The *Create Model* operator is used to initialize an empty model that serves as a container for subsequent operations. It implements the *Create a model* operation from the set of basic modeling operations.

The *Create Model Element* operator creates any model elements except connectors. To construct both the visual and conceptual parts of the element, it receives a reference to the concept in the Palette Ontology that the user intends to instantiate. The meta-model mapping then provides the corresponding concept from the Meta-Model Ontology to instantiate the conceptual element. The instantiation type-whether as a class or an instance-is specified by a parameter of the operator. Finally, visual management information such as coordinates and a UUID is received from the canvas library. This operator implements the basic modeling operations *Create a model element*, *Model A can include elements of Model B*, and *The user can choose to instantiate classes as instances*.

The *Create Connection* operator is a specialization of the *Create Model Element* operator. In addition to the model element, it requires both the target and source elements for the connection. This operator implements the situations *Connect two model elements* and *The user can choose to instantiate classes as instances*.

The *Delete Model* operator clears data in the ontology. It directly depends on the *Delete Model Element* operator to remove its elements.

The *Delete Model Element* operator deletes model elements, including both their shapes and conceptual elements. A shape is always deleted, whereas a conceptual element is only deleted if no other shape is referencing it. This operator implements the situation *Delete a model element or connection*.

The *Update Model Element* operator is the most complex operator, as it requires numerous read and write queries for different parts of the model elements and their relationships in various ontologies. It receives the new representation of the model element, including the relations of the conceptual part, as input. A read operation fetches the current representation, a delete operation clears it, and a write operation creates the nodes and relations for the new representation of the model element. Being the most complex operator, it also implements the most modeling situations: *Position the model element, Scale the shape of the model element, Label the model element, Add a note to the model element, An element can represent a model, An element A can be declared the same as element B from a different modeling language, An element can overwrite inherited attributes from the meta-model, The visualization for a model element can be changed*, and *Elements of a model can be placed into containers*.

The operator *Meta-Model: Delete sub-class* already exists in AOAME. It is updated with restrictions to ensure that no concepts in the meta-model can be deleted, which have been instantiated in one of the models.

4.2 Semantic Mechanisms

For the sake of brevity, Fig. 1 illustrates only the update for creating a model element. This is invoked by the operator *Create Model Element*. The operator generates the model element and returns its updated representation in the ontology.

As input, the operator requires the identifier of the Palette Ontology concept (e.g., po:Task), the coordinates, and the ID of the shape.

```
INSERT {
    mod:Task_203184e1        rdf:type ?type .
    mod:Task_203184e1        rdf:type mod:ConceptualElement .
    mod:Task_203184e1        lo:elementIsMappedWithDOConcept ?concept .
    mod:Task_Shape_b0a1b81f  rdf:type mod:Shape .
    mod:Task_Shape_b0a1b81f  mod:shapePositionsOnCoordinateX 0 .
    mod:Task_Shape_b0a1b81f  mod:shapePositionsOnCoordinateY 0 .
    mod:Task_Shape_b0a1b81f  mod:shapeHasHeight ?height .
    mod:Task_Shape_b0a1b81f  mod:shapeHasWidth ?width .
    mod:Task_Shape_b0a1b81f  mod:shapeInstantiatesPaletteConstruct po:Task .
    mod:Task_Shape_b0a1b81f  mod:shapeVisualisesConceptualElement mod:Task_203184e1 .
    mod:Task_Shape_b0a1b81f  rdfs:label "Task" .
    mod:Model_99b74b9e       mod:modelHasShape mod:Task_Shape_b0a1b81f .
} WHERE {
    po:Task po:paletteConstructIsRelatedToModelingLanguageConstruct ?type .
    po:Task po:paletteConstructHasHeight ?height .
    po:Task po:paletteConstructHasWidth ?width .
    OPTIONAL { ?type lo:elementIsMappedWithDOConcept ?concept }
}
```

Fig. 1. Update to create a model element including a shape and a conceptual element

4.3 User Interface and Results

The aforementioned operators are implemented as Java methods within the web service and are invoked from the user interface. For example, Fig. 2 shows the user interface using BPMN 2.0 as the modeling language. Here, the user instantiates a 'bpmn:Task' with the element 'Create Invoice'. As soon as the instantiation

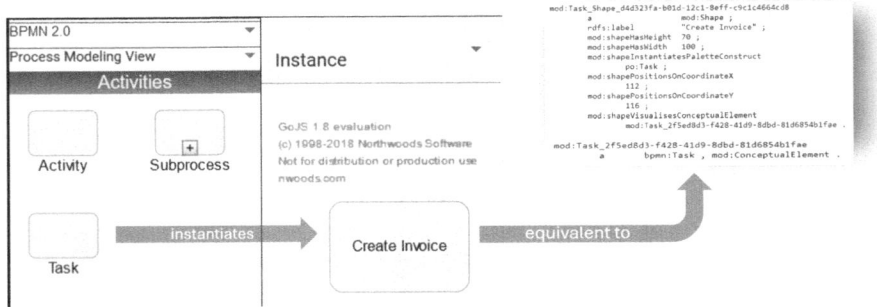

Fig. 2. Creating a model element in the UI

occurs, a SPARQL update[6] is triggered to generate the corresponding RDF triples.

The JavaScript library implementing the canvas is goJS[7].

The ontology-based modeling approach has already been validated in various domains, with two of the most recent being building energy management systems [17] and IoT applications [18].

5 Conclusion

This paper presents an ontology-based modeling approach, implemented in the tool AOAME, which allows the creation of knowledge graphs in RDF(S) from enterprise models.

A set of modeling operators has been implemented in AOAME to apply changes from the graphical model to the knowledge graph. For this, semantic mechanisms in the form of SPARQL updates were incorporated into the modeling operators. Finally, the new operators were implemented in the user interface of AOAME to enable the modeler to create and maintain ontology-based models.

AOAME is open-source software licensed under the GPL-3.0. It is currently used for both research and teaching purposes at the University of Applied Sciences and Arts Northwestern Switzerland and the University of Camerino (UNI-CAM), Italy.

Current limitations of AOAME include a modeling user experience that lacks smoothness, and the need for additional engineering effort whenever a new modeling language-one not already represented as an ontology-must be supported. These enhancement needs are left for future work.

References

1. Fox, M.S., Gruninger, M.: Enterprise modeling. AI Mag. **19**(3), 109 (1998)
2. Guarino, N.: Formal ontology and information systems. In: FOIS, Trento, pp. 6–8. IOS Press, Amsterdam (1998)
3. Buchmann, R., et al.: Large language models: expectations for semantics-driven systems engineering. Data Knowl. Eng. **152**, 102324 (2024)
4. Laurenzi, E.: An agile and ontology-based meta-modelling approach for the design and maintenance of enterprise knowledge graph schemas. In: Enterprise Modelling and Information Systems Architectures (EMISAJ), vol. 19 (2024)
5. Azzini, A., Braghin, C., Damiani, E., Zavatarelli, F.: Using semantic lifting for improving process mining: a data loss prevention system case study. In: SIMPDA, pp. 62–73. Citeseer (2013)
6. Hrgovcic, V., Karagiannis, D., Woitsch, R.: Conceptual modeling of the organisational aspects for distributed applications: the semantic lifting approach. In: 2013 IEEE 37th Annual Computer Software and Applications Conference Workshops, pp. 145–150 (2013)

---

[6] https://www.w3.org/TR/sparql11-query/.
[7] https://gojs.net/.

7. Kappel, G., et al.: Lifting metamodels to ontologies: a step to the semantic integration of modeling languages. In: Nierstrasz, O., Whittle, J., Harel, D., Reggio, G. (eds.) MODELS 2006. LNCS, vol. 4199, pp. 528–542. Springer, Heidelberg (2006). https://doi.org/10.1007/11880240_37
8. Hinkelmann, K., Laurenzi, E., Martin, A., Thönssen, B.: Ontology-based metamodeling. In: Dornberger, R. (ed.) Business Information Systems and Technology 4.0. SSDC, vol. 141, pp. 177–194. Springer, Cham (2018). https://doi.org/10.1007/978-3-319-74322-6_12
9. Laurenzi, E., Hinkelmann, K., van der Merwe, A.: An agile and ontology-aided modeling environment. In: Buchmann, R.A., Karagiannis, D., Kirikova, M. (eds.) PoEM 2018. LNBIP, vol. 335, pp. 221–237. Springer, Cham (2018). https://doi.org/10.1007/978-3-030-02302-7_14
10. Fill, H.-G.: Using semantically annotated models for supporting business process benchmarking. In: Grabis, J., Kirikova, M. (eds.) BIR 2011. LNBIP, vol. 90, pp. 29–43. Springer, Heidelberg (2011). https://doi.org/10.1007/978-3-642-24511-4_3
11. Emmenegger, S., Hinkelmann, K., Laurenzi, E., Thönssen, B.: Towards a procedure for assessing supply chain risks using semantic technologies. In: Fred, A., Dietz, J., Liu, K., Filipe, J. (eds.) IC3K 2012. CCIS, vol. 415, pp. 393–409. Springer, Heidelberg (2013). https://doi.org/10.1007/978-3-642-54105-6_26
12. Buchmann, R.A., Karagiannis, D.: Enriching linked data with semantics from domain-specific diagrammatic models. Bus. Inf. Syst. Eng. **58**(5), 341–353 (2016). https://doi.org/10.1007/s12599-016-0445-1
13. Gailly, F., Alkhaldi, N., Casteleyn, S., Verbeke, W.: Recommendation-based conceptual modeling and ontology evolution framework (CMOE+). Bus. Inf. Syst. Eng. **59**(4), 235–250 (2017). https://doi.org/10.1007/s12599-017-0488-y
14. Karagiannis, D., Kühn, H.: Metamodelling platforms. In: Bauknecht, K., Tjoa, A.M., Quirchmayr, G. (eds.) EC-Web 2002. LNCS, vol. 2455, pp. 182–182. Springer, Heidelberg (2002). https://doi.org/10.1007/3-540-45705-4_19
15. Nikles, S., Brander, S.: Separating conceptual and visual aspects in metamodelling. In: Workshop on Advanced Enterprise Architecture and Repositories (2009)
16. Laurenzi, E.: A methodological approach for ontology-based meta-modelling. In: Joint Proceedings of the BIR 2023 Workshops and Doctoral Consortium Co-located with 22nd International Conference on Perspectives in Business Informatics Research, pp. 55–64. CEUR-WS.org (2023)
17. Laurenzi, E., Allan, J., Campos, N., Stoller, S.: An ontology-based meta-modelling approach for semantic-driven building management systems. In Almeida, J.P.A., Di Ciccio, C., Kalloniatis, C. (eds.) Advanced Information Systems Engineering Workshops, pp. 200–211. Springer, Cham (2024). https://doi.org/10.1007/978-3-031-61003-5_18
18. Fedeli, A., Peraic, M., Laurenzi, E., Polini, A.: AOAME4floware: ontology-based feature models for context-aware configurations in IoT applications. In: BIR-WS 2024: BIR 2024 Workshops and Doctoral Consortium, 23rd International Conference on Perspectives in Business Informatics Research, CEUR Workshop Proceedings (2024)

OpenBPT: An Extensible Platform for Conceptual Modeling and Analysis

Tom Lichtenstein[✉][iD], Maximilian König[iD], Maximilian Körner[iD], Anjo Seidel[iD], Arsalan Ghasemi[iD], and Mathias Weske[iD]

Hasso Plattner Institute, University of Potsdam, Potsdam, Germany
{Tom.Lichtenstein,maximilian.koenig,maximilian.koerner,Anjo.Seidel, Arsalan.Ghasemi,Mathias.Weske}@hpi.de

Abstract. This paper introduces the OpenBPT platform, which provides conceptual modeling and analysis capabilities to the academic community. The purpose of this project is to support teaching and research in information systems engineering and business process management by integrating existing open-source tools and providing additional services, where appropriate. The web-based platform offers multiple graphical modelers and model management. In addition, an extensible software architecture based on microservices enables the integration of research prototypes for model analysis. This paper discusses the current state of OpenBPT and plans for future development.

Keywords: Conceptual modeling · Extensible platform · Model analysis · Business process management

1 Introduction and Motivation

Conceptual modeling is an important cornerstone of information systems engineering [12], enabling the specification of systems from multiple perspectives, including architecture, data, and processes. Consequently, it is widely taught in higher education classes at universities worldwide [2]. To appreciate the value of modeling information systems, it is essential that students engage in practical exercises to design, analyze, and critically discuss conceptual models [2].

Over the years, the academic community has developed a wide range of tools for different conceptual modeling tasks, including model creation, analysis, and simulation. Although these tools provide excellent functionality, they often create silos as they are primarily developed by individual research groups. Therefore, different types of conceptual models, such as process and data models, are typically designed in separate tools, making consistency checking cumbersome.

Particularly in academic teaching, the use of research software can be challenging due to its complexity or installation requirements. In addition, as it is often only needed for a short period of time, such as for an exercise, teaching staff may not have the resources to provide adequate support to students in overcoming installation and usage issues, which can ultimately prevent the use of such software in this context.

Even for researchers who use these tools regularly, the fragmented landscape requires manual creation and maintenance of workflows and data pipelines to handle configuration and file format changes. This challenge extends beyond the software itself to the models designed within these tools.

This paper introduces OpenBPT, a web-based platform for the conceptual modeling community. It is based on three key principles: (i) offering fundamental modeling functionality with extensibility for additional modeling languages, (ii) providing standardized interfaces for invoking services to operate on models, such as soundness checking for workflow nets, and (iii) integrating existing open-source tools where appropriate.

In the following, we position OpenBPT in relation to other tools and outline its core requirements in Sect. 2. Section 3 presents the platform's design and architecture, followed by a use case scenario in Sect. 4. The paper concludes with a discussion of the current maturity level in Sect. 5 and the future development plans in Sect. 6.

2 Related Tools and Requirements

In the area of conceptual modeling, several software solutions have emerged from both academic and commercial initiatives. Tools such as ADOxx (www.adoxx.org), webgme (webgme.org), or MetaEdit+ (www.metacase.com) offer powerful features that allow expert users to define custom domain-specific languages while providing modeling support for models based on these custom languages.

At the other end of the spectrum, web-based modeling tools such as Lucidchart (www.lucidchart.com) and draw.io (www.drawio.com) provide a modeling canvas and predefined shapes for various popular modeling notations. However, unlike the former, these tools lack a metamodel of the respective notation, offering little modeling support and allowing arbitrary connections between shapes.

Other conceptual modeling tools seek to balance these two approaches by supporting a limited set of established—and typically standardized—modeling languages along with their respective metamodels. These tools ensure that only syntactically correct models can be created and typically allow for the import and export of models that adhere to the respective standards. Examples of these tools include Visual Paradigm (www.visual-paradigm.com) and Modelio (www.modelio.org), which support standards such as UML [10] and BPMN [9].

We aim to design OpenBPT as a modeling tool of the latter type, with a distinct focus on research and teaching activities that extend beyond model creation and management by enabling model analysis and transformation. Therefore, OpenBPT differs from the aforementioned tools in two ways: (i) it supports additional modeling languages commonly used in research, such as Petri nets, and (ii) it allows integrating various model processing capabilities, including existing tools developed in the academic community, such as LoLA [13] for Petri net analysis.

Inspired by the discontinued web-based process modeling platform Oryx [3], first introduced in 2008, OpenBPT is intended to serve as a central, extensible platform for the creation and management of conceptual models, while

OpenBPT: An Extensible Platform for Conceptual Modeling and Analysis   191

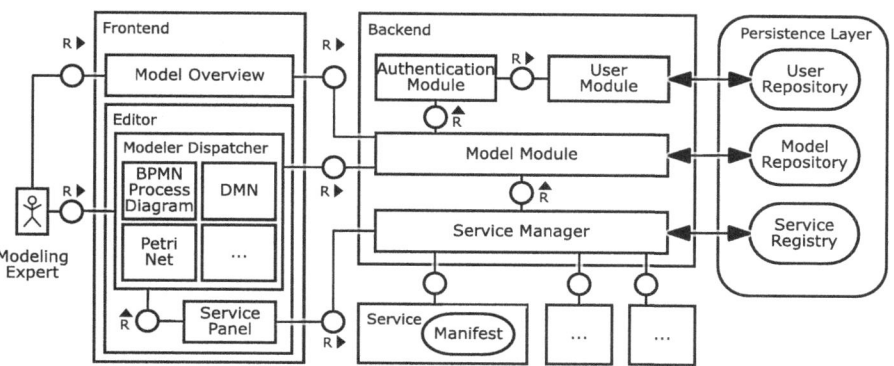

Fig. 1. OpenBPT architecture illustrating the frontend, backend, and persistence layer, as well as the service interface for platform extension.

enabling the integration of and uniform access to model processing services. To achieve this, OpenBPT is designed to meet the following requirements:

R_1 *Web-based application* to ensure easy accessibility without local installation.
R_2 *Multi-type model creation and management* in a centralized manner.
R_3 *Consistent user experience* across modeling languages and analysis features.
R_4 *Comprehensive model processing* including the analysis, transformation, and simulation of models.
R_5 *Extensibility* to integrate additional modeling languages and tools for model processing.

3 Platform Design

OpenBPT is designed with modularity and extensibility in mind. This section provides an overview of the platform architecture, extensibility endpoints, and implementation details, highlighting key components and design choices.

3.1 Architecture

OpenBPT follows a layered architectural style comprising a frontend, a backend, and a persistence layer. Additionally, it incorporates elements of service-oriented architecture to support the integration of loosely coupled services within the backend. Designed for extensibility, this architecture supports multiple conceptual model types and enables the integration of programming language-agnostic services for model processing. The overall architecture is illustrated in Fig. 1.

The frontend is accessible via a web browser (R_1) and consists of two primary components: the *model overview* and the *editor*. The model overview lists available models, while the editor enables model creation, visualization, and modification (R_2). The editor includes an extensible *modeler dispatcher* that dynamically selects the appropriate modeler based on the model type (R_5), and a *service panel* that lists available services for the currently loaded model, allowing users to invoke them. The frontend is implemented using React (react.dev).

The backend is structured into four core modules dedicated to user, model, authentication, and service management. To address R_2, the *model module* handles the creation, updates, and retrieval of models, making them accessible to the frontend and the service manager. Model access is controlled by the *authentication module*, which verifies user identities and interfaces with the *user module*, responsible for storing and managing user data. Both the user and model modules persist their respective data in dedicated repositories within the persistence layer, which is implemented using the PostgreSQL (www.postgresql.org) relational database. Furthermore, the authentication module supports the integration of authentication providers via OAuth 2.0 [6]. The *service manager* enables extending the functionality of OpenBPT by allowing services with model processing capabilities to register at the platform (R_4, R_5), and coordinates interactions between the frontend and the services. The backend implementation builds on the Nest.js framework (nestjs.com).

3.2 Platform Extensibility

To satisfy R_5, the platform offers multiple endpoints for extensibility. In the following, we describe two key mechanisms for facilitating the extension of modeling and model processing capabilities.

Modeler Framework. To integrate modelers for different modeling languages, we use the open-source library *diagram-js*, which was created in the context of the bpmn.io project (bpmn.io/about). The library provides a canvas and basic modeling capabilities, including navigation, modeling workflow support, and keyboard shortcuts. It also specifies an interface for defining the metamodel of the implemented modeling language. By using diagram-js as a basis for all modelers, we ensure a consistent user experience across all model types (R_3). Currently, the modeler dispatcher (cf. Figure 1) integrates existing modelers based on the diagram-js library, including bpmn-js and dmn-js, both developed as part of the bpmn.io project, as well as chor-js [8] for BPMN choreography diagrams and ptn-js (github.com/MaximilianKoenig/ptn-js) for Petri nets. Building on our experience developing ptn-js, we are developing a generic template for diagram-js-based modelers to provide an interface for supporting additional modeling languages (R_2). The modeler dispatcher enables the seamless integration of new diagram-js-based modelers with little configuration overhead (R_5).

Service Integration. OpenBPT enables extending its model processing capabilities through an HTTP-based interface that allows external services to connect. Since extensions are not limited to specific programming languages, a wide range of existing libraries and tools can be integrated into one coherent ecosystem (R_5). Services can remain independent and stateless, as OpenBPT manages authentication, data retrieval, input validation, and output management. An overview of the integration and invocation of services is depicted in Fig. 2.

OpenBPT: An Extensible Platform for Conceptual Modeling and Analysis 193

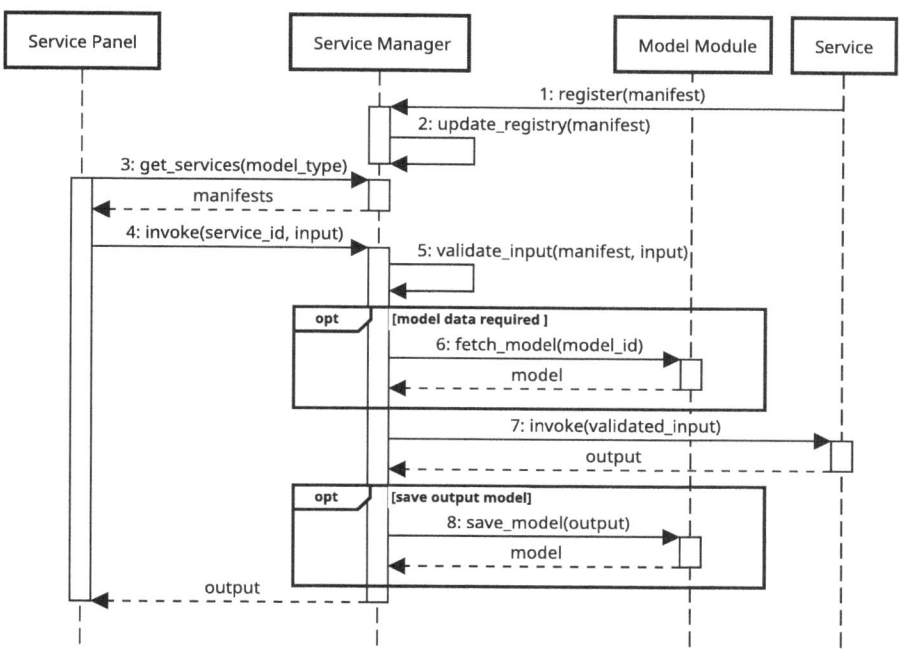

Fig. 2. Service integration in OpenBPT, highlighting the service manager's role in service registration, input validation, data retrieval, and service invocation.

The service manager acts as a central orchestration layer, handling service registration and invocation requests by the frontend, thus mitigating security risks by preventing unauthorized access. Once a service is deployed, it registers with the service manager by providing a *manifest* that defines the service's metadata, including name, description, version, and expected input and output payloads, which consist of models and primitive data types (1). The service manager keeps records of all registered services (2) and monitors their availability.

The service panel dynamically retrieves the manifests of available services based on the type of model currently loaded in the editor and presents these services to the user (3). The user interface for invoking services and visualizing outputs is automatically generated based on the manifests, providing a consistent user experience across different services (R_3).

After receiving an invocation request by the service panel (4), the service manager validates all input against the service manifest, preventing malformed requests from reaching the service (5). When a service requires additional model-related information, the service manager retrieves the necessary input from the respective module, ensuring that the service does not have to handle access control or data retrieval (6). Please note that for brevity, Fig. 2 abstracts from the interactions with the authentication module. After invoking the service (7), the output, e.g., a transformed model, may be stored if specified in the manifest (8). Finally, the output is forwarded to the service panel. By decoupling services

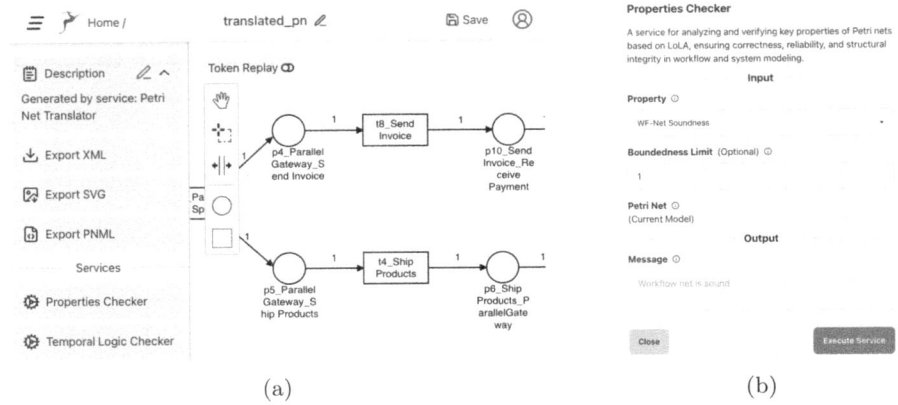

Fig. 3. OpenBPT's editor interface showing the translated Petri net (a) and a service panel for the Petri net properties service (b).

from authentication, access control, and data management, the service manager improves security and facilitates service development.

4 Use Case Scenario

This section illustrates the application of OpenBPT in a typical business process management scenario, including the creation and verification of process models, as well as ensuring their compliance with business rules [7]. This scenario involves three services connected to OpenBPT: (i) a *Petri net translator*, which converts a BPMN process diagram into an equivalent Petri net [4], (ii) a *Petri net properties* service, which analyzes Petri net properties such as workflow net soundness, and (iii) a *temporal logic checker*, which verifies compliance between business rules and modeled behavior.

OpenBPT allows users to create or upload BPMN process models, which can be edited using the BPMN process diagram modeler. The service panel displays the Petri net translator service as the only available option for the given BPMN model. Once executed, this service generates a Petri net file, which can be opened in the Petri net modeler. The service panel then loads the Petri net properties and temporal logic checker services from the service manager, both powered by LoLA [13]. These services enable the formal analysis of the Petri net. Using the graphical UI, users may refine the model to correct its behavior and verify it again. Additionally, the modeler supports manual token replay to simulate the net. All models—whether uploaded, designed, or generated—are persisted within OpenBPT and can be exported as SVG or standard-compliant XML files. Figure 3 illustrates OpenBPT's editor interface, featuring (a) the modeler view for a translated Petri net and (b) the service panel for configuring the Petri net properties service, along with its execution output. A screencast demonstrating the use case is available online[1].

---

[1] https://youtu.be/_t9AQnYUqUM.

5 Maturity

OpenBPT has been successfully used in a conceptual modeling lecture at the Hasso Plattner Institute (HPI), where 116 students created over 700 models. It is also being used in classes by colleagues from Munich, Ulm, and Bolzano. Stable features include model creation, storage, and modification through a consistent interface, ensuring a unified user experience across different modeling languages. Currently, OpenBPT supports BPMN process and choreography diagrams (omg.org/spec/BPMN/2.0.2), DMN decision requirements diagrams and decision tables (omg.org/spec/DMN/1.6/Beta1), and Petri nets (pnml.org), including XML import and export capabilities compliant with the respective standards. The behavior of BPMN process diagrams and Petri nets can be explored using the token replay feature. Additionally, the platform integrates an HPI-internal identity provider and Auth0 (auth0.com) for authentication.

The generic service interface provides the foundation for integrating existing community tools while enabling the development of new services for processing supported model types. To facilitate service development, we offer templates in JavaScript, TypeScript, Java, and Python that handle communication with the service manager and provide example manifests. These templates are available in a GitHub repository[2]. Services integrating the Scylla simulation engine [11], the PM4Py process mining library [1], and support for storing XES event logs [5] have been implemented but are not yet released due to licensing considerations.

The development of OpenBPT is coordinated by a group of researchers, with several working students and student projects contributing to different aspects of the system. To ensure high code quality, all contributions require thorough reviews by core team members. Over the past two years, more than 20 contributors have contributed to the project. OpenBPT is publicly accessible online[3].

6 Conclusion and Future Work

This paper introduces OpenBPT, an online modeling and analysis platform for conceptual and process models. Its extensible architecture bridges the silos of existing open-source tools, making integrated modeling and analysis more accessible for teaching and research.

Future developments will extend support for additional modelers based on the diagram-js framework described in Sect. 3, including but not limited to entity-relationship diagrams, UML class diagrams, FMC architecture diagrams, automata, and various Petri net classes. For better teaching support, we plan to integrate a directory structure, model-sharing, and collaborative modeling capabilities. Additionally, to support multi-model approaches, we are designing a project-based structure that connects multiple related models.

We invite fellow researchers to contact us to collaborate on OpenBPT by integrating their research prototypes as services, making them more accessible to the academic community.

---

[2] https://github.com/bptlab/openbpt-service-templates.
[3] https://openbpt.org/.

Acknowledgments. We acknowledge the open-source projects that form the foundation of OpenBPT, with special thanks to the bpmn.io project initiated and maintained by Camunda. We also thank the members of the Business Process Technology research group and the students who contributed to OpenBPT. In particular, we thank Florian Papsdorf and Franka Traupe for their significant contributions.

Disclosure of Interests. The authors have no competing interests to declare that are relevant to the content of this article.

References

1. Berti, A., van Zelst, S.J., Schuster, D.: PM4Py: a process mining library for Python. Softw. Impacts **17** (2023). https://doi.org/10.1016/J.SIMPA.2023.100556
2. Bork, D.: A framework for teaching conceptual modeling and metamodeling based on bloom's revised taxonomy of educational objectives. In: HICSS 2019, pp. 1–10. ScholarSpace (2019)
3. Decker, G., Overdick, H., Weske, M.: Oryx – an open modeling platform for the BPM community. In: Dumas, M., Reichert, M., Shan, M.-C. (eds.) BPM 2008. LNCS, vol. 5240, pp. 382–385. Springer, Heidelberg (2008). https://doi.org/10.1007/978-3-540-85758-7_29
4. Dijkman, R.M., Dumas, M., Ouyang, C.: Semantics and analysis of business process models in BPMN. Inf. Softw. Technol. **50**(12) (2008). https://doi.org/10.1016/J.INFSOF.2008.02.006
5. Gunther, C.W., Verbeek, H.: XES-standard definition. In: BPM Reports, vol. 1409. BPMcenter.org (2014)
6. Hardt, D. (ed.): RFC 6749 - The OAuth 2.0 Authorization Framework. Technical report. IETF (2012). https://tools.ietf.org/html/rfc6749
7. Kunze, M., Weske, M.: Behavioural Models: From Modelling Finite Automata to Analysing Business Processes. Springer, Heidelberg (2016)
8. Ladleif, J., von Weltzien, A., Weske, M.: chor-js: a modeling framework for BPMN 2.0 choreography diagrams. In: ER Forum and Poster & Demos Session. CEUR Workshop Proceedings, vol. 2469. CEUR-WS.org (2019)
9. OMG: Business Process Model and Notation (BPMN), Version 2.0.2. Technical report. Object Management Group (2014). https://www.omg.org/spec/BPMN/2.0.2/
10. OMG: Unified Modeling Language (OMG UML), Version 2.5.1. Technical report. Object Management Group (2017). https://www.omg.org/spec/UML/2.5.1/
11. Pufahl, L., Wong, T.Y., Weske, M.: Design of an extensible BPMN process simulator. In: Teniente, E., Weidlich, M. (eds.) BPM 2017. LNBIP, vol. 308, pp. 782–795. Springer, Cham (2018). https://doi.org/10.1007/978-3-319-74030-0_62
12. Wand, Y., Monarchi, D.E., Parsons, J., Woo, C.C.: Theoretical foundations for conceptual modelling in information systems development. Decis. Support Syst. **15**(4), 285–304 (1995). https://doi.org/10.1016/0167-9236(94)00043-6
13. Wolf, K.: Petri net model checking with LoLA 2. In: Khomenko, V., Roux, O.H. (eds.) PETRI NETS 2018. LNCS, vol. 10877, pp. 351–362. Springer, Cham (2018). https://doi.org/10.1007/978-3-319-91268-4_18

SecBPMN2BC Online Editor: A Web-Based Tool for Designing Secure Business Processes on Blockchains

Giovanni Meroni[1(✉)], Anders Dalskov[2], and Alex Norta[3,4,5]

[1] Technical University of Denmark, Kgs. Lyngby, Denmark
giom@dtu.dk
[2] Partisia ApS, Aarhus, Denmark
anderspkd@partisia.com
[3] Tallinn University, Tallinn, Estonia
alex.norta.phd@ieee.org
[4] Dymaxion OÜ, Viimsi Parish, Estonia
[5] Department of Informatics, University of Pretoria, Pretoria, South Africa

Abstract. SecBPMN2BC has been proposed as a model-driven approach to support the execution of business processes that span multiple organizations on a blockchain. In particular, SecBPMN2BC allows one to formalize the security requirements that hold for process elements. Based on such requirements, SecBPMN2BC can identify which process elements would benefit from running on a blockchain and which ones would cause security violations if running on a blockchain. However, SecBPMN2BC offered limited tool support. In particular, it lacked an intuitive editor for visually creating and editing process models annotated with security requirements.

The SecBPMN2BC Online Editor addresses this gap by offering a Web-based visual editor to support SecBPMN2BC. Users can create process models annotated with security requirements either from scratch or by importing existing BPMN models. They can also invoke algorithms to determine which process elements to deploy on a blockchain and to check for conflicting security requirements. The SecBPMN2BC Online Editor has been conceived and evaluated with industry partners using real-world case studies.

Keywords: Secure Business Processes · BPMN · Blockchain · Model-driven Security Annotations

1 Introduction

With the rise in popularity of blockchains, several approaches have been proposed that take advantage of the trusted smart contract execution environment offered by this technology to enforce collaborative business processes. In fact, collaborative business processes can be viewed as a form of smart contracts. In particular, collaborative business processes can formalize agreements between multiple parties on when tasks should be executed and by whom, and on how physical and digital objects should be manipulated. However, relying on a blockchain to automate the execution of a collaborative process significantly affects the security requirements of that process. For instance, running the process on a public blockchain can enforce some requirements (e.g., non-repudiation) while being detrimental for others (e.g., confidentiality). Therefore, care should be taken to identify, based on the security requirements, which process elements should be deployed on a blockchain and which ones should not.

To this end, SecBPMN2BC [3] has been proposed as a model-driven approach to design business processes with security requirements that are meant to be deployed on blockchains. To support SecBPMN2BC, the following artifacts were conceived: SecBPMN2BC-ML, an extension of Business Process Modeling Notation (BPMN) 2.0 [2] that allows the design of secure smart contracts; SecBPMN2BC-Tools, a set of algorithms and their implementation that check incompatible security requirements and help the design of smart contracts. Regarding SecBPMN2BC-Tools, although it was able to validate the approach, it suffered from several limitations from the usability point of view. In particular, it did not allow to visually create and edit SecBPMN2BC-ML models.

To address such limitations, a new tool has been developed, named the SecBPMN2BC Online Editor, which is presented in this paper. The SecBPMN2BC Online Editor has been released open-source[1] and is also publicly accessible at https://secbpmn2bc.compute.dtu.dk. A screencast demonstrating the SecBPMN2BC Online Editor can be viewed at https://youtu.be/f-TuOJrCkbc.

This paper is structured as follows. Section 2 briefly introduces SecBPMN2BC and its artifacts. Section 3 describes how the requirements for SecBPMN2BC Online Editor were elicited, the architecture of the tool, and how to use it. Section 4 discusses the maturity of SecBPMN2BC Online Editor. Finally, Sect. 5 draws conclusions and describes future work.

2 The SecBPMN2BC Approach

To make this paper self-contained, this section briefly introduces the SecBPMN2BC approach. The reader should refer to [3] for further details.

SecBPMN2BC is a model-driven framework to support the development of blockchain-based applications. One of the prerequisites for this framework is that the application or parts of it can be represented as a business process, which in turn could be implemented as a business process. This assumption is justified by the fact that many information systems are process-aware [8], and that tools have been proposed to execute business processes on a blockchain–either by translating them into smart contract code [7] or by interpreting the model at runtime [10]. SecBPMN2BC is organized as shown in Fig. 1 in four steps: Requirements Elicitation, On-Chain Elements Identification, Model Revision, and Implementation.

---

[1] Source code is accessible at https://github.com/meronig/secbpmn2bc-online-editor and https://github.com/meronig/secbpmn2bc-rest-service.

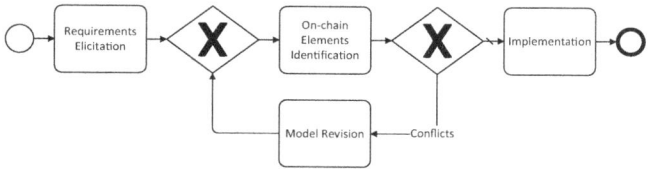

Fig. 1. Steps composing the SecBPMN2BC approach.

Requirements Elicitation. In this step, the user takes as input an informal description of functional and security requirements for the application to be developed (e.g., as textual documentation) and produces a formal description of the application and its security requirements using the SecBPMN2BC-ML modeling language.

SecBPMN2BC-ML extends the SecBPMN language [9], which is in turn an extension of the BPMN 2.0 language commonly used to model business processes. Compared to BPMN, SecBPMN2BC-ML introduces annotations to represent security requirements, which can be attached to activities (units of work that make up the process), data objects (information consumed and/or produced by activities), and messages (information exchanged between different organizations).

Although the graphical notation shown in Fig. 3 has already been defined for SecBPMN2BC-ML annotations, until now no tool was available to display and visually edit a SecBPMN2BC-ML model.

On-Chain Elements Identification. In this step, the user takes as input the SecBPMN2BC-ML model created during the previous step and determines which elements of the application would benefit from being implemented as smart contracts on the blockchain. In addition, the user also identifies conflicting security requirements. As a result, the model is updated with this information.

To support this step, a set of enforcement rules, as well as an algorithm to identify the affected elements and merge the rules, has been introduced. These components enrich the SecBPMN2BC-ML model by specifying which process element should be implemented on a blockchain and how (e.g., storing data in unencrypted or encrypted form).

The algorithm has already been implemented in SecBPMN2BC-Tools as an Eclipse plugin. However, SecBPMN2BC-Tools lacked a graphical front-end to visually show the revised process model and the results of reasoning.

Model Revision. This step is needed only if security conflicts are identified or if the user disagrees with the decisions being made after the On-chain Elements Identification step. In this step, the user takes as input the automatically enriched SecBPMN2BC-ML model, and manually revises the security annotations and/or the on-chain properties. Then, the On-chain Elements Identification step is repeated to check if all conflicts are resolved.

Regarding the requirement elimination step, no tool was available to visually edit the automatically enriched SecBPMN2BC-ML model.

Implementation. In this step, the user takes as input the final SecBPMN2BC-ML model and uses it as a blueprint to produce the smart contract code responsible for running the application. Currently, this step is entirely manual. In addition, no tool was available to display the final SecBPMN2BC-ML model.

3 SecBPMN2BC Online Editor

To address the limitations of SecBPMN2BC-Tools to support the approach, a new tool, named SecBPMN2BC Online Editor, has been developed. This section discusses how the requirements for SecBPMN2BC Online Editor have been elicited, how its architecture was conceived, and how it can be used by end users.

3.1 Application Requirements

Together with industry partners, the most critical limitations of SecBPMN2BC-Tools have been identified and, consequently, the requirements of SecBPMN2BC Online Editor have been elicited. To this end, industry partners identified two case studies, namely blockchain-based platforms for trading luxury products [11] and for exchanging humanitarian tokens [1]. For both case studies, industry partners evaluated to what extent SecBPMN2BC-Tools could have been used to support design decisions and what features were missing. To prioritize the features to be introduced and the requirements of the SecBPMN2BC Online Editor, the MoSCoW method [4] was adopted.

Industry partners identified the lack of a graphical user interface to visualize and edit SecBPMN2BC-ML models as a critical limitation of SecBPMN2BC-Tools. Therefore, providing such an interface (R1) was a **must-have**. They also mentioned that the transition between the different steps of the SecBPMN2BC approach **must** be simplified in the new tool. In particular, the same user interface should allow one to model the process, invoke the algorithms to check for conflicts and to identify on-chain elements, visually see the on-chain elements, and if necessary directly edit the annotated model (R2).

The partners also commented that SecBPMN2BC-Tools **should** be available as a web application, without requiring the user to locally deploy it on his/her own computer (R3). In fact, in many corporate environments, the ability to install and run applications autonomously is restricted. Instead, applications must undergo a strict vetting process before being installed. Offering the new tool as a web application would overcome this limitation. Another requirement that **should** be addressed was the ability to reuse the existing code of SecBPMN2BC-Tools (R4), in particular the algorithms to identify conflicts and determine which process elements to move on-chain. In this way, it would have been possible to shorten the development time of the new tool and reduce the risk of introducing bugs into existing features.

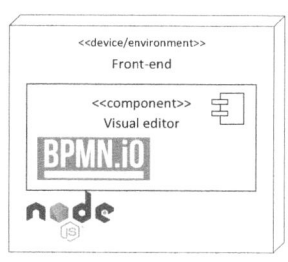
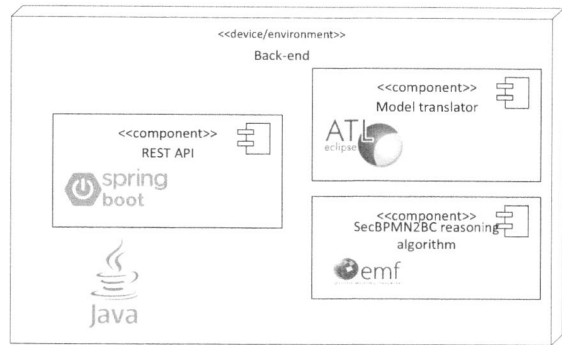

Fig. 2. Architecture of SecBPMN2BC Online Editor.

One requirement that **could** have been nice to have was the possibility of importing existing BPMN models (R5). In this way, the end user would not have been forced to model the process again if a BPMN model already existed.

Finally, industry partners agreed that, although potentially useful, automatic generation of smart contract code from annotated SecBPMN2BC-ML models (R6) was **not** required for the first release version of the SecBPMN2BC Online Editor. In fact, it was considered more beneficial for the adoption of the SecBPMN2BC approach to prioritize the other requirements, to fully support the first three steps of the approach.

3.2 Architecture

Based on the application requirements identified in Sect. 3.1, the SecBPMN2BC Online Editor architecture was designed as shown in Fig. 2. To address R3, SecBPMN2BC Online Editor was developed as a two-tier web application.

For the front-end, to address R1 and R2, bpmn-js[2], a well-established open-source JavaScript library was adopted to display and edit BPMN process models. bpmn-js supports custom extensions to the BPMN language, making it possible to add SecBPMN2BC-ML elements while maintaining compatibility with BPMN models. In this way, it was also possible to address R5 with minimal effort. The front-end relies on node.js[3] to run.

For the back-end, to address R4, a Representational State Transfer (REST) API was developed to expose the original implementation of SecBPMN2BC-Tools. To do so, the Spring Boot framework[4] was used, since the existing tools were implemented as an Eclipse plugin. In this way, it was possible to reuse the existing code. However, bpmn-js uses a different approach to define BPMN extensions (custom properties) than the one originally adopted by SecBPMN2BC-Tools (EMF metamodel extensions[5]). This caused the front-end models to be

---

[2] See https://bpmn.io/toolkit/bpmn-js.
[3] See https://nodejs.org/en.
[4] See https://spring.io/projects/spring-boot.
[5] See https://projects.eclipse.org/projects/modeling.emf.emf.

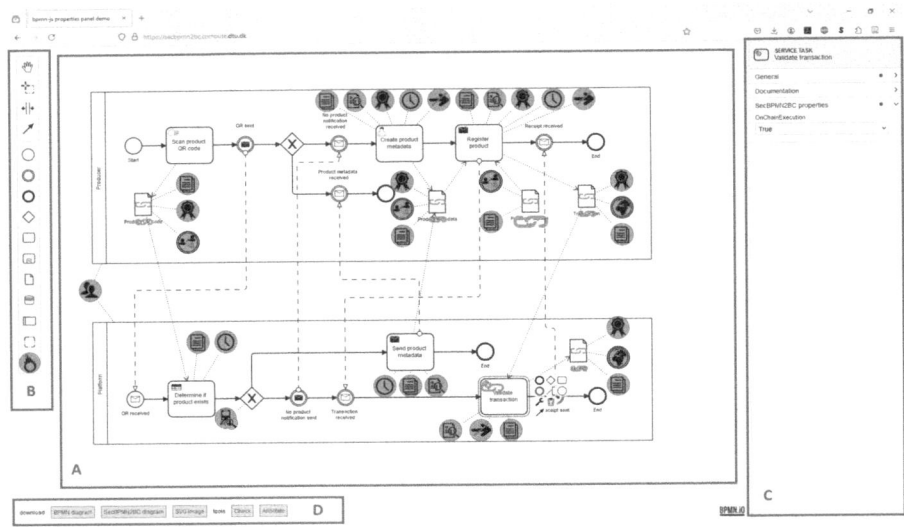

Fig. 3. User interface of SecBPMN2BC Online Editor.

in a different format than those consumed by SecBPMN2BC-Tools. To address this, a set of rules was implemented to translate the models between the two formats through the ATL framework[6] and exposed by the REST API.

3.3 User Interface

When the user opens SecBPMN2BC Online Editor, they are asked to either start creating a new SecBPMN2BC-ML model or open an existing one by dragging the corresponding file over the Web browser window. Then, the user interface shown in Fig. 3 is displayed. The user interface consists of a canvas (A), a toolbar (B), a property panel (C), and a button bar (D).

The canvas shows the SecBPMN2BC-ML model. In particular, besides showing the BPMN process model, it also shows SecBPMN2BC-ML annotations. In addition, whenever a BPMN element is marked as on-chain, a chain symbol is shown on top of that element to visually communicate this decision to the user.

The toolbar is used to add process elements to the canvas, select process elements, and move the diagram. Its behavior is similar to other bpmn-js derived applications, with the exception of the last tool, which is used to add SecBPMN2BC-ML annotations (e.g., immutability) to the model. SecBPMN2BC annotations can then be associated to BPMN elements with the association flow, either by choosing the arrow icon from the contextual tooltip shown when a SecBPMN2BC annotation is highlighted, or the arrow icon from the toolbar.

---

[6] See https://projects.eclipse.org/projects/modeling.mmt.atl.

The properties panel is used to change the type of SecBPMN2BC annotation and to manually override the decision of the enforcement algorithm over the BPMN process elements. For example, by selecting a SecBPMN2BC annotation, one can change the security property it represents (e.g., from immutability to integrity) by selecting the appropriate value from the Type combo box under SecBPMN2BC properties. Similarly, by selecting a BPMN activity, one can specify whether it should run on-chain or off-chain by selecting the appropriate value from the OnChainExecution combo box under SecBPMN2BC properties. Also, by selecting a BPMN data object or message flow, one can specify if an how it should be stored on-chain by selecting the appropriate value from the OnChainData combo box under SecBPMN2BC properties.

The button bar is used to save the model (1) as a BPMN model file, (2) as a SecBPMN2BC model file, or (3) as a picture. When choosing (1) or (2), the SecBPMN2BC-ML extensions are retained. In fact, (2) is made available to provide backward compatibility with the original version of SecBPMN2BC-Tools. The button bar is also used to (4) check if the model contains conflicting SecBPMN2BC elements and (5) run the algorithm to identify elements in the chain. To perform (2), (4), and (5), the REST services provided by the back-end are invoked. Also, when running (5), the user is asked if any manually specified on-/off-chain assignment should be preserved or not.

4 Maturity

To evaluate whether the SecBPMN2BC Online Editor could be used for real-world applications, a preliminary evaluation involving two industry partners—each belonging to a different organization—was conducted. Industry partners were asked to use the SecBPMN2BC Online Editor to model, enrich, and evaluate the processes belonging to their case studies [6]. More in detail, industry partners were asked to (1) import an existing BPMN model and extend it with SecBPMN2BC-ML annotations, (2) run the algorithm to identify on-chain elements, (3) create a SecBPMN2BC-ML model from scratch, and (4) manually identify on-chain elements and run the algorithm to check for conflicts. After each part was over, the partners were asked if they were able to complete it and how easy it was, and if they agreed with the outcome provided by the tool [5].

Both industry partners were able to complete all the tasks, and they found the tool easy to use despite having different levels of expertise in BPMN and process modeling in general. They also agreed with the decisions taken by the tool on which BPMN elements to move on-chain. Although the user experience has been significantly improved with respect to SecBPMN2BC-Tools, both partners found it difficult to remember by heart the association between security properties and the corresponding icons. To address this issue, one partner suggested that the icon and a short text description be shown in the properties panel.

5 Conclusion and Future Work

This paper introduced the SecBPMN2BC Online Editor, a tool to support the SecBPMN2BC approach. The tool was able to address all the most pressing requirements identified by industry partners, who were positively impressed by the tool. Future work will focus on conducting a more extensive evaluation involving more partners from industry and academia. The minor issues identified by the partners will also be addressed, the architecture revised to support horizontal scalability in the back-end, and the tool extended to support the generation of smart contract code from SecBPMN2BC-ML models.

Acknowledgments. This work has been partially funded by the project "Improving Business Processes with Blockchain: Model-driven Generation of Secure Smart Contract Code", funded by Copenhagen Fintech (https://www.copenhagenfintech.dk/projects/improving-business-processes-with-blockchain), and also by Estonian "Personal research funding: Team Grant (PRG)" project PRG1641.

References

1. Humanitarian token solution: Digital cash assistance that preserves privacy. https://blogs.icrc.org/inspired/2023/06/27/humanitarian-token-solution-digital-cash-assistance-preserves-privacy. Accessed 04 Mar 2025
2. Fundamentals of Business Process Management. Springer, Heidelberg (2018). https://doi.org/10.1007/978-3-662-56509-4_9
3. Köpke, J., Meroni, G., Salnitri, M.: Designing secure business processes for blockchains with SecBPMN2BC. Future Gener. Comput. Syst. **141**, 382–398 (2023)
4. Kravchenko, T., Bogdanova, T., Shevgunov, T.: Ranking requirements using Moscow methodology in practice. In: Computer Science On-line Conference, pp. 188–199. Springer (2022)
5. Meroni, G.: Improving business processes with blockchain - evaluation results (2024). https://doi.org/10.5281/zenodo.15170516
6. Meroni, G., Dalskov, A., Norta, A.: Improving business processes with blockchain - secbpmn2bc case studies (2024). https://doi.org/10.5281/zenodo.14508508
7. Pintado, O., García-Bañuelos, L., Dumas, M., Weber, I., Ponomarev, A.: Caterpillar: a business process execution engine on the ethereum blockchain. Pract. Experience, Softw. (2019)
8. Reichert, M., Weber, B.: Enabling Flexibility in Process-Aware Information Systems - Challenges, Methods, Technologies Springer, Cham (2012)
9. Salnitri, M., Paja, E., Giorgini, P.: Maintaining secure business processes in light of socio-technical systems' evolution. In: Proceedings of IEEE MoDRE, pp. 155–164 (2016)
10. Tran, A.B., Lu, Q., Weber, I.: Lorikeet: a model-driven engineering tool for blockchain-based business process execution and asset management. In: Proceeedings of BPM, pp. 56–60 (2018)
11. Zimmermann, R., Udokwu, C., Kompp, R., Staab, M., Brandtner, P., Norta, A.: Methods to authenticate luxury products: identifying key features and most recognized deficits. SN Comput. Sci. **4**(6), 747 (2023)

A3S3 - Automated Android Audit of Safety and Security Signals

Guillaume Nguyen(✉)[iD] and Xavier Devroey[iD]

NADI - University of Namur, Namur, Belgium
{guillaume.nguyen,xavier.devroey}@unamur.be

Abstract. Android devices and related applications are increasingly prevalent in our daily routines. Furthermore, these technologies are being used for more than just connecting people around the world. Indeed, Android devices are more and more connected to external sensors or used as sensors, directly gathering data from their environment, which brings them closer to *Cyber Physical Systems (CPS)*. When used for specific purposes such as health, Android devices and related applications can be life-critical (insulin pumps, heart monitoring, etc.), requiring guarantees specific to the application domain. Interestingly, when considering the technical security in domains related to operational technologies, we can see that many *standards* are available while not directly intended for Android applications. Other *regulatory texts* can also be valuable to drive an audit process, although they need more effort to reach technically testable requirements from the legal requirements they define. In particular, Android applications are developed using various device permissions (i.e., resource access), external libraries, etc. In this paper, we present A3S3 a tool to link requirements from industry standards and regulatory texts to Android features to drive a security audit. Following research in the cyber-security community, we suggest an approach based on static code analysis of Android applications to retrieve good and bad *signals*, denoting potential violations, related to non-functional requirements.

Keywords: android · compliance · static analysis · tool · safety · security

1 Introduction and Motivation

The Android Operating System (OS) makes up approximately 70% of the market share in terms of mobile operating systems [23]. With its development, Android-based devices are now commonly used for many different purposes than initially intended. Indeed, it started as an OS for mobile devices such as phones and tablets when Google released it in 2007, 2 years after their acquisition [7]. And now *Android is an open source, Linux-based software stack created for a wide array of devices and form factors* [11]. This new definition includes way more device types than previously. Many of those devices are part of our daily routines and are being used as means of data collection, among other things. This includes serving as an intermediary with Internet of Things (IoT) devices such as smart home devices, smartwatches, smart TVs, projectors, etc.

Highlighting the sensor capabilities of Android devices and their integration with external sensors, we can see that their use is closer to *Cyber Physical Systems (CPS)*, which relies on sensor data and real-time computing to have an effect on the real world than regular Android applications. CPSs share similarities with *Embedded Systems, Internet of Things (IoT)* or *Operational Technology* (OT) in the industry. Gartner defines OT as *hardware and software that detects or causes a change through the direct monitoring and/or control of industrial equipment, assets, processes, and events* [10].

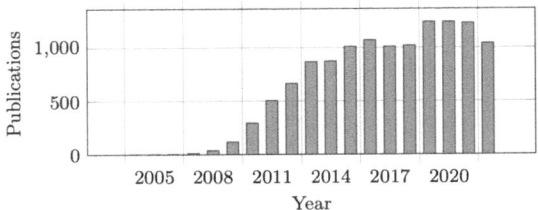

Fig. 1. Evolution of the number of papers based on search results for *"Android device"* + *"health"* on Google Scholar.

In particular, the number of Android devices used in the health sector for medical purposes is rising. Indeed, as shown in Fig. 1, we can see that the number of papers associated with *Android device* and *Health* has been growing quite steadily since Google released Android. Of course, this is only a light indicator of evolution. Yet, it remains interesting to focus our efforts on ensuring patients' safety when such technologies are used for medical purposes. Furthermore, when talking about Android Smartphones, we can see that they also have their utility as sensors. Indeed, they could also be used as *Fall Detection systems*, a significant issue for elderly people regarding life risks and hospital costs [3]. Other well-known embedded sensors, such as the camera and the microphone, can also serve various purposes in the health sector (e.g., respiratory monitoring) [18]. We can already see Android applications supporting the control of Unmanned Aerial Vehicles (UAV).

Practically, A3S3 is developed as a platform to generate, using static code analysis [17], a report enabling an auditor to decide whether an Android application passes specific audit controls based on the collected *signals* (i.e., indications of a potential violation, extracted using static analysis). Concretely, we want to help developers (or quality assurance) tick audit boxes (called *audit controls*) based on automatically retrieved Android features in specific applications. Once checked, the report produced by A3S3 can be used as an additional input for an audit process supporting the production of a proof of (non-)conformity. In short, we aim at detecting non-conformity risks similar to the efforts of the Software Engineering community in detecting security risks through audits [22]. A non-referenced demonstration video of the tool is available[1], and the source code is openly available[2]. A3S3 is a static code analyser for non-conformity risks on Android application with respect to a specific framework (regulation or standard) based on URL's, Imports and Permissions found in the decompiled code of an application.

2 Related Work

In this section we discuss the various work related to assessing an android application such as previous work in malware detection, static security analysis, non-functional properties and medical applications.

Malware Detection - Most Android application assessment focuses on malware detection [6]. For example, if a video game is requesting access to text messages, to the storage of the device, the camera, the Bluetooth devices connected to the phone, etc., it might be a signal that this video game is trying to collect data unlawfully [25]. Exploiting this relationship between permissions and malware, Aswini et al. [2] created *Droid Miner* to extract relevant permissions as *features* and determine whether those *features* are signals of a *malicious* or a *benign* application using machine learning classification techniques.

Static Security Analysis - Going deeper into Android application code analysis, we can see that there is an extensive collection of tools. Indeed, when trying to determine if an application is *benign* or *malicious*, popular tools like *FlowDroid* perform a taint analysis using *sources* (data, user input, etc.) and *sinks* (where it goes) [1]. There is also the *FEST* tool that acts as an extractor of API calls and URLs within the code [26]. As a helping tool within the *Intellij* IDE, *SWANassist* takes known *Common Weakness Enumeration* (CWE) from the *MITTRE corporation* [4] and identifies Security Relevant Method from a Java source code [20]. Finally, *SootFX*, a tool developed as a Java API, extracts a tremendous amount of features, manifest, packages, and methods from Android *.apk* files [15].

Non-functional Properties - When speaking about non-functional requirements, work is emerging from the well-known (European) *General Data Protection Regulation* (GDPR) [8] and its privacy concerns. Indeed, Tan et al. [24] use Flowdroid to find discrepancies between the declared privacy policies of some applications and the actual collection and processing of personal data within the .apk file. They actually found that application providers sometimes did not declare everything or even did not classify personal data as such. On a more precise matter, Khedar et al. [16] propose the use of static analysis on .apk files to identify

---

[1] https://youtu.be/8GB6Fcq9rII.
[2] https://github.com/sabredefable/A3S3_python.

where data anonymization was necessary and not performed or not sufficiently performed. At a higher abstraction level, Sacre et al. use metamodels to assess the conformity of a system by comparing a theoretical and compliant model to the model of the system under conformity assessment [21].

Medical Applications - Looking more specifically at the security of medical applications, Hussain et al. [12] proposed a framework accompanied by a set of tools to help developers enhance the security maturity of their applications.

As we can see, the main concern is identifying malware or data leakage within the applications. All the existing tools either provide ways of retrieving features, classifying *malicious* and *benign* applications, or finding more general *bugs*. Encouraging work is being done concerning privacy matters on Android applications. However, we look for conformity signals and propose a way to audit non-functional requirements.

3 Approach

Our solution aims to retrieve *signals* for audit controls, presented in a structured data format, and produce an audit report. In a nutshell, the assessment of conformity to a regulation or industrial standard (i.e., the audit) is usually carried out by non-technical auditors who require: (1) inputs from technical experts and (2) thorough documentation from the audited party or both. For example, conformity audits in the European Union are based on technical reports, which must include *"proof of conformity"* based on a specific legal framework [5]. Our approach allows technology-agnostic audit controls of the legal requirements by external non-technical auditors to be interpreted in technology-specific signals (here, Android).

Assessment of Medical Application. As mentioned earlier, life-critical data analysis safety concerns based on sensor collection share CPS-related concerns. So, for example, in terms of technical security, we can look at manufacturing industry standards such as IEC 62443-4-2 [13], which has been declined into multiple industry-specific variations and lays out seven technology-agnostic *Foundational Requirements* (FR's): *Identification and Authentication Control, Use Control, System Integrity, Data Confidentiality, Restrict Data Flow, Timely Response to Events* and *Resource Availability*. Those FR's have multiple controls that must be performed for a FR's to be validated. For each control, the auditor has to decide on a Security Level for each of the following categories (as defined in IEC 62443-4-2): the *target level*, the *achieved level*, and the *capability level* of a specific component. The levels range from 0 to 4, the latter being the highest level of security, indicating resilience to cyber attacks using *sophisticated means, great resources*, and *motivation*.

For this first application of A3S3, we focus on Android applications working with medical data gathered from a device connected to the Android phone using Bluetooth, any other Android Application Programming Interface (API) used to retrieve data from existing services, or the device itself. Fortunately, the IEC 62443 standard has been adapted into different versions to suit better the needs of specific manufacturing industries (here, the production of medical devices). Specifically, we use the IEC 60601-4-5 [14] that specifies the technical security requirements for Medical Devices (MD). While costs to access such documents quickly add up in the balance, we can assume that it includes the relevant security levels for each MD use case. Thus, we can use the foundational requirements as an audit base. Despite industry standards being easier than regulatory texts to use when assessing the conformity of a *product*, they do not constitute a basis for (technical) audit documents. While they give valuable information to engineers or any interested party on what to aim for when building, developing, producing, testing, etc. *products*, standards must be interpreted for each specific use case to link FR's to implementation. In our example, this means linking FR's related to Data Confidentiality and Restrict Data Flow to specific Android API calls gathering data from connected devices.

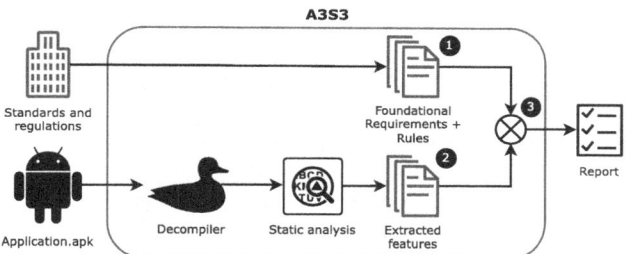

Fig. 2. A3S3 analysis pipeline overview.

Assessment Process Using A3S3. Figure 2 presents an overview of the A3S3 approach. First, we must identify the various **FRs** and their link to the different *features* that can be extracted based on defined **rules** (1 in Fig. 2). For instance, Android permissions can be easily collected and linked to the various FR's related to data management, like Data Confidentiality and Restrict Data Flow. Second, we need to apply static analysis to the Android application to collect various features (2 Fig. 2) that can be used to identify signals based on the rules defined in (1). We consider Android executables stored as .apk and .xapk files. Those files must be decompiled (from executable in binary to human-readable files) before being analyzed. For instance, for our evaluation, we consider Android applications from the Google Play store and search for applications with medical purposes to download a set of .apk and .xapk files. Finally, A3S3 assesses each FR individually based on its rules (3 Fig. 2) and produces a report with the various signals (i.e., combinations of extracted features) for each FR. In this paper, we reach level 3 on the Technology Readiness Level (TRL) scale [19].

4 Preliminary Evaluation

For our preliminary evaluation, we performed a reduced audit of an application with medical purposes to test our tool. Specific applications might have to comply with MD requirements [9]. Indeed, when looking at smartphones, we can quickly see that multiple applications offer "medical" follow-up in one form or another. While many applications include a disclaimer saying users should not be considered a replacement for a health professional, they still gather and correlate health data to provide recommendations.

Using requirements extracted from the MDR for devices with a medical purpose (monitoring, prevention or monitoring of disease) and requirements laid out in points 17 and 18 of Annex I we decided to focus on 17.2 stating *"For devices that incorporate software or for software that are devices in themselves, the software shall be developed and manufactured in accordance with the state of the art taking into account the principles of development life cycle, risk management, including information security, verification and validation"* [9, p. 100]. As previously introduced, we decided to use IEC 60601 as state of the art which has a specific application for medical devices. We focused on the fifth one: *Restrict Data Flow (RDF)*, stating that a limited number of data sources is desirable. While not an exhaustive list, we identified 8 possible data sources. By auditing 12 randomly selected health-related applications available on *Google Play*, we found that the average number of data sources per application is 3.75 and that the most common sources are Internet (12/12), Bluetooth (11/12) and Firebase (10/12). Google supports all APIs identified in the source code.

The auditor can decide whether the FR is met for each application based on the data collected. For instance, when considering *FibriCheck*, we identify the three data sources using the following features collected by the static analyzer: (i) Internet, identified from the manifest that has the '`android.permission.INTERNET`' permission;[3] (ii) Bluetooth, identified from the import of the '`android.bluetooth`' library somewhere in the code;[4] (iii) Firebase API, identified from the presence of the '`https://firebase.google.com`' URL in the code and the import of the '`com.google.firebase`' library.[5] Based on those signals, an auditor can assess if the RDF requirement is satisfied.

5 Conclusion and Future Work

We presented A3S3, a tool that performs static code analysis on Android applications following specific controls from various sources to look for *signals* that an auditor or any interested party might interpret. We showed that linking non-functional controls (i.e., FRs) to specific Android features was possible. Indeed, by auditing 12 Android applications, we looked into various data sources by performing a static code analysis and helping an auditor decide if the control

---
[3] https://developer.android.com/develop/connectivity/network-ops/connecting.
[4] https://developer.android.com/reference/android/bluetooth/package-summary.
[5] https://firebase.google.com/docs/build?hl=fr.

was satisfied. The compliance or non-compliance with a specific control remains within the auditor's power.

While we believe this tool has great potential in assessing Android applications, it will be upgraded to extract even more features. For static code analysis, we will use SootFX, which allows a broader range of static analyses, like the extraction of methods called within the application. For signal generation, we will look for additional technical regulations. For instance, we believe that the controls from IEC 62443 might act as a good cornerstone between high-level and technical requirements for CPS-related safety and security concerns.

We will also work with users to develop coherent dashboards to display the audit results in a user-friendly and adapted way (e.g., for auditors, developers, managers, etc.). We will add information on the various signals found in the assessed application to limit as much as possible the technical knowledge required to understand what the signals mean in the context of a specific regulation.

Acknowledgments. This research was funded by the CyberExcellence by Digital-Wallonia project (No. 2110186), funded by the Public Service of Wallonia (SPW Recherche).

References

1. Arzt, S., et al.: Flowdroid: precise context, flow, field, object-sensitive and lifecycle-aware taint analysis for android apps. ACM SIGPLAN Notices **49**(6), 259–269 (2014). https://doi.org/10.1145/2666356.2594299
2. Aswini, A.M., Vinod, P.: Droid permission miner: mining prominent permissions for android malware analysis. In: The Fifth International Conference on the Applications of Digital Information and Web Technologies (ICADIWT 2014). IEEE (2014). https://doi.org/10.1109/icadiwt.2014.6814679
3. Casilari, E., Luque, R., Morón, M.J.: Analysis of android device-based solutions for fall detection. Sensors **15**(8), 17827–17894 (2015). https://doi.org/10.3390/s150817827
4. Corporation, M.: CWE - Common Weakness Enumeration - cwe.mitre.org. https://cwe.mitre.org/. Accessed 10 Sept 2024
5. EC: EUR-Lex - commission notice the 'blue guide' on the implementation of EU product rules 2022 (2022). https://eur-lex.europa.eu/. Accessed 19 Nov 2024
6. Ehsan, A., Catal, C., Mishra, A.: Detecting malware by analyzing app permissions on android platform: a systematic literature review. Sensors **22**(20), 7928 (2022). https://doi.org/10.3390/s22207928
7. Elgin, B.: Google Buys Android for Its Mobile Arsenal - web.archive.org (2005). https://shorturl.at/Qoh2p. Accessed 06 Sept 2024
8. EU: Regulation - 2016/679 - EN - gdpr - EUR-Lex - eur-lex.europa.eu (2016). https://eur-lex.europa.eu/eli/reg/2016/679/oj. Accessed 20 Sept 2024
9. EU: Regulation - 2017/745 - EN - Medical Device Regulation - EUR-Lex - eur-lex.europa.eu (2017). https://eur-lex.europa.eu/legal-content/EN/TXT/?uri=CELEX%3A32017R0745. Accessed 18 Sept 2024
10. Gartner: Definition of Operational Technology (OT) - Gartner Information Technology Glossary - gartner.com. https://www.gartner.com/en/information-technology/glossary/operational-technology-ot. Accessed 04 Jul 2023

11. Google: Platform architecture — Android Developers - developer.android.com. https://developer.android.com/guide/platform?hl=en. Accessed 05 Sept 2024
12. Hussain, M., et al.: Conceptual framework for the security of mobile health applications on android platform. Telematics Inform. **35**(5), 1335–1354 (2018). https://doi.org/10.1016/j.tele.2018.03.005
13. IEC: IEC 62443-4-2:2019 (2019). https://webstore.iec.ch/en/publication/34421. Accessed 30 Aug 2024
14. IEC: IEC TR 60601-4-5:2021 (2021). https://webstore.iec.ch/en/publication/64703. Accessed 30 Aug 2024
15. Karakaya, K., Bodden, E.: Sootfx: a static code feature extraction tool for java and android. In: 2021 IEEE 21st International Working Conference on Source Code Analysis and Manipulation (SCAM). vol. 14, pp. 181–186. IEEE (2021). https://doi.org/10.1109/scam52516.2021.00030
16. Khedkar, M., Bodden, E.: Toward an android static analysis approach for data protection (2024). https://doi.org/10.48550/ARXIV.2402.07889
17. Louridas, P.: Static code analysis. IEEE Softw. **23**(4), 58–61 (2006). https://doi.org/10.1109/ms.2006.114
18. Majumder, S., Deen, M.J.: Smartphone sensors for health monitoring and diagnosis. Sensors **19**(9), 2164 (2019). https://doi.org/10.3390/s19092164
19. Mankins, J.C., et al.: Technology readiness levels. White Paper, April **6**(1995), 1995 (1995)
20. Piskachev, G., Nguyen Quang Do, L., Johnson, O., Bodden, E.: Swanassist: semi-automated detection of code-specific, security-relevant methods. In: 2019 34th IEEE-ACM International Conference on Automated Software Engineering (ASE). IEEE (2019). https://doi.org/10.1109/ase.2019.00110
21. Sacre, A., Colin, J.N., Hosselet, B.: ARRCIS: évaluation et renforcement de la conformité réglementaire d'un système d'information, pp. 159–176. No. 52 in Collection du CRIDS, Larcier (2021)
22. Sanchez-Garcia, I.D., Rea-Guaman, A.M., Gilabert, T.S.F., Calvo-Manzano, J.A.: Cybersecurity Risk Audit: A Systematic Literature Review, p. 275-301. Springer (2024). https://doi.org/10.1007/978-3-031-50590-4_18
23. Statista: Mobile OS market share worldwide 2009-2024 — Statista - statista.com (2024). https://www.statista.com/statistics/272698/global-market-share-held-by-mobile-operating-systems-since-2009/. Accessed 09 Sept 2024
24. Tan, Z., Song, W.: PTPDROID: detecting violated user privacy disclosures to third-parties of android apps. In: 2023 IEEE/ACM 45th International Conference on Software Engineering (ICSE), pp. 473–485. IEEE (2023). https://doi.org/10.1109/icse48619.2023.00050
25. Zhang, Y., et al.: Vetting undesirable behaviors in android apps with permission use analysis. In: Proceedings of the 2013 ACM SIGSAC Conference on Computer & Communications Security - CCS '13. CCS '13, pp. 611–622. ACM Press (2013)
26. Zhao, K., Zhang, D., Su, X., Li, W.: Fest: a feature extraction and selection tool for android malware detection. In: 2015 IEEE Symposium on Computers and Communication (ISCC). IEEE (2015). https://doi.org/10.1109/iscc.2015.7405598

FIREPRIME App: A Self-assessment Tool to Evaluate Home Risk to Wildfires

Marc Oriol[✉], Lidia López, Huihui Xu, and Xavier Franch

Universitat Politècnica de Catalunya, Barcelona, Spain
{marc.oriol,lidia.lopez,xavier.franch}@upc.edu,
huihui.xu@estudiantat.upc.edu

Abstract. Wildfires are an increasing global threat due to climate change and environmental factors. Communities in high-risk areas often lack the necessary knowledge and resources to assess and mitigate their vulnerability to wildfires. To address this issue, we developed the FIREPRIME app, a mobile application designed to evaluate home wildfire risk and provide personalized mitigation recommendations. The app integrates a structured questionnaire assessing house vulnerability factors with real-time hazard data from the Copernicus Fire Weather Index (FWI). The house vulnerability factor is computed using a fault tree model. The application was developed as part of the FIREPRIME European research project, incorporating feedback from three pilot sites in Spain, Sweden, and Austria. This paper presents the design, implementation, and evaluation of the FIREPRIME app, highlighting its usability and effectiveness in guiding homeowners toward improved wildfire resilience. A formative evaluation was conducted with project stakeholders, resulting in usability improvements and feature enhancements. Our findings indicate that the FIREPRIME app is a valuable tool for raising awareness and promoting proactive risk reduction in wildfire-prone regions.

Keywords: Wildfire risk assessment · house vulnerability · app · recommender system

1 Introduction

Wildfires have become an increasingly frequent and severe threat across the world, driven by climate change and other environmental factors. Rising temperatures, reduced humidity, and prolonged dry seasons have significantly heightened wildfire risks, even in regions that previously faced little to no threat. For instance, data from 2024 indicate that the number of recorded wildfires has surpassed the 2010–2020 average in multiple European countries[1]. Heatwaves create ideal conditions for wildfire outbreaks, as seen in past incidents such as the devastating wildfires in Greece in 2018, Canada in 2023, or California in 2025, to name a few examples.

---

[1] EFFIS Statistics: https://forest-fire.emergency.copernicus.eu/apps/effis.statistics/.

© The Author(s), under exclusive license to Springer Nature Switzerland AG 2025
L. Pufahl et al. (Eds.): CAiSE 2025, LNBIP 557, pp. 213–220, 2025.
https://doi.org/10.1007/978-3-031-94590-8_26

Beyond their devastating environmental impact, wildfires pose serious risks to human lives, infrastructure, and economies. As these incidents grow in frequency and intensity, effective prevention and mitigation strategies are more critical than ever. A key challenge in wildfire management is improving the preparedness and self-protection capacity of rural communities, which are often the most vulnerable. Many residents in high-risk areas lack the necessary knowledge and resources to respond effectively, complicating prevention efforts and increasing overall danger. Addressing this issue requires the development of targeted tools and strategies to enhance community resilience and response capabilities in the face of escalating wildfire threats.

To tackle this growing challenge, we have developed the FIREPRIME app, a mobile application that features a structured questionnaire that evaluates key factors influencing the house vulnerability to wildfires combined with the inherent wildfire risk of the area (hazard). In addition to this risk assessment, the application provides personalized recommendations to improve the safety of the house, guiding users on effective measures to reduce the wildfire risk.

The development of this app has been conducted as part of the FIREPRIME European research project[2] comprising three pilot sites: Collserola (Barcelona, Spain), the Swedish west coast (Göteborg, Sweden), and Tyrol (Haiming, Austria). FIREPRIME is an interdisciplinary project that brings together expertise from civil protection, environmental science, social sciences, and digital technologies to build fire resilience in diverse wildland-urban interface (WUI) communities across Europe. The first version of the tool is complete, successfully tested internally by project partners, and will soon be deployed at the pilot sites. The app and a video material demoing the tool in use is available at: https://github.com/FIREPRIME-APP.

The FIREPRIME app embodies the "Bridging Silos" theme of CAiSE'25 by integrating multiple domains—technology, environmental science, risk management, and human-centric design—into a cohesive information system for wildfire risk assessment.

The rest of the paper is organized as follows: Sect. 2 describes the app functionalities. Section 3 provides the architecture details. Section 4 includes the evaluation methodology and results. Section 5 explores the related work. Finally, Sect. 6 presents the conclusions and future work.

2 Software Description

This section illustrates, via an example, the use of the FIREPRIME app main functionalities. The non-functional requirements for this app are critical because of the final users' diversity and the possibility of being used in a low-connectivity area. The application should support multi-language, be adapted to the country, be really easy to use, be functional even if there is no connection to the Internet, and be available for both Android and iOS systems.

To start with the risk assessment, the homeowner needs to register the house in the application, providing the address where the house is located. Once a house is registered, the homeowner is requested to answer a questionnaire that includes a total of 25 multichoice questions. The first set of questions are related to the house characteristics and

---

[2] https://civil-protection-knowledge-network.europa.eu/projects/fireprime.

the second set to the house surroundings. Questions include a description and a set of images to make it easier for the user to understand what is being asked (see Fig. 1a); those images can be different depending on the country defined in the house address. When all the questions are answered, the app shows the risk assessment result representing the wildfire risk index: a number from 0 to 100 where 0 represents the lower risk and 100 the higher risk. Figure 1b shows the assessment result; the risk index value is complemented with a graphical representation using a gauge chart coloured from green (values near to 0 representing low risk) to red (values near to 100 representing high risk).

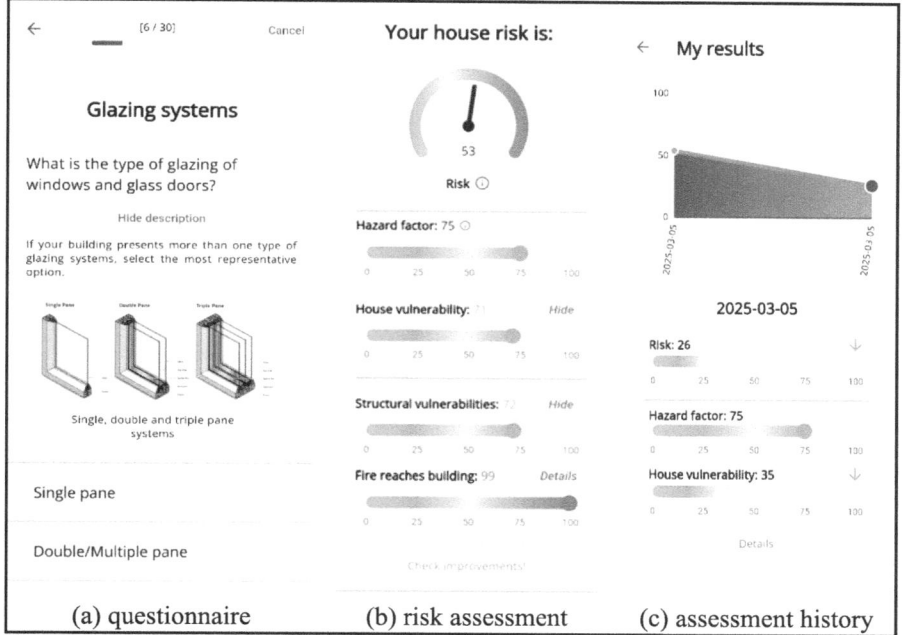

Fig. 1. FIREPRIME app questionnaire and results

The risk index is calculated as the multiplication of two components: fire hazard level of the area where the house is located and house vulnerability factor. The hazard level is based on the Fire Weather Index[3] provided by Copernicus[4,5], the Earth Observation component of the European Union's space programme. The vulnerability factor is calculated using a fault tree model [1], whose input are the answers from the questionnaire. In the example shown in Fig. 1b, the homeowner can see a risk index value equals to 53 that is the result of multiplying 0.75 (fire hazard level as a percentage) and 71 (vulnerability

---

[3] The Fire Weather Index (FWI) is a meteorologically based index used worldwide to estimate fire danger. The concrete value used is the "Danger by weather" data that corresponds to the number of days with high-to-extreme fire danger by weather (FWI >= 30).

[4] https://www.copernicus.eu/.

[5] https://forest-fire.emergency.copernicus.eu/apps/fire.risk.viewer/.

factor), both numbers being shown using a progress chart just below the gauge. The risk index value 53 is near the midpoint of the scale, suggesting a moderately concerning state, but the vulnerability factor is 71, near to the risky area. In order to understand the house characteristics that are negatively affecting the vulnerability, the user can see the detailed assessment that is shown just below (Fig. 1b). The details correspond to the result of the evaluated properties defined on the fault tree model; likewise, these properties' evaluations are numerical values from 0 to 100, also represented graphically using a progress chart using green for low good values and red for high bad values. In this example, the vulnerability property worst ranked is the house glazing system, with a value of 59 (Fig. 2a).

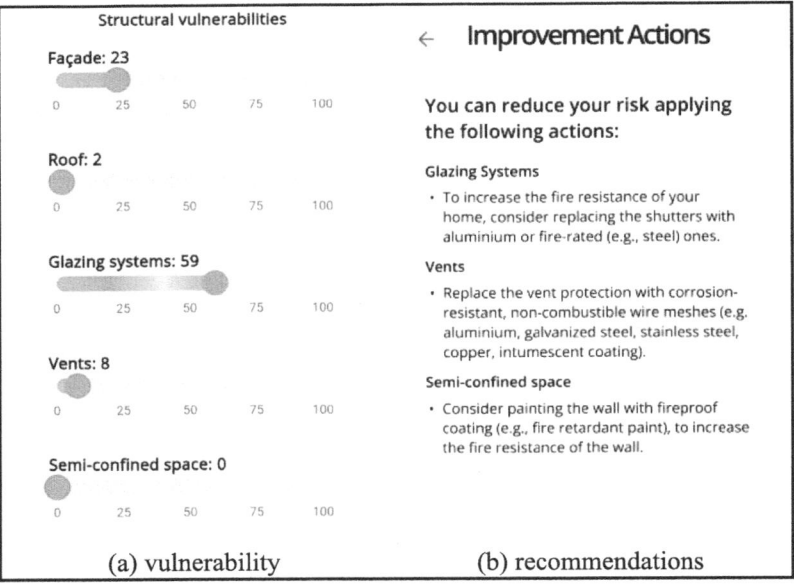

Fig. 2. Assessment details and improvement actions

Based on the answers from the questionnaire, using the button "Check improvements" just below the risk assessment (see Fig. 1b), the user obtains a list of recommendations of changes on the house to decrease the fire vulnerability (see Fig. 2b). For example, to improve the glazing systems, the app recommends *"replacing the shutters with aluminium or fire-rated"*. When the homeowner performs the suggested renovations, they should change one or more answers in the questionnaire to reflect the new house or surrounding characteristics, and then ask the app to reevaluate the risk assessment.

When the user performs more than one risk assessment, the app provides a historical risk assessment view (Fig. 1c), using a chart to provide graphical representation of the risk factor evolution over time. In the example used in this section, selecting the last evaluation, the user can see that the risk index value (26) is better than the previous one (53).

The application also includes usage monitoring, storing anonymised information on how the final users navigate through the screens and options, providing valuable feedback to be used to enhance the user experience.

3 Architecture

The FIREPRIME app is a mobile application with a modular, loosely coupled and extensible layered architecture to provide flexibility and ease of integration of new components (see Fig. 3). It is worth mentioning that the entire execution takes place locally on the user's mobile device, whilst having a cache-based resilient communication with external services, ensuring a smooth experience independent of internet connectivity issues.

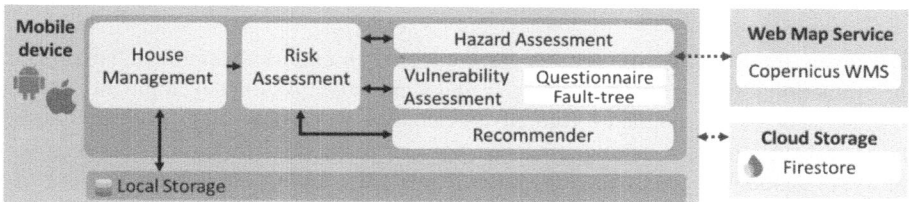

Fig. 3. FIREPRIME App architecture

The *House Management* component is the main entry-point of the app and responsible for managing the different houses of the end-user. This component interacts with *Risk Assessment* whenever a new risk assessment is initiated by the end-user. The *Risk Assessment* component orchestrates the *Hazard Assessment*, and the *Vulnerability Assessment*.

The *Hazard Assessment* component computes the hazard level of the area where the house is located. It communicates with an external *Web Map Service* (WMS) that provides data related to the hazard level of an area. In the current implementation, the FIREPRIME app is integrated with the *Copernicus WMS*, which provides the hazard level from any area in Europe. Nevertheless, the app can be easily extended with additional WMS if needed. In case that the *Hazard Assessment* can't connect to the *Web Map Service*, it uses the hazard level of the area, previously stored in cache.

The *Vulnerability Assessment* component computes the vulnerability of the house. It is composed of a *Questionnaire* to interact with the end-user and a *Fault-tree* to compute the vulnerability of the house based on the questionnaire's responses. The *Fault-tree* component uses fault-tree analysis to compute the vulnerability of the house based on the user's responses. The topology of the faul-tree, which comprises the vulnerability values associated for each response, along with their weights and relationships affecting the overall vulnerability of the house, is based on the fault-tree from Alba et al. [1].

When the risk value is obtained, the *Recommender* is triggered to suggest recommendations to the end-user on how to mitigate the vulnerability of their houses. The *Recommender* follows a rule-based approach, in which, based on the responses of the user and the values obtained in the assessment, it provides a list of actionable recommendations to reduce the risk of their houses.

Finally, the application tracks the user interactions with its functionalities and securely stores this data in the cloud using Firestore[6]. To protect the privacy of the end-users, all information is anonymized, and only interaction patterns—excluding responses or risk-related data—are recorded. This information enables the collection of implicit feedback, helping to refine and guide the app's future development.

The app has been implemented using Flutter[7]. Flutter is a cross-platform framework that enables the development of apps for multiple platforms using a single codebase. This feature enabled the FIREPRIME app to be available for both Android and iPhone devices seamlessly.

4 Evaluation

To evaluate the FIREPRIME app, we have adopted an empirical approach, structuring our evaluation into two phases: formative and summative. As the development is being done iteratively, we designed a formative evaluation workshop to be conducted at the end of each development iteration, involving project members. The formative workshops consist of 2-hour sessions where the participants are asked to use the app to complete specific tasks and then answer a questionnaire to evaluate quality properties of the app (e.g. usability, visualisation, understandability). This structured evaluation is followed by an open session to identify nice features and potential improvements. Following this structured evaluation, an open session takes place where the participants are asked to write in cards nice features, potential improvements, and other comments. The moderator reads all the cards, asking for clarification when needed, and asks the participants to vote (each participant has 3 votes). The most voted improvements are discussed to obtain concrete actions to be developed in the next development iteration. Currently, we have performed part of the formative evaluation.

This paper reports the results of the first formative evaluation workshop, which was performed virtually by September 23rd, 2024. A total of 12 people participated from all the project partners, five of them representatives from the use cases, four from technical partners, and three of the papers' authors. To assess the quality of the app, 9 participants filled a questionnaire to analyse the app usability using the System Usability Scale (SUS), widely recognized as a commonly used tool for assessing usability [2]. The SUS score obtained in the evaluation was 75 (in the range [0..100]). According to Bangor et al. [3], scores over 68 are considered above average, with a score of 75 being considered good, though still leaving some room for improvement.

The app version reported in this paper includes two major improvements based on the reported evaluation: (a) the functionality of recommending improvements, which is related to the most voted improvement "*... help the user understand which are the best options to improve her/his home*" with nine votes, and (b) the hazard factor in the risk index computation supporting the "*... A home with the same conditions could have*

---

[6] https://firebase.google.com/docs/firestore.
[7] https://flutter.dev/.

different vuln depending on the community" with 4 votes. There were also some minor improvements to enhance the user experience, such as including the arrows next to the assessment in the historical view.

The most voted nice features were: "*It is nice to see the history of the vulnerability … It is a way to reinforce the commitment of homeowners*" and "*Very helpful with the photos and photos change for each country*", both with seven votes, followed by "*vulnerability score showed very clearly*" with two.

The complete details of the workshop structure, the responses of participants and subsequent analysis can be found in the replication package [4].

5 Related Work

Several tools and mobile apps have been developed to help prevent or mitigate wildfire risks in rural areas. Kamilaris et al. [5] introduced EscapeWildFire, an app that predicts wildfire movement in real time, to facilitate safe evacuations. Monedero et al. [6] developed the Wildfire Analyst Pocket Edition, an app designed for firefighters, offering real-time fire visualization and behaviour analysis. Similarly, Ottolini et al. [7] introduced WilfireWatch, an app that tracks wildfires in Spanish regions.

Regarding house vulnerability, apps like the FireSmart Begins at Home, developed as part of the FireSmart project [8], help homeowners to assess the wildfire risks to their houses. Through a series of property-related questions, the app helps homeowners identify steps they can take to reduce the vulnerability of their houses. Other apps out of the scientific community, such as Fire Risk Assessment & Audit[8], RiskBase[9], or QuidvisRisk Fire Assessments[10] also offer self-assessment questionnaires to identify the fire vulnerabilities. However, these applications are designed primarily for auditing purposes rather than wildfire risk assessment in rural areas.

All the aforementioned tools lack a comprehensive approach, as they do not aggregate data holistically to generate a hazard or risk indicator based on a robust model. Instead, they typically focus on a few aspects of either hazard or vulnerability in isolation, without integrating them into a unified, data-driven assessment that provides a complete picture of home risks to wildfire. To the best of our knowledge, the FIREPRIME app is the only app that integrates both vulnerability and hazard assessment. By implementing a model capable of computing a hazard indicator, it provides a more advanced data-driven and holistic approach to wildfire risk assessment.

6 Conclusions and Future Work

In this paper we have presented the FIREPRIME app, a mobile application that represents a significant step forward in wildfire risk assessment and mitigation for homeowners. By integrating house vulnerability analysis and hazard data from the Copernicus FWI, FIREPRIME provides users with actionable recommendations tailored to their specific

---
[8] https://play.google.com/store/apps/details?id=com.platinumproperty.fra.
[9] https://riskbase.uk/.
[10] https://apps.apple.com/gb/app/quidvisrisk-fire-assessments/id1503338827.

risk conditions. The evaluation results demonstrate that users find the app useful, particularly its ability to visualize risk evolution, and suggest targeted improvements. The usability assessment yielded a System Usability Scale (SUS) score of 75, indicating a strong foundation while also revealing areas for refinement.

The iterative development process, involving stakeholders from three European pilot sites, ensured that the app addresses diverse environmental conditions and user needs. The results from the evaluation workshop led to meaningful enhancements, such as incorporating a hazard factor in the risk computation and providing clearer improvement recommendations.

As future work, we will conduct additional evaluations during a second formative workshop with project partners, followed by the deployment of the app at the pilot sites with real end-users. These activities will include both qualitative and quantitative validations, incorporating structured surveys and usage analytics to assess the app's effectiveness, usability, and impact.

Overall, FIREPRIME demonstrates how digital tools can empower communities to proactively manage wildfire risks, bridging the gap between scientific hazard assessments and practical homeowner actions.

Acknowledgments. This research was partially funded by the European Union Civil Protection (Project GA101140381, FIREPRIME UCPM-2023- KAPP) anb by the AGAUR program SGR-Cat 2021, project 2021 SGR 01531.

Disclosure of Interests. The authors declare that they have no known competing financial interests or personal relationships that could have appeared to influence the work reported in this paper.

References

1. Àgueda, A., Vacca, P., Planas, E., Pastor, E.: Evaluating wildfire vulnerability of Mediterranean dwellings using fuzzy logic applied to expert judgement. Int. J. Wildland Fire **32**, 1011–1029 (2023)
2. Lewis, J.R.: The system usability scale: past, present, and future. Int. J. Hum. Comput. Interact. **34**(7), 577–590 (2018)
3. Bangor, A., Kortum, P.T., Miller, J.T.: An empirical evaluation of the system usability scale. Int. J. Hum. Comput. Interact. **24**(6), 574–594 (2008)
4. Oriol, M., López, L.: Replication package for paper "FIREPRIME app: a self-assessment tool to evaluate home risk to wildfires" (2025). https://doi.org/10.5281/zenodo.15200056
5. Kamilaris, A., et al.: EscapeWildFire: assisting people to escape wildfires in real-time. In: PerCom Workshops, pp. 129–134 (2021)
6. Monedero, S., Ramirez, J., Cardil, A.: Predicting fire spread and behaviour on the fireline. Wildfire analyst pocket: a mobile app for wildland fire prediction. Ecol. Model. **392**, 103–107 (2019)
7. Ottolini, I., Arenas, M., Prat-Guitart, N., Uyttewaal, K., Pandey, P., Rodríguez-Giralt, I., Cifre-Sabater, M.: A toolkit for fostering co-creation and participative community engagement with vulnerable communities at risk. PyroLife Project, deliverable D17 (2023)
8. Ergibi, M., Hesseln, H.: Awareness and adoption of FireSmart Canada: barriers and incentives. For. Policy Econ. **119**, 102271 (2020)

Doctoral Consortium – Enterprise Architecture

Toward Improving the Quality of Enterprise Architecture Models

Jan Schoonderbeek[✉]

Maastricht University, Maastricht, The Netherlands
j.schoonderbeek@architecting.nl

Abstract. In the field of Enterprise Architecture (EA), the EA model (EAM) plays a crucial role. However, the topic of EAM quality is not well researched, negatively impacting not only actual practitioners in the field of EA, but also educators and researchers in EA.

This research proposal outlines addressing this issue by investigating the attributes and corresponding guidelines that influence EAM quality. To support this investigation, a theory for EAM quality needs to be devised. Furthermore, it is highly desirable to obtain a quality framework specifically geared to support EAM quality. All these research activities require establishing at least a basic theory of EAMs and EA modelling, as well as an applied ontology that can serve to express the relevant topics.

Keywords: Enterprise Architecture Model Quality · Enterprise Architecture Modelling theory · Applied Ontology

1 Introduction

In order for the enterprise architects to prepare their advice to the decision makers, they require analysis of the required change. To enable such analysis, they usually capture and use different architectures, such as the baseline and target architectures, as well as relevant reference architectures [6,31]. Depending on the needs at hand, the capture of such architectures is carried out by constructing and documenting one or more enterprise architecture models (EAMs). These models are underpinning many of the architects' professional products and services. On top of that, models often play an important role in communicating with the decision makers, implementers, and other stakeholders [14, ch. 3–4].

2 Problem Definition

2.1 The Problem Itself

The EAM plays a crucial role in the endeavour of Enterprise Architecture (EA), since EAMs are contained in, or provide an underpinning of, many of the architects' professional products and services [9,14,25,30]. But while the quality of

EA services is a regular topic of research, e.g. [17,20,32], the quality of EAMs themselves is not [26].

Here, the term "quality" itself cannot be left at the level of implicit understanding [26, p.9]. In this research, the following definition for quality will be employed: *"Quality is meeting and/or exceeding customers' expectations"* [24, pp. 432–433]. The motivation for using this definition is outlined in [26, ch. 3.2].

Given this, the problem of EAM quality can succinctly be put as follows: outside of visualization, there is little theory on what constitutes EAM quality, how one could determine the quality of an EAM, or how one could obtain sufficient quality in the creation of an EAM to meet and/or exceed the expectations of the EAM's consumers.

That is not to say that *no* materials exist to help with creating EA models, just that these materials are based overwhelmingly on "good practice", rather than a theory of model quality.

2.2 The Groups that Are Affected by This Problem

The lack of research results on which to build an EA modelling praxis leads to many problems for the **actual practitioners** in the discipline of EA. Just to name a few:

- An EAM may be of insufficient quality to contribute to an organization's decision making process for change initiatives, but practitioners of EA have no objective way to determine this. When practitioners of EA use such (possibly) lacking EAMs to support the decision makers, the quality of the outcome of the decision making process may suffer. To put that more bluntly: if an EA practitioner is making use of a bad EAM, business decisions on change that rely on their advice are impacted.
- Not knowing what makes an EAM "good" means a practitioner cannot objectively determine when to stop improving the model. But if an EAM is developed beyond the point of "good enough", then every bit of that additional work unnecessarily diminishes the Return on modelling Effort (RoME) [22] for that EAM.

Furthermore, the lack of EA modelling theory also affects the **educators that teach EA modelling**. Not knowing what influences model quality makes it challenging to teach EA modelling as a discipline to (aspiring or practising) EA modellers. As a result, educators teach the use of specific modelling languages, focusing on the language particulars (such as syntax) instead of the modelling acts that would promote EA model quality.

And finally, the lack of understanding of EAM quality is problematic for **researchers into EAMs and EA modelling**, because there is very little material on which they can build. Not every researcher has the expertise, time, and/or resources to themselves create the very scientific foundations they require for further research. Consequentially, these researchers then might base their work on incomplete or inapt foundations, are forced to spend time and effort creating their own foundations (for which they might lack time and resources, and/or may be ill equipped), or find themselves leaving the problem area of EAM quality altogether.

2.3 The State of the Practice on This Issue

There is little theory on obtaining/maintaining sufficient quality [30] (notwithstanding works like [13,15,29]). Even practical guidance based on scientific research, such as [14, ch.7], seems to be thin on the ground[1]. Thus, the creation of EA models must currently be considered a best-effort affair, for which the quality of its results cannot be objectively determined.

Consequently, most of the guidance available to EA modellers is of a practical nature, and based largely or entirely on the opinion and experience of its writer. That guidance may actually be sound, and the quality of the results therefore sufficient (maybe even excellent), but without scientific underpinning and an objective standard for EAM quality, there is no way to tell such material apart from other works that do *not* lead to improving an EAM's quality.

In prior work, the author has contributed via [26], a bachelor thesis that presents an initial investigation into the problem of enterprise architecture model quality. This has been followed by [27], a master's thesis that provides the first part of an ontology with which to discuss enterprise architecture models and their quality, and [28], a paper that summarises the master's thesis.

2.4 The Challenges to Overcome

Lack of EAM Quality Attributes and of a Theory for EAM Quality: Earlier work by the author [26] notes that on the topic of EAM quality, not much research material is available. For example, see this quote:

> "... we identify a lack of work regarding quality assessment of enterprise architecture models in general and frameworks or methods on that account in particular." [30, p.14]

In [26, ch.4.2], a set of EAM quality attributes was presented that were extracted from the literature. However, it was noted that the set is a first approximation, that cannot be considered complete, and that it is lacking in empirical validation [26, p.37].

For a theory for EAM quality, the above also holds. Theoretical approaches such as [15] have not yielded generally accepted theories for the quality of specifically EAMs, and neither have pragmatic approaches such as [14].

---

[1] As an illustration, a search on Google Scholar conducted in February 2025, and combining the three terms `"practical guidance"`, `"modelling"`, and `"enterprise architecture"` (including the quotation marks) returned 359 results. Of these, none had as its main topic the practical guidance for EA *modelling* itself. Incidentally, the query did return my own paper [28] published in 2024, but that is because it mentions "modellers *lack* practical guidance".

Lack of a Quality Framework for EAM Quality: Any discussion on quality can gain extra support from using a quality framework [15]. Such a framework can provides a systematic structure to categorise and evaluate quality attributes. In author's earlier work [26], a number of quality frameworks were investigated. It was concluded that none directly addresses EAM quality – although identifying CMQF [19] as a promising candidate, while discounting EAQF [30]. Furthermore, validation of each of these frameworks is limited or wholly absent.

Lack of a Theory for EAMs and for EA Modelling: When searching for either a theory for EAMs, or one for EA modelling, the results of the search fall into one of several categories.

- They describe a method by which to construct EAMs, but either without theory sufficiently substantiating it (e.g. [25]), or with scientific underpinning limited to (domain-)specific detail (e.g. [14]).
- They provide theories on modelling, but for a domain that is either (much) more general than the domain of EA (e.g. [1]), or for a domain that differs significantly from EA (e.g. [8]), and thus are not readily applicable to EAMs.
- They provide theories on modelling that might be applied to the domain of EA (e.g. [13]), but provide little or no guidance on how an EA modeller is to apply the theory in practice.

Lack of an Applied Ontology for EAMs: Any type of scientific research requires a suitable conceptual framework. Such a framework is expected to contain an ontology [4, p.130]. Scientific research into EAM quality is in no way exempt of this requirement [23].

> "An ontology is a conceptual model of (a fragment of) an observed reality; it is, in essence, a repository of interlinked concepts pertaining to a given application domain." [5, p.79]

> "An ontology specifies a rich description of the
> - terminology, concepts, nomenclature;
> - relationships among and between concepts and individuals; and
> - sentences distinguishing concepts, refining definitions and relationships (constraints, restrictions, regular expressions)
>
> relevant to a particular domain or area of interest" [11, pp.2-3]

Despite its relevance to research into EAM quality, no suitable applied[2] ontology for EA modelling and EAM quality readily presents itself.

---

[2] The term "applied" is used to distinguish between on the one hand a *foundational* ontology, which provides terms to describe metadata, basic knowledge such as the concept of time, and core domain-level content, and on the other hand *applied* ontology, which deals with the adequate presentation of a specific domain for scientific and practical purposes [18, p. 21].

A sizeable hurdle to researching EAM quality is the absence of a comprehensive, consistent, and tested applied ontology, suitable for researching and practising EA. As a consequence, a researcher looking into EAMs and EAM quality must either make use of an existing but ill suited (or even wholly unsuitable) ontology, or by necessity create their own ontology. This severely impedes relating different pieces of research into EA modelling and EAM quality.

3 Problem Statement

Given the challenges as indicated above, the research problem is captured as:
There exists no pragmatic guidance fully backed by theory by which an EA modeller can create EA models of sufficient quality.

- There is an absence of practical guidance for EA modellers that is both supported by theory and explicitly aims to improve Enterprise Architecture model quality.
- There is also a lack of a comprehensive theory for Enterprise Architecture model quality.
- There are multiple competing but unvalidated model quality frameworks.
- There is a distinct lack of an applied ontology that can serve the researchers of Enterprise Architecture models, let alone the practitioners that work with such models.

4 Research Questions

To tackle the problem as described in the problem statement, this thesis work will address the following research question, with subordinate and coordinate research questions:
How can a practising EA modeller improve EA model quality?

1. What does "EA model quality" entail?
   (a) What constitutes an applied ontology, suitable for describing EA models and their quality?
      i. Which terms and relations of more generic types of modelling are applicable to EA modelling?
      ii. Which theory or theories describe relevant aspects of EA modelling and EA model quality?
      iii. What are the relevant terms and relations of an applied ontology for EA model quality?
   (b) Which quality attributes of an EA model have a major influence on their quality?
      i. What are (the) quality attributes of an EA model?
      ii. How do the quality attributes of an EA model influence EA model quality?
      iii. What quality framework can provide a systematic structure to categorise and evaluate quality attributes?
2. What modelling guidelines contribute in improving EA model quality?

5 Research Objectives and Deliverables

The objective that follows from research sub-question 1(a) and its own sub-questions is to create and present an applied ontology, suitable for describing EAMs and their quality, and including those pieces of EA modelling theories that are relevant to EAM quality[3]. Deliverables that realise this objective:

- An applied ontology suitable for describing EAMs, including their quality, creation, usage, and lifecycle.
- A coherent theory, or set of theories, that cover the creation, usage, and lifecycle of EAMs.

The objective that follows from research sub-question 1(b) and its own sub-questions is to establish the criteria or aspects that determine EAM quality. Deliverables that realise this:

- A qualitative description of EAM quality.
- A quality framework specifically geared to support EAM quality.
- A set of quality attributes that have a major influence on EAM quality.

The objective and deliverable from research sub-question 2 is to obtain a set of guidelines for EA modellers that assist in attaining sufficient EAM quality for its intended use. This last deliverable, supported by the other deliverables, then answers the main research question.

6 Research Approach/Methodology

6.1 Research Approach and Strategy

The desired end result of the thesis research is a set of guidelines for EA modellers. This constitutes an artefact, and thus a suitable means to conduct the research is to employ a design science approach [10]. The overall plan for conducting the research is by means of two strategies:

- Deductive analysis [21]: apply existing theoretical and conceptual frameworks, including a suitable foundational ontology, to obtain an applied ontology and a set of theories covering EAM quality, including a qualitative description of EAM quality.
- Surveys [10, ch. 3.2.3]: validate the results from the deductive analysis work by means of purposive sampling.

---

[3] Note: this research deliverable already has been partially realized in [28].

6.2 Research Methods

The methods by which the research will be conducted mainly fall in three categories:

- Systematic literature review (SLR) [3, pp. 94–100]: to uncover existing knowledge and data, material to this research.
- Deductive thematic analysis [21, ch. 2]: using the theory from the SLR to qualitatively analyse the research problem.
- Delphi panels [2], comprising seasoned practitioners in the field of EA modelling. This instrument will be employed for the following purposes:
  - To evaluate the obtained ontology for usability in practice in a focus group
  - To test the selected EAM quality framework, so as to validate its efficacy0. This is done using questionnaires, and employing SPL-SEM [7] for the data analysis.
  - To evaluate and improve the drafted EA modelling guidelines.
- A case study [3, pp. 63–69]: to test the EA modelling guidelines by employing them in practice.

References

1. Apostel, L.: Towards the formal study of models in the non-formal sciences. In: The Concept and the Role of the Model in Mathematics and Natural and Social Sciences: Proceedings of the Colloquium sponsored by the Division of Philosophy of Sciences of the International Union of History and Philosophy of Sciences organized at Utrecht, January 1960, by H. Freudenthal, pp. 1–37. Springer (1961)
2. Avella, J.R.: Delphi panels: research design, procedures, advantages, and challenges. Int. J. Dr. Stud. **11**, 305–321 (2016)
3. Bell, E., Bryman, A., Bill, H.: Business Research Methods, 6th edn. Oxford University Press (2022)
4. Berman, J., Smyth, R.: Conceptual frameworks in the doctoral research process: a pedagogical model. Innov. Educ. Teach. Int. **52**(2), 125–136 (2015)
5. De Nicola, A., Missikoff, M.: A lightweight methodology for rapid ontology engineering. Commun. ACM **59**(3), 79–86 (2016)
6. Greefhorst, D., Proper, E.: Architecture principles: the cornerstones of enterprise architecture. In: The Enterprise Engineering Series, vol. 4. Springer, Heidelberg (2011)
7. Hair, J., Hult, G., et al.: A Primer on Partial Least Squares Structural Equation Modeling (PLS-SEM), 2nd ed. Sage (2016)
8. Hestenes, D.: Modeling theory for math and science education. In: Lesh, R., Galbraith, P.L., Haines, C.R., Hurford, A. (eds.) Modeling Students' Mathematical Modeling Competencies: ICTMA 13, pp. 13–41. Springer, US (2010)
9. International Organization for Standardization. Systems and software engineering-Architecture description, No. 42010; 2nd edn. (2022)
10. Johannesson, P., Perjons, E.: An Introduction to Design Science. Springer (2021)
11. Kendall, E., McGuinness, D.: Ontology Engineering. In Synthesis Lectures on the Semantic Web: Theory and Technology, vol. 9. Springer (2019)
12. Kenyon, G., Sen, K.: The Perception of Quality. Springer (2015)

13. Krogstie, J.: Quality in Business Process Modeling. Springer (2016)
14. Lankhorst, M., Hoppenbrouwers, S., et al.: Enterprise Architecture at Work: Modelling, Communication and Analysis (2017)
15. Lindland, O., Sindre, G., Solvberg, A.: Understanding quality in conceptual modeling. IEEE Softw. **11**(2), 42–49 (1994)
16. Mayr, H.C., Thalheim, B.: The triptych of conceptual modeling. Softw. Syst. Model. **20**(1), 7–24 (2020)
17. Mirsalari, S., Ranjbarfard, M.: A model for evaluation of enterprise architecture quality. Eval. Program Plann. **83**, 101853 (2020)
18. Munn. Applied Ontology-An Introduction. Ontos (2013)
19. Nelson, H., Poels, G., Genero, M., Piattini, M.: A conceptual modeling quality framework. Software Qual. J. **20**(1), 201–228 (2011)
20. Niemi, E., Pekkola, S.: Enterprise architecture quality attributes: a case study. In: 2013 46th Hawaii International Conference on System Sciences, pp. 3878–3887 (2013)
21. Pearse, N.: An illustration of deductive analysis in qualitative research. In: 18th European Conference on Research Methodology for Business and Management Studies, pp. 264–270 (2019)
22. Proper, H., Guizzardi, G.: Modeling for Enterprises: Let's go to RoME ViA RiME, vol. 3327, pp. 4–15. CEUR (2022)
23. Recker, J., Niehaves, B.: Epistemological perspectives on ontology-based theories for conceptual modeling. Appl. Ontol. **3**(1–2), 111–130 (2008)
24. Reeves, C., Bednar, D.: Defining quality: alternatives and implications. Acad. Manag. Rev. **19**(3), 419–445 (1994)
25. Sandkuhl, K., Stirna, J., Persson, A., Wißotzki, M.: Enterprise Modeling: Tackling Business Challenges with the 4EM Method. Springer (2014)
26. Schoonderbeek, J.: Quality Attributes of Enterprise Architecture models. Bachelor's Thesis, NOVI University of Applied Sciences (2020)
27. Schoonderbeek, J.: Toward an Ontology for EA Modeling and EA Model Quality Master's Thesis, Antwerp Management School (2023)
28. Schoonderbeek, J., Proper, H.: Toward an ontology for EA modeling and EA model quality. Softw. Syst. Model. **23**, 535–558 (2024)
29. Spence, C.: Factors Affecting the Quality of Enterprise Architecture Models. Ph.D. Thesis, University of Reading (2020)
30. Timm, F., Hacks, S., Thiede, F., Hintzpeter, D.: Towards a quality framework for enterprise architecture models. Quant. Approaches Software Qual. **2017**(38), 14–21 (2017)
31. The Open Group. The TOGAF Standard, 10th Edition - Architecture Development Method. Van Haren (2022)
32. Van den Berg, M., Slot, R., et al.: How enterprise architecture improves the quality of IT investment decisions. J. Syst. Softw. **152**, 134–150 (2019)

Designing Consistent Business Capability Models: A Method for Aligning Value Streams, Capabilities, and Information Concepts

Sefanja Severin[1,2]

[1] Open Universiteit, Valkenburgerweg 177, 6419 AT Heerlen, The Netherlands
sefanja.severin@ou.nl
[2] Stedin Groep, Blaak 8, 3011 TA Rotterdam, The Netherlands

Abstract. In today's competitive landscape, organizations must align strategic goals with operational execution to swiftly adapt to market changes. Business architecture management offers a structured framework for understanding and improving various facets of an organization through models like value stream maps, business capability maps, and information maps. Although several enterprise architecture frameworks promote the use of such models, they lack systematic methods to align them. This leads to confusion, redundant investments, and increased regulatory risks. This research addresses this gap by developing a design science-based method to ensure greater consistency across business architecture models, facilitating more effective decision-making and organizational adaptability.

Keywords: Business capability modeling · Enterprise architecture · Business architecture · TOGAF · ArchiMate

1 Problem Statement and Research Questions

In today's competitive business landscape, organizations face growing pressure to align their strategic goals and operational execution to quickly adapt to market shifts. Business architecture has become increasingly critical to realizing this alignment, as it provides a structured framework for understanding the various facets of an enterprise [7]. A key part of business architecture is a set of interrelated models—including value stream maps, business capability maps, and information maps—that are meant to equip leaders with the insights necessary to make informed decisions in response to these challenges [4].

These models are vital tools for visualizing and analyzing how an organization functions. Business capability maps have seen growing adoption as they provide a structured representation of an organization's core functions, making them a key reference for strategic planning [1]. However, capabilities cannot be fully understood in isolation. Value stream maps are essential for understanding how capabilities contribute to stakeholder value. Information maps, in turn, specify the business objects that undergo transformation to create this value. Together, these three models offer a holistic framework for structuring and aligning business capabilities, making them essential focal points for this research.

However, despite the widespread adoption of business architecture practices [1], a significant challenge persists in existing frameworks: the lack of a systematic method to closely align these disparate models. Because each model represents a different aspect of the organization and can do so in various correct ways, integrating them into one architectural view typically results in inconsistencies.

This lack of consistency—illustrated in Sect. 2.1—undermines the effectiveness of business architecture: it causes confusion, misalignment, redundant investments, inconsistent customer experiences, and compliance risks. The need for a systematic approach to integrating these models is, therefore, critical. Current frameworks do not define formal semantic relations between model types, leaving practitioners without clear guidance for establishing or validating internal consistency. This research addresses this gap by explicitly introducing such relations. However, once defined, checking whether models conform to these relations remains a non-trivial task—manual verification is time-consuming, error-prone, and often infeasible in complex settings. To alleviate the problem, this research aims to answer four main questions:

- **RQ1**. What requirements can be formulated for consistent business architecture models, comprising of business capability, value stream and information maps?
- **RQ2**. What method can be used to automatically check for consistency between these models?
- **RQ3**. What method can be designed to support the construction of a consistent set of capability, value stream, and information models?
- **RQ4**. To what extent do the proposed artifacts demonstrate utility and robustness when applied in field contexts beyond the original design environment?

The artifact developed for RQ2 provides a method for automatically checking the consistency of business architecture models by assessing them against a subset of the requirements identified in RQ1. This method focuses specifically on identifying inconsistencies within an existing set of models, acting as a diagnostic tool. In contrast, the artifact for RQ3 goes a step further by offering a method that supports the design of consistent models from the outset, reducing the need for extensive checks afterward. The artifact for RQ2 will also function as a component within the artifact for RQ3, allowing for consistency checks during the design process. Finally, to assess the generalizability of the artifacts developed in RQ2 and RQ3, RQ4 focuses on their applicability in organizational contexts different from the one in which they were designed. This validation step ensures that the artifacts are not overfitted to their design context but offer broader practical relevance.

The remainder of this paper is structured as follows. Section 2 identifies common inconsistencies and reviews existing solutions. Section 3 outlines the methods used to develop artifacts that address these inconsistencies. Finally, Sect. 4 highlights this research's contributions to both academia and practice.

2 Problem Domain and Related Solutions

2.1 Examples of Inconsistency

Figure 1 shows inconsistency examples found in the Business Architecture Guild's Industry Reference Models [3]. From top to bottom, the figure shows a value stream map, business capability map, and an information map. These models adhere to widely accepted frameworks such as TOGAF [21] and BIZBOK [4].

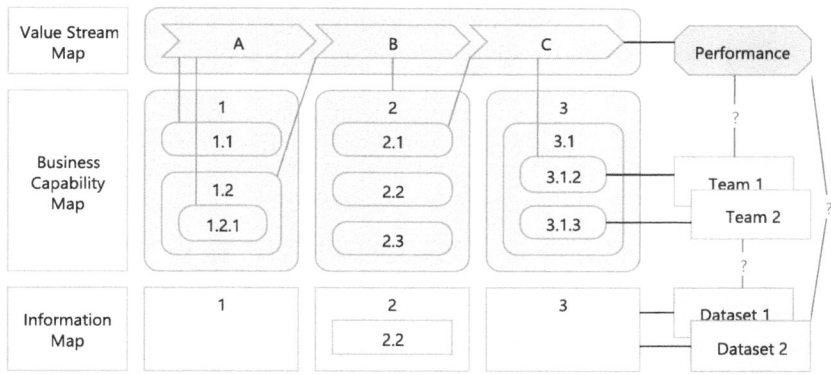

Fig. 1. Examples of inconsistency

The figure illustrates some critical issues in the model. First, it exhibits **inconsistent decomposition levels**: while business capability *3* is refined into more granular sub-capabilities, the corresponding information concept *3* remains at a highly abstract level. This discrepancy obstructs essential tasks such as performance management for value stream stage *C*, as there is no clear traceability from the value stream stage to the specific data required, which pertains exclusively to capability *3.1.2*. The problem is worsened by **unrestricted multiplicities**: value stream stage *C* can be associated with numerous business capabilities, such as *2.1* and *3.1.2* in the figure, which are themselves defined at varying levels of decomposition. This lack of structural coherence makes systematic business analysis nearly impossible.

2.2 Existing Solutions and Limitations

Several business architecture frameworks have emerged, such as TOGAF, DoDAF, NAF, UAF, VDML, and Capability-Driven Development (CDD) [10].

Despite advocating interrelated models, these frameworks lack explicit semantic relations between capabilities, value streams, and information concepts. For example, TOGAF defines a business capability as "a particular ability that a business may possess or exchange to achieve a particular purpose" [22, p. 12]. This research clarifies this 'purpose' by interpreting it as the transformation of business objects into more valuable states, enabling consistency constraints such as: 'Each capability must be the ability to transform at least one business object.'

Moreover, these frameworks do not support automated consistency verification. While modeling tools (e.g., ArchiMate) facilitate visualization, they lack built-in mechanisms to detect inconsistencies, making manual validation error-prone. This research addresses these limitations by introducing explicit consistency rules and automated verification, ensuring a structured and verifiable business architecture.

Although multiview consistency has been addressed in fields such as UML modeling [24], goal-oriented requirements [25], and enterprise modeling [18], these approaches typically assume a fixed metamodel with stable semantics. In contrast, this research redefines core modeling semantics through ontological analysis, allowing consistency to be structurally derived rather than imposed post hoc.

3 Research Methods and Expected Artifacts

3.1 Research Approach

This research aims to develop and evaluate two related methods based on a set of requirements: one to check for consistency between business architecture models and one to create a consistent set of such models. Although consistency problems are widely recognized, current frameworks do not provide operational mechanisms to systematically enforce or verify them.

This research is grounded in the Design Science Research (DSR) framework as articulated by Hevner et al. [8] and follows the structured process defined by Peffers et al. [16], ensuring a rigorous approach from problem identification to artifact evaluation. Our knowledge base consists of the following elements:

- The foundational design of the method will be informed by the existing business architecture frameworks from both the professional and academic knowledge base, such as TOGAF [21], BIZBOK [4], For Enterprise Modelling (4EM) [18], Architecture for Integrated Information Systems (ARIS) [19], and ArchiMate [23].
- The problem of model consistency is not exclusive to business architecture models. The knowledge base, therefore, also includes research on multi-view consistency in modeling languages such as Knowledge Acquisition in autOmated Specification (KAOS) [25], EXecuTable Requirements Management and Evolution (ExtREME) [17], and the Unified Modeling Language (UML) [24].

- To ensure model consistency, it is crucial to refine and align the semantics of modeling elements. Ontological analysis, using foundational ontologies like UFO [6], provides a formal basis for clarifying key concepts and their relationships. Complementing this with frameworks such as value chains, business model canvases, and customer journeys [15] ensures both semantic precision and practical relevance in value creation modeling.

This research will be applied within the operators of the Dutch energy system. The industry's NBility model [14] provides access to practitioners and allows historical model analysis. Importantly, the NBility initiative explicitly incorporates value stream thinking as part of its modeling approach, confirming the relevance of value-based structuring in this context. Its broad applications, including data governance, enterprise architecture, and decision making, support diverse artifact evaluations. The open source nature of NBility ensures accessibility for other researchers.

3.2 Formulation of Requirements

The artifacts will be developed based on the requirements established by the identified problems, the business environment, and the literature. We use an adaptation of requirements engineering [2] to structure the problem space and systematically derive requirements. This makes the design process comprehensible and transparent. To formulate the requirements, we will:

- Perform a semantic analysis of metamodels in existing business architecture frameworks such as TOGAF [21], ArchiMate [23], and BIZBOK [4].
- Use the output of the semantic analysis to create a refined metamodel with well-defined elements and relationships.
- Use the refined metamodel as a basis for the formulation of precise requirements, many in the form of consistency rules and guidelines.

This research builds on previous reviews [10] and applies focused semantic analyses rather than conducting a complete review of the literature. An initial version has already been developed by the author in [20], so it will be used as a basis for further formulation of the requirements throughout the remainder of the research process.

3.3 Development of Artifact 1 and 2

This research produces two artifacts to ensure consistency in business architecture models. Artifact 1 provides an automated approach to checking consistency and is planned to be developed and validated in 2025–2026, while Artifact 2 offers a structured method for creating consistent models and is scheduled for development and validation in 2026–2028. Both artifacts are built upon ArchiMate [23], selected due to its widespread adoption in enterprise architecture [27], suitability for expressing business architectures [13], and built-in support for consistency checking [11].

Artifact 1 automates model checking against a suitable subset of the requirements. The artifact will be built using Ampersand [9]. Ampersand is appropriate since it has been used successfully to check consistency in ArchiMate models.

Artifact 2 guides users through the design of business architecture models, ensuring consistency. It will be developed by researching the following aspects:

- **Modeling process**: This establishes a process for building capability, value stream, and information models, such that internal consistency is ensured, but not at the cost of external consistency (or validity). For example, the process will instruct users to initially build each model in isolation and focus on creating an accurate representation of the business domain. Inconsistencies between models are to be resolved only afterwards.
- **Templates**: To ensure that each model (value stream, capability, information) is composed of the correct elements, templates will be developed that prompt users to accurately identify and categorize foundational elements. This aid simplifies the design process, reducing errors in early stages and creating a uniform baseline for each model type.
- **Checklists**: A checklist specifies the requirements for consistency as a list of items that users can apply at each stage of model creation. For example, users will get specific incentives to verify that each element has the correct level of decomposition, is accurately cross-mapped, and aligns with value delivery goals. These checklists serve as quick references, helping users implement requirements step-by-step as they design and validate the models.

3.4 Evaluation

This research adopts Technical Action Research (TAR) [26] to evaluate the artifacts. Although the method is developed in close collaboration with Dutch energy grid operators, the TAR evaluation will be conducted in a different domain—specifically, in higher education. This cross-sector application enables validation under varied organizational conditions, increasing external validity. Unlike other action research methods that aim to solve a problem, TAR is artifact-driven: it is used to validate artifacts before scaling them to broader practice. To ensure objectivity, a research logbook is maintained to document the researcher's influence on the assessment process. Additionally, all evaluation results will be independently reviewed by research supervisors, reducing subjective bias and increasing rigor.

Artifact evaluations may prompt further improvements, requiring iterative reassessment. The knowledge goal is to determine whether the artifacts are effective and efficient. To this end, we employ the Technology Acceptance Model (TAM) [12] and in-depth interviews [5], both suited to eliciting rich qualitative insights from a limited number of participants.

4 Contributions

This work advances theory and methodology by addressing a key shortcoming in current frameworks: the absence of clear consistency rules and guidelines to align different business architecture models. By systematically defining the relationships between value stream, capability, and information models, this research provides a structured approach to ensure their consistency.

This contributes to the Enterprise Architecture field by refining the underlying metamodels used in business architecture, offering a more precise method for checking and designing consistent models. Such advancements enable both researchers and practitioners to analyze organizations with greater clarity, reducing ambiguity and improving the reliability of business architecture as a strategic tool.

The uniqueness of this research lies in its focus on the integration of multiple business architecture models, which, despite their common use, have been treated separately in existing frameworks like TOGAF and BIZBOK. By proposing a systematic method, this research challenges the conventional siloed approaches to business architecture. This research has the potential to redefine how organizations perceive and utilize business architecture, ultimately contributing to a more holistic understanding of enterprise operations and architecture.

References

1. Aleatrati Khosroshahi, P., Hauder, M., Volkert, S., Matthes, F., Gernegroß, M.: Business capability maps: current practices and use cases for enterprise architecture management. In: Proceedings of the 51st Hawaii International Conference on System Sciences, vol. 51, pp. 4603–4612 (2018)
2. Braun, R., Benedict, M., Wendler, H., Esswein, W.: Proposal for requirements driven design science research. In: Donnellan, B., Helfert, M., Kenneally, J., VanderMeer, D., Rothenberger, M., Winter, R. (eds.) DESRIST 2015. LNCS, vol. 9073, pp. 135–151. Springer, Cham (2015). https://doi.org/10.1007/978-3-319-18714-3_9
3. Business Architecture Guild: Industry reference models (2022). https://www.businessarchitectureguild.org/page/INDREF
4. Business Architecture Guild: A guide to the business architecture body of knowledge, version 13.0 (2024). https://www.businessarchitectureguild.org/page/BIZBOK
5. Guion, L.A., Diehl, D.C., McDonald, D.: Conducting an in-depth interview: Fcs6012/fy393, rev. 8/2011. Edis **2011**(8) (2011). https://doi.org/10.32473/edis-fy393-2011
6. Guizzardi, G., Botti Benevides, A., Fonseca, C.M., Porello, D., Almeida, J.P.A., Prince Sales, T.: UFO: unified foundational ontology. Applied ontology **17**(1), 167–210 (2022). https://doi.org/10.3233/AO-210256
7. Hadaya, P., Gagnon, B.: Business Architecture: The Missing Link in Strategy Formulation, Implementation and Execution. ASATE Publishing Inc. (2017)
8. Hevner, A.R., March, S.T., Park, J., Ram, S.: Design science in information systems research. MIS Quart. 75–105 (2004). https://doi.org/10.2307/25148625
9. Joosten, S., Roubtsova, E.: Enterprise modeling with conventions. In: International Symposium on Business Modeling and Software Design. pp. 56–73. Springer (2023). https://doi.org/10.1007/978-3-031-36757-1_4
10. Koutsopoulos, G., Henkel, M., Stirna, J.: An analysis of capability meta-models for expressing dynamic business transformation. Software Syst. Model. **20**, 147–174 (2021). https://doi.org/10.1007/s10270-020-00843-0

11. Lankhorst, M.M., Proper, H.A., Jonkers, H.: The architecture of the archimate language. In: International Workshop on Business Process Modeling, Development and Support, pp. 367–380. Springer (2009). https://doi.org/10.1007/978-3-642-01862-6_30
12. Marangunić, N., Granić, A.: Technology acceptance model: a literature review from 1986 to 2013. Universal access in the information society **14**, 81–95 (2015). https://doi.org/10.1007/s10209-014-0348-1
13. Meertens, L.O., Iacob, M.E., Nieuwenhuis, L.J., van Sinderen, M.J., Jonkers, H., Quartel, D.: Mapping the business model canvas to archimate. In: Proceedings of the 27th Annual ACM Symposium on Applied Computing, pp. 1694–1701 (2012). https://doi.org/10.1145/2245276.2232049
14. Netbheer Nederland: Nbility model (2025). https://nbility-model.github.io/
15. Ojasalo, J., Ojasalo, K.: Service logic business model canvas. J. Res. Mark. Entrep. **20**(1), 70–98 (2018). https://doi.org/10.1108/JRME-06-2016-0015
16. Peffers, K., Tuunanen, T., Rothenberger, M.A., Chatterjee, S.: A design science research methodology for information systems research. J. Manag. Inf. Syst. **24**(3), 45–77 (2007). https://doi.org/10.2753/MIS0742-1222240302
17. Roubtsova, E.: Interactive Modeling and Simulation in Business System Design. Springer (2016). https://doi.org/10.1007/978-3-319-15102-1
18. Sandkuhl, K., Stirna, J., Persson, A., Wißotzki, M.: Enterprise modeling. Springer (2014). https://doi.org/10.1007/978-3-662-43725-4
19. Scheer, A.W.: The Composable Enterprise: Agile, Flexible, Innovative: A Gamechanger for Organisations. Digitisation and Business Software. Springer (2023). https://doi.org/10.1007/978-3-658-43089-4
20. Severin, S., Roubtsova, E., Roelens, B., Joosten, S.: A method to align business capability maps and enterprise data models. In: International Symposium on Business Modeling and Software Design, pp. 48–64. Springer (2024). https://doi.org/10.1007/978-3-031-64073-5_4
21. The Open Group: Togaf® standard, 10th edn. (2022). https://www.opengroup.org/library/c220
22. The Open Group: Togaf® standard - architecture content (2022). https://publications.opengroup.org/c220
23. The Open Group: Archimate® 3.2 specification (2023). https://pubs.opengroup.org/architecture/archimate3-doc/
24. Torre, D., Genero, M., Labiche, Y., Elaasar, M.: How consistency is handled in model-driven software engineering and UML: an expert opinion survey. Software Qual. J. **31**(1), 1–54 (2023). https://doi.org/10.1145/1125944.1125949
25. Van Lamsweerde, A.: Goal-oriented requirements engineering: a guided tour. In: Proceedings fifth IEEE International Symposium on Requirements Engineering, pp. 249–262. IEEE (2001). https://doi.org/10.1109/ISRE.2001.948567
26. Wieringa, R.: Design Science Methodology for Information Systems and Software Engineering. Springer (2014). https://doi.org/10.1007/978-3-662-43839-8
27. Zhou, Z., Zhi, Q., Morisaki, S., Yamamoto, S.: A systematic literature review on enterprise architecture visualization methodologies. IEEE Access **8**, 96404–96427 (2020). https://doi.org/10.1109/ACCESS.2020.2995850

A Modeling Method for Work Systems Knowledge Capture and Traceability

Andrei Chiş(✉)

OMILAB@UBB-FSEGA, Babeş-Bolyai University, Cluj-Napoca, Romania
andrei.chis@econ.ubbcluj.ro

Abstract. This is the Ph.D. research plan and progress report on a project aiming to make a Design Science contribution that comprises a modeling method and a model-driven architectural proposition for operationalizing the Work Systems Framework (WSF) by means of knowledge engineering. WSF practitioners have traditionally used semi-structured document templates for work system briefings, while academic works often emphasized the requirement for granular machine readability and traceability of such descriptions.

The goal of this work is to achieve this by model-driven streamlining between (a) a domain-specific modeling language (DSML) founded on the WSF conceptualization and (b) large language model (LLM) services informed by diagrammatic work system descriptions, using (c) RDF graphs as a mediator format. This represents a convergence of artifact-oriented research agendas emerging in recent literature – the synergy of conceptual modeling with LLMs, and the GraphRAG patterns for enhancing LLM response quality with the help of knowledge graphs.

The research follows a standard Design Science process that also encapsulates a DSML engineering cycle employing the Agile Modeling Method Engineering (AMME) methodology. Current results include the diagramming environment implemented on the ADOxx metamodeling platform including model-to-RDF transformation scripts to satisfy competency and traceability requirements. The second half of the Ph.D. timeline focuses on refining and deploying an evaluation protocol to measure the LLM responses quality (informed by the WSF diagrams as opposed to WSF documents) and to evaluate modeling language qualities.

Keywords: Work Systems Framework · Knowledge Graphs · Large Language Models · Domain-specific Modeling · GraphRAG

1 Introduction

This Ph.D. thesis work follows a Design Science research (DSR) process to develop a knowledge engineering treatment based on the enterprise conceptualization provided by the Work Systems Framework (WSF) [1], and an architecting proposition for a knowledge system governed by it. The proposed system aims to expose diagrammatic designs - captured through the WSF lens employed as a "domain-specific language" - to LLM services, by employing RDF graphs as a mediator format. The overarching goal is to fill a gap between (a) *enterprise conceptualizations* that are established in systems analysis and design but only serving a conceptual work level (i.e. WSF), and (b) *granular semantic structures* that enable data traceability, machine reasoning, semantic querying and ingestion by LLM services. This gap can be recognized in several conceptual unpacking efforts – from the initial coarse concepts of WSF down across layers of increasingly granular metamodels and taxonomies [2], including an early-stage proposition of a Work Systems Modeling Method [3]. At the same time, knowledge graph (KG) engineering shows an on-going preoccupation with leveraging enterprise conceptualizations – see e.g. supply chain KGs informed by SCOR [4].

This work is also motivated by recent research agendas: a call to shift the role of conceptual modeling from representation to mediation [5]; a call to action on building artifacts that operationalize WSF by knowledge engineering means [2] in contrast to the practice based on document templates and frontends [3, 6].

2 Problem Statement and Contribution Summary

To balance the need for new prescriptive knowledge with practical problem solving, we are looking both at the DSR research question (RQ) taxonomy of [7], and the design problem template recommended by [8]. The project pursues the following questions: **RQ1.** *How can we capture work system (WS) descriptions by means of machine-readable knowledge representation?* The envisioned solution is a KG whose ontological layer is informed by the WSF conceptualization and competency, with an early draft already published in [9]. **RQ2.** *How can we facilitate the KG development for enterprise modelers familiar with WSF but lacking technical KG skills?* The envisioned solution is to adopt the model-driven paradigm and to design a DSML that offers a diagrammatic design experience that produces WSF-informed semantic graphs. **RQ3.** *How does a traditional WS description (based on Word templates) compare with our DSML-based description, in terms of LLM answering quality based on them?* This last question assumes the LLM involvement in communication flows related to system analysis tasks (WS briefings) and knowledge transfers (i.e. LLMs as partners in socialization, internalization or other phases of Nonaka's knowledge conversion spiral [10]). The answer will be pursued by comparative experimentation with evaluating LLM responses between different retrieval-based generative AI setups – first based on semi-structured WSF documents, then leveraging the traceability of the model-driven KG in the so-called GraphRAG interaction patterns [11].

As encouraged by DSR, each RQ generate **nested subquestions** referring to artifact qualities: *how competent is the KG in terms of traceability and reasoning; how suitable is the DSML in terms of modeling language qualities; how do different subgraph patterns perform when exposed to the GraphRAG interaction with the LLM?*

The RQs lead to the practical problem statement formulated below, and anchored in artifact requirements: diagrammatic mapping of WSs through a drag-and-drop experience; semantic linkage to traditional enterprise modeling grammars; viewpoints of different granularities navigable through hyperlinks; interoperability with triplestores and LLMs to allow both SPARQL and natural language querying.

The resulting contribution, with some elements already developed, will comprise:

> Enhance **work system design and analysis capabilities** *(problem context)*
> ... by treating them with a **modeling method derived from the WST conceptualization and an architecture to streamline WS designs to LLM services** *(artifact)*
> ... to facilitate **visual design, granular semantic traceability and natural language WS briefings** *(artifact service/requirements)*
> ... in order to support WSF practitioners **who need a design space complemented by generative AI interpretation** *(stakeholder goals)*

(a) Artifact innovations: (i) *A visual modeling language* that deploys, through a metamodeling approach, the WSF conceptualization, in more structured designs than the semi-structured briefing templates or frontend forms that were the basis of operationalizing WSF in the past. For prototyping, the ADOxx metamodeling platform[1] is employed; (ii) *Model transformation and interoperability mechanisms* for converting WSF models into semantic graphs exposed to a GraphRAG [11] setup to enable natural language queries. For demonstration, OpenAI[2] and Ontotext GraphDB[3] are employed;

(c) Artifact experimentation: (i) *DSML quality evaluations*, from the perspective of established frameworks for cognitive effectiveness and modeling language quality (Moody's physics of notation [12], Krogstie's SEQUAL [13]); (ii) *LLM response quality evaluations*, varying different prompting strategies and metamodel terminological choices, and in comparison with traditional narrative and templated WS descriptions.

While generative AI services provide computer vision features[4] that can inspect diagrammatic models, we favor model transformation and serialization (as RDF graphs) because not all information captured in domain-specific models is visually manifested – some is only perceived by user interaction (e.g. hyperlinks to BPMN subprocesses), or in annotation attributes (e.g. times and costs). Secondly, domain-specific models face an implicit scarcity of training content, which justifies the decision to employ GraphRAG as it can be easily redeployed for different LLMs and design variations.

3 Related Works

WSF imposes a work system perspective to enterprise architecting in simpler terms compared to multi-layered frameworks (TOGAF-Archimate, Zachman), while supporting a drill-down decomposition centered on value-creating activities for concrete customers within a constraining environment. Successful application and case study reports over the years [14] are still deterred by a lack of knowledge engineering treatments, except for some conceptual propositions of taxonomies and metamodels [15]. An early attempt as part of this doctoral project was to build a KG employing a schema inspired by the WSF concepts [9], however the means how such as KG can be populated and interrogated remains a major challenge that this thesis approaches from two directions – model-driven

---

[1] https://adoxx.org/.
[2] https://platform.openai.com/.
[3] https://graphdb.ontotext.com/.
[4] https://platform.openai.com/docs/guides/vision?lang=node.

knowledge capture, and LLM services as a querying interface. Their integration is made possible by the GraphRAG family of architecting patterns [11], therefore semantic graphs are employed for DSML-LLM interoperation.

Even before the advent of LLM services, there has been a long-term preoccupation with treating diagrammatic models as graphs, or to repurpose graph databases as model repositories – i.e. proposing non-XML alternatives to the traditional model interchange and storage formats (XMI, BPMN XML etc.). BPMN2KG [16] is an example of such an RDF treatment applied to BPMN, while [17] used KGs to detect enterprise architecture model "smells". In earlier works, diagram-to-RDF generation patterns were defined at metamodeling level to make them applicable to arbitrary DSMLs [18].

This Ph.D. work tailors its own WSF schema as an intermediate representation between the metamodel governing the diagramming experience and the KG to be exposed to LLMs via the GraphRAG integration patterns - diverse KG platform vendors advertised diverse integration patterns included under this umbrella. We work with the patterns promoted by Ontotext [11], i.e. employing a KG as subject-of-matter expert.

The literature shows a growing preoccupation with how enterprise modeling can interact with LLMs. Most works focus on empirical observations on how LLMs augment certain modeling tasks [19]. Such observations must inform design-oriented propositions and novel knowledge flows, potentially leading to LLM-supported metamodeling [20], model generation [21] or augmentation of the business process management lifecycle [22, 23]. The mentioned works place the LLMs at the forefront of design tasks, while we shift the LLM role to the receiving end of model-driven semantic structures, keeping a pro-active human involvement in system design.

4 Research Methodology: DSR with AMME Subprocess

Due to the artifact-oriented nature of this work, the Peffers DSR process [24] is adopted, and also adapted in its *Development* phase by resorting to a DSML engineering "subprocess" - the framework of AMME (Agile Modeling Method Engineering) [25], the engineering approach commonly used for ADOxx metamodeling:

1. In the **Problem Identification** phase a preoccupation with the WSF conceptual "unpacking" was identified, towards making WS descriptions machine interpretable for system analysis toolkits. The opportunity to move away from narrative templates to knowledge engineering means was thus pursued; **2.** In the **Objectives Statement** phase we formulated RQs and artifact features (Sect. 2) to outline the nature of the artifact and pick variation criteria for experimentation; **3.** The **Design and Development** phase was decomposed in parallel development tasks: (3a) on one hand, the *engineering of a DSML* and a modeling tool with RDF model interchange, relied on AMME [25]; (3b) on the other hand, *GraphRAG streamlining* between semantic graphs and LLM services using Ontotext integration patterns and custom Python mediator scripts with OpenAI services. The parallel developments are currently converging into the complete architecture (Fig. 1); **4.** In the **Demonstration** step we picked scenarios from our academic environment to model and use in evaluation tasks - examples are maintained outside of this paper content (link in Sect. 6); **5.** During the **Evaluation** phase, the ingredients are analyzed by different criteria – at front-end we focus on the modeling language evaluation; at

the knowledge ingestion end we focus on LLM responses quality (details in Sect. 6);
6. The **Communication** phase involved preliminary reports in [9] (on WSF-based KG development) and [26] (on model-driven knowledge streamlining).

5 Current Results: Design Decisions and Artifact Deployments

The architecting proposition is shown in Fig. 1 (top) as an integration between the diagrammatic modeling tool, a triplestore acting as a diagram repository and an LLM service. Python components act as interchange mediator and retriever to facilitate the natural language queries according to the GraphRAG interaction flow.

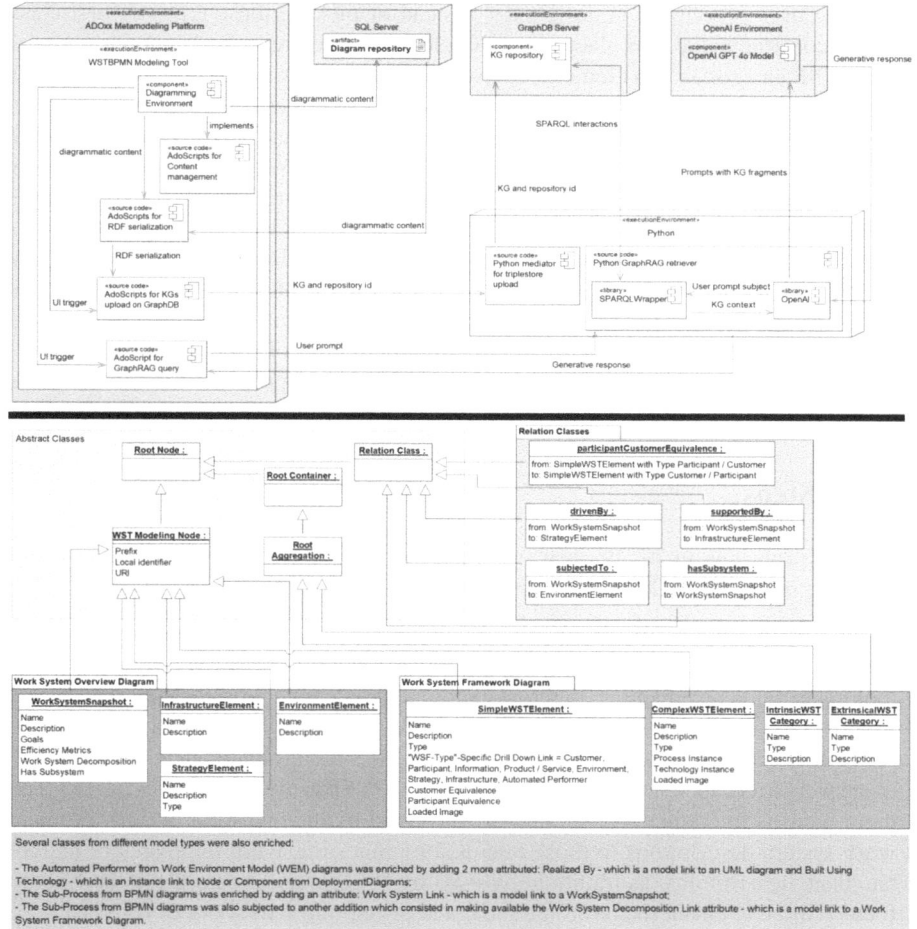

Fig. 1. Architecture for a model-driven WSF knowledge system (top) and ADOxx metamodel of the WSF DSML (bottom)

Fragmentary artifacts have been developed over the progress of the Ph.D. project, filling various technological functions of this architecture. A standalone KG whose ontology was aligned with WSF was evaluated in terms of scalability and WSF competency questions in [9]. In parallel, a diagrammatic modeling tool was implemented on the ADOxx metamodeling platform. A recent iteration of the metamodel is shown in the bottom half of Fig. 1 and due to space limitations we provide a link to exemplary diagrams for demonstrative scenario: https://github.com/andreichis97/WSTBPMN.

The DSML is partitioned between two model types: the *Work System Overview* is the external view gathering the Environment, Strategy and Infrastructure elements around a WS; the core *WSF diagram* provides the internal view mapping elements of WSF categories: Product/Service, Process/Activity, Customer, Participant, Information & Technology element. The WSF element types are not distinguished in the metamodel because of how the user experience is designed – instead of picking these types as first-class language constructs, the user places (simple) elements into prescribed containers representing WSF categories. An element receives its WSF type from the container where it was dropped, and specific properties according to that type become active.

Besides WSF concepts, the DSML drills down certain descriptions through legacy notations. By extending the Bee-Up open modeling tool [27], we are repurposing BPMN and UML diagram types as a means of drilling down some WSF concepts – process/activity (links to BPMN), infrastructure elements (links to UML deployment diagrams and nodes) and work systems participants (links to Bee-Up organigrams). By doing this, the conceptual schema of WSF becomes a semantic layer that unifies legacy models with traceability links in WSF terms – allowing semantic queries to navigate between levels of detail and abstraction for different aspects of a work system. Furthermore, a decomposition mechanism also allows a BPMN subprocess to be detailed as a work system – i.e. as a semantically richer alternative to embedded subprocesses.

6 Next Steps

The Ph.D. project is in its 3rd year, with the last segment focusing on refining and deploying a multi-criterial evaluation protocol:

1. At the **knowledge capture front-end**, the modeling language is evaluated through the lens of established criteria for modeling language quality (SEQUAL [13]), primarily looking at syntax, semantics (in terms of competency/model queries) and pragmatics (model transformation performance and scalable interoperability with an RDF store);
2. At the **knowledge retrieval end**, the LLM responses are evaluated in terms of quality of answers to competency questions derived from WSF analysis scenarios [9, 14]. The main focus is to compare LLM answers informed by the ingestion of diagrammatic work system descriptions to those obtained by ingesting Word templates of natural language descriptions, as traditionally used by WSF practitioners [3]. A secondary focus will be to check the terminological and prompting sensitivity of responses.

For the first part, partial evaluations are iteratively encapsulated in the nested tool development cycle (AMME) to ensure the quality of RDF serialization - from a software quality perspective and from a semantic coherence/competency perspective. User-oriented evaluation involves management practitioners and business administration students for whom we track: the *effort* of describing a WS by diagrammatic means (as time and number of clicks); *model understandability* (grasping the narrative of a situation by looking at models); and preference of *visual notation* in relation to Moody's principles [12]. Examples of design decisions already incorporated from intermittent evaluations are: layers of notation – a default, semantically transparent, visual shape is seconded by the option for loading user-provided icons to trade off graphical economy with expressivity; a flexible typing system where the WSF types, instead of being hardcoded in the metamodel, are applied dynamically depending on where an element is dropped in containers representing WSF categories – Environment, Strategy etc. (their properties are consequently activated or deactivated). This emulates the traditional template filling experience of WS briefings.

In the second part, response quality is evaluated through RAGAs framework [28], measuring similarities between embeddings of the *response*, of *provided context* (serialized graph fragments around a focal node), and/or a reference *ground truth*. Besides traditional Precision/Recall, we also use more specialized metrics [28]: *Response Relevancy* (alignment with question intent, irrespective of factual correctness and penalizing redundancy), *Answer Semantic Similarity* (cosine similarity to the ground truth), and *Faithfulness* (the fraction of claims supported or inferable via Turtle triple embeddings). These metrics are then compared across prompting strategies based on the TELeR taxonomy [29], contrasting responses generated via ingesting narrative Word templates with those resulted from ingesting diagrammatic designs.

References

1. Alter, S.: Work system theory: overview of core concepts, extensions, and challenges for the future. J. Assoc. Inf. Syst. **14**(2), 72 (2013)
2. Bork, D., Alter, S.: Satisfying four requirements for more flexible modeling methods: theory and test case. Enterp. Model. Info. Syst. Archit. **15**, 3–1 (2020). https://doi.org/10.18417/emisa.15.3
3. Alter, S., Bork, D.: Systems analysis and design toolkit based on work system theory and its extensions. J. Database Manag. **31**(3), 1–13 (2020)
4. Ramzy, N., Auer, S., Ehm, H., Perier, B.: SENS: semantic synthetic integrated model for sustainable supply chain analysis and benchmarking. Enterp. Model. Info. Syst. Archit. **19** (2024). https://doi.org/10.18417/emisa.19.5
5. Recker, J., Lukyanenko, R., Jabbari Sabegh, M.A., Samuel, B.M., Castellanos, A.: From representation to mediation: a new agenda for conceptual modeling research in a digital world. MIS Q. **45**(1), 269–300 (2021)
6. Alter, S., Bolloju, N.: A work system front end for object-oriented analysis and design. Int. J. Inf. Technol. Syst. Approach **9**(1), 1–18 (2016)
7. Thuan, N., Drechsler, A., Antunes, P.: Construction of design science research questions. Commun. Assoc. Inf. Syst. **44** (2019)
8. Wieringa, R.J.: Design Science Methodology for information systems and software engineering. Springer, Heidelberg (2014). https://doi.org/10.1007/978-3-662-43839-8

9. Chiș, A., Ghiran, A.-M., Alter, S.: Informing enterprise knowledge graphs with a work system perspective. Enterp. Model. Info. Syst. Archit. **19** (2024). https://doi.org/10.18417/emisa.19.7
10. Nonaka, I., von Krogh, G.: Tacit knowledge and knowledge conversion: controversy and advancement in organizational knowledge creation theory. Organ. Sci. **20**, 635–652 (2009)
11. Ontotext, What is Graph RAG. https://www.ontotext.com/knowledgehub/fundamentals/what-is-graph-rag/. Accessed 05 Mar 2025
12. Moody, D.L.: The "physics" of notations: towards a scientific basis for constructing visual notations in software engineering. IEEE Trans. Softw. Eng. **35**(5), 756–779 (2009)
13. Krogstie, J., Sindre, G., Jørgensen, H.: Process models representing knowledge for action: a revised quality framework. Eur. J. Inf. Syst. **15**, 91–102 (2006)
14. Köhler, T., Alter, S., Cameron, B.H.: Enterprise modeling at the work system level: evidence from four cases at DHL express Europe. In: Buchmann, R., Karagiannis, D., Kirikova, M. (eds.) PoEM 2018, pp. 303–318. LNBIP, vol. 335. Springer, Cham (2018). https://doi.org/10.1007/978-3-030-02302-7_19
15. Alter, S., Recker, J.C.: Using a work system perspective to expand BPM research use cases. J. Inf. Technol. Theory Appl. **18**(1), 47–71 (2017)
16. Bachhofner, S., Kiesling, E., Revoredo, K., Waibel, P., Polleres, A.: Automated process knowledge graph construction from BPMN models. In: Strauss, C., Cuzzocrea, A., Kotsis, G., Tjoa, A.M., Khalil, I. (eds.) DEXA 2022. LNCS, vol. 13426, pp. 32–47. Springer, Cham (2022). https://doi.org/10.1007/978-3-031-12423-5_3
17. Smajevic, M., Hacks, S., Bork, D.: Using knowledge graphs to detect enterprise architecture smells. In: Serral, E., Stirna, J., Ralyté, J., Grabis, J. (eds.) PoEM 2021. LNBIP, vol. 432, pp. 48–63. Springer, Cham (2021). https://doi.org/10.1007/978-3-030-91279-6_4
18. Buchmann, R.A., Karagiannis, D.: Pattern-based transformation of diagrammatic conceptual models for semantic enrichment in the web of data. In: KES 2015, Procedia CS 60, pp. 150–159. Elsevier (2015)
19. Gutschmidt, A., Nast, B.: Assessing model quality using large language models. In: Paja, E., Zdravkovic, J., Kavakli, E., Stirna, J. (eds.) PoEM 2024. LNBIP, vol. 538, pp. 105–122. Springer, Cham (2025). https://doi.org/10.1007/978-3-031-77908-4_7
20. Challa, G., Gartini, A., Muff, F., Fill, H.-G.: An architecture for integrating large language models into metamodeling platforms: the example of MM-AR. In: ER Forum 2024, CEUR-WS 3849 (2024). https://ceur-ws.org/Vol-3849/poster-demo1.pdf
21. Härer, F.: Conceptual model interpreter for large language models. In: ER Forum 2023, CEUR-WS 3618 (2023). https://ceur-ws.org/Vol-3618/forum_paper_11.pdf
22. Vidgof, M., Bachhofner, S., Mendling, J.: Large language models for business process management: opportunities and challenges. In: Di Francescomarino, C., Burattin, A., Janiesch, C., Sadiq, S. (eds.) BPM 2023. LNBIP, vol. 490, pp. 107–123. Springer, Cham (2023). https://doi.org/10.1007/978-3-031-41623-1_7
23. Dolha, D.N., Buchmann, R.A.: Generative AI for BPMN process analysis: experiments with multi-modal process representations. In: Řepa, V., Matulevičius, R., Laurenzi, E. (eds.) BIR 2024. LNBIP, vol. 529, p. 19–35. Springer, Cham (2024). https://doi.org/10.1007/978-3-031-71333-0_2
24. Peffers, K., Tuunanen, T., Routenberger, M., Chatterjee, S.: A design science research methodology for information systems research. J. Manag. Inform. Syst. **24**(3), 45–77 (2008)
25. Karagiannis, D.: Agile modeling method engineering. In: PCI 2015, pp. 5–10. ACM (2015)
26. Chiș, A., Stoica, O., Ghiran, A.-M., Buchmann, R.A.: A knowledge graph approach to cyber threat mitigation derived from data flow diagrams. In: AQTR 2024, pp. 1–6. IEEE (2024)
27. OMILAB NPO, Bee-Up. https://bee-up.omilab.org/activities/bee-up/. Accessed 12 Apr 2025
28. RAGAs Framework Documentation. https://docs.ragas.io/en/stable/. Accessed 28 Feb 2025
29. Karmaker, S.K., Feng, D.: TELeR: a general taxonomy of LLM prompts for bench-marking complex tasks. In: EMNLP 2023, pp. 14197–14203. ACL (2023)

CAiSE 2025 Doctoral Consortium – Digital Transformation

Enhancing Occupational Health and Safety for Healthcare Workers Through Digital Innovation

Xavier Portell[(✉)] [iD]

aMSP, Esteve Terrades 30, 08023 Barcelona, Spain
xportell@amsp.cat

Abstract. Ensuring the safety and well-being of healthcare workers is essential for improving the quality of care. This paper presents an ongoing study at a real non-profit organization that provides occupational safety and health services for healthcare and social healthcare centers. To strengthen its strategic position, the organization aims to become more data-driven and process-oriented. Digital transformation can significantly improve its services, but it may also involve a profound shift in its operations, processes and culture. This study explores the challenge of digitally improving the company through an applied action-research project focused on enterprise modeling, architecture, and IS strategic planning. Our literature review suggests that this may be the first reported case of using these tools in occupational risk prevention, offering valuable insights for similar organizations.

Keywords: Digital enterprise transformation · Enterprise modeling · Enterprise architectures · IS strategic planning · Action-research · Occupational safety and health in healthcare

1 Context and Motivation

According to the World Health Organization (WHO) [1], health workers are essential to any health system and must have safe and healthy working conditions. They are exposed to numerous occupational risks such as infections, chemicals, or psychosocial hazards. Protecting their well-being is essential to prevent work-related diseases and injuries, enhance job satisfaction, and improve the quality of care.

Traditional methods of managing these risks often fall short in addressing the dynamic and complex nature of healthcare settings. This is where digital transformation comes into play. Technologies offer such organizations a unique opportunity to improve their services, by helping them to become more data-intensive and process-oriented. This article examines the challenges of implementing such changes, considering not only technology but also key factors like organizational structure, work culture, and political dynamics.

This project is being conducted in collaboration with the company aMSP under an Industrial Doctorate program. One of the main challenges was integrating the business environment and academic research, which operate at different speeds and have distinct requirements. Business emphasizes fast decision-making and strict deadlines, while academic research follows a more deliberate and methodical approach. For more details on the project refer to the published paper [2].

The Commonwealth Health Prevention association (aMSP, after its Catalan name, associació Mancomunitat Sanitària de Prevenció) is a nonprofit organization established in 1998. It aims to provide occupational safety and health services for healthcare and social healthcare centers in the Catalan public sector, within a context of innovation and change. aMSP is the result of an alliance between 35 entities covering more than 23,900 professionals.

Its strategy is based on consolidating a skilled and versatile human team, deploying occupational health and prevention units in each associated entity. Thus, aMSP provides direct and exclusive services to its associates, who contribute their part of the common expenses through a proportional fee system based on the number of employees being covered.

aMSP detected some areas of improvement when reviewing its strategic plan in 2021, specifically in knowledge and data sharing from associated entities. A key factor was the failure of the implementation of the new (at that moment; now discontinued) Prevenet software application for health surveillance and monitoring. Most entities decided not to use it because they found it excessively rigid and lacking flexibility.

The plan was then updated. Goals related to the digital transformation were added to the initial objective of improving service delivery, quality, and efficiency. It was decided to launch a new tender to replace the core software application and to create a new position of head of information systems. The management of aMSP sought assistance from the Universitat Politècnica de Catalunya (UPC) to both finding someone to lead their digital transformation and provide counselling advice on:

- Assisting aMSP in their future digital transformation based on their current situation.
- Helping aMSP in its digital transformation to evolve into a data-driven organization.

2 Background

The two key needs of aMSP outlined above can be translated into two main academic research streams, namely digital transformation and digital business strategy.

Digital Transformation Definition and Description. There is a lack of common understanding of what Digital Transformation (DT) is [3]. In this paper, we adopt the definition from Morakanyane and Grace: "[DT is] an evolutionary process that leverages digital capabilities and technologies to enable business models, operational processes and customer experiences to create value" [3].

Digital Business Strategy and IS/IT Strategic Planning. Digitalization, driven by rapid technological development, fundamentally changes how organizations operate, compete, and strategize [4]. The strategies for Information Systems (IS) and Information Technologies (IT), attainable through IS/IT strategic planning, are evolving into Digital Business Strategy (DBS). It has moved from exploiting existing technologies to exploring new innovative opportunities enabled by digital technologies. This proactive shift positions IS as a driver of business innovation and transformation.

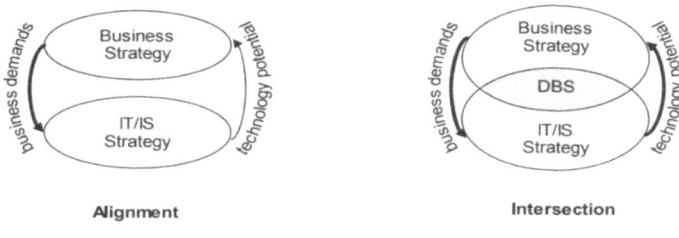

Fig. 1. DBS between the poles of business and IS/IT strategy. [4]

In Fig. 1, the traditional alignment view perceives IS/IT strategy as subordinate to business strategy, which is true for the "departmental plan" and "strategy support" conceptions but not for the "shared view" and "master plan" conceptions. Now digital strategy drives business strategy beyond just supporting it.

3 Research Design

Digital Transformation (DT) may involve a profound shift in organizational operations, processes, and culture driven by the integration of digital technologies. Our research focuses on key success factors, challenges, and outcomes. Research in this area is usually practical, often involving models and the development of new tools, approaches, processes, or methods beneficial to organizations or specific institutions [5].

An IS/IT strategic plan is essential to align DT efforts with business goals and manage organizational change. It ensures technology initiatives support performance, competitiveness, and innovation. Based on the challenges highlighted by aMSP in the previous section, we identified the following research question:

- **RQ1.** How to design, plan and execute a successful DT effort for improving the key processes of a healthcare risk prevention organization?

The proposed main methodology to address the research is Action Research (AR) in several iterations of diagnosing, action planning, action taking, evaluating and specific learning according to Baskerville's description [5]. AR was chosen since it addresses real-world problems and issues while simultaneously aiming to expand scientific knowledge [6]. Unlike other research methodologies, which involve the researcher studying but not altering organizational phenomena, AR aims to create organizational change while studying the change process.

We decided to conduct three iterations with well-defined goals: cover key processes, include support processes, and refine. We also had an initial exploratory phase with a literature review. Each of the iterations inside the AR cycles are inspired in Design Science Research (DSR), for which we follow the principles defined in [7].

To ensure research rigor and quality, we follow McKay and Marshall's framework [8] which emphasizes reflective and reasoned action around four categories: research conduct, conceptual significance, practical significance and presentation.

4 aMSP Digital Strategic Review, Challenges and Objectives

In response to RQ1, this section provides a strategic review of aMSP and highlights key challenges and objectives.

4.1 aMSP Digital Strategy Current State Assessment (as of 2023)

How the Assessment Was Done. To establish an initial strategic analysis, we have adapted the PENSI methodology [9] for DBS planning, enhancing the traditional SWOT framework with IS/IT analytical methods. The SWOT analysis was conducted through participative sessions with representatives from technical, healthcare, IS and aMSP management areas. The sessions followed an adapted Metaplan methodology [10] a structured method for group discussions and idea generation. We also identified current IS/IT usage across key processes.

Current IS/IT Usage Across Key Processes. Processes have been categorized by responsibility-either to aMSP or to the associated entities. A total of 7 groups of processes were covered.

SWOT Analysis. The questions were structured using a SWOT matrix across the business, application, and technology dimensions. Priorities and proposed actions were established in the second session, considering what were the processes involved.

4.2 aMSP Main Challenges and Objectives

A final participative session was held with the same team to develop a list of potential challenges related to the DT effort, to be presented to aMSP management. Using SWOT analysis as a foundation, participants proposed and discussed objectives for each challenge. The following challenges and objectives were endorsed by aMSP management:

- **Challenge 1: Aligning business and IS/IT strategy by using the new core application GeISS and improving the key business processes.**

    1. O1: Define/implement new business processes to improve the quality of the service.
    2. O2: Implement new core application according to defined processes

- **Challenge 2: Strengthen the links with the associated entities.**

    3. O3: Expand new core application usage to associated entities, as a common platform.
    4. O4: Involve the board of directors in the DT process. DT steering committee.

- **Challenge 3: Reduce dependency on the software provider.**

    5. O5: Model processes, operations and applications.
    6. O6: Explore alternatives.

5 Enterprise Modeling and Architecture for aMSP

aMSP business challenges cannot be addressed by simply adding or changing a few systems [11]. Instead, a complete restructuring of the organization's operational and organizational framework is necessary. We propose the use of Enterprise Architecture (EA) to drive this transformation.

5.1 Using Enterprise Architecture for Digital Transformation

As stated in Section 3.2, DT begins with developing a DBS, integrating IT-based processes that enhance capabilities and complexity, requiring new methods and tools [12]. EA aims to transform the enterprise from complexity to efficiency [11]. This transformation requires significant changes to eliminate duplication, reduce costs, improve reliability, and increase agility.

EA describes comprehensively an enterprise, detailing essential business artifacts and their relationships [12]. It provides a strategic foundation for business enablement.

Criticism of EAs as an Instrument for DT. EA appears to be a promising support for DT, but it is not widely used in this context [12]. Key reasons include:

- Gap between EA and business transformation: EA is IT-centric and does not adequately consider strategy, while business transformation focuses on processes.
- Complexity: Frameworks like TOGAF are complex and require extensive training, making them difficult to implement.
- Inflexibility: EA follows a traditional, detailed planning approach, conflicting with the agile, iterative methods needed for digital transformation.

DT requires rapid time-to-market, customer inclusion, and deep integration of digital strategies and business models, not currently supported by EA. There is a need for new, lightweight, business-focused planning tools that support agile methods and are understandable by all stakeholders.

Approach for DT. Goerzig and Bauernhansl [12] proposed a new EA approach for DT for solving the above-mentioned weaknesses emphasizing agility and customer proximity. The approach is divided into a macro and micro cycles, as shown in Fig. 2 [12].

The macro cycle defines the architecture of the entire organization, while in the micro cycle single functions are implemented and tested.

5.2 Proposed Methodology

Based on the previous approach we propose a methodology for driving aMSP digital transformation comprising an initial exploratory phase followed by three iterations. The methodology is depicted in Fig. 3. The initial exploratory phase includes design of the research plan, research approach and the initial digital business strategic review (DBS). Each iteration uses the DBS from the previous iteration, and the current architecture,

254 X. Portell

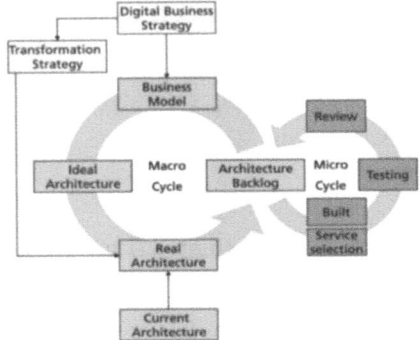

Fig. 2. Agile enterprise architecture for digital transformation [12]

initially described in the exploratory phase and updated after each iteration. The output is the new real architecture, that becomes the current architecture for the next iteration.

The first and second iterations focuses on key processes, while the third one involves refining the systems and processes implemented in previous iterations.

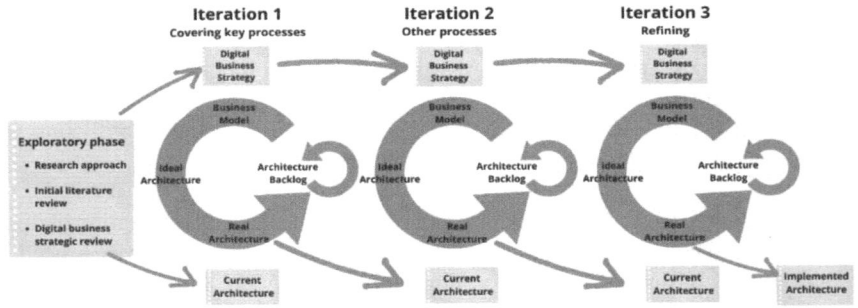

Fig. 3. Proposed methodology based on three AR iterations

The proposed methodology will be tested, evaluated and refined in aMSP case. Its applicability to similar organizations will be assessed based on the results.

6 Research Planning and Status

6.1 First Year: Exploratory Phase

In the first year of the research project we have covered the exploratory phase. Key activities included developing the research plan, defining the approach, and conducting an initial literature review on digital transformation (DT) in nonprofits and healthcare, DT challenges, IS/IT strategic planning, and enterprise architecture in healthcare risk prevention. A digital strategy review of aMSP was carried out, assessing its current state, conducting SWOT analysis, identifying key processes, and evaluating business challenges and objectives. The research plan was then updated based on findings. Additional activities included research training, preparing and defending the thesis plan.

6.2 Second and Third Years: First Iteration for Key Processes

In the second and third years, the project focuses on the first iteration of key processes. This includes prioritizing processes and deriving the business model from DBS, already completed, as well as modeling both the current and ideal architectures for the seven key processes, currently in process. Next, the real architecture will be derived, implemented, and updated in the information systems. Once the new architecture is tested, users will be trained, services will be launched, and results will be measured according to the indicators defined during the exploratory phase. Finally, the activities will be documented.

6.3 Fourth Year: Refining and Improving

In the fourth year, the focus will be on refining and improving the work from previous iterations. The DBS will be updated, prioritized and planned according to the feedback from previous iterations. The business model will be derived from the revised DBS, and the architecture and business model for each key process will be updated. Changes will be implemented, tested, and integrated into the information systems. Updated services will be launched, results measured, and activities documented in reports.

7 Conclusions

Ensuring the safety and well-being of healthcare workers is crucial for improving the quality of care. Technologies offer such organizations a unique opportunity to improve their services, by helping to become more data-intensive and process-oriented. DT can significantly improve those services, but may involve a profound shift in its operations, processes and culture. This restructuring of the enterprise's operational and organizational framework is the main challenge of our project, and we believe that it can be done successfully with the help of an EA.

After intensive research, we could not find any documentation describing references of an EA in risk prevention for healthcare professionals, not even in occupational risk prevention in general. As far as we know, this project will develop the first documented EA for risk prevention for healthcare professionals.

Thus, although this research is based on improving a concrete case, we believe that it may offer valuable insights and inspiration for similar cases, such as for-profit prevention services.

References

1. World Health Organization: World Health Organization fact-sheets: Occupational health: health workers. https://www.who.int/news-room/fact-sheets/de-tail/occupational-health--health-workers. Accessed 29 July 2024

2. Portell, X., Franch, X., Pastor, J.A.: The challenge of digitally improving a nonprofit associative enterprise for the occupational risk prevention of healthcare professionals. In: Paja, E., Zdravkovic, J., Kavakli, E., Stirna, J. (eds.) PoEM 2024. LNBIP, vol. 538, pp. 19–34. Springer, Cham (2025). https://doi.org/10.1007/978-3-031-77908-4_2
3. Morakanyane, R., Grace, A., O'Reilly, P.: Conceptualizing digital transformation in business organizations: a systematic review of literature. In: Digital Transformation – From Connecting Things to Transforming Our Lives, pp. 427–443. University of Maribor Press (2017). https://doi.org/10.18690/978-961-286-043-1.30
4. Teubner, R.A., Stockhinger, J.: Literature review: understanding information systems strategy in the digital age. J. Strateg. Inf. Syst. **29**, 101642 (2020). https://doi.org/10.1016/j.jsis.2020.101642
5. Baskerville, R.L.: Investigating information systems with action research. Commun. Assoc. Inf. Syst. **2** (1999). https://doi.org/10.17705/1CAIS.00219
6. Varajão, J., Magalhães, L., Freitas, L., Rocha, P.: Success management – from theory to practice. Int. J. Proj. Mang. **40**, 481–498 (2022). https://doi.org/10.1016/j.ijproman.2022.04.002
7. Hevner, M.: Park, ram: design science in information systems research. MIS Q. **28**, 75 (2004). https://doi.org/10.2307/25148625
8. McKay, J., Marshall, P.: Quality and rigour of action research in information systems. In: European Conference on Information Systems (ECIS) (2000). http://aisel.aisnet.org/ecis2000/38
9. Pastor, J.A., Sánchez, F.: Método integral de planificación estratégica de SI-TI. Nota técnica 2 (2007)
10. Metaplan SARL: Moderating group discussions using the Metaplan approach (2019)
11. Bente, S., Bombosch, U., Langade, S.: Enriching EA with lean, agile, and enterprise 2.0 practices. In: Collaborative Enterprise Architecture, pp. i–ii. Elsevier (2012). https://doi.org/10.1016/B978-0-12-415934-1.00016-9
12. Goerzig, D., Bauernhansl, T.: Enterprise Architectures for the digital transformation in small and medium-sized enterprises. Procedia CIRP **67**, 540–545 (2018). https://doi.org/10.1016/j.procir.2017.12.257

Integrating Real-Time Worker Wellbeing into IoT-Enhanced Business Process Orchestration for Industry 5.0

Mathis Wyffels[✉]

Research Centre for Information Systems Engineering (LIRIS), KU Leuven, Warmoesberg 26, 1000 Brussels, Belgium
mathis.wyffels@kuleuven.be

Abstract. Business Process Management (BPM) aims to optimize task execution and sequencing to enhance efficiency and create value. With Industry 4.0 and the Internet of Things (IoT), real-time process monitoring and dynamic adaptations have become possible, leading to IoT-enhanced business processes. However, despite these advancements, current BPM technology overlooks real-time human factors, particularly worker wellbeing, when orchestrating manufacturing processes. This gap is critical as Industry 5.0 emphasizes a human-centric approach, recognizing that worker physical and cognitive wellbeing directly impacts productivity, sustainability, and workforce retention. This research project addresses this challenge by integrating real-time worker wellbeing data into IoT business processes for automatic process orchestration. A dynamic worker profile will be developed, leveraging IoT wearables to capture physical and cognitive wellbeing metrics. These real-time insights will then be incorporated into BPM technology to enhance actor assignment and execution, ensuring a balance between worker wellbeing, organizational constraints, and economic objectives. Following the design science research methodology, this project is structured into four work packages, covering wellbeing monitoring, actor assignment extension, mechanism prototyping, and evaluation. By embedding worker wellbeing into process orchestration, this research aims to enhance productivity, reduce accidents and errors, and promote a healthier, more sustainable, and resilient workforce.

Keywords: process orchestration · Internet of Things · worker wellbeing · Industry 5.0

1 Introduction

For a company to create value for customers through products or services, a series of tasks and activities must be performed. Beyond executing individual tasks, companies strive to optimize the sequencing of these tasks, i.e., their business processes, to maximize efficiency. Companies that manage their processes more effectively than competitors can create additional value [7]. This is where the field of business process management (BPM) plays a crucial role.

A core focus of BPM is ensuring processes run correctly while minimizing errors. With the advent of Industry 4.0 (I4.0) and its associated technologies, such as the Internet of Things (IoT), real-time process monitoring and dynamic adjustments have become possible. IoT-enhanced business processes leverage contextual data to support informed decision-making [31]. Additionally, analyzing collected data can uncover new insights for process optimization. As a result, IoT is recognized as a key driver of digital transformation in organizations [17].

Building upon I4.0, the European Commission introduced Industry 5.0 (I5.0) in 2021, emphasizing a human-centric approach to industrial operations. Despite increasing automation, human workers remain essential in the execution of industrial processes due to their dexterity and cognitive abilities, which are crucial for production in mass customization [9,22]. However, industrial tasks often negatively impact workers' physical and cognitive wellbeing, as the duration and repetitiveness of tasks create significant physical and mental demands [5,35]. Over time, these challenges contribute to an unsustainable work system that affects both employees and organizational performance [18]. Additionally, manufacturing industries face increasing difficulties in attracting and retaining skilled workers due to an aging workforce and a shrinking pool of qualified graduates [2]. Prioritizing worker wellbeing would not only support employee health and engagement but also enhances productivity and long-term competitiveness, ensuring a sustainable and resilient workforce [18].

Despite the recognized importance of worker wellbeing, integrating human factors into IoT business processes remains a challenge [10]. Current BPM technology that automatically orchestrates process executions overlooks real-time worker data when assigning workers, ignoring key factors that affect effectiveness and flexibility [10]. In particular, worker wellbeing should be monitored continuously to maintain optimal working conditions, detect potential issues early, and enable real-time interventions that prevent disruptions and errors while sustaining productivity. Current research on worker wellbeing in an industry setting focuses on improving the work environment or product design and thus focuses on long-term modifications rather than real-time changes [1,26].

Although real-time tracking of worker wellbeing is crucial for both IoT business processes and I5.0, no research has yet explored its integration into process orchestration. Nevertheless, existing research in BPM underscores this need to integrate worker wellbeing into decision-making, with [11] emphasizing its role in human resource allocation, [13] advocating for intelligent systems that consider wellbeing, and [20] highlighting its impact on both productivity and worker health.

To integrate worker wellbeing into IoT business processes and I5.0, this research project will extend IoT business processes to consider workers' physical and cognitive wellbeing at real-time during manufacturing process orchestration. Specifically, a dynamic worker profile will be developed, capturing real-time physical and cognitive wellbeing information through IoT devices. This real-time wellbeing profile of workers will be integrated into BPM technology for automatic orchestration of manufacturing processes, ensuring that the human factor is considered in process modeling and execution.

This paper is structured as follows. Section 2 reviews relevant literature. Section 3 defines the research goal, based on the literature and introduction. Section 4 outlines the design science research methodology and four work packages. Section 5 presents six key deliverables and their expected academic and industrial impact. Section 6 concludes with a summary and current research status.

2 Related Work

This project aims to advance IoT business processes by leveraging real-time physical and cognitive wellbeing data into process orchestration. The following section outlines the state of the art in BPM and technology, IoT business processes, and IoT-measured wellbeing in manufacturing.

BPM technology aims to efficiently orchestrate the execution of the various activities of a business process. Manual activities performed by workers are automatically coordinated by assigning the most appropriate worker at that time to a particular task. This assignment of workers to tasks (actor assignment) currently only uses basic organizational characteristics such as role [33]. A few works extend this with additional information about expertise, experience or capabilities [23,25,33]. However, this information is specified at design-time [16] and only to a limited extent incorporates runtime data such as immediate availability [8]. Similarly, research on scheduling optimization (problem) primarily focuses on machine utilization in operations research (OR) and is largely constrained to design-time specifications [25,36]. This results in a clear gap in integrating real-time worker data into process orchestration, restricting flexibility in actor assignment and ultimately reducing overall process efficiency.

IoT integration in BPM enables real-time data-driven decision-making. Most research in this area has focused on extending the BPMN modeling language to incorporate IoT elements [6,29], with fewer works addressing execution, monitoring, or analysis of IoT business processes [28]. Recent literature review confirmed that challenges related to real-time human resource monitoring, as identified by [10] and [17], remain unaddressed in IoT business processes [21]. This project will build upon a state-of-the-art approach developed by [31,32], which enables the modeling and execution of IoT business processes in a decoupled manner, yet it does not address human factors. Therefore, a critical gap persists in real-time monitoring of human factors and their influence on IoT business processes [10,17].

Researchers have explored various methods for measuring wellbeing using IoT devices. Wearables can track physiological indicators such as heart rate, skin conductivity, and breathing rate, providing insights into stress levels, physical fatigue, and attention [20]. While some studies within ergonomics use wellbeing data to improve workstation or product design in OR [1,19,26], these efforts focus on long-term optimization rather than real-time adaptation. Additionally, the emerging concept of the Human Digital Twin (HDT) aims to digitize human attributes, including wellbeing data, yet remains largely theoretical with limited practical applications [34]. Consequently, no existing approaches integrate real-time worker wellbeing data to dynamically adjust process execution and proactively address potential issues.

3 Research Goal

Currently, IoT business processes and automatic process orchestration lack real-time integration of human factors such as worker wellbeing. While IoT enables real-time data collection, existing approaches focus on modeling or long-term optimization rather than real-time execution and adaptation, limiting process flexibility and efficiency. This project addresses this gap with the following research goal:

> *This project aims to develop an innovative process orchestration mechanism that leverages real-time IoT-based physical and cognitive wellbeing data, along with organizational worker characteristics (e.g. roles) and economic objectives, to enhance the workforce effectiveness and sustainability in manufacturing.*

This research goal drives two key contributions: (1) developing a wellbeing profile of workers, considered a partial HDT, by leveraging IoT wearables within a manufacturing context, and (2) enhancing process orchestration in BPM by integrating real-time physical and cognitive wellbeing data of workers.

4 Research Methodology

This research takes a design science research (DSR) approach and follows the well-known frameworks for DSR methodology of [15] and [24], as shown in Fig. 1. The project is organized into four work packages (WPs) in line with the steps of the DSR procedure [24].

4.1 WP1: Conceptualizing Measurable Wellbeing in I5.0

A systematic literature review (SLR) will map the state of the art in wellbeing monitoring within manufacturing, focusing on IoT devices, the data they collect, and how this data can be processed to derive wellbeing indicators. Unlike prior work that centers on algorithms, this SLR emphasizes the underlying data. The model will be validated through semi-structured interviews and observations in industrial partner companies, integrating insights from workers, HR, and managers to assess feasibility, relevance, and ethical considerations. The qualitative analysis will be conducted using techniques such as In Vivo coding. The outcome is a structured, reusable framework for the next work packages, based on

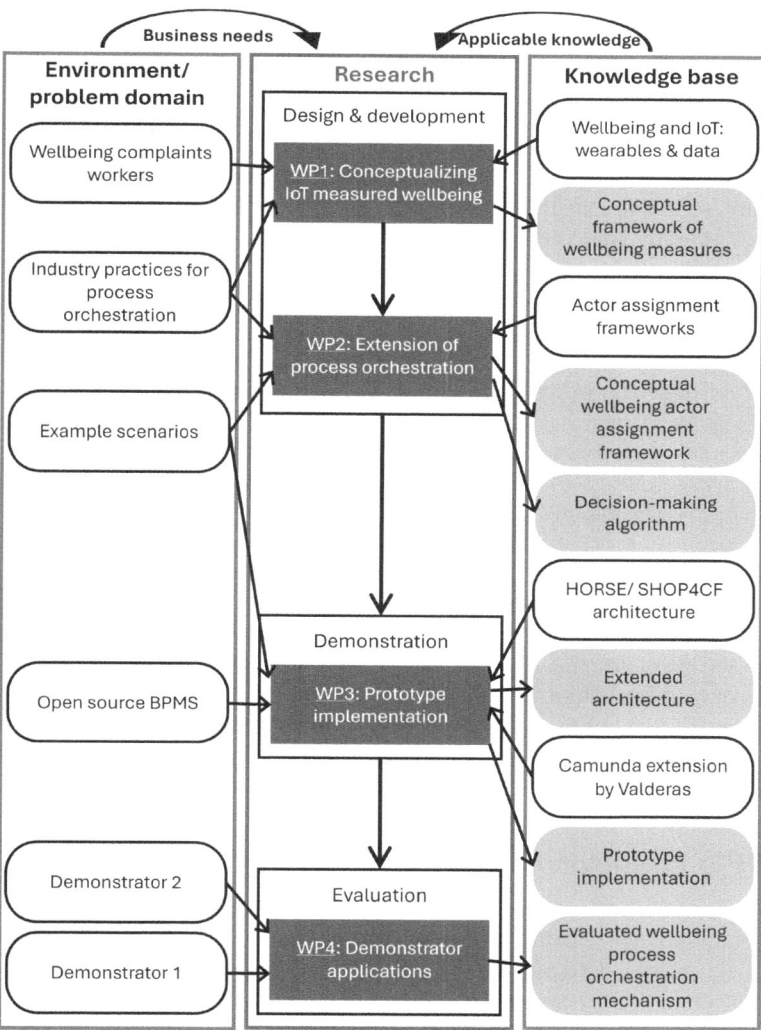

Fig. 1. Visualization of the research methodology: showing the three pillars from [15] (Environment, Research and Knowledge base) and the research process steps from [24] (Design and development, Demonstration, Evaluation). A flow diagram of the four WPs is visible in the research pillar (in blue boxes). Note that for the sake of clarity, only the main inputs (in white ovals) and outputs (in green ovals) of the project are shown. (Color figure online)

an extension of the IoT process log ontology by [4] to include worker wellbeing metrics. Exploratory interviews have been conducted, and the SLR is nearing submission to a journal.

Preliminary findings of the SLR already indicate that stress and mental workload are the most monitored aspects-stress is typically measured via skin conductivity and heart rate using wristbands like Empatica E4, while mental workload is assessed through pupil diameter using glasses such as Tobii Pro 3. Finally, in this work package, ethical approval will be sought from the Social and Societal Ethics Committee at KU Leuven for the proposed handling of personal and potentially sensitive data. All data will be fully anonymized, securely stored within the system, and only used from participants who have provided explicit consent.

4.2 WP2: Extension of the Process Orchestration Mechanism

This WP extends the process orchestration mechanism by integrating wellbeing metrics from WP1 into actor assignment frameworks. First, existing frameworks, which focus on organizational data and process performance indicators, will be enhanced with wellbeing factors from WP1 such as stress and mental workload. To achieve this, the general framework in the BPM domain by [25] and [3] will be utilized. Secondly, worker wellbeing assessment processes will be modeled as IoT business processes using the BPMN-IoT microservice architecture developed in [31] and [32], enabling real-time collection of raw IoT data and its transformation into actionable wellbeing metrics. Finally, an algorithm will be developed to optimize actor assignment by balancing worker wellbeing with process objectives such as cost and lead time. The development will follow a step-by-step approach, progressing from rule-based methods (e.g. priority rules) to heuristic techniques (e.g., variable neighborhood search) and ultimately to stochastic search methods (e.g., Monte Carlo Tree Search).

4.3 WP3: Prototype Implementation

This WP develops a prototype system to implement the process orchestration mechanism from WP2. First, a conceptual information system architecture will be designed based on the reference architecture for the HORSE and SHOP4CF projects [12,30]. Next, the prototype system will be implemented as a Camunda extension, leveraging the BPMN-IoT tool. The microservice architecture will enable flexible and dynamic process orchestration by integrating the key advancements from WP2: (1) microservices for executing worker wellbeing assessment tasks, (2) integration of all relevant data sources from the developed framework, and (3) the decision-making algorithm for real-time actor assignment. The goal is to reach Technology Readiness Level (TRL) 4 (validated in lab setting), with validation conducted through small-scale simulated scenarios informed by interviews and observations from WP1 and WP2.

4.4 WP4: Evaluation with Industrial Demonstrators

This WP focuses on implementing and evaluating the process orchestration mechanism in real-world manufacturing settings. Two demonstrators will be selected from collaborating companies, each targeting different wellbeing metrics. Before deployment, IoT wearables will be tested in a simulated environment to ensure accuracy, feasibility, and compatibility with the orchestration mechanism. Wearable selection will be based on criteria such as cost, real-time data accessibility, and the range of wellbeing factors they cover. The demonstrators will integrate relevant wellbeing factors identified in WP1 and apply the developed system from WP3. To assess the impact, stakeholders, such as workers, management, and HR, will be surveyed using semi-structured interviews and standard questionnaires such as the System Usability Scale (SUS) and Technology Acceptance Model (TAM), while cognitive workload will be assessed through NASA-TLX questionnaires before and after implementation [14]. This evaluation will highlight benefits, potential challenges, and areas for improvement. Finally, insights gathered will be used to refine the process orchestration mechanism in the final task.

5 Expected Contributions

Following the comprehensive research methodology from previous section, this project aims to contribute six deliverables to the knowledge base, as illustrated in Fig. 1.

1. WP1: A conceptual framework (ontology) that outlines real-time worker wellbeing indicators relevant to Industry 5.0, measurable through IoT technologies.
2. WP2.1: An actor assignment framework enhanced with real-time wellbeing metrics, with assessment processes modeled as IoT business processes using a BPMN-IoT microservice architecture.
3. WP2.2: A multi-objective decision-making algorithm for process orchestration that considers worker wellbeing and existing organizational aspects.
4. WP3.1: Dynamic process orchestration reference architecture.
5. WP3.2: Prototype implementation of the dynamic process orchestration mechanism.
6. WP4: A refined process orchestration mechanism, validated through two demonstrators, with a prototype implementation for each. Additionally, a demonstrator report will discuss the application and evaluation of the process orchestration mechanism.

Overall, with a focus on worker wellbeing, this project contributes to the needs of 1) I5.0 to make industries more human-centric, (socially) sustainable and resilient and 2) the Operator 4.0 paradigm, which focuses, among other things, on healthier workers in manufacturing industries [27]. In addition, this project contributes to several of the United Nations Sustainable Development Goals (i.e., 3-good health and wellbeing, 8-decent work and economic growth and 9-industry innovation and infrastructure). Finally, this solution is made possible by leveraging recent advances in the combined fields of BPM and IoT.

In addition to its contributions to the knowledge base, this project is expected to have a broad range of positive impacts on industry. Worker wellbeing will be improved by reducing excessive fatigue, stress, and other factors that negatively affect health. Companies will benefit from increased productivity, fewer accidents, and reduced defects, resulting from better working conditions. Finally, the industry will be better positioned to attract young talent by improving the public image of the sector, helping to address workforce shortages.

6 Conclusion

This research project aims to develop a dynamic process orchestration mechanism that incorporates real-time worker physical and cognitive wellbeing data, captured through IoT wearables, alongside existing worker characteristics and economic objectives. The project makes two key contributions: (1) the development of a wellbeing profile for workers, considered a partial HDT, using IoT wearables within a manufacturing context, and (2) the enhancement of process orchestration in BPM by integrating real-time worker wellbeing data. This approach addresses the existing gap in the lack of real-time integration of worker wellbeing into IoT business processes and automatic process orchestration. The project follows the Design Science Research (DSR) methodology and is currently in its early stages, with substantial progress in WP1. Exploratory interviews have been conducted, and the SLR on devices, data, and wellbeing indicators is nearing submission to a journal. As WP1 concludes, the project is transitioning to WP2 and the next development phases.

Acknowledgments. I would like to thank my supervisors, Prof. Irene Vanderfeesten and Prof. Estefanía Serral Asensio, for their continuous support and guidance throughout this research project.

References

1. Antonaci, F.G., et al.: Workplace well-being in industry 5.0: a worker-centered systematic review. Sensors **24** (2024)
2. Arasanmi, C.N., Krishna, A.: Employer branding: perceived organisational support and employee retention - the mediating role of organisational commitment. Ind. Commer. Train. (2019)
3. Arias, M., Munoz-Gama, J., Sepúlveda, M.: Towards a taxonomy of human resource allocation criteria. In: Teniente, E., Weidlich, M. (eds.) BPM 2017. LNBIP, vol. 308, pp. 475–483. Springer, Cham (2018). https://doi.org/10.1007/978-3-319-74030-0_37
4. Bertrand, Y., Veneruso, S., Francesco, L., Mecella, M., Serral, E.: Nice: the native IoT-centric event log model for process mining. Technical report (2024)
5. Breque, M., Nul, L.D., Petridis, A.: Industry 5.0: towards a sustainable, human-centric and resilient European industry. Technical report (2021)

6. Compagnucci, I., Corradini, F., Fornari, F., Polini, A., Re, B., Tiezzi, F.: A systematic literature review on IoT-aware business process modeling views, requirements and notations. SoSyM (2023)
7. Dumas, M., Rosa, M.L., Mendling, J., Reijers, H.A.: Fundamentals of Business Process Management (2018)
8. Erasmus, J., Vanderfeesten, I., Traganos, K., Grefen, P.: The case for unified process management in smart manufacturing. In: EDOC (2018)
9. Erasmus, J., Vanderfeesten, I., Traganos, K., Keulen, R., Grefen, P.: The horse project: the application of business process management for flexibility in smart manufacturing. Appl. Sci. (2020)
10. Fornari, F., et al.: Digital twins of business processes: a research manifesto (2024)
11. Goel, K., Fehrer, T., Roglinger, M., Wynn, M.T.: Not here, but there: human resource allocation patterns, vol. 14159 (2023)
12. Grefen, P., Vanderfeesten, I., Boultadakis, G.: Architecture design of the horse hybrid manufacturing process control system (2016)
13. Grillo, H., Alemany, M.M., Caldwell, E.: Human resource allocation problem in the industry 4.0: a reference framework. Comput. Ind. Eng. **169** (2022)
14. Hart, S.G., Staveland, L.E.: Development of NASA-TLX (task load index): results of empirical and theoretical research. Adv. Psychol. (1988)
15. Hevner, A.R., March, S.T., Park, J., Ram, S.: Design science in information systems research. Des. Sci. IS Res. MIS Q. **28**, 75 (2004)
16. Ihde, S., Pufahl, L., Völker, M., Goel, A., Weske, M.: A framework for modeling and executing task-specific resource allocations in business processes. Computing (2022)
17. Janiesch, C., et al.: The internet of things meets business process management: a manifesto. IEEE Syst. Man Cybern. Mag. **6**, 34–44 (2020)
18. de Jonge, J., Peeters, M.C.: The vital worker: towards sustainable performance at work (2019)
19. Kolus, A., Wells, R., Neumann, P.: Production quality and human factors engineering: a systematic review and theoretical framework. Appl. Ergon. **73** (2018)
20. Loizaga, E., Eyam, A.T., Bastida, L., Lastra, J.L.: A comprehensive study of human factors, sensory principles, and commercial solutions for future human-centered working operations in industry 5.0 (2023)
21. Luzi, F.D., Leotta, F., Marrella, A., Mecella, M.: On the interplay between business process management and internet-of-things: a systematic literature review. BISE (2024)
22. Miqueo, A., Torralba, M., Yagüe-Fabra, J.A.: Lean manual assembly 4.0: a systematic review. Appl. Sci. **10**, 1–37 (2020)
23. Padella, A., Mannhardt, F., Vinci, F., de Leoni, M., Vanderfeesten, I.: Experience-based resource allocation for remaining time optimization. In: BPM, vol. 14940 (2024)
24. Peffers, K., Tuunanen, T., Rossi, M.: The design science research process: a model for producing and presenting information systems research. Technical report (2006)
25. Pufahl, L., Stiehle, F., Ihde, S., Weske, M., Weber, I.: Resource allocation in business process executions-a systematic literature study. Inf. Syst. **132** (2025)
26. Reiman, A., Kaivo-oja, J., Parviainen, E., Takala, E.P., Lauraeus, T.: Human factors and ergonomics in manufacturing in the industry 4.0 context - a scoping review. Technol. Soc. **65** (2021)
27. Romero, D., Mattsson, S., Åsa Fast-Berglund, Wuest, T., Gorecky, D., Stahre, J.: Digitalizing occupational health, safety and productivity for the operator 4.0. IFIP AICT (2018)

28. Tair, K., Boukhedouma, S.: Integration of internet of things in bpm lifecycle: concepts and comparison of approaches. In: BIWA (2022)
29. Torres, V., Serral, E., Valderas, P., Pelechano, V., Grefen, P.: Modeling of IoT devices in business processes: a systematic mapping study. In: CBI 2020, vol. 1, pp. 221–230 (2020)
30. Traganos, K., Grefen, P., Vanderfeesten, I., Erasmus, J., Boultadakis, G., Bouklis, P.: The horse framework: a reference architecture for cyber-physical systems in hybrid smart manufacturing. J. Manufact. Syst. **61**, 461–494 (2021)
31. Valderas, P., Torres, V., Serral, E.: Modelling and executing IoT-enhanced business processes through BPMN and microservices. JSS **184** (2022)
32. Valderas, P., Torres, V., Serral, E.: Towards an interdisciplinary development of IoT-enhanced business processes. BISE (2023)
33. Vanderfeesten, I.: Advanced Dynamic Actor Assignment (2024)
34. Wang, B., et al.: Human digital twin in the context of industry 5.0. Robot. Comput.-Integr. Manuf. **85** (2024)
35. Wang, Z., Liu, H., Yu, H., Wu, Y., Chang, S., Wang, L.: Associations between occupational stress, burnout and well-being among manufacturing workers: mediating roles of psychological capital and self-esteem. BMC Psychiatry **17** (2017)
36. Xiong, H., Shi, S., Ren, D., Hu, J.: A survey of job shop scheduling problem: the types and models (2022). https://doi.org/10.1016/j.cor.2022.105731

Security in Automated Manufacturing: A Function-Driven Approach

Vjatšeslav Antipenko[✉][iD]

University of Tartu, Ülikooli 18, 50090 Tartu, Estonia
vjatseslav.antipenko@ut.ee

Abstract. The digital transformation of manufacturing introduces new security challenges as interconnected cyber-physical systems (CPS) and the Industrial Internet of Things (IIoT) expand the attack surface. This research presents FAST (Functions, Assets, Security Threats, and Treatments), a structured and adaptable security framework for automated manufacturing. FAST prioritises mitigations based on operational dependencies, balancing industrial functionality with security resilience. Developed through a design science methodology, it integrates literature review, regulatory analysis, simulation, and pilot implementations. Preliminary results show that FAST improves risk classification by linking threats to functional impact, bridging compliance requirements with practical application. It contributes a scalable, function-driven model to guide security decision-making in manufacturing contexts.

Keywords: Industry 4.0 · Cyber-Physical System · Industrial Automation · Risk Management · Security

1 Introduction

The European manufacturing sector is a key driver of economic stability, contributing approximately 15% of the EU's Gross Domestic Product (GDP) and employing around 30 million people [3,10]. The European Industrial Strategy emphasises sustainability, global competitiveness, and resilience, with a strong focus on digitalisation and green innovation [5]. As manufacturing integrates Industry 4.0 technologies, cyber-physical systems (CPS), and the Industrial Internet of Things (IIoT), it benefits from enhanced efficiency, predictive maintenance, and supply chain optimisation [14]. However, this transformation has also significantly expanded the attack surface, increasing the vulnerability of manufacturing systems to cyber threats [8,11,21].

The interconnected nature of manufacturing and global supply chains further exacerbates security risks. The latest ENISA Threat Landscape report highlights that 6% of all reported security incidents in 2024 targeted the manufacturing sector, underscoring its vulnerability alongside other critical industries [7]. These threats extend beyond Information Technology (IT) systems, posing direct risks to Operational Technology (OT) and leading to production disruptions, equipment damage, and financial losses [17].

In response, the EU has introduced regulatory frameworks such as the NIS2 Directive (NIS2) [6] and the Cyber Resilience Act (CRA) [4] to bolster the security of critical infrastructure. Yet their implementation remains inconsistent across member states and primarily targets large enterprises, leaving smaller manufacturers with limited practical guidance [16,19].

While security standards such as ISO 27001 and the NIST Framework offer formal guidance, their resource intensity and generality often hinder adoption in manufacturing contexts [14]. Vendor dependence and constrained security budgets further compound the challenge [3,7,10].

This research addresses these gaps by introducing FAST (Functions, Assets, Security Threats and Treatments), a structured yet adaptable security framework that aligns mitigations with operational dependencies to support functionally resilient manufacturing environments.

The remainder of this paper is structured as follows: Sect. 2 outlines the problem domain; Sect. 3 presents the research approach and key questions; Sect. 4 summarises current findings; Sect. 5 discusses ongoing validation efforts; and Sect. 6 concludes.

2 Background

As manufacturing continues its digital evolution, security has emerged as a critical factor influencing operational stability. Unlike conventional IT security, security in manufacturing must address digital and physical threats, where security breaches can lead to cascading effects, including production halts, equipment malfunctions, and compromised worker safety [8,11,21]. The convergence of IT and OT has further expanded the cyber threat landscape, necessitating security solutions that bridge these domains.

Security in industrial environments spans three primary domains: the physical domain, where attacks target sensors, actuators, and industrial hardware; the cyber domain, which includes network-based threats such as false data injection, malware intrusions, and man-in-the-middle attacks as well as non-networked vulnerabilities like design flaws and improper access control configurations; and the cyber-physical domain, where threats propagate from cyberspace to disrupt physical processes [11,12].

Existing research on industrial security has explored multiple approaches. Still, these remain fragmented in addressing the complexity of manufacturing environments [8,9,11,20]. Krotofil's work [12] on cyber-physical security highlights the limitations of conventional IT security in industrial contexts by introducing a process-aware security approach that analyses cyber threats in relation to physical system behaviours. Her research identifies attack strategies that exploit control system dynamics to manipulate industrial processes, demonstrating how adversaries can induce physical damage through cyber intrusions [12].

The security challenges introduced by IT/OT convergence have led to research on network segmentation, zero-trust architectures, and anomaly detection. While these approaches improve industrial network security, they introduce operational constraints that reduce their practical feasibility [8]. Intrusion detection systems designed for industrial environments suffer from false positive rates, limiting their effectiveness in reliability-critical manufacturing settings [21].

Efforts to enhance security risk classification have led to function-based security models, which assess security risks based on operational impact rather than static vulnerability evaluations. Unlike conventional models, function-oriented security frameworks prioritise asset protection relative to production continuity, ensuring security investments align with industrial processes [21]. However, these models remain largely conceptual and lack practical methodologies for implementation in dynamic manufacturing environments [8]. While existing research provides theoretical underpinnings, it does not offer scalable security frameworks applicable across diverse manufacturing environments.

This research addresses these gaps by introducing FAST—Functions, Assets, Security Threats, and Treatments—an adaptive security framework that explicitly anchors security assessment in the operational functions performed by automated systems. FAST adopts Alter's classification of information-processing work functions [1], defining functions as operations such as capturing, transmitting, storing, retrieving, manipulating, and displaying information. These functions may be realised through physical processes (e.g., robot arms capturing sensor data), digital activities (e.g., PLCs manipulating production metrics), or hybrid interactions that bridge cyber-physical boundaries (e.g., transmitting control data from a machine to a monitoring station). By linking these function types to specific assets, associated threats, and appropriate treatments, FAST enables a structured and scalable risk classification that foregrounds operational impact and business relevance.

3 Research Approach

Managing security risks in automated manufacturing requires an approach grounded in theoretical foundations and empirical validation. This study follows a **design science methodology** [15], developing the **FAST** framework through iterative phases: systematic literature review, regulatory analysis, simulation-based testing, and pilot deployments in industry. The research is structured around four key phases (Fig. 1), each linked to a core research question.

3.1 Research Questions and Contributions

The research is guided by four questions, each contributing to a functionally grounded, scalable security framework.

RQ1: How can security risks in automated manufacturing systems be managed?

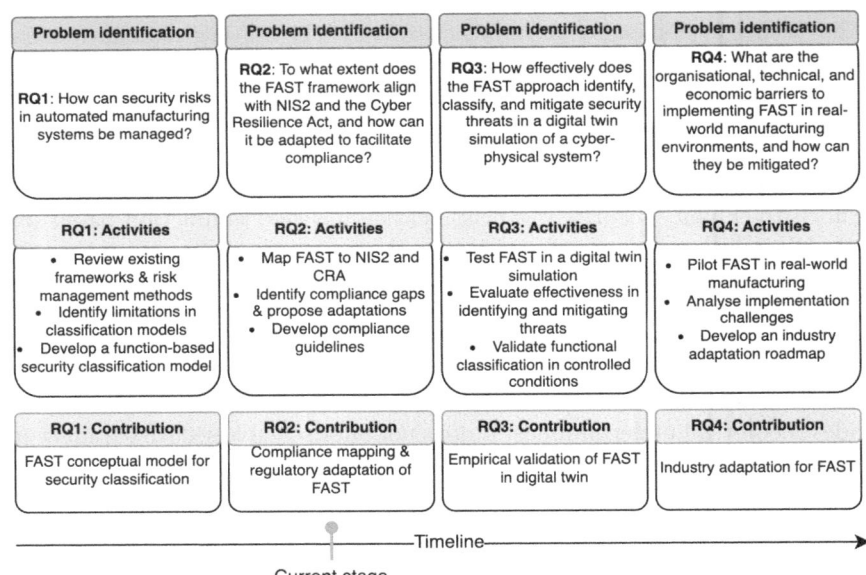

Fig. 1. Research structure linking questions, activities, and contributions of the FAST framework.

Phase: *Conceptual Development* – Existing frameworks focus on static assets and often lack operational context. A systematic literature review identifies classification gaps in cyber-physical risk modelling.

Contribution: This research develops **FAST**, a function-based model that classifies risks based on operational dependencies and threat exposure. This enables dynamic risk prioritisation grounded in real-world functional impact.

RQ2: To what extent does FAST align with NIS2 and the Cyber Resilience Act, and how can it be adapted to support compliance?

Phase: *Regulatory Alignment* – NIS2 and CRA introduce security obligations that are often difficult to interpret and implement consistently. This phase assesses how FAST maps to these requirements and identifies necessary adaptations.

Contribution: The study develops a compliance framework that translates regulatory obligations into concrete operational controls, enabling manufacturers to align security efforts with legal requirements.

RQ3: How effectively does FAST identify, classify, and mitigate threats in a digital twin simulation of a cyber-physical system?

Phase: *Simulation-Based Validation* – A digital twin simulates cyber-physical attack scenarios, testing FAST's ability to assess and mitigate threats.

Contribution: FAST's effectiveness is evaluated regarding situational awareness, risk classification, and treatment guidance. The simulation is based on realistic industrial scenarios with known vulnerabilities, providing a ground truth for validation. While FAST structures threat-treatment mapping, final decisions remain human-led.

RQ4: What are the organisational, technical, and economic barriers to implementing FAST in manufacturing environments, and how can they be mitigated?

Phase: *Industry Adaptation* – Pilot studies identify barriers to real-world implementation, including resource constraints, workforce readiness, and integration feasibility.

Contribution: The research develops an adoption roadmap that offers structured guidance for integrating FAST into diverse manufacturing settings, ensuring its practical scalability and adaptability.

FAST is designed to scale with system complexity, vendor diversity, and functional scope while remaining adaptable to changes in regulatory and operational context. A unified modelling structure supports consistent analysis across IT/OT systems. These properties are validated through simulation (RQ3) and pilot studies (RQ4), evaluating usability, effort, and mitigation effectiveness across scenarios.

4 Preliminary Results

The research on security risk management in automated manufacturing has followed a structured approach, leading to the development of the FAST framework. Introduced in *Functional Security in Automation: The FAST Approach* [2], FAST was built upon a literature review identifying key security risks and mitigation strategies in automated manufacturing.

By aligning assets and functions with identified threats and tailored mitigation measures, FAST structures security risk management into three core phases:

- **System Function and Asset Identification** – Classifying assets and functions using the Information Systems Security Risk Management (ISSRM) model [13], covering both digital (data processing) and physical (sensors, actuators) components.
- **Threat Categorisation** – Using the STRIDE model [18] to classify security threats into six categories: *Spoofing, Tampering, Repudiation, Information Disclosure, Denial of Service, and Elevation of Privilege*.
- **Mitigation Techniques Application** – Mapping targeted security controls to identified threats, ensuring security measures align with function-specific vulnerabilities.

To illustrate the function-driven security approach, Fig. 2 demonstrates how business assets are linked to functions, security threats, and countermeasures.

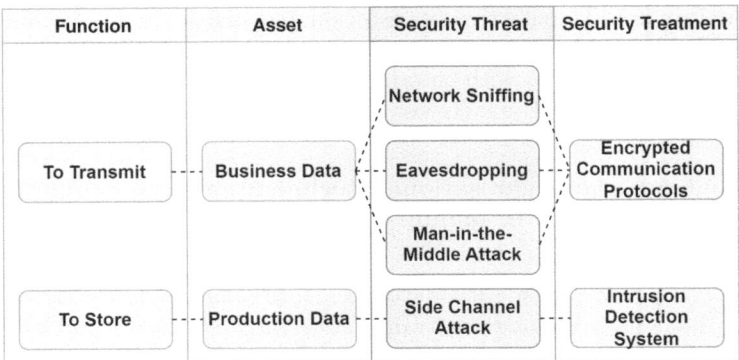

Fig. 2. Information Disclosure - FAST

This scenario highlights a vulnerability to eavesdropping attacks, where unauthorised entities may intercept confidential information, compromising data confidentiality. This risk is mitigated through encrypted communication protocols, ensuring the protection of sensitive data in transmission.

FAST enables a structured risk prioritisation approach by integrating security considerations into functional dependencies.

5 Work in Progress

The next stage of this research focuses on assessing FAST's alignment with EU security regulations, specifically NIS2 and CRA. This study evaluates FAST's applicability for regulatory compliance, aiming to reduce implementation burdens for enterprises by providing structured security guidance.

Preliminary findings indicate that while FAST aligns with core principles of NIS2 and CRA, gaps remain in governance and reporting obligations. Its functional classification model complements the risk-based approach in NIS2, but refinements are needed to support incident reporting and supply chain security requirements.

Following regulatory assessment, the research shifts to empirical validation and industry adaptation. A digital twin simulation will test FAST's effectiveness in identifying and mitigating security risks in cyber-physical environments. Simultaneously, pilot implementations in manufacturing enterprises are being prepared, with ongoing industry engagement addressing concerns such as cost-effectiveness, integration feasibility, and compliance alignment.

The findings from these validation efforts will refine FAST to ensure scalability, regulatory compliance, and operational viability. These ongoing efforts bridge the gap between theoretical development and real-world security management, equipping manufacturers with a structured and efficient security assessment framework.

6 Concluding Remarks

This paper presented ongoing PhD research on FAST (Functions, Assets, Security Threats, and Treatments), a function-based security framework for automated manufacturing. The research has defined FAST's classification model (RQ1) and is currently assessing its regulatory alignment with NIS2 and CRA (RQ2). The next phase involves empirical validation (RQ3), including digital twin simulations to evaluate FAST's effectiveness in mitigating cyber threats in cyber-physical systems. Pilot implementations (RQ4) in manufacturing enterprises will assess adoption feasibility, usability, and integration challenges.

FAST provides a structured, scalable risk assessment model that bridges the gap between compliance-driven security and function-based risk management. By aligning security measures with industry needs and regulatory requirements, FAST enables manufacturers to prioritise security investments while minimising operational disruptions. Future work will refine the framework based on validation outcomes and explore its integration with security automation for real-time risk management in Industry 4.0 environments.

Acknowledgments. This PhD thesis is supervised by Prof. Raimundas Matulevičius at the Institute of Computer Science, University of Tartu, Estonia. The European Union funds this research under Grant Agreement No. 101087529. However, views and opinions expressed are those of the author(s) only and do not necessarily reflect those of the European Union or European Research Executive Agency. Neither the European Union nor the granting authority can be held responsible.

References

1. Alter, S.: The Work System Method: Connecting People, Processes, and IT for Business Results. Work System Method (2006)
2. Antipenko, V., Matulevičius, R.: Functional security in automation: the FAST approach. In: IFIP Working Conference on the Practice of Enterprise Modeling, pp. 244–261. Springer (2024)
3. European Commission: Reassessing the decline of EU manufacturing (2019). https://op.europa.eu/en/publication-detail/-/publication/5f21b462-1a33-11ea-8c1f-01aa75ed71a1. Accessed 5 Mar 2025
4. European Commission: The cyber resilience act: Ensuring secure digital products in the EU. Digital Strategy of the European Commission (2024). https://digital-strategy.ec.europa.eu/en/policies/cyber-resilience-act. Accessed 5 Mar 2025
5. European Commission: EU industry strategy: accelerating the twin transitions. European Commission Website (2024). https://single-market-economy.ec.europa.eu/industry/strategy_en#accelerating-the-twin-transitions. Accessed 5 Mar 2025
6. European Commission: The NIS2 directive: strengthening Europe's cybersecurity. Digital Strategy of the European Commission (2024). https://digital-strategy.ec.europa.eu/en/policies/nis2-directive. Accessed 5 Mar 2025
7. The European Union Agency for Cybersecurity (ENISA): ENISA threat landscape 2024. ENISA Report (2024). https://www.enisa.europa.eu/sites/default/files/2024-11/ENISA%20Threat%20Landscape%202024_0.pdf. Accessed 5 Mar 2025

8. Duo, W., Zhou, M., Abusorrah, A.: A survey of cyber attacks on cyber physical systems: recent advances and challenges. IEEE/CAA J. Automatica Sinica **9**(5), 784–800 (2022). https://doi.org/10.1109/JAS.2022.105548
9. El-Kady, A.H., Halim, S., El-Halwagi, M.M., Khan, F.: Analysis of safety and security challenges and opportunities related to cyber-physical systems. Process Saf. Environ. Prot. **173**, 384–413 (2023). https://doi.org/10.1016/j.psep.2023.03.012
10. Eurostat: Businesses in the manufacturing sector. Eurostat Statistics Explained (2024). https://ec.europa.eu/eurostat/statistics-explained/index.php?title=Businesses_in_the_manufacturing_sector. Accessed 5 Mar 2025
11. Kim, S., Park, K.J., Lu, C.: A survey on network security for cyber-physical systems: from threats to resilient design. IEEE Commun. Surv. Tutor. **24**(3), 1534–1573 (2022). https://doi.org/10.1109/COMST.2022.3187531
12. Krotofil, M.: Security of cyber-physical systems: process-aware approach. Ph.D. thesis (2023)
13. Matulevičius, R.: Fundamentals of Secure System Modelling. Springer, Cham (2017)
14. Oks, S.J., et al.: Cyber-physical systems in the context of industry 4.0: a review, categorization and outlook. Inf. Syst. Front. 1–42 (2022)
15. Peffers, K., Tuunanen, T., Rothenberger, M.A., Chatterjee, S.: A design science research methodology for information systems research. J. Manag. Inf. Syst. **24**(3), 45–77 (2007). https://doi.org/10.2753/MIS0742-1222240302
16. Schmittner, C., Veledar, O., Faschang, T., Macher, G., Brenner, E.: Fostering cyber resilience in Europe: an in-depth exploration of the cyber resilience act. In: Yilmaz, M., Clarke, P., Riel, A., Messnarz, R., Greiner, C., Peisl, T. (eds.) Systems, Software and Services Process Improvement, pp. 390–404. Springer, Cham (2024). https://doi.org/10.1007/978-3-031-71139-8_26. Accessed 5 Mar 2025
17. Shilenge, M., Telukdarie, A.: Optimization of operational and information technology integration towards industry 4.0. In: 2022 IEEE 31st International Symposium on Industrial Electronics (ISIE), pp. 1076–1081 (2022). https://doi.org/10.1109/ISIE51582.2022.9831605
18. Shostack, A.: Threat Modeling: Designing for Security. Wiley (2014)
19. Vandezande, N.: Cybersecurity in the EU: how the NIS2 directive stacks up against its predecessor. Comput. Law Secur. Rev. **52**, 105890 (2024). https://doi.org/10.1016/j.clsr.2023.105890
20. Yaacoub, J., Salman, O., Noura, H.N., Kaaniche, N., Chehab, A., Malli, M.: Cyber-physical systems security: limitations, issues and future trends. Microprocess. Microsyst. **77**, 103201 (2020). https://doi.org/10.1016/j.micpro.2020.103201
21. Yu, Z., Gao, H., Cong, X., Wu, N., Song, H.H.: A survey on cyber-physical systems security. IEEE Internet Things J. **10**(24), 21670–21686 (2023). https://doi.org/10.1109/JIOT.2023.3289625

CAiSE 2025 Doctoral Consortium – LLM for Business Process Modelling

Integrating LLMs and Symbolic Reasoning for Framed Autonomy in AI-Augmented Business Process Management

Angelo Casciani(✉)

Department of Computer, Control, and Management Engineering, Sapienza University of Rome, Rome, Italy
casciani@diag.uniroma1.it

Abstract. The rapid advancement of Artificial Intelligence (AI) has prompted the vision of AI-Augmented Business Process Management Systems (ABPMSs), which aim to enhance process adaptability, explainability, and user interaction. This research proposes a hybrid framework integrating Large Language Models (LLMs) with Symbolic AI reasoners to support ABPMSs framed autonomy in a conversationally actionable way. Drawing an analogy to Kahneman's theory of cognition, LLMs (System 1) enable intuitive, natural language interactions, while reasoners (System 2) ensure precise, rule-based decision-making and compliance with process constraints. This framework functions as a Decision Support System, explaining decisions, enabling what-if analysis, and identifying optimal trade-offs that minimize violation costs while ensuring process progression. By formalizing the frame, the framework enables precise reasoning and autonomous reframing of processes. The research also addresses fostering trust and collaboration between the ABPMS and human users. Initial results demonstrate the potential of this approach to improve decision support and dynamically align process execution with evolving constraints.

Keywords: AI-augmented BPM · Large Language Model · Symbolic Reasoning · Framed Autonomy · Decision Support System

1 Introduction

The rapid evolution of Artificial Intelligence (AI) has opened new frontiers in Business Process Management (BPM), particularly with the emergence of *AI-Augmented BPM Systems* (ABPMSs). A recent research manifesto [6] defines the vision for ABPMSs, extending the traditional BPMS lifecycle in two ways. Firstly, traditional lifecycle phases (e.g., modeling, analysis, execution, monitoring) are iteratively enhanced with AI capabilities. Secondly, the lifecycle includes additional AI-dependent tasks such as adaptation, explanation, and continuous improvement.

ABPMSs introduce a paradigm shift from traditional business process (BP) modeling to the broader notion of *process framing*, which involves establishing multiple constraints including procedural rules, best practices, and norms to guide the BP's execution [14]. Hence, an ABPMS should be *framed autonomous*, i.e., making independent decisions about the execution within the boundaries of the established frame. Unlike conventional BPMSs where framed autonomy rigidly adheres to the prescriptive interpretation and enactment of a predefined BP model, ABPMSs must simultaneously take into account multiple (potentially conflicting) constraints regulating strict (procedural) and/or flexible (declarative) aspects of a BP execution. Besides, they should violate the frame whenever needed to complete a partial process execution with the minimum cost.

Regarding autonomy within the frame, an ABPMS can proactively *reframe* itself as it acquires new knowledge during adaptation, explanation, or improvement stages. Alternatively, the designer can restrict it, determining which parts of the frame it can modify independently and which require human intervention. Furthermore, the ABPMS's autonomy depends on its knowledge of the environment: the more information it has about the process' context and constraints, the more it can make informed decisions and act accordingly. Hence, the ABPMS should ask its human agent for additional information whenever needed.

Indeed, despite the autonomous nature of ABPMSs, *human involvement* remains essential [15], particularly for maintaining *trust* and a sense of *control* within the workforce, known barriers to the adoption of automated technologies in Information Systems [11]. To address these concerns while minimizing human effort, an ABPMS should be *conversationally actionable*, engaging with users through natural language when the constraints of the frame cannot be met, discussing the BP progression and the benefits and drawbacks of actions.

However, achieving this vision requires the system to reason about the current state of the process, predict future situations, and make decisions that align with the frame, always interacting with human agents to provide actionable insights and recommendations in natural language. Users must also be able to understand and trust the ABPMS's decisions, especially when it autonomously adapts or reframes the BP constraints.

To address these challenges towards *achieving framed autonomy in a conversationally actionable way*, this research proposes a *hybrid framework* that combines the strengths of *Large Language Models* (LLMs) and *Symbolic AI reasoners*. The key idea is to use LLMs for natural language understanding and generation, enabling the system to interact with users in a conversational manner, while relying on symbolic reasoning for precise, rule-based decision-making and process execution. This vision aligns with Kahneman's dual-process theory of cognition [8]: *System 1* (fast, intuitive, and automatic) and *System 2* (slow, deliberative, and analytical). Translating this analogy to ABPMSs, LLMs embody the strengths of System 1, i.e., rapid pattern recognition, natural language interaction, and adaptability to unstructured inputs. Formal reasoners, on the other hand, mirror System 2, with their structured, rule-based reasoning that ensures compliance, consistency, and explainability.

By combining the strengths of both technologies, this framework should act as a *Decision Support System* (DSS), providing explanations for the ABPMS's decisions and enabling *what-if* analysis on the process. It helps users understand the implications of breaking specific constraints and identify the optimal trade-offs, minimizing violation costs while ensuring the BP progression.

Differently from traditional user interfaces (UIs) for DSSs, our work would enable intelligent and insightful interactions between users and ABPMSs. To further motivate this claim, we examine a manufacturing scenario involving production planning. The frame includes procedural guidelines for production scheduling, declarative constraints representing resource utilization limits, and customer delivery deadlines. During the process enactment, violations of these constraints may occur, and the ABPMS must find the *near-optimal frame*, interacting with production managers to discuss the nature and severity of the violations.

For instance, when a sudden machine breakdown during production happens, the ABPMS notifies the production manager and provides a what-if analysis to explore the consequences of different recovery strategies: (*i*) pause production and wait for the machine to be repaired, minimizing costs but delaying all pending orders; (*ii*) reassign the affected tasks to another machine, increasing operational strain but keeping production on schedule; and (*iii*) outsource the affected tasks to a third-party supplier, ensuring timely delivery but incurring additional costs. The ABPMS explains that reassigning tasks to another machine could lead to overloading that machine, increasing the risk of future breakdowns. However, outsourcing the tasks would ensure timely delivery but at a higher cost for the company. Thus, the production manager might decide to violate the constraint of minimizing operational strain, opting to reassign tasks to another machine while closely monitoring its workload.

This manufacturing scenario exemplifies how our dual-layer framework could enable effective collaboration between the ABPMS and production managers in a *trustworthy* manner. Thus, building on the previous considerations, the following research questions (RQs) can be drawn:

RQ1: *What are the challenges in enabling actionable conversations in BPM, and what existing techniques have been developed to address them?*
RQ2: *How can the integration of LLMs and formal reasoners support framed autonomy in ABPMSs?*
RQ3: *What is the impact of the hybrid framework on human trust and the adoption of ABPMSs?*

2 Related Work

Despite LLMs demonstrating impressive performance across diverse tasks and benchmarks [22], emerging research highlights critical shortcomings in their planning, reasoning, and verification abilities. Studies demonstrate that even state-of-the-art LLMs struggle with basic reasoning tasks, exhibiting high variability in performance due to minor problem variations, overconfidence in incorrect solutions, and an inability to benefit from multi-step re-evaluation [16]. Similarly, LLMs display significant performance drops in mathematical reasoning when faced with slightly altered problem parameters or increased complexity, suggesting that their reasoning is more simulated than logical [13]. Indeed, LLMs are argued to function more as *approximate knowledge retrievers* than true reasoning agents, raising doubt on their capacity for tasks requiring planning or self-verification [9]. These findings emphasize the need for more robust frameworks and rethinking LLMs application in reasoning-intensive domains.

Recent research has explored integrating LLMs with formal reasoners and verifiers to address their limitations. For instance, combining LLMs with Linear Temporal Logic (LTL) representations has enhanced their ability to interpret and execute natural language instructions in temporally extended tasks, demonstrating superior performance in text-based games [18]. The LLM-Modulo framework proposes a tighter integration of LLMs with symbolic verifiers, enabling bidirectional interactions that extend planning and reasoning capabilities beyond mere translation tasks [9]. Other approaches incorporate Answer Set Programming (ASP) solvers to structure user queries for traditional AI planners, significantly outperforming LLM-only strategies in orchestrating complex API tasks [2]. Neuro-symbolic systems such as AlphaGeometry further highlight the potential of integrating neural LLMs with symbolic deduction engines, achieving state-of-the-art results in mathematical theorem proving [17].

Building on these advancements that underscore the potential of hybrid architectures in overcoming the inherent reasoning deficits of standalone LLMs, our work introduces a novel framework integrating LLMs with symbolic reasoners to enable actionable conversations in BPM. This approach leverages formal representations of BPs to ensure framed autonomy, adaptability, and faithful interactions with the ABPMS, bridging the gap between natural language understanding and rigorous reasoning in a unified system.

3 Methodology

This PhD thesis follows the *Design Science* methodology [19], which is the design and investigation of artifacts in context to improve some aspect of it. Here, the proposed artifacts include a hybrid framework for integrating LLMs and symbolic reasoners to achieve framed autonomy in an ABPMS, as well as a taxonomy and an assessment framework for evaluating the trustworthiness of ABPMSs in BPM.

The previously introduced RQs driving this research reflect the three main stages of the *design cycle*, namely *Problem Investigation*, *Treatment Design*, and *Treatment Validation*, as reported in Fig. 1. We do not consider the *Treatment Implementation* according to the Wieringa definition, i.e., the transfer of the treatment to the problem context [19].

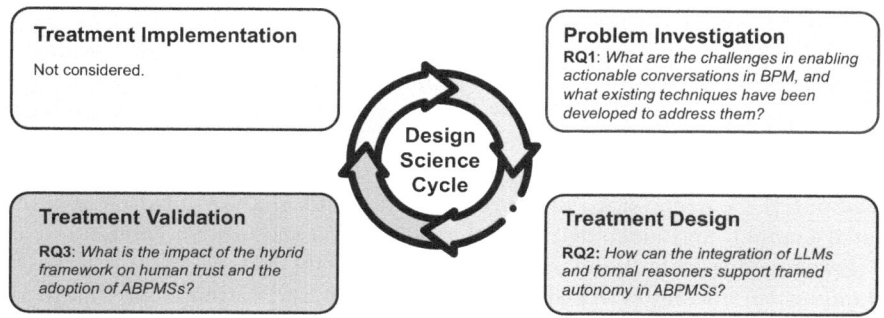

Fig. 1. The Design Science Cycle for this PhD thesis according to [19].

3.1 Problem Investigation

In the Problem Investigation, we addressed **RQ1** through an extensive and structured review of the state-of-the-art approaches facilitating actionable conversations to back framed autonomy in ABPMSs. Thus, we developed a survey [4] applying a rigorous and reproducible search protocol across recognized academic databases inspired by [10], and we categorized the findings following the BPM taxonomy drawn in [5].

This initial work allowed us to identify the challenges addressed by this research to achieve ABPMSs framed autonomy through actionable conversations and to determine the techniques that could be employed to tackle these issues.

3.2 Treatment Design

In this phase, we tackle **RQ2** through the design of the main artifact, i.e., the hybrid framework enabling actionable conversations to support framed autonomy in ABPMSs. Building on the manufacturing example in Sect. 1, the integration of LLMs and reasoners in the ABPMS vision should act as a DSS, providing real-time decision support, interactive what-if scenario evaluation, and proactive process adaptations. It should detect exogenous actions violating the frame and converse with human agents to reframe accordingly, adhering to a *human-in-the-loop* approach where the final decision rests with the human [20].

We already experimented with LLMs by implementing a conversational process-aware DSS for answering BP-related questions, combining fine-tuning to incorporate domain-specific knowledge and *Retrieval-Augmented Generation* (RAG) to embed the contextual knowledge for accurate answers [3]. We also explored RAG-based approaches for object-centric analysis on OCEL 2.0 logs and next activity prediction in Predictive Process Monitoring.

Nevertheless, solely relying on LLMs "reasoning" capabilities can be detrimental due to their *poor explainability* and *hallucinations* [21]. We posit that integrating symbolic AI reasoners can enhance the reliability and transparency of ABPMSs, making their reasoning more faithful and human-understandable. Thus, we envisage this *neuro-symbolic framework* leveraging *LLMs as System 1*, for natural language interaction and rapid pattern recognition, and *symbolic reasoners as System 2*, for structured, rule-based decision-making and process execution. Such a framework, adopting a common communication format to facilitate the interaction between the two systems, enables the ABPMS to reason about the current state of the BP, predict and analyze future states in a what-if manner, and make decisions that align with the process frame.

However, this PhD thesis introduces several challenges, such as: (*i*) creating techniques to translate between natural language and formal representations, ensuring seamless mapping of user queries and generation of natural language responses; (*ii*) developing efficient algorithms to support real-time reasoning over complex processes, balancing computational demands with system responsiveness; and (*iii*) designing methods to foster trust in the system for human users.

Thus, to realize this vision, we need a formalization for the process frame. Specifically, we are exploring a formal representation of BPMN using *Situation Calculus* (SitCalc), a first-order logic language for reasoning about actions in AI, and *ConGolog*, a high-level programming language built on top of the latter. A SitCalc basic action theory can model the state of a BP as a sequence of actions (i.e., a *situation*), while a ConGolog program can specify complex process dynamics. The formalization can support reasoning tasks about the sequence of activities and on the objects manipulated during the BP execution, and to check the presence of deadlocks. This modular formalization can also enable the ABPMS to *reframe* the process autonomously, adding or adapting constraints and goals as they emerge during execution in response to exogenous events.

3.3 Treatment Validation

Finally, we validate the main artifact and its effects on the stakeholders in terms of their fostered trust towards ABPMSs, addressing **RQ3**.

To date, the dynamics of human-AI collaboration in decision-making processes, particularly in high-stakes environments, is not well understood. Hence, we plan to conduct empirical studies to explore interactions between the human and the framework in various domains and scenarios. Insights from these studies will guide the design of interaction protocols with the ABPMS to improve its efficiency and foster trust.

Trust plays a crucial role in framed autonomy since, instead of merely presenting actions to select for the human agent as in traditional UIs, it supports intelligent decision-making by providing actionable insights into the choices through conversations. Nevertheless, the ABPMS's decisions in sensitive contexts, e.g., in healthcare, might not be trusted. Thus, the human agent remains essential for building trust in these systems. For this reason, in [1], inspired by established principles for trustworthy AI [12], we explored factors that foster human trust in these systems. We developed and validated a *classification framework* to assess the trustworthiness of ABPMSs, linking specific trust principles to each step of the system. Adopting this framework can lead to the implementation of more accountable, reliable, and transparent ABPMSs, capable of handling modern BP complexities.

Moreover, users may distrust decisions made by ABPMSs if they do not understand the reasoning behind them. Integrating Symbolic AI reasoners, which are *inherently explainable* due to their rule-based reasoning, can help mitigate this issue.

Future research will address the lack of standardized metrics for evaluating the trustworthiness of ABPMSs and the impact the proposed artifact has on them. First, we plan to develop a taxonomy of autonomy for these systems, as trust is often *inversely proportional* to the level of autonomy. Specifically, we will devise comprehensive metrics that encompass both qualitative and quantitative aspects, such as user satisfaction surveys, adherence to ethical guidelines, and performance benchmarks, to rigorously assess the effectiveness and trustworthiness of the ABPMS. The evaluation will combine a real-world case study, conducted on a manufacturing production line, with controlled experiments to compare user trust in BPMSs with and without the framework.

4 Conclusion

This work proposes a *hybrid framework* for ABPMSs that integrates LLMs with symbolic reasoning to support framed autonomy through actionable conversations and enhance user interaction. By providing a formal representation for the BP frame, it enables precise, rule-based reasoning through the *System 2-like reasoners*, while *System 1-like LLMs* provide a natural language interface for intuitive, context-aware communication. This combination addresses key challenges such as explainability, faithfulness, and real-time adaptability, fostering trust and collaboration between the ABPMS and human users. Initial results demonstrate the framework's potential to improve decision support, provide accurate answers and dynamically align process execution with evolving constraints.

This dual-layer framework represents a significant advancement in BPM, enabling adaptive and reliable systems. By grounding LLMs in formal reasoning, this work moves closer to AI that aligns with human values like compliance, transparency, and trust. This research lays the foundation for the new generation of ABPMSs that can transform industries such as manufacturing, driving their wider adoption to reduce costs and increase productivity in the era of Industry 5.0 [7].

Acknowledgments. This work has been carried out while Angelo Casciani was enrolled in the Italian National Doctorate on Artificial Intelligence run by Sapienza University of Rome. This research work is supervised by Prof. Andrea Marrella (marrella@diag.uniroma1.it) and Prof. Marta Cimitile (marta.cimitile@unitelma.it).

References

1. Acitelli, G., Agostinelli, S., Casciani, A., Marrella, A.: The role of trust in AI-augmented business process management. In: Artificial Intelligence for Business Process Management (AI4BPM) Workshop - BPM 2024. Springer (2024)
2. Agarwal, S., Sreepathy, A., Alonso, D.H., Lamba, P.: LLM+reasoning+planning for supporting incomplete user queries in presence of APIs. arXiv (2024)
3. Bernardi, M.L., Casciani, A., Cimitile, M., Marrella, A.: Conversing with business process-aware large language models: the BPLLM framework. J. Intell. Inf. Syst. **62**(6), 1607–1629 (2024)
4. Casciani, A., Bernardi, M.L., Cimitile, M., Marrella, A.: Conversational systems for AI-augmented business process management. In: 18 International Conference on Research Challenges in Information Science (RCIS 2024), vol. 513, pp. 183–200. Springer (2024)
5. Chapela-Campa, D., Dumas, M.: From process mining to augmented process execution. Softw. Syst. Model. **22**(6), 1977–1986 (2023)
6. Dumas, M., Fournier, F., Limonad, L., Marrella, A., et al.: AI-augmented business process management systems: a research manifesto. ACM Trans. Manag. Inf. Syst. **14**(1), 1–19 (2023)
7. He, L., Gao, J., Leng, J., Wu, Y., et al.: Disassembly sequence planning of equipment decommissioning for industry 5.0: prospects and retrospects. Adv. Eng. Inform. **62**, 102939 (2024)
8. Kahneman, D.: Thinking, Fast and Slow. Macmillan (2011)
9. Kambhampati, S., Valmeekam, K., Guan, L., Verma, M., et al.: Position: LLMs can't plan, but can help planning in LLM-modulo frameworks. In: Forty-First International Conference on Machine Learning, ICML 2024. OpenReview.net (2024)
10. Kitchenham, B.: Procedures for performing systematic reviews. Keele University, Keele, UK, vol. 33, pp. 1–26 (2004)
11. Lee, J.D., See, K.A.: Trust in automation: designing for appropriate reliance. Hum. Factors **46**(1), 50–80 (2004)
12. Mariani, R., Rossi, F., et al.: Trustworthy AI - part 1. Computer **56**(2), 14–18 (2023)
13. Mirzadeh, S., Alizadeh, K., Shahrokhi, H., Tuzel, O., et al.: GSM-symbolic: understanding the limitations of mathematical reasoning in large language models. arXiv (2024)
14. Montali, M.: Constraints for process framing in AI-augmented BPM. In: 20th International Conference on Business Process Management (BPM 2022 Workshops), vol. 460, pp. 5–12. Springer (2022)
15. Muthusamy, V., Unuvar, M., Völzer, H., Weisz, J.D.: Do's and Don'ts for Human and Digital Worker Integration. arXiv abs/2010.07738 (2020)
16. Nezhurina, M., Cipolina-Kun, L., Cherti, M., Jitsev, J.: Alice in wonderland: simple tasks showing complete reasoning breakdown in state-of-the-art large language models. arXiv (2024)
17. Trinh, T.H., Wu, Y., Le, Q.V., He, H., Luong, T.: Solving olympiad geometry without human demonstrations. Nature **625**(7995), 476–482 (2024)
18. Tuli, M., Li, A.C., Vaezipoor, P., Klassen, T.Q., et al.: Learning to follow instructions in text-based games. In: Advances in Neural Information Processing Systems 35 (NeurIPS) (2022)
19. Wieringa, R.J.: Statistical Difference-Making Experiments. Springer (2014)

20. Zanzotto, F.M.: Viewpoint: human-in-the-loop artificial intelligence. J. Artif. Intell. Res. **64**, 243–252 (2019)
21. Zhang, Y., Li, Y., Cui, L., Cai, D., et al.: Siren's Song in the AI Ocean: A Survey on Hallucination in Large Language Models. arXiv abs/2309.01219 (2023)
22. Zhao, W.X., Zhou, K., Li, J., Tang, T., et al.: A Survey of Large Language Models. arXiv abs/2303.18223 (2023)

Towards an LLM-Based Conversational Framework for Business Process Modeling: Research Approach and Preliminary Results

Luca Franziska Hörner(✉)[iD]

Institute of Databases and Information Systems, Ulm University, Ulm, Germany
luca.hoerner@uni-ulm.de

Abstract. Business process modeling is a crucial task for organizations to document, analyze, and optimize their business processes. However, creating process models requires modeling expertise, aggravating this knowledge-intensive task for non-experts. Recent advancements in Natural Language Processing and artificial intelligence offer new possibilities for automating the generation of process models from natural language descriptions. This doctoral research aims to address these emerging possibilities by developing BPMNGen, an LLM-based conversational framework that enables users to generate and iteratively evolve BPMN 2.0 process models using natural language input. By leveraging NLP techniques, BPMNGen translates the process descriptions entered by the user into BPMN 2.0 process models and then allows for real-time modifications through interactive prompts. The research follows the Design Science Research Methodology to develop and evaluate the conversational framework in a structured manner. A key focus of future work will be the evaluation of the generated BPMN 2.0 process models to ensure their quality, correctness, and usefulness. Additionally, different techniques (including prompt engineering) will be explored to improve the accuracy and quality of the model generation process. The main goal of this research is to make process modeling with BPMN 2.0 more accessible and convenient for a broader audience, including domain experts, process participants, and business analysts.

Keywords: LLM · Chatbot · Conversational Process modeling · BPMN

1 Introduction

BPMN 2.0 has established itself as the de facto standard for modeling business processes, enabling organizations to document, visualize, analyze, and optimize their business processes [13]. Many domain experts, business analysts, and process participants often lack the modeling skills needed to manually create BPMN 2.0 process models with corresponding modeling tools, resulting in a gap between the design of a process and its formal representation and implementation [15,17]. At the same time, recent advancements in Natural Language Processing (NLP) and artificial intelligence (AI) have demonstrated that chatbots and large language models (LLMs) can bridge this gap by translating natural language text into structured formats that computers can process (e.g. JSON and XML) [7–9]. While NLP has been widely applied in text automation, conversational agents, and knowledge extraction, its application in the conversational generation of BPMN 2.0 process models remains an underexplored area of research [4,6].

This PhD research addresses this gap by developing BPMNGen, an LLM-based conversational framework, capable of generating BPMN 2.0 process models from natural language process descriptions provided by humans. Many process participants and domain experts are frequently involved in process design but lack the technical expertise to translate their domain knowledge into formal BPMN 2.0 process models. The framework to be developed shall support the human modeler by decreasing the technical barriers and simplify the creation of BPMN 2.0 process models. Instead of manually creating process models, users of the framework shall be enabled to input natural language process descriptions in BPMNGen, which will then attempt to translate these descriptions into BPMN 2.0 models. Beyond the initial process model generation, BPMNGen shall enable users to iteratively refine and enhance their process models by providing additional prompts. This interactive prompting shall allow for a dynamic and flexible approach to process modeling. Another promising use case of the framework concerns the migration of existing textual process documentations, as prevalent in many organizations and enterprises, to BPMN 2.0 process models, which can then be imported in existing modeling tools and suites.

The remainder of this paper is structured as follows: Sect. 2 describes the methodology of my PhD research. Section 3 presents the proposed solutions applied on each phase of the Design Science Research Methodology. Finally, Sect. 4 closes this paper with a conclusion.

2 Methodology

My PhD research follows the Design Science Research Methodology (DSRM), as introduced by [14], which provides a structured framework for conducting research that leads to the creation and validation of innovative artifacts. The DSRM was designed to address the lack of a widely accepted methodology for conducting design science research, particularly in the Information Systems (IS) discipline.

- **Phase 1: Problem identification and motivation** - Defines the research problem, its significance, and the gaps in existing knowledge.
- **Phase 2: Objective of solution** - Establishes the goals the solution must achieve, based on literature insights and problem analysis.
- **Phase 3: Design and development** - Involves creating an innovative artifact, such as a framework, model, method, or system.
- **Phase 4: Demonstration and evaluation** - Tests and evaluates the artifact in a real or simulated environment to assess its effectiveness, relevance, and impact.

3 Proposed Solution and Preliminary Results

After discussing the methodology driving this PhD research, which is at the end of its first year, this section presents its proposed solutions. The latter are structured according to the previously outlined phases of the methodology. Figure 1 illustrates my PhD research approach along the DSRM phases.

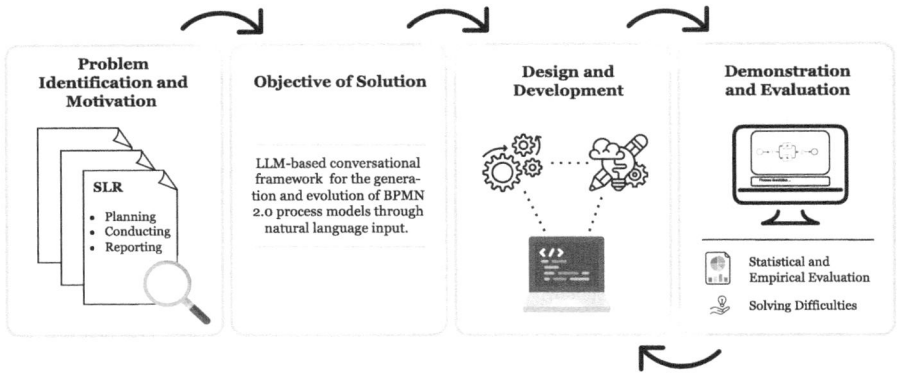

Fig. 1. PhD Research Approach

3.1 Problem Identification and Motivation SLR

To establish a solid foundation for the proposed solution in Phase 1, I conducted a systematic literature review (SLR) following the methodology by Kitchenham [5] to identify the state of the art in generating BPMN 2.0 process models from natural language input. This SLR [4], focused specifically on process models and did not cover multi-perspective conceptual models such as enterprise or systems models. Relevant broader work, e.g., by [3], was not considered.

While significant advancements have been made in both business process management and LLM-based chatbot technologies, the literature reveals a notable gap in integrating these two domains. To structure the analysis, the SLR differentiates between two key transformation approaches: generating BPMN 2.0 process models from natural language input (Text-to-Model) and generating textual descriptions from BPMN 2.0 models (Model-to-Text). Although existing studies neither fully address Text-to-Model nor Model-to-Text, the most common techniques in related work involve NLP, sentence analysis, and mapping rules. These findings highlight the need for a novel approach that bridges this gap, which will form the basis for Phases 2–4 of my research.

3.2 Objective of Solution Chatbot

The primary objective of this research is to develop an LLM-based conversational framework for generating and evolving BPMN 2.0 process models through natural language input. This addresses the identified research gap where no existing approaches fully integrate NLP and BPMN 2.0 process modeling in an interactive and iterative manner. The proposed solution, BPMNGen, is designed to ensure theoretical relevance and practical applicability.

3.3 Design and Development - BPMNGen Framework

This section gives first insights into the BPMNGen framework, including its architecture as well as an interaction scenario, aligning with Phase 3 of the DSRM. This phase focuses on the design and development of the LLM-based conversational framework, providing a detailed overview of the various components of BPMNGen and illustrating how users interact with this framework to generate and refine BPMN 2.0 process models.

Architecture. The architecture of BPMNGen (see Fig. 2) consists of four components: a user interface, a custom assistant, a server, and a database.

The user begins by interacting with BPMNGen through a graphical interface, where he or she inputs natural language instructions into a dedicated input panel. These instructions are then sent to the custom assistant, which interprets the user input. The custom assistant processes the instructions and translates them into a structured JSON representation of a BPMN 2.0 process model. The generated JSON is then forwarded to the server, which handles the communication between the custom assistant, the database, and the user interface. The server converts the JSON to BPMN-compliant XML format and ensures proper database management. Finally, the database stores the generated BPMN 2.0 process models, allowing users to retrieve, edit, and manage their models over time, providing persistent storage and a history of the generated models.

Interaction Scenario. A user wants to generate a BPMN 2.0 process model using BPMNGen. The modeling starts when he or she enters a process description in natural language. BPMNGen processes the input and generates an initial BPMN 2.0 process model, which is displayed in the central workspace (cf. Fig. 3) using the BPMN-js viewer [1]. To further refine the model, the user interacts with the prompt history panel on the right, entering additional prompts. BPMNGen updates the process model accordingly during the interaction. Throughout the modeling session, the left panel provides access to previously generated BPMN 2.0 models and an option to generate new ones. Once a process model is finalized, the user can utilize the elements at the top bar to save, export, or delete the process model. This simple scenario shall demonstrate how BPMNGen aims to enable an intuitive and dynamic approach to process modeling, allowing users to generate and refine BPMN 2.0 models interactively through natural language.

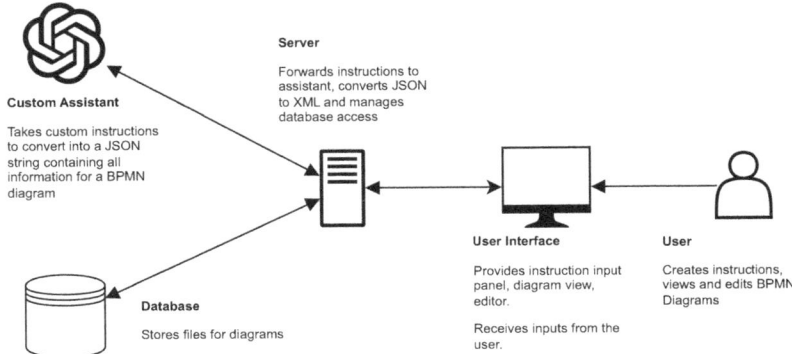

Fig. 2. Architecture of BPMNGen

3.4 Demonstration and Evaluation - Statistical and Empirical Studies

The implemented BPMNGen framework shall provide a functional approach to generate and evolve BPMN 2.0 process models from natural language input. This leads to the overarching research question: *RQ0: Is it possible to generate sound BPMN 2.0 process models or to evolve existing ones based on natural language input?* To answer RQ0, several areas require further exploration, (1)–(3), aligning with Phase 4 of the DSRM (cf. Sect. 2).

(1) Quality Evaluation of Generated BPMN 2.0 Models. One area of this investigation is assessing the quality of the generated BPMN 2.0 models. To ensure soundness, the process models generated with BPMNGen will be evaluated based on the quality aspects defined by the well-established SEQUAL Framework [10,11]:

- **Syntactic Quality**: Verifying structural correctness and compliance with BPMN 2.0 standards.
- **Semantic Quality**: Ensuring that models accurately represent the intended process logic, avoiding inconsistencies and misinterpretations.
- **Pragmatic Quality**: Evaluating the clarity, readability, and usability of the generated models.

This leads to the first research question:

RQ1: How well do chatbot-generated BPMN 2.0 process models conform to syntactic, semantic, and pragmatic quality?

(2) Exploration of Different Prompting Strategies. Another crucial area is the role of prompt engineering in enhancing the generation of process models. By systematically refining the prompts inputted by humans, the quality and

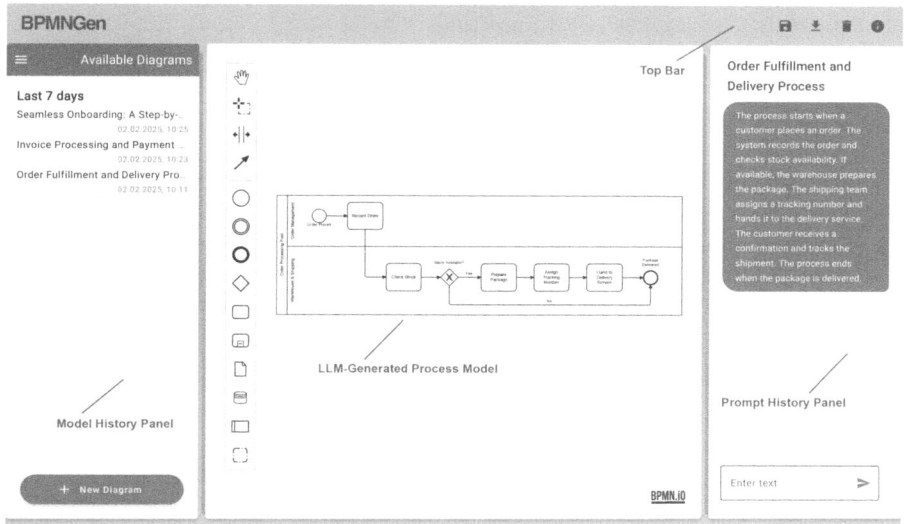

Fig. 3. User Interface of BPMNGen

consistency of the resulting process models shall be improved. The quality of BPMN 2.0 model generation is significantly influenced by how effectively the chatbot interprets and processes user input. Future research will focus on systematically testing and comparing various prompting strategies to improve the accuracy of generated process models and minimize errors in output generation. The following approaches could be explored:

- **Zero-shot prompting** [2]: Evaluating the ability of BPMNGen to generate BPMN 2.0 process models without any prior examples, relying solely on its pre-trained knowledge to interpret user instructions. This approach will help assess the baseline capabilities of the model in understanding and structuring process flows.
- **Few-shot prompting** [12]: Providing BPMNGen with a limited number of structured examples before generating a BPMN 2.0 process model. This strategy aims to enhance consistency and guide BPMNGen toward producing more accurate and contextually relevant models, particularly for complex or domain-specific processes.
- **Chain-of-thought prompting** [16]: Encouraging BPMNGen to break down the process description into intermediate reasoning steps before constructing the process model. This method may improve logical consistency and reduce errors caused by implicit assumptions or incomplete information in the user input.
- **Experimenting with diverse textual inputs**: Assessing the ability of BPMNGen by utilizing a heterogeneous set of process descriptions varying in length, complexity, and linguistic quality. This approach aims to systematically evaluate the quality of the process model across different input scenarios.

This leads to the second research question:

RQ2: How can the quality of the generated process models be improved through sophisticated prompt engineering?

(3) Continuous Improvement of BPMNGen. Finally, to ensure that BPMNGen produces comprehensive and accurate process models, it becomes necessary to examine how well these models capture all relevant aspects and elements of the process description. To increase the expressiveness and applicability of the chatbot, future research could explore its ability to handle additional BPMN 2.0 elements. Areas for expansion include:

- **Artifacts and Data Objects**: Investigating how the chatbot can incorporate BPMN 2.0 artifacts, such as data objects and annotations, to provide richer contextual information in generated models.
- **Advanced Gateways**: Enhancing BPMNGen to support additional BPMN 2.0 gateway types, such as event-based gateways, to improve the accuracy of decision modeling and process flow control.
- **Message Flows**: Extending the capabilities of BPMNGen to generate multi-pool BPMN 2.0 diagrams with message flows and choreography diagrams, enabling it to represent interactions between different process participants and external entities.

These improvements shall allow the (current) chatbot to generate more complex and realistic process models, making it more applicable for real-world BPM use cases. This leads to the third research question:

RQ3: How complete are BPMN 2.0 process models compared to the textually specified processes and the various aspects they cover?

4 Conclusion

This PhD research follows the Design Science Research Methodology (DSRM) to explore the potential of integrating NLP and LLM to facilitate business process modeling through conversational AI. BPMNGen, the proposed chatbot, aims to bridge the gap between non-experts in process modeling and BPMN 2.0 process modeling by enabling the generation and modification of process models using natural language input. Preliminary results demonstrate the feasibility of generating BPMN 2.0 process models from process descriptions. Nonetheless, further research is needed to improve the quality of BPMNGen, explore different prompting strategies, and extend its support for additional BPMN 2.0 elements to achieve a more effective and user-friendly business process modeling.

References

1. BPMN.io: Bpmn.js - the BPMN 2.0 viewer and modeler (2025). https://bpmn.io/toolkit/bpmn-js/. Accessed 02 Feb 2025
2. Brown, T., et al.: Language models are few-shot learners. Adv. Neural. Inf. Process. Syst. **33**, 1877–1901 (2020)
3. Fill, H.G., Fettke, P., Köpke, J.: Conceptual modeling and large language models: impressions from first experiments with chatgpt. Enterp. Model. Inf. Syst. Archit. (EMISAJ) **18**, 1–15 (2023)
4. Hörner, L.F., Reichert, M.: Generating process models by interacting with chatbots-a literature review. Future Internet **16**(10) (2024)
5. Kitchenham, B., et al.: Systematic literature reviews in software engineering-a tertiary study. Inf. Softw. Technol. **52**(8), 792–805 (2010)
6. Klievtsova, N., Benzin, J.V., Kampik, T., Mangler, J., Rinderle-Ma, S.: Conversational process modeling: can generative AI empower domain experts in creating and redesigning process models? arXiv preprint arXiv:2304.11065 (2023)
7. Klievtsova, N., Benzin, J.V., Kampik, T., Mangler, J., Rinderle-Ma, S.: Conversational process modelling: state of the art, applications, and implications in practice. In: International Conference on Business Process Management, pp. 319–336. Springer (2023)
8. Kourani, H., Berti, A., Schuster, D., van der Aalst, W.M.: Process modeling with large language models. In: International Conference on Business Process Modeling, Development and Support, pp. 229–244. Springer (2024)
9. Kourani, H., Berti, A., Schuster, D., van der Aalst, W.M.: Promoai: process modeling with generative AI. arXiv preprint arXiv:2403.04327 (2024)
10. Krogstie, J.: Sequal as a framework for understanding and assessing quality of models and modeling languages. In: Encyclopedia of Information Science and Technology, Third Edition, pp. 1611–1620. IGI Global (2015)
11. Krogstie, J., Krogstie, J.: Quality of Business Process Models. Springer (2016)
12. Liu, P., Yuan, W., Fu, J., Jiang, Z., Hayashi, H., Neubig, G.: Pre-train, prompt, and predict: a systematic survey of prompting methods in natural language processing. ACM Comput. Surv. **55**(9), 1–35 (2023)
13. Object Management Group (OMG): Business Process Model and Notation (BPMN) Version 2.0 (2011). https://www.omg.org/spec/BPMN/2.0/. Accessed 04 Feb 2025
14. Peffers, K., Tuunanen, T., Rothenberger, M.A., Chatterjee, S.: A design science research methodology for information systems research. J. Manag. Inf. Syst. **24**(3), 45–77 (2007)
15. Recker, J.: Opportunities and constraints: the current struggle with BPMN. Bus. Process. Manag. J. **16**(1), 181–201 (2010)
16. Wei, J., et al.: Chain-of-thought prompting elicits reasoning in large language models. Adv. Neural. Inf. Process. Syst. **35**, 24824–24837 (2022)
17. Zimoch, M., Pryss, R., Probst, T., Schlee, W., Reichert, M.: Cognitive insights into business process model comprehension: preliminary results for experienced and inexperienced individuals. In: Reinhartz-Berger, I., Gulden, J., Nurcan, S., Guédria, W., Bera, P. (eds.) BPMDS/EMMSAD -2017. LNBIP, vol. 287, pp. 137–152. Springer, Cham (2017). https://doi.org/10.1007/978-3-319-59466-8_9

Towards the Comprehensibility of Manually, Automatically, and Semi-automatically Created Process Models: A Conceptual Framework

Maximilian Möller(✉)

Institute of Databases and Information Systems, University of Ulm, Ulm, Germany
maximilian.moeller@uni-ulm.de

Abstract. The conversational generation of business process models with LLM-based chatbots offers promising perspectives for involving non-experts in process modeling. However, corresponding approaches will not be successful if the created models are of bad quality and, are therefore not comprehensible. While cognitive factors play a crucial role in the comprehension of process models, research on the specific factors that foster or affect the comprehensibility of process models created by humans, LLM-based bots, or a combination of them remains limited. This PhD research aims to systematically investigate the cognitive factors (e.g. perception, attention, memory, problem-solving, and metacognition) relevant in this context. Following the Design Science Research Methodology, this PhD research develops the conceptual framework *ComprehenGen*, which shall integrate the cognitive factors to systematically assess and provide guidelines for enhancing the comprehensibility of LLM-generated process models. The evaluation of this framework will incorporate methods from both cognitive neuroscience (e.g., eye tracking) and cognitive psychology (e.g., *Cognitive Load Theory*) to enable a comprehensive understanding of how humans process and interpret these models. Ultimately, this PhD research seeks to provide a structured approach to improve the comprehensibility of LLM-generated process models and their practical applicability in business process management.

Keywords: Process Model · BPMN 2.0 · Comprehensibility · Cognition · Chatbot · Large Language Model · Design Science Research

1 Introduction

The increasing availability of LLM-based chatbots to generate and iteratively refine conceptual models in general and process models in particular, raises questions about their cognitive impact on the comprehensibility of the generated models. Cognitive factors such as perception, attention & concentration, memory & knowledge representation, problem solving & decision making, language, emotion & motivation, and metacognition & self-regulation play a crucial role in understanding process models [5,9,16]. However, a systematic literature review (SLR) conducted in the context of this PhD research revealed that not all of these factors have been thoroughly examined in the context of human-created process models. Furthermore, the SLR by Hörner and Reichert [6] indicates that research on LLM-generated process models is still in its early stages, with only few LLM-based chatbots currently being capable of generating such models.

Building upon these findings, this PhD research investigates the cognitive factors that influence the comprehensibility of process models, which leads to the overarching research question **RQ0: Is it possible to generate comprehensible process models using an LLM?** In particular, how these factors shape the comprehensibility of process models depending on whether they are created manually by humans, automatically by LLM-based bots, or by a combination of both, will be investigated with **RQ1: How does the comprehensibility of LLM-generated process models differ from that of human-created process models?** Additionally, I aim to examine how prompting strategies can be leveraged to enhance the comprehensibility of LLM-generated process models – this research is expressed by **RQ2: How can prompting strategies enhance the comprehensibility of LLM-generated process models?**

To answer these research questions, the research follows the Design Science Research Methodology (DSRM) [12] and proposes the development of a conceptual framework called *ComprehenGen*. *ComprehenGen* aims to develop a set of guidelines based on the cognitive factors contributing to the comprehensibility of process models. In particular, the framework provides insights into how the comprehensibility of LLM-generated process models can be optimized.

The remainder of this paper is structured as follows: Sect. 2 presents the research methodology. Section 3 outlines the research approach, focusing on the development of *ComprehenGen*. Section 4 concludes the paper.

2 Methodology

This PhD research follows the Design Science Research Methodology (DSRM) [12], ensuring a structured and iterative approach for developing solutions and investigating the comprehensibility of LLM-generated process models. The research process is divided into four phases (cf. Fig. 1).

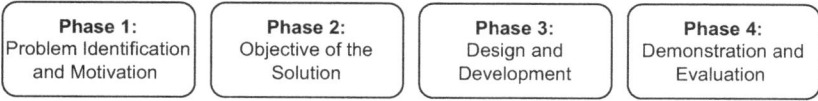

Fig. 1. Design Science Research Methodology

3 Research Approach

This section outlines the proposed solutions, addressing each phase in accordance with the PhD research approach (see Fig. 2).

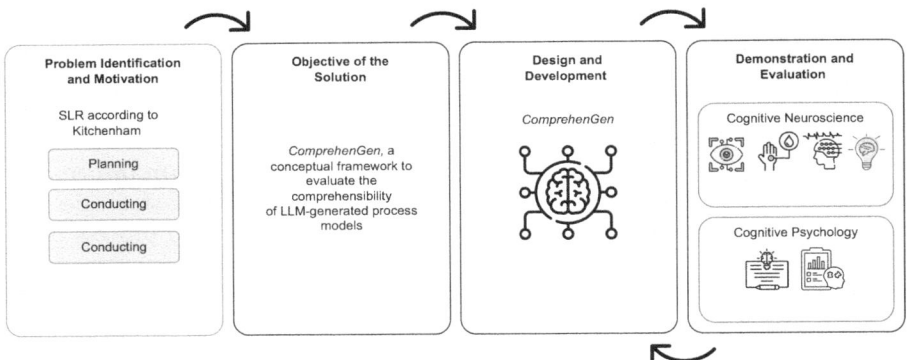

Fig. 2. PhD Research Approach

3.1 Problem Identification and Motivation

Process models play a crucial role in business process management and software engineering, serving as essential tools for representing and managing process models. Their effective use, however, depends on how well the various stakeholders (e.g., business analysts or domain experts) are able to comprehend these process models. Previous research has thoroughly examined a number of factors that shall foster the comprehension of process models [2], including, for example, the used process modeling notation [18,19] (e.g., BPMN 2.0), process model characteristics [1,4,13] (e.g., layout, complexity), and secondary notations [3,8,14] (e.g., colors).

A systematic literature review (SLR) [10] conducted in the context of this PhD research has revealed that cognitive factors in process model comprehension still remain underexplored.

While research on process model comprehensibility has primarily focused on purely human-created models, it remains unclear to what extent the same cognitive factors influence the comprehensibility of LLM-generated process models. Although it can be assumed that established frameworks for assessing comprehensibility also apply to LLM-generated models, this assumption has not yet been empirically validated. Existing studies on the use of LLM-based chatbots in Business Process Management (BPM) indicate that the generation of process models through natural language input constitute an emerging area of research [7,11]. The systematic literature review by Hörner & Reichert [6] explores the intersection of BPM and chatbot technologies, identifying approaches for text-to-model and model-to-text transformations. However, their findings indicate that research on LLM-based chatbots for process model generation is still evolving, with only a limited number of studies and implementations available.

Building on these findings, this PhD research is dedicated to investigate the cognitive factors influencing the comprehensibility of process models, and to utilize the resulting insights to allow for the generation of more comprehensible process models, regardless of whether they are human-created, bot-generated or human-bot-generated.

3.2 Objective of the Solution

The primary objective of this research is to develop *ComprehenGen*, a conceptual framework that aims to guide the generation of more comprehensible process models. As the core solution of the DSRM, *ComprehenGen* aims to provide structured guidelines, fostering the creation of better comprehensible process models.

3.3 Design and Development

The design and development of *ComprehenGen* is based on seven cognitive factors (cf. Fig. 3), which provide the foundation for systematically organizing the comprehensibility guidelines for generating better comprehensible process models, created manually by humans, automatically by LLM-based bots or semi-automatically by a combination of both. To systematically capture the cognitive factors influencing process model comprehension, *ComprehenGen* will be iteratively refined and extended through findings from empirical studies. Through this iterative process, *ComprehenGen* shall accumulate empirically validated guidelines, ensuring that its content is grounded on scientific evidence and is practically as well.

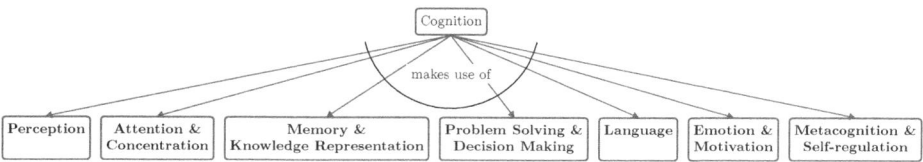

Fig. 3. Cognitive Factors on Process Model Comprehension

3.4 Demonstration and Evaluation

The demonstration and evaluation of ComprehenGen will be conducted through empirical studies to answer the overarching research question RQ0, i.e., whether it is possible to generate comprehensible process models using an LLM?

One crucial aspect, addressed in RQ1, concerns the investigation whether there is a difference in comprehending process models depending on how these models were created. The three groups considered in this investigation are ① models solely created by humans (with the use of a standard process modeling tool), ② models entirely generated by an LLM-based bot (i.e., without human interaction), and ③ hybrid models created by humans interacting with an LLM-based chatbot.

Another crucial aspect, addressed in RQ2, concerns the investigation of how different prompting strategies, which utilize insights into the cognitive factors considered by *ComprehenGen* might enhance the comprehensibility of LLM-generated process models (cf. RQ2).

The empirical studies conducted in the context of the above mentioned investigations are based on methodologies from cognitive neuroscience and cognitive psychology (see Fig. 4).

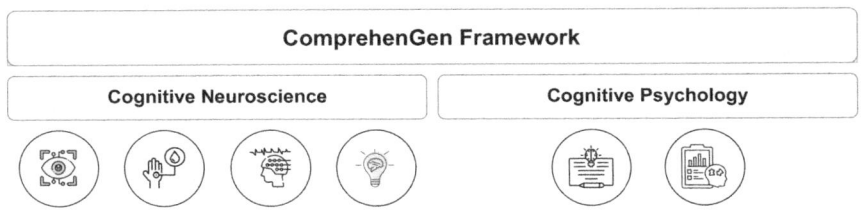

Fig. 4. *ComprehenGen* based on Empirical Studies

Cognitive neuroscience enables an objective evaluation of how the brain processes process models and how different modeling approaches impact comprehension during their reading. This can be measured using the following methods:

- **Eye Tracking**: Enables the analysis of visual attention distribution when interpreting process models [15]. Metrics such as fixation duration, saccadic movements, and heatmaps provide insights into how users navigate through models and on what their attention focuses. By comparing gaze patterns across human-created, bot-generated, and human-bot-generated models, this method helps to assess differences in the comprehensibility (RQ1) and evaluates how prompting strategies may influence the comprehensibility of the created models (RQ2).
- **Electrodermal Activity (EDA)**: Captures the physiological arousal by measuring changes in skin conductance, which serves as an indicator of cognitive load and emotional engagement [17]. Differences in arousal levels across different created models can reveal whether LLM-generated models impose higher cognitive load (RQ1), while variations in prompting strategies can indicate whether some approaches produce more comprehensible process models (RQ2).

- **Electroencephalography (EEG)**: Records brain activity to assess cognitive workload, attentional focus, and comprehension difficulty. EEG frequency analysis can determine whether LLM-generated models require more cognitive effort compared to human-created or hybrid models (RQ1) and whether different prompting strategies lead to variations in cognitive processing efficiency (RQ2).
- **Functional Magnetic Resonance Imaging (fMRI)**: Examines neural activation patterns to understand how different brain regions contribute to process model comprehension. Differences in brain activation between human-created, bot-generated, and human-bot-generated models can provide insights into their alignment with natural cognitive processing (RQ1), while variations based on prompting strategies can reveal whether certain input formulations facilitate better comprehension (RQ2).

In addition to cognitive neuroscience methods, established theories from cognitive psychology will be applied to assess how users process and comprehend process models.

- **Cognitive Load Theory**: Evaluates *intrinsic*, *extraneous*, and *germane* cognitive load to determine how effectively process models are comprehended. Comparing cognitive load across human-created, bot-generated, and human-bot-generated models helps to assess differences in comprehensibility (RQ1), while analyzing variations in cognitive load across different prompting strategies reveals their impact on human-bot-generated models (RQ2).
- **Cognitive Fit Theory**: Examines how well the representation of process models aligns with users' cognitive processing needs. Differences in cognitive fit between the three model types indicate their suitability for effective problem-solving (RQ1), while analyzing how different prompting strategies shape model clarity provides insights into optimizing process models (RQ2).
- **Technology Acceptance Model (TAM)**: Assesses user acceptance by measuring perceived ease of use and usefulness of process models. Evaluating TAM factors across human-created, bot-generated and human-bot-generated models highlights potential barriers to adoption (RQ1), while examining how prompting strategies influence perceived usability provides recommendations for improving human-bot-generated models (RQ2).
- **Think-Aloud Protocol**: Captures the real-time thought processes of users, the reasoning, and the metacognitive strategies while interpreting process models. Observing how users describe their difficulties with different model types helps to assess their comprehensibility (RQ1). Additionally, analyzing user feedback on human-bot-generated models with different prompting strategies provides insights into which approaches improve clarity and understanding (RQ2).

By integrating methodologies from both cognitive neuroscience and cognitive psychology, the empirical studies ensure a comprehensive assessment of process model comprehensibility across the three different groups and diverse prompting strategies.

4 Conclusion

This PhD research aims to evaluate and enhance the comprehensibility of bot-generated and human-bot-generated process models by systematically investigating the cognitive factors. While previous studies have explored cognitive aspects in human-created process models, the impact of these factors on bot-generated and human-bot-generated models remains underexplored. By following the Design Science Research Methodology, this work introduces *ComprehenGen*, a conceptual framework designed to evaluate and enhance the comprehensibility of the process models created by the three different groups.

To achieve this, the PhD research aims to apply empirical studies using methodologies from cognitive neuroscience (e.g., eye tracking) and cognitive psychology (e.g., *Cognitive Load Theory*).

Ultimately, this research contributes to the broader field of Business Process Management by providing structured guidelines in the *ComprehenGen* framework to improve the comprehensibility of bot-generated and human-bot-generated process models. By bridging the gap between cognitive science and LLM-based process modeling, this work paves the way for more comprehensible and better process modeling.

Acknowledgments. I would like to thank the supervisor of this work, Prof. Manfred Reichert, for his support and review on this paper.

Compliance with Ethical Standards
Disclosure of Interests. The authors have no competing interests to declare that are relevant to the content of this article.

References

1. Bernstein, V., Soffer, P.: How Does it look? exploring meaningful layout features of process models. In: Persson, A., Stirna, J. (eds.) CAiSE 2015. LNBIP, vol. 215, pp. 81–86. Springer, Cham (2015). https://doi.org/10.1007/978-3-319-19243-7_7
2. Figl, K.: Comprehension of procedural visual business process models: a literature review. Business Inform. Syst. Eng. **59**, 41–67 (2017)
3. Figl, K., Mendling, J., Strembeck, M.: The influence of notational deficiencies on process model comprehension. J. Assoc. Inf. Syst. **14**(6), 1 (2013)
4. Figl, K., Recker, J., Mendling, J.: A study on the effects of routing symbol design on process model comprehension. Decis. Support Syst. **54**(2), 1104–1118 (2013)
5. Franceschetti, M., Abbad-Andaloussi, A., Schreiber, C., López, H.A., Weber, B.: Exploring the cognitive effects of ambiguity in process models. In: International Conference on Business Process Management, pp. 493–510. Springer (2024)
6. Hörner, L.F., Reichert, M.: Generating process models by interacting with chatbots-a literature review. Future Internet **16**(10) (2024)
7. Klievtsova, N., Benzin, J.V., Kampik, T., Mangler, J., Rinderle-Ma, S.: Conversational process modeling: Can generative ai empower domain experts in creating and redesigning process models? arXiv preprint arXiv:2304.11065 (2023)

8. Kummer, T.F., Recker, J., Mendling, J.: Enhancing understandability of process models through cultural-dependent color adjustments. Decis. Support Syst. **87**, 1–12 (2016)
9. Mandelburger, M.M., Mendling, J.: Cognitive diagram understanding and task performance in systems analysis and design. MIS Q. **45**(4), 2101–2157 (2021)
10. Möller, M., Winter, M., Reichert, M.: Cognitive factors in process model comprehension-a systematic literature review. Authorea Preprints
11. Nour Eldin, A., Assy, N., Anesini, O., Dalmas, B., Gaaloul, W.: Nala2bpmn: Automating bpmn model generation with large language models. In: International Conference on Cooperative Information Systems, pp. 398–404. Springer (2024)
12. Peffers, K., Tuunanen, T., Rothenberger, M.A., Chatterjee, S.: A design science research methodology for information systems research. J. Manag. Inf. Syst. **24**(3), 45–77 (2007)
13. Petrusel, R., Mendling, J., Reijers, H.A.: How visual cognition influences process model comprehension. Decis. Support Syst. **96**, 1–16 (2017)
14. Reijers, H.A., Freytag, T., Mendling, J., Eckleder, A.: Syntax highlighting in business process models. Decis. Support Syst. **51**(3), 339–349 (2011)
15. Winter, M., Neumann, H., Pryss, R., Probst, T., Reichert, M.: Defining gaze patterns for process model literacy-exploring visual routines in process models with diverse mappings. Expert Syst. Appl. **213**, 119217 (2023)
16. Winter, M., Pryss, R., Probst, T., Baß, J., Reichert, M.: Measuring the cognitive complexity in the comprehension of modular process models. IEEE Trans. Cogn. Develop. Syst. **14**(1), 164–180 (2020)
17. Winter, M., Pryss, R., Probst, T., Reichert, M.: Towards the applicability of measuring the electrodermal activity in the context of process model comprehension: Feasibility study. Sensors **20**(16), 4561 (2020)
18. Zimoch, M., Mohring, T., Pryss, R., Probst, T., Schlee, W., Reichert, M.: Using insights from cognitive neuroscience to investigate the effects of event-driven process chains on process model comprehension. In: Business Process Management Workshops: BPM 2017 International Workshops, Barcelona, Spain, September 10-11, 2017, Revised Papers 15 pp. 446–459. Springer (2018)
19. Zimoch, M., Pryss, R., Schobel, J., Reichert, M.: Eye Tracking experiments on process model comprehension: lessons learned. In: Reinhartz-Berger, I., Gulden, J., Nurcan, S., Guédria, W., Bera, P. (eds.) BPMDS/EMMSAD -2017. LNBIP, vol. 287, pp. 153–168. Springer, Cham (2017). https://doi.org/10.1007/978-3-319-59466-8_10

CAiSE 2025 Doctoral Consortium – Software Engineering

Generation of User Interfaces for Different Context of Use from Conceptual Models

Susel María Matos Claro[1,2](✉)

[1] University of Holguin, XX Anniversary, 80100 Holguin, Cuba
smatosc@uho.edu.cu
[2] KU Leuven, Naamsestraat 69, 3000 Leuven, Belgium
suselmaria.matosclaro@kuleuven.be

Abstract. User Interfaces (UIs) are the first point of interaction between humans and systems. Effective UI design can reduce errors, enhance task efficiency, and provide an enjoyable user experience. However, current software development cycles often prioritize technical requirements over user experience, leading to UIs that are functional but not intuitive. Model-Driven Engineering (MDE) is a well-known approach to automate the development of UIs. However, most of the solutions found are not capable of generating UIs for diverse contexts of use or taking in considerations diverse types of user or their needs. This article proposes an overview of a PhD research project that is motivated by this limitation. To address the lack of user and context adaptation, we propose to combine an explicit user model, context model and presentation model with application models (such as the class diagram, state charts, etc.). To demonstrate the effectiveness of the approach, a proof of concept will be developed based on the tools associated to the MERODE methodology.

Keywords: User Interfaces · Model-Driven Engineering · Context of Use · Conceptual Model · Accessibility

1 Introduction

User interfaces (UIs) serve as the primary point of interaction between humans and technology, playing a pivotal role in shaping user perceptions and overall experiences. Well-designed UIs can minimize errors, enhance task efficiency, and deliver a satisfying user experience. However, the development of UIs is a time-intensive process, often consuming nearly half of the total time within the software development lifecycle. Frequently, developers prioritize technical requirements over user experience, resulting in UIs that, while functional, lack intuitiveness and usability [1, 2].

In today's context, software and UIs are no longer confined to a single environment or user group. Software is an integral part of our daily lives and must be universally accessible. In accordance with the principle of "Leave No One Behind"[1] as set out in

---
[1] https://unsdg.un.org/2030-agenda/universal-values/leave-no-one-behind.

the Sustainable Development Goals (SDGs) of the 2030 Agenda of the United Nations (UN), the software industry must align its practices with this objective. The overarching ambition is to eradicate all forms of discrimination, exclusion and reduce inequality in all aspects of society. Therefore, diverse contexts, including varying environments, user types, domain applications, and platforms, must be considered from the initial stages of the software development process. Consequently, developing UIs that adapt to multiple contexts of use has become even more resource- and time-intensive [3, 4].

Over the past decades, Model-Driven Engineering (MDE) has gained prominence as a strategy to accelerate software production. This approach emphasizes the creation and use of platform independent models to automate the generation of code, configurations, and other artifacts, thereby reducing manual effort while enhancing consistency and productivity. From an MDE perspective, models can encapsulate critical information about UI characteristics, behaviours, and layouts, and can potentially reduce inherent complexity and decrease the effort required for UI development [5, 6].

An alternative approach with considerable potential to accelerate software development is the adoption of Low-Code/No-Code (LCNC) platforms. These tools allow application creation through models, drag-and-drop components, and configuration-based logic, significantly reducing or eliminating traditional coding. LCNC platforms enable non-technical users, or citizen developers, to build functional applications, decreasing reliance on professional programmers. A defining feature of these tools, and a major driver of their increasing adoption, is their capacity to streamline the rapid development, deployment, and iteration of applications [7–9].

Leveraging the advantages of MDE, numerous modelling tools have emerged, including commercial tools such as Mendix[2] and open source tools such as the Eclipse Modeling Framework[3]. These tools enable the modelling of problems and the subsequent generation of corresponding code. Among these, MERODE represents an MDE approach specifically tailored for developing enterprise information systems and the didactic support of modelling education. MERODE is supported by a tool called Merlin for facilitates the modelling of system characteristics and behaviours, ensuring a robust structure and functionality for business logic. Additionally, a Code Generator is included, capable of producing software prototypes in the form of Java desktop applications. This allows the testing of functionalities and logic modelled in Merlin before the full implementation of the application. This approach offers the possibility of implementing other models to obtain more flexibles and usable UIs [10, 11].

The research undertaken is based on the following problem definition: "How to improve the automatic generation of UIs for different context of use from conceptual models with the ultimate goal to accelerate software development, enhance UI quality, and reduce costs?". The motivation behind this PhD research is to investigate the development of accessible and multi-context UIs through MDE. The goal is to enable the generation of fully functional applications featuring adaptable UIs that can be tailored to different contexts of use while incorporating user preferences, including users with disabilities and special needs. To validate the proposal, an implementation of the solution

---

[2] www.mendix.com.

[3] www.eclipse.dev/modeling/emf/.

in the MERODE tool kit will be made to extend its capabilities beyond prototyping, and it will be tested in two case studies.

This paper is structured as follows: Sect. 2 reviews the state of art of UI generation and identifies existing gaps and important limitations found in the literature; Sect. 3 discusses problem, motivation, objective, demonstration and evaluation of the research proposal; Sect. 4 presents the research planning for the PhD.

2 State of Art

Before embarking on a research endeavour, it is essential to conduct a thorough investigation of the state of the art in the relevant field. One of the most effective methods for achieving this is through the execution of a Systematic Literature Review (SLR). For this research, we have adhered to the guidelines proposed by [12]. The primary objective of this review was to identify existing gaps and limitations in the literature that could be addressed through our research.

To systematically search for scientific papers, we utilized the Scopus database, which contains over 90 million records and covers a wide range of specialized databases and meta-databases such as Web of Science [13]. The keywords and search strings were formulated based on the research questions.

The initial search in the Scopus database yielded 690 documents. After applying inclusion and exclusion criteria, a set of 94 papers was obtained. From this initial set of papers, two additional inclusion criteria were applied to categorize the papers into two distinct group as shows Fig. 1. The first group focused on MDE-based methods for the generation of UIs tailored to different contexts of use, and resulted in the identification of 11 papers. The second group concentrated on LCNC tools designed for the same purpose, leading to the identification of 3 papers. The complete selection process is illustrated in Fig. 1, and some interesting findings are detailed below.

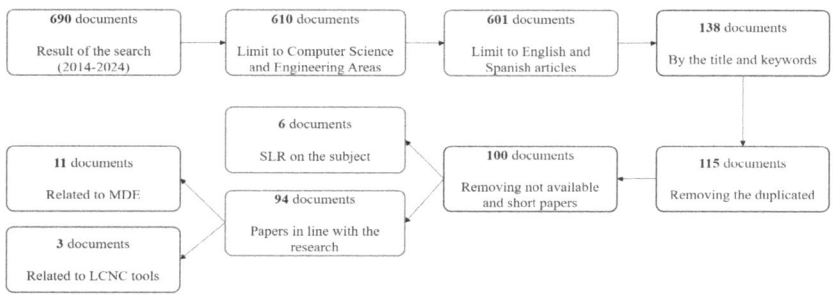

Fig. 1. Steps and activities in the reviewing process

In [14] an MDE-based approach for generating adaptable UIs with a focus on accessibility contexts is proposed. This approach relies on metamodel transformations and is demonstrated through a case study that illustrates its effectiveness in supporting UI adaptation for blind users. Another MDE approach for UI adaptation, specifically addressing accessibility contexts, is proposed in [15]. This approach is structured into four steps, with meta-model transformations based on mapping and adaptation. The study includes an empirical evaluation of the usability using the case of visually impaired users. Additionally, [16] introduces the Adaptive User Interface to Accessibility Context framework that employs a sequential and layered transformation process from Platform-Independent Models (PIM) to Platform-Specific Models (PSM), supported by adaptive transformation rules tailored to specific disabilities and interaction modalities. Furthermore, [17] introduces OSTRICH, a strongly typed rich templating language designed for the OutSystems low-code platform. OSTRICH leverages metamodel annotations to enable the correct instantiation of templates for different platforms.

The SLR[4] identified key limitations in MDE-based UI generation. While numerous solutions exist, few address the challenges of diverse contexts of use, such as variations in platforms, environments, and domain applications, highlighting a significant research gap. Additionally, the literature insufficiently considers diverse user types, including differences in age, disabilities, experience levels, and preferences. Moreover, current MDE models often overlook critical design and layout aspects, such as element positioning, font type, alignment, color, and visual hierarchy, hindering the creation of flexible, intuitive, and navigable UIs.

LCNC tools are widely acknowledged for enabling individuals with minimal or no software development experience to create functional, multiplatform applications. However, existing literature and practical experience highlight notable limitations. A significant drawback is vendor lock-in, as changes or disruptions to the platform can heavily impact the developed software. Additionally, LCNC tools often restrict developers' control over the source code, a limitation exacerbated by the commercial nature of many platforms, which may require payment for access or essential features.

3 Research Proposal

The PhD proposal follows the Design Science Research Methodology proposed in [18], a recognised framework for conducting design science research in the field of information systems. The objective is to incorporate the principles, practices and procedures necessary to conduct design research. The steps that guide the research are shown in Fig. 2 and explained specifically for this research below.

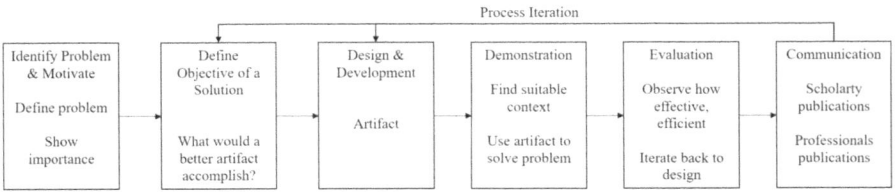

Fig. 2. DSRM Process Model as proposed in [18]

---

[4] The full SLR has been submitted as paper to EMMSAD 2025.

Identify the Problem and Motivation

The development of UIs is a complex and time-consuming process that is frequently not integrated into software development from the initial stages. The development of UIs capable of adapting to different contexts of use or taking into consideration user preferences and needs as well as environmental factors is an even more challenging process. The proposed research is based on the following problem definition: "How to improve the automatic generation of UIs for different context of use from conceptual models with the ultimate goal to accelerate software development, enhance UI quality, and reduce costs?".

Beside the main problem of the investigation, this proposal is guide by the following Research Questions (RQ):

RQ1: What are the main limitations on MDE and LCNC approaches in the generation of adaptative and flexible UIs?

RQ2: How can presentation, context and user models be integrated in the MERODE toolkit to enhance UIs usability and quality of UIs?

RQ3: What impact would the implementation of the presentation, context and user model in MERODE toolkit have on the rapid software production and the education of software developers?

Define Objective of a Solution

The objectives of this research is, firstly, to develop the necessary methods and proof-of-concept tools allowing to develop software with higher levels of usability and flexibility, considering different contexts of use. The relevance of this research is motivated by both a cost perspective and sustainable development goals. From the cost perspective, the implementation of the proposed solution has the potential to enhance the agility of software production, leading to substantial savings in time and resources dedicated to the development of quality software. From the sustainable development goal perspective, the research is motivated by the importance of adaptability in UI design for software success and better user experience for all (leave no one behind). Design principles and guidelines for including different types of users according to diverse disabilities, demographic factors and personal expertise will be considered, and will allow to support diversity and achieve better equality.

Design and Development

Some of the existing model-based approaches for UI design make use of user models besides task, dialog, presentation and domain models, but never use all models, and the user models do not always capture context [19]. To achieve the required broader coverage to deal with different contexts of use, the initial design of the solution will involve the definition of three new platform independent models that can be combined with application models to generate code.

The *presentation model* will be dedicated to the technological aspects of the UI, with the purpose of defining the organisation and display of information. Its function is to facilitate the creation of reusable components that can be combined in different ways to adapt to various designs, while ensuring visual and functional coherence across all elements of the UI.

The *user model* will be designed to address the human aspects of the UI, capturing user characteristics, skills, and preferences to customise the interface to individual needs. It should include the definition of profiles based on demographic characteristics (age, gender), technical skills (beginner, advanced), and preferences (light/dark mode, font size). Furthermore, it should consider accessibility requirements, such as support for users with visual, hearing, or motor disabilities.

The *context model* will be designed to defines the environment within which the application is utilised, encompassing physical, social and technological factors with the capacity to exert influence on the UI design. In order to optimise the user experience, it is imperative that these factors are given due consideration, including but not limited to location (indoor/outdoor), lighting and ambient noise. Furthermore, it is essential to ascertain the nature of the task being performed by the user (e.g. work, entertainment, education) in order to facilitate a targeted and personalised interface design.

Demonstration and Evaluation

In order to test the proposal, it is necessary to implement a MDE UI-generation environment and use it in practice. We aim for two case studies in a real software production environment in order to verify the possible advantages of applying the solution. The first case study will re-implement an existent software and compare the results of the UI satisfaction of both software versions. The second case study aims to compare the development time, developer's perceived usability and end-user's usability by developing a new software both in the traditional way and making use of the MDE UI-generation environment. The implementation of the latter will be based on the MERODE toolkit: the tools already allow to generate code from a domain model, and a proof of concept of presentation models has already been developed. It thus provides a sound base to start from. Figure 3 illustrates the operational dynamics of Merlin and the Code Generator indicating the additions with a red box.

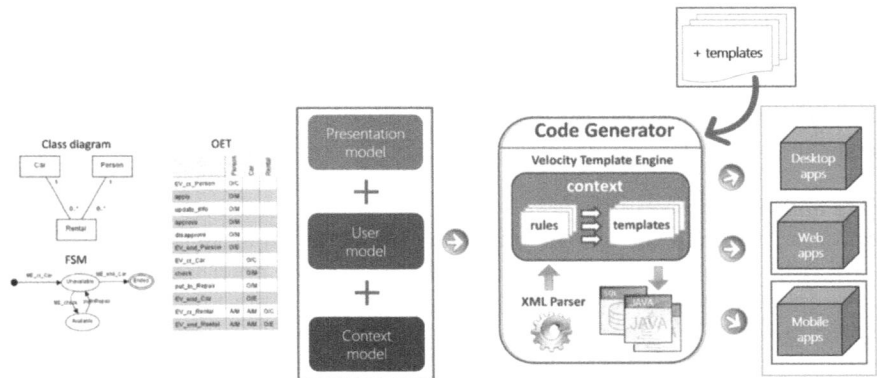

Fig. 3. Model and function of Merlin and Code Generator with the proposed improvement (Color figure online)

In addition to the case studies, the MDE-UI generation tool will also be used to train bachelor's and master's students, who will be the future software developers. The use of the artefact in the educational context is expected to facilitate student comprehension of the significance of developing UIs that cater to a diverse range of users and their diverse needs. Furthermore, it is anticipated that the solution will promote awareness among students of the pivotal role that UIs play in the success of software applications. This awareness is to be cultivated from the outset of the software development process.

4 Research Planning

The present PhD research is divided into three phases, with a duration of one year each.

First Year: in the initial (ongoing) year, the focus is on defining and designing the foundations for the entire research project. A significant activity in this year has been the investigation of the current state of the art of generating UIs in the contexts of MDE and LCNC tools. This study has enabled the identification of existing gaps and limitations in the field, which this research aims to address.

Second Year: will be devoted to designing and implementing an initial version of the three new models in Merlin and the Code Generator. This will also require designing templates and components for the generation of UI for different contexts of use, following design principles and guidelines for each environment or platform.

Third Year: following the development and implementation of the proof of concept of the solution, the final stage of the PhD process will entail the testing and evaluation of the proposal. As previously mentioned, the plan is to implement two case studies in a real software production environment and to introduce them to bachelor's and master's students. The evaluation process will allow for the validation of the developed solution, and all feedback received will be used to improve it.

References

1. Paternò, F.: Concepts and design space for a better understanding of multi-device user interfaces. Univers. Access. Inf. Soc. **19**(2), 409–432 (2020)
2. Abrahão, S., Insfran, E., Sluÿters, A., Vanderdonckt, J.: Model-based intelligent user interface adaptation: challenges and future directions. Softw. Syst. Model. **20**(5), 1335–1349 (2021)
3. Yigitbas, E., Sauer, S., Engels, G.: Adapt-UI: an IDE supporting model-driven development of self-adaptive UIs. In: Proceedings of the ACM SIGCHI Symposium on Engineering Interactive Computing Systems, EICS 2017, pp. 99–104. Association for Computing Machinery, Inc., June 2017
4. Zouhaier, L., Hlaoui, Y.B., Ben Ayed, L.J.: Generating accessible multimodal user interfaces using MDA-based adaptation approach. In: Proceedings - International Computer Software and Applications Conference, pp. 535–540. IEEE Computer Society, September 2014. https://doi.org/10.1109/COMPSAC.2014.76
5. Brambilla, M., Cabot, J., Wimmer, M.: Model-Driven Software Engineering in Practice, 2nd edn. (2017)
6. Roubi, S., Erramdani, M., Mbarki, S.: Generating graphical user interfaces based on model driven engineering. Int. Rev. Comput. Softw. (IRECOS) **10**(5), 520–528 (2015)

7. Bucaioni, A., Cicchetti, A., Ciccozzi, F.: Modelling in low-code development: a multi-vocal systematic review. Softw. Syst. Model. **21**(5), 1959–1981 (2022). https://doi.org/10.1007/s10270-021-00964-0
8. Ajimati, M.O., Carroll, N., Maher, M.: Adoption of low-code and no-code development: a systematic literature review and future research agenda. J. Syst. Softw. **222** (2025)
9. Hagel, N., Hili, N., Schwab, D.: Turning low-code development platforms into true no-code with LLMs. In: Proceedings: MODELS 2024 - ACM/IEEE 27th International Conference on Model Driven Engineering Languages and Systems: Companion Proceedings, pp. 876–885. Association for Computing Machinery, Inc., October 2024. https://doi.org/10.1145/3652620.3688334
10. Snoeck, M.: Enterprise Information Systems Engineering. The MERODE Approach. Springer, Cham (2014). https://doi.org/10.1007/978-3-319-10145-3
11. Ruiz, J., Asensio, E.S., Snoeck, M.: Learning UI functional design principles through simulation with Feedback. IEEE Trans. Learn. Technol. **13**(4), 833–846 (2020)
12. Kitchenham, B., Charters, S.M.: Guidelines for performing systematic literature reviews in software engineering (2007). https://www.researchgate.net/publication/302924724
13. Deeva, G., Bogdanova, D., Serral, E., Snoeck, M., De Weerdt, J.: A review of automated feedback systems for learners: classification framework, challenges and opportunities. Comput. Educ. **162** (2021)
14. Zouhaier, L., Hlaoui, Y.B., Ayed, L.J.B.: Methodology for the development of accessible user interfaces based on meta-model transformations: the case of blind users. In: Saeed, K., Homenda, W., Chaki, R. (eds.) CISIM 2017. LNCS, vol. 10244, pp. 73–84. Springer, Cham (2017). https://doi.org/10.1007/978-3-319-59105-6_7
15. Bendaly Hlaoui, Y., Zouhaier, L., Ben Ayed, L.: Model driven approach for adapting user interfaces to the context of accessibility: case of visually impaired users. J. Multimodal User Interfaces (2019)
16. Zouhaier, L., BenDalyHlaoui, Y., Ben Ayed, L.: Adaptive user interface based on accessibility context. Multimed. Tools Appl. **82**(23), 35621–35650 (2023). https://doi.org/10.1007/s11042-023-14390-5
17. Lourenço, H., Ferreira, C., Costa Seco, J., Parreira, J.: OSTRICH: a rich template language for low-code development (extended version). Softw. Syst. Model. **22**(5), 1645–1663 (2023)
18. Peffers, K., Tuunanen, T., Rothenberger, M.A., Chatterjee, S.: A design science research methodology for information systems research. J. Manag. Inf. Syst. **24**(3), 45–77 (2007)
19. Ruiz, J., Serral, E., Snoeck, M.: Evaluating user interface generation approaches: model-based versus model-driven development. Softw. Syst. Model. **18**(4), 2753–2776 (2019). https://doi.org/10.1007/s10270-018-0698-x

Adopting Large Language Models to Automated System Integration

Robin D. Pesl

University of Stuttgart, Stuttgart, Germany
robin.pesl@iaas.uni-stuttgart.de

Abstract. Modern enterprise computing systems integrate numerous subsystems to resolve a common task by yielding emergent behavior. A widespread approach is using services implemented with Web technologies like REST or OpenAPI, which offer an interaction mechanism and service documentation standard, respectively. Each service represents a specific business functionality, allowing encapsulation and easier maintenance. Despite the reduced maintenance costs on an individual service level, increased integration complexity arises. Consequently, automated service composition approaches have arisen to mitigate this issue. Nevertheless, these approaches have not achieved high acceptance in practice due to their reliance on complex formal modeling. Within this Ph.D. thesis, we analyze the application of Large Language Models (LLMs) to automatically integrate the services based on a natural language input. The result is a reusable service composition, e.g., as program code. While not always generating entirely correct results, the result can still be helpful by providing integration engineers with a close approximation of a suitable solution, which requires little effort to become operational. Our research involves (i) introducing a software architecture for automated service composition using LLMs, (ii) analyzing Retrieval Augmented Generation (RAG) for service discovery, (iii) proposing a novel natural language query-based benchmark for service discovery, and (iv) extending the benchmark to complete service composition scenarios. We have presented our software architecture as Compositio Prompto, the analysis of RAG for service discovery, and submitted a proposal for the service discovery benchmark. Open topics are primarily the extension of the service discovery benchmark to service composition scenarios and the improvements of the service composition generation, e.g., using fine-tuning or LLM agents.

Keywords: Service composition · Service discovery · Large language models · OpenAPI

1 Introduction

Automated service composition describes the emergence of combining multiple services to a composite service [10]. Automating this process yields the advantages of reduced manual effort, faster time-to-market, and agile adoption to changed business needs, resulting in an overall strategic benefit for the company. An example would be an automotive vendor wanting to integrate roadside services like parking spot booking. An automated approach allows for the integration of services that are not available during design time without further manual development effort.

Previous approaches to automated service composition rely on formal models, always producing correct results while requiring extensive manual modeling. With the advent of Large Language Models (LLMs), it has become feasible to process natural language queries and semi-structured documentation automatically, i.e., formal and natural language parts, while considering syntax and semantics. Employing LLMs for automated service composition could mitigate the issue of complex formal modeling by allowing developers to express their requirements in natural language while generating a code recommendation fully automatically.

This leads to our overarching research question:

How well can LLMs be employed for automated service composition?

The remainder of the paper is structured as follows. In Sect. 2, we give an overview of the current literature regarding service composition in Information System Engineering (ISE) and Service-Oriented Computing (SOC) and the application of LLMs for service compositions. Then, we state our research methodology in Sect. 3. In Sect. 4, we clarify our contributions. Section 5 shows what we already achieved. We elaborate on our planned work in Sect. 6 and conclude with Sect. 7.

2 State of the Art

We provide a short literature overview to motivate the topic's relevancy and explain the current state of the art. This includes a brief description of classical service composition approaches, the subfield of service discovery, its relevance for ISE, and initial ideas to apply LLMs in SOC.

2.1 Service Composition

Automated service composition has been a field of research in ISE and SOC for more than two decades. While ISE mainly focuses on its positioning in automating parts of the requirement engineering process to reduce workload and decrease time-to-market [4,8,32], SOC concentrates on its technical implementation [10]. This contains aspects like *component access, conversation management, control flow, dataflow,* and *data transformation* [10]. While there was initially high creativity in creating solution approaches, the research slowed down. Nevertheless, there is still a lack of a comprehensive, viable solution.

Famous classical approaches rely on AI planning, which computes a plan, i.e., a sequence, of service invocations based on formal modeling of the service and the composition requirements. These approaches can be domain-specific [27] or domain-independent [12]. Further approaches rely on finite state automata to model the service interaction known as the "Roman model" [3,6]. While always producing correct results, these classical approaches require laborious and erroneous formal modeling, leading to brittle solutions and low application in practice.

In contrast, services are often documented using a semi-structured OpenAPI specification [17] in JSON or YAML. It consists of general information about the service, like name or host, and the endpoints, i.e., the APIs that offer the actual functionality. The endpoint specification again contains natural language elements like a description and structured elements like input and output schemas. Our approach relies on OpenAPI specifications for implementations as these are the state of practice.

A subfield of automated service composition is service discovery, which identifies relevant services within a potentially vast set of all available services. Initial ideas concentrate on centralized registries across vendors implement, e.g., in the Universal Description, Discovery, and Integration (UDDI) specification [5]. These share the same drawbacks of requiring extensive laborious manual modeling and opposing workload reduction efforts.

More recent approaches try to leverage already present OpenAPI documentation [28]. In our work, we analyze the application of Retrieval Augmented Generation (RAG) with OpenAPI to realize service discovery to allow automated natural language processing, sidestepping any manual effort.

The relevancy of service composition and service discovery is backed by a long list of literature in the ISE community, e.g., [1,2,8,9,13,18,30,32]. It enables steering system design, streamlining development, dynamic system changes, reduced manual labor, increased scalability, avoids human-induced errors, and allows agil reactions to changed business needs. Often, it is considered as part of the requirement engineering process [8,13,32], e.g., using ontologies [18] or formal models [30]. Domains include Smart Cities [2] or cloud computing [9]. Recent implementations also support OpenAPI specifications [1]. Our work contributes to this knowledge corpus by analyzing how LLMs can be applied to the problem.

2.2 LLMs for Automated Service Composition

LLMs achieve remarkable results in natural language understanding, processing, and generation. Initial ideas adopt an encoder-decoder architecture [25]. Newer approaches use a decoder-only approach for text generation [26] and encoder-only (embedding) models for similarity computation [7].

Within SOC, we proposed initial concepts of using LLMs for service composition. These still face the issues of input token limitations, imperfect results, and hallucinations [20,23,24].

Another approach to integrating LLMs with services (tools) is LLM agents. These incorporate tool invocations into the chat interaction [14,16,31]. While facing similar problems like tool/service selection, the main difference to service composition is that the result of service composition is an executable, reusable artifact, e.g., as code. In contrast, LLM agents invoke the tools directly during the answer creation [24].

A significant problem is the lack of appropriate benchmarks. Although some initial proposals like RestBench [29] exist, a general benchmark across numerous domains is still missing. We add to this by introducing generalized benchmarks.

3 Research Method

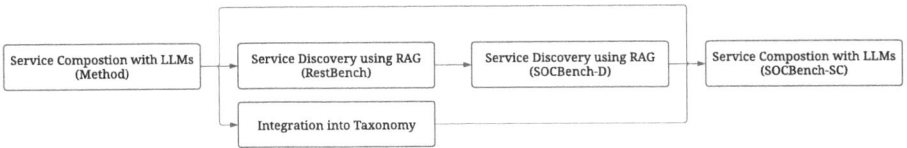

Fig. 1. Research Methodology

Figure 1 shows our research methodology from left to right. The first item is a general software architecture, i.e., a method to employ LLMs for automated service compositions. Using this architecture, we can implement a prototype and measure the performance and implications of the approach.

Next, we look into the literature and analyze how to classify our method in the existing taxonomy of Lemos, Daniel, and Benatallah [10] and how the taxonomy needs to be extended. In parallel, we examine service documentation chunking, i.e., extracting the most relevant parts to allow using RAG for service discovery. This allows us to mitigate prompt input token limitations. We evaluate the RAG chunking approaches first by employing the exiting RestBench benchmark [29], then by introducing our custom SOCBench-D benchmark generalized across all domains of the Global Industry Classification Standard (GICS) [15].

Finally, we bridge the gap between service discovery and our software architecture by creating a benchmark comprising services based on the GICS domains, measuring the end-to-end performance from prompt to final service composition. Further experiments could contain user studies to measure the time-saving of employing LLMs versus manual labor or applying LLM agents to improve reasoning.

4 Contributions

Following our research methodology from Fig. 1, we introduce four contributions. The contributions are as follows:

1. The Compositio Prompto software architecture.
2. Our extension to Lemos' taxonomy, which results in an extended taxonomy.
3. The service discovery using RAG. This comprises the analysis of RAG using the existing RestBench [29] and the creation of the SOCBench-D benchmark. The resulting artifacts are a query-based service discovery benchmark and an algorithm that can dynamically create such a benchmark.
4. The SOCBench-SC service composition benchmark. It contains the analysis of current LLMs, the benchmark itself, and the benchmark creation algorithm.

5 Preliminary Results

We already worked on the method, the taxonomy, and the service discovery with RAG. Open points are in the full service composition and subsequent studies.

5.1 Compositio Prompto

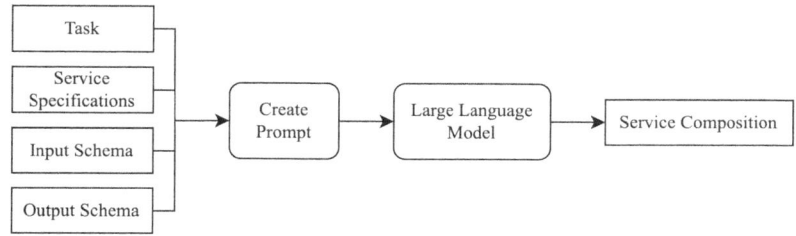

Fig. 2. Compositio Prompto Architecture [24]

First, we introduce our architecture "Compositio Prompto" to employ LLMs for automated service composition shown in Fig. 2 [24]. It uses a task, service documentation, and an in- and output schema as input to create a prompt. The prompt is then fed into the LLM, creating an executable service composition.

To evaluate Compositio Prompto, we implemented a fully operation prototype and performed a case study from the automotive domain. Our prototype uses a natural language query as a task, OpenAPI specifications as service documentation, JSON schemas as in- and output schemas, and Python code for the executable service composition. The results show that currently, only large models with more than 70B parameters can solve at least some tasks perfectly. Nevertheless, even small models like Llama 3 8B produce close approximations of our manually crated sample solution. Therefore, we conclude that current LLMs can be used to create a code recommendation that only needs little adaption, i.e., working time, to become operational. Further research is needed to achieve full automation.

5.2 Extended Taxonomy

To analyze whether service composition with LLMs can already be expressed using the well-known taxonomy of Lemos, Daniel, and Benatallah [10], we examine for each category if it already covers the LLM capabilities adequately. The result is an extended taxonomy, which comprises the additional subcategories needed to include the LLM capabilities in natural language understanding, semantic processing, and text generation [19] (submitted).

We validated our taxonomy extension using four existing LLM-based approaches for service composition from literature. They show that each introduced new subcategory is indeed necessary. Limitations are primarily in the original methodology, which only includes taxonomy elements that stem from actual service composition approaches. Further extensions may be necessary once novel service composition approaches arise.

5.3 OpenAPI RAG

The Compositio Prompto experiments highlight the challenge of the limited input token length of LLMs. It leads to only being able to input parts of the service documentation. An example is that the OpenAPI of Spotify alone does not fit into the context size of OpenAI's GPT4o, leaving alone inputting additional services. A technique to mitigate this issue is RAG, which splits the input data into smaller chunks. The RAG system performs a semantic search using an embedding model based on these chunks and inserts the most relevant chunks into the prompt. The benefit is that the inserted chunks are much smaller than the complete input data while revealing only the most relevant information [11].

We apply RAG to service discovery to determine the influence of the model and chunking strategy [21] (to appear). We rely on the RestBench benchmark [29], which consists of the Spotify and TMDB OpenAPI specification and pairs of natural queries with expected endpoints. Our results show that it is beneficial to split the OpenAPI by endpoints [21].

Nonetheless, the lack of general benchmarks arises. Therefore, we extended our evaluation further by introducing the novel service discovery benchmark SOCBench-D, which generalizes across the GICS domains [22] (submitted). We execute it using OpenAI's *text-embedding-3-large*, Nvidia's *NV-Embed-v2*, and BGE's *bge-small-en-v1.5*. Our results show that the choice of the chunking strategy is insignificant across all domains. The number of received chunks is particularly relevant to the overall performance. The second factor is the embedding model. The Nvidia model outperforms the OpenAI model, which outperforms the BGE model. Nonetheless, the BGE model reveals reasonable results. In practice, this leads to the consideration that when resources are sparse, the BGE model can be used; when familiar with the OpenAI tooling, the OpenAI model can be used; and when interested in the best results, the Nvidia model can be employed.

6 Future Work

Our next research effort will comprise the analysis of complete service compositions incorporating the RAG-based service discovery. The basic idea is to use a query-based service discovery benchmark like RestBench or SOCBench-D and extend it to code analysis. This can be done by static code analysis, unit test-like testing, or creating custom mock instances of the services and tracking invocations. The optimal approach has still to be determined. The result is a benchmark for natural language service composition approaches, generalized across the GICS domains.

Further, we want to measure actual implications on development time savings, sustainability aspects, and advanced approaches like LLM agents. These allow logical reasoning, which may reduce hallucinations and improve the composition quality.

7 Concluding Remarks

With this Ph.D. thesis, we want to analyze the potential of employing LLMs for the well-known yet unresolved problem of automated service composition. We introduced the Compostio Prompto architecture to realize automated service composition with LLMs in practice. Further, we examined the usage of RAG for service discovery first by using the real-world RestBench benchmark and then by our cross-domain SOCBench-D benchmark. Next, we will create a benchmark for general service composition cases and analyze how well current LLMs perform. Other open points are the improvement of the result generation, e.g., by employing LLM agents, and the analysis of applicability in practice, e.g., by performing a user study.

Acknowledgments. I want to thank my supervisor, Prof. Dr. Marco Aiello, for his ongoing support throughout my Ph.D. journey.

Disclosure of Interests. The author is listed as inventors of a patent [20], which covers Compositio Prompto for the automotive domain.

References

1. Apostolakis, I., Mainas, N., Petrakis, E.G.: Simple querying service for OpenAPI descriptions with semantic extensions. Inf. Syst. **117**, 102241 (2023)
2. Ben-Sassi, N., et al.: Service discovery and composition in smart cities. In: Information Systems in the Big Data Era, pp. 39–48. Springer (2018)
3. Berardi, D., et al.: Automatic composition of E-services that export their behavior. In: ICSOC, pp. 43–58 (2003)
4. Bianchini, D., et al.: Ontology-based methodology for e-service discovery. Inf. Syst. **31**(4), 361–380 (2006)
5. Curbera, F., et al.: Unraveling the web services web: An introduction to SOAP, WSDL, and UDDI. IEEE Internet Comput. **6**(2), 86–93 (2002)
6. De Giacomo, G., Patrizi, F., Sardiña, S.: Automatic behavior composition synthesis. Artif. Intell. **196**, 106–142 (2013)
7. Devlin, J., Chang, M.W., Lee, K., Toutanova, K.: BERT: Pre-training of deep bidirectional transformers for language understanding. In: NAACL-HLT 2019, pp. 4171–4186 (2019)
8. Dourdas, N., et al.: Discovering remote software services that satisfy requirements: Patterns for query reformulation. In: CAiSE, pp. 239–254. Springer Berlin Heidelberg, Berlin, Heidelberg (2006). https://doi.org/10.1007/11767138_17
9. Jerbi, I., et al.: Request relaxation based-on provider constraints for a capability-based naas services discovery. In: CAiSE, pp. 611–627. Springer (2023)
10. Lemos, A.L., Daniel, F., Benatallah, B.: Web service composition: A survey of techniques and tools. ACM Comput. Surv. **48**(3) (dec 2015)

11. Lewis, P., et al.: Retrieval-augmented generation for knowledge-intensive NLP tasks. In: NeurIPS. vol. 33, pp. 9459–9474. Curran Associates (2020)
12. McDermott, D.V.: Estimated-regression planning for interactions with web services. In: AIPS, pp. 204–211. AAAI (2002)
13. Mehandjiev, N., Lécué, F., Carpenter, M., Rabhi, F.A.: Cooperative service composition. In: CAiSE pp. 111–126. Springer (2012)
14. Mialon, G., et al.: Augmented language models: a survey (2023). https://arxiv.org/abs/2302.07842
15. MSCI Inc., Standard & Poor's: Global industry classification standard (GICS). https://www.msci.com/gics (August 2024)
16. OpenAI: Function calling and other API updates (Jun 2024). https://openai.com/index/function-calling-and-other-api-updates/. Accessed 18 July 2024
17. OpenAPI Initiative: OpenAPI specification. https://www.openapis.org/ (2021), version 3.1.0. Accessed 15 Mar 2025
18. Oriol, X., Teniente, E.: An ontology-based framework for describing discoverable data services. In: CAiSE, pp. 220–235. Springer, Cham (2018)
19. Pesl, R.D., Aiello, M.: Revisiting Lemos' taxonomy for service compositions with large language models. In: ICWS (2025), submitted
20. Pesl, R.D., Klein, K., Aiello, M.: Verfahren zur Nutzung von unbekannten neuen Systemdiensten in einer Fahrzeuganwendung (2024), Patent DE102024108126A1
21. Pesl, R.D., Mathew, J.G., Mecella, M., Aiello, M.: Advanced system integration: Analyzing OpenAPI chunking for retrieval-augmented generation. In: CAiSE (2025). https://arxiv.org/abs/2411.19804, to appear
22. Pesl, R.D., Mathew, J.G., Mecella, M., Aiello, M.: Retrieval-augmented generation for service discovery: Chunking strategies and benchmarking. TSC (2025), submitted
23. Pesl, R.D., Stötzner, M., Georgievski, I., Aiello, M.: Uncovering LLMs for service-composition: Challenges and opportunities. In: ICSOC 2023 WS. Springer (2024)
24. Pesl, R.D., et al.: Compositio Prompto: An architecture to employ large language models in automated service computing. In: ICSOC 2024, pp. 276–286. Springer (2025)
25. Radford, A., et al.: Better language models and their implications. OpenAI blog **1**(2) (2019). https://openai.com/index/better-language-models/. Accessed 28 Nov 2024
26. Radford, A., et al.: Improving language understanding by generative pre-training (2018)
27. Sheshagiri, M., DesJardins, M., Finin, T.: A planner for composing services described in DAML-S. In: 13th ICAPS WS on planning for Web services (2003)
28. Soki, A.T., Siqueira, F.: Discovery of RESTful Web services based on the OpenAPI 3.0 standard with semantic annotations. In: AINA, pp. 22–34. Springer (2024)
29. Song, Y., et al.: RestGPT: Connecting large language models with real-world RESTful APIs (2023). https://arxiv.org/abs/2306.06624
30. Wang, H.H., et al.: A formal model of the semantic web service ontology (WSMO). Inf. Syst. **37**(1), 33–60 (2012)
31. Yao, S., et al.: React: Synergizing reasoning and acting in language models (2023), https://arxiv.org/abs/2210.03629
32. Zachos, K., et al.: Discovering web services to specify more complete system requirements. In: CAiSE, pp. 142–157. Springer (2007)

Bridging Agile Software Development and Modeling

Yaimara Granados Hondares(✉)

Central University of Las Villas, Camajuaní Km 5 1/5, Santa Clara, Villa Clara, Cuba
ygranados@uclv.edu.cu

Abstract. While Agile Software Development (ASD) has been embraced by software development teams and helps them to focus on customer value, ASD also faces challenges related to requirements changes and technical debt. While conceptual models may help to mitigate this challenges, conceptual modelling is not a common Agile practices. As practitioners recognize the importance of conceptual models for enhancing requirement understanding, their ability to represent different aspects of software (data, functional, behavior), and the effectiveness of domain-driven development in agile environments, we propose to develop a framework to integrate the practice of conceptual modelling in ASD as a solution to the main challenges that ASD faces: requirements management and technical debt. The research follows the Design Science Research framework from Peffers respecting the seven guidelines proposed by Hevner. This is a research project that is still in the beginning stages. We are providing a summary of the first result from the project's first phase.

Keywords: Agile Software Development · ASD · Conceptual Models · ASD Challenges

1 Introduction

Software development is a multidisciplinary process that has a major impact on every sector of society. Software is constantly evolving and focuses on solving problems of all kinds, motivated by the efficiency of processes, the optimization of resources and the proximity of services to the people [1]. As software evolves, so does the way it is built. The field of software engineering research is very rich in studies aimed at making the development process more efficient, focusing on the rapid and valuable delivery of products, as well as their quality [2–5]. In this sense, the challenges are growing exponentially, and by responding to the demands of speed, quality, and adaptability, new approaches to software development have emerged. One such approach, that has become a dominant force in the industry, is Agile Software Development (ASD). ASD promotes team autonomy, leadership, the continuous delivery of valuable increments, efficient management of changing requirements [6], and replacement of extensive documentation with lightweight but sufficient documentation. In addition, agile emphasizes face-to-face communication, fostering collaboration and rapid problem-solving. This agile transformation represents a cultural shift toward adaptability, collaboration, and innovation across multiple domains [7].

Despite their many benefits, agile methods face challenges that are well documented in the literature. Two recurring issues stand out: requirements management, as balancing evolving requirements with project schedule and scope can be complex, and technical debt, as the emphasis on rapid delivery sometimes leads to shortcuts in code quality, that can accumulate and cause long-term problems [8, 9]. These challenges highlight the need for complementary approaches, such as conceptual modelling (CM), to address these challenges and improve outcomes in agile development.

Numerous studies have identified and described the challenges of ASD, and some have proposed solutions. Among these solutions, we find the use of tools such as Natural Language Processing (NLP) to improve the quality and format of requirements (mainly formulated as user stories), as well as the creation of conceptual models (CMs) to optimize the communication and understanding of user stories [5, 10, 11].

However, while user stories are the primary requirements artifact used in agile development, they serve different purposes and operate at different levels of abstraction compared to CMs. They are user-centric and focus on system behavior, while CMs focus on the structure of the domain and provide a long-term view of the domain, creating a gap between CMs and ASD. This gap raises fundamental questions about how to integrate them effectively without compromising agile principles.

In the context of software development, CMs are abstract representations of a system or domain that help to understand and communicate its structure, behavior and relationships. They can be graphical, such as class diagrams, flowcharts, or entity-relationship diagrams, textual, or a combination of graphics and text. Their main purpose is to capture and express the essence of the problem, and to help the team share a common understanding. According to [12], "A model is a selective, simplified, and structured form of knowledge. An appropriate model makes sense of information and focuses it on a problem". Conceptual models improve the understanding of the domain problem, help to structure the software design, promote requirements agreement, and are considered to provide a common language between stakeholders and the development team. It is also true that CMs can add additional complexity to the software process due to a high learning curve and the need for model maintenance. Therefore, considering the strengths and challenges of ASD and the benefits and threats of CMs, we define the research problem as follows: *How can modelling and agile software development be reconciled to address the challenges of requirements and technical debt, while respecting agile values and principles?*

Works such as "*Domain-driven design*"[12], and research that investigates using CMs in ASD as a possible solution to requirements engineering challenges [13] are examples of integrating the use of conceptual model into agile software processes. However, there remains a practical gap and a lack of real evidence on how effective the use of models can be in agile development. Therefore, the specific objective of the present research is: "*Develop a framework to integrate CMs in Agile Software Development, with the goal of evaluating the practical impact*".

The remainder of the paper is structured as follows: Sect. 2 describes the project's organization according to Design Science Research Frameworks. Section 3 describes the preliminary results so far. Section 4 concludes with some general insights.

2 Design Science Research Methodology

2.1 General Methodology

The design of this research follows the guidelines of Design Science Research (DSR), combining Hevner's and Peffers's frameworks. From Hevner we took as a patterns the seven guidelines [14] and research positioning of the research in the contribution framework [15]. Peffers proposes an iterative methodology to structure the research as a process [16]. The integration of these frameworks ensures that the research is scientifically rigorous and has practical impact, achieving the proposed objectives both in terms of academic knowledge and solving real world problems.

Peffers defines six iterative phases in the DSR methodology: problem identification and motivation, definition of objectives for a solution, design and development, demonstration, evaluation, and communication. In our research, the central problem addresses the persistent challenges in ASD, particularly those related to evolving requirements and technical debt, and how conceptual models (CMs) can be leveraged to mitigate them. Understanding the current perceptions and practices of industry professionals regarding the use of CMs reinforces both the motivation and relevance of this study.

The initial phase focuses on identifying and characterizing these challenges through focus groups with practitioners and a review of existing literature. Concurrently, this phase includes the selection or adaptation of modeling techniques and supporting components to be integrated into the proposed framework. The design and development phase will begin with the synthesis of prior research and empirical data to define key elements and guide the construction of a preliminary version of the framework. Subsequent phases will adopt an iterative approach. The framework will be applied in a real-world, controlled setting to enable demonstration and refinement based on feedback and observations. A comprehensive evaluation will follow, using both formative and summative methods, supported by quantitative and qualitative metrics. Finally, the results and contributions will be communicated through academic and practitioner-oriented channels, ensuring both theoretical impact and practical relevance.

According to the framework proposed by Hevner [14], this research is positioned in the "Improvement" quadrant, characterized by high application maturity and low solution maturity. While it may not fully fit the concept of a "new solution to a known problem", it is important to note that the greatest impact of the solution lies in selecting elements from existing frameworks and unifying the most impactful ones, which can be considered a new solution. Regarding the "known problem", we identify the challenges currently faced in ASD, in particular requirements management and technical debt. However, the proposed solution may also address additional challenges that require further analysis.

The knowledge contribution comes from the development of a framework for using CMs in a way that is compatible with agile practices. We will also provide guidelines and best practices for integrating CMs into agile workflows, resulting in academic contribution with new insights and methods applied in academia.

2.2 Problem Identification and Motivation

Given the iterative development process and potentially expanding scope inherent in ASD, requirements management and technical debt accumulation are significant challenges. The initial phase of this research is dedicated to fully understanding these challenges through the following research questions:

RQ1: What is the current perception of ASD professionals regarding CMs?
RQ2: What factors influence the willingness of agile teams to adopt conceptual modeling practices?
RQ3: How can conceptual modeling techniques be systematically mapped to specific agile challenges?
RQ4: What are the existing components that could be leveraged or extended to support CMs in ASD?
RQ5: How does the proposed framework improve key agile outcomes such as requirements clarity, communication, productivity, maintainability, and technical debt management?

To answer RQ1 and RQ2, a mixed-methods approach is proposed: an initial survey of agile practitioners has been conducted (see Sect. 3) and a series of focus groups are planned to gather rich, context-sensitive insights. For RQ3 and RQ4 a systematic literature review combined with bibliometric analysis will be conducted to identify existing research on the use of CM in ASD, including networks of authorship and relevant modeling components. The goal is to map agile development problems to suitable modeling approaches and identify gaps in current practice. Based on these insights, the research aims to design and validate a model-driven framework tailored to agile environments (RQ5). This framework will offer guidance for selecting and applying conceptual models aligned with specific agile challenges.

As expected contributions, we plan to provide:

A classification of ASD problems based on empirical data from focus groups.
A mapping between agile challenges and suitable CM-based solutions.
A structured model-driven framework adaptable to agile contexts.
A case study validation within a deployed software project.
Empirical evidence on the impact of conceptual modeling in agile practices.

2.3 Design, Development and Iterative Validation

To answer RQ3 and RQ4, the intended artifact, a "Unified Framework to bridging ASD-CM", will be developed. The framework will propose a list of CM practices that can be combined with agile practices with the goal of addressing and resolving ASD challenges. The framework may take a shape similar to the subway map of agile practices[1] or to the interactive map of SAFe[2].

An initial version of the framework will be developed based on literature. To further develop and validate the framework we propose two main projects.

---

[1] https://www.agilealliance.org/agile101/subway-map-to-agile-practices/.
[2] https://framework.scaledagile.com/.

First we will conduct a case study based on a deployed and operational project, developed according to ASD process. The first step is to characterize the context of the project's development, taking into account specific aspects such as the working methodology, as well as cultural and social factors that may influence the results. The tasks to be performed are to elicit and update functional requirements through reverse engineering and interviews, critically analyze the existing schema using conceptual modeling techniques, identify potential improvements in the models that support better alignment with quality. The study of the project aims to identify areas of risk and improvement (technical debt) in the project. A retrospective analysis will investigate if and how the risks and threats could have been mitigated through CM practices identified in literature or other CM practices. We expect to obtain a critical analysis of the potential benefits of the systematic use of CMs, and valid information on what kind of model or combination could be introduced in the agile workflow, measuring its impact on technical debt and agile values. These identified opportunities for CM (combinations) will be used to adjust the initial version of the framework.

A second project will be an action research, based on an early development project, also from Cuban software industry. The objective is to study the integration of the use of the framework's suggested CM practices in the agile development process in real time. The expected outcome is an evaluation of the perceived and actual effectiveness of using the suggested CM practices to manage requirements and reduce technical debt, as well as the willingness of agile practitioners to use them. This outcome will be used to develop a third improved version of the framework.

2.4 Demonstration and Evaluation

The designed framework (version 3) will be validated in two different contexts. The formative evaluation will be based on expert feedback sessions with agile and modeling specialists, focus group feedback during iterative cycles and walkthroughs using example scenarios and models to assess usability. The summative evaluation will focus on measuring the impact of the framework deployment through the application of quantitative and qualitative metrics (Table 1). This evaluation phase will be iterative, and post-release feedback will be integrated to refine the core framework (version 4, final version).

3 Preliminary Results

3.1 Design of a Practitioners' Survey

As a first step to explore and motivate the research problem in more detail, we designed a questionnaire to investigate software industry professionals' perceptions of CM (RQ1) and the factors that influence their willingness to use modelling (RQ2). The survey design was based on the Technology Acceptance Model (TAM) and the Unified Theory of Acceptance for Use of Technology version 2 (UTAUT2). The purpose of this study is to explore practitioners' perceptions of the use and creation of CMs in contemporary

Table 1. Dimensions and metrics to evaluate the proposed framework

Dimension	Metrics	Observations
Requirements Completeness	% of validated functional requirements	Measures how modeling helps in uncovering missing features
Requirements Volatility	Changes per sprint or release	A decline would show modeling supports better requirement clarity
Developer Productivity	Story points completed/iteration	Agile metrics, reflect model-supported task execution
Model Usefulness	Likert-scale responses from developers	Based on TAM; captures perceived value of models
Documentation Quality	Checklist	
	Readability	Evaluates clarity and usefulness of generated documentation
	Satisfaction Survey	

software development, specifically in ASD. Th results of this survey will allow us to answer to RQ1 and RQ2 as defined in Sect. 2[3].

The design instrument includes questions around the constructs: habit, enjoyment, ease of use, usefulness, social influence and intention to use. Social influence represents the environmental characteristics that can change behavior and attitude. This construct is analyzed according to external elements such as the opinions of colleagues, company policy and the vision of the project manager. The analysis of motivation to comply provides insights on what is more influential in taking action to use models in software development. On the other hand we designed the questions related to usefulness along three perspectives: 1) Addressing the ASD challenge of "requirements management"; 2) Addressing the ASD challenge of "technical debt": assessing the impact on software quality such as design and architecture improvements, and 3) Addressing the impact on agile delivery: assessing the alignment with agile values and principles.

This survey allows for the assessment of perceptions about CMs in the context of ASD challenges, specifically those related to requirements, technical debt and agility. Participant demographics were also collected, including age, country, and gender, as well as information on company size, software development experience, and client/team characteristics.

---

[3] A full report of this research is submitted as paper to EMMSAD 2025.

3.2 Results of Conducted Survey

A total of 88 valid responses were received from participants from different regions of the world. Of these, 57.3% were from Cuba, 14.6% from the United States, 13.5% from Belgium, and smaller contributions came from countries such as Canada, Mexico, Uruguay, Ecuador, Iran, Germany, and Chile. The sample is characterized by the participants' involvement in software development. A significant 96.62% of them hold roles such as project manager (42%), software developer (52%), software architect (20%), software analyst (33%), software tester (12%). In all cases, participants manifest that they play multiple roles. In addition, the sample highlights the frequent use of agile approaches, with 93.3% of the participants using such methodologies. Scrum is used by 70% of respondents, establishing it as the dominant software development methodology. Conversely, the Rational Unified Process (RUP) is used by 6.8% of respondents.

Although CM is not one of the recommended agile practices, the perceived usefulness of CM amongst practitioners (RQ1) is high: about 90% of participants believe that CMs are important for software development. In addition, there is a high agreement about the positive impact of models on understanding requirement and better software quality and design. Conversely, there is more disagreement about a positive impact on rapid delivery and agile practices. Considering the willingness to use (RQ2), the study revealed that habit, ease of use, and usefulness are the most influential factors in the adoption of conceptual models. In terms of social influence, company policy and peer opinion can influence the intention to use conceptual models.

4 Conclusion

This research proposes a structured, model-driven framework for integrating CM into ASD, addressing key challenges such as requirements and technical debt. Grounded in design science research, this research aims to provide both theoretical and practical contributions. The main result achieved so far are the results from the a survey that explores the perception of CM use among ASD practitioners. Initial results indicate a positive attitude, confirming the motivation and direction of the research. Future work includes framework design, and two case studies: one retrospective and one action research. These will guide iterative refinement and allow evaluation of the relevance and adaptability of the framework in different organizational and cultural settings.

Acknowledgments. This research is funded by the VLIRUOS TEAM-project "Capacity building for the Cuban software industry's use of Model-Driven Engineering" (CU2024TEA542A101).

References

1. Khan, H.U., et al.: Revolutionizing software developmental processes by utilizing continuous software approaches. J. Supercomput. **80**(7), 9579–9608 (2024). https://doi.org/10.1007/s11227-023-05818-8
2. Mornie, M.N., Jali, N., Junaini, S.N., Mit, E., Shiang, C.W., Saee, S.: Visualisation of user stories in UML models: a systematic literature review. Prague Univ. Econ. Bus. (2023). https://doi.org/10.18267/j.aip.212

3. Umar, M.A., Lano, K.: Advances in automated support for requirements engineering: a systematic literature review. Requir. Eng. **29**(2), 177–207 (2024). https://doi.org/10.1007/s00766-023-00411-0
4. Guerrero-Calvache, M., Hernández, G.: Team productivity factors in agile software development: an exploratory survey with practitioners. In: Florez, H., Leon, M. (eds.) ICAI 2023. CCIS, vol. 1874, pp. 261–276. Springer, Cham (2024). https://doi.org/10.1007/978-3-031-46813-1_18
5. Gunes, T., Aydemir, F.B.: Automated goal model extraction from user stories using NLP. In: Proceedings of the IEEE International Conference on Requirements Engineering, pp. 382–387. IEEE Computer Society, August 2020. https://doi.org/10.1109/RE48521.2020.00052
6. Beck, K.: Manifesto for agile software development (2001). Accessed 16 Dec 2024. https://agilemanifesto.org/
7. Al-Saqqa, S., Sawalha, S., Abdelnabi, H.: Agile software development: methodologies and trends. Int. J. Interact. Mob. Technol. **14**(11), 246–270 (2020). https://doi.org/10.3991/ijim.v14i11.13269
8. Fissalma, H., Ferdinansyah, A., Purwandari, B.: Investigating challenges in Agile software development: a cross-country comparative analysis. Int. J. Electr. Comput. Eng. **15**(1), 855–869 (2025). https://doi.org/10.11591/ijece.v15i1.pp855-869
9. Dias Canedo, E., et al.: On the Challenges to Documenting Requirements in Agile Software Development: A Practitioners' Perspective (2024). https://www.google.com/forms
10. Georges, T., Rice, L., Huchard, M., König, M., Nebut, C., Tibermacine, C.: Guiding feature models synthesis from user-stories: an exploratory approach. In: ACM International Conference Proceeding Series, pp. 65–70 (2023). https://doi.org/10.1145/3571788.3571797
11. Tsilionis, K., Amna, A.R., Heng, S., Poelmans, S., Poels, G.: Controlled experiments on user stories' modeling: past, present, and future. In: CEUR Workshop Proceedings, pp. 27–32 (2022)
12. Evans, E.: Domain-Driven Design: Tackling Complexity in the Heart of Software. Addison-Wesley Professional (2004)
13. Gupta, A., Poels, G., Bera, P.: Using conceptual models in Agile software development: a possible solution to requirements engineering challenges in agile projects. IEEE Access **10**, 119745–119766 (2022). https://doi.org/10.1109/ACCESS.2022.3221428
14. Hevner, A.R., March, S.T., Park, J., Ram, S.: Design science in information systems research. MIS Q., 75–105 (2004)
15. Gregor, S., Hevner, A.R.: Positioning and presenting design science research for maximum impact. MIS Q., 337–355 (2013)
16. Peffers, K., Tuunanen, T., Rothenberger, M.A., Chatterjee, S.: A design science research methodology for information systems research. J. Manag. Inf. Syst. **24**(3), 45–77 (2007). https://doi.org/10.2753/MIS0742-1222240302

Correction to: Pondering on Capability Brokering with LLM

Jelena Zdravkovic, Janis Stirna, and Chen Hsi Tsai

Correction to:
Chapter 20 in: L. Pufahl et al. (Eds.): *Intelligent Information Systems*, **LNBIP 557, https://doi.org/10.1007/978-3-031-94590-8_20**

In the originally published version of chapter 20, there was a spelling error in the last name of the first author. This has been corrected.

The updated version of this chapter can be found at
https://doi.org/10.1007/978-3-031-94590-8_20

© The Author(s), under exclusive license to Springer Nature Switzerland AG 2025
L. Pufahl et al. (Eds.): CAiSE 2025, LNBIP 557, p. C1, 2025.
https://doi.org/10.1007/978-3-031-94590-8_39

Author Index

A

Alfonso, Iván 3
Alter, Steven 12
Antipenko, Vjatšeslav 267
Armas Cervantes, Abel 62
Ayite, Komlan 145

B

Barret, Nelly 20
Barthe-Delanoë, Anne-Marie 145
Beecks, Christian 103
Bemthuis, Rob H. 29
Bénaben, Frédérick 145
Bernasconi, Anna 20
Bork, Dominik 145
Buchmann, Robert Andrei 45
Buss, Alina 37

C

Cabot, Jordi 3
Calvanese, Diego 137
Cappiello, Cinzia 20
Casciani, Angelo 277
Chiş, Andrei 239
Chiş, Andrei 45
Conrardy, Aaron 3
Corradini, Flavio 53

D

Dalskov, Anders 197
De Michele, William 62
Decker, Stefan 103
Deshmukh, Rohit A. 103
Devroey, Xavier 205
Di Ciccio, Claudio 173
Díaz, Oscar 70
Ding, Yuntian 78

E

Engelberg, Gal 86
Eshuis, Rik 119

F

Famelis, Michalis 153
Franch, Xavier 213
Frermann, Lea 62
Friolo, Daniele 173

G

Garmendia, Xabier 70
Ghasemi, Arsalan 189
Ghiran, Ana-Maria 45
Gill, Asif Qumer 95
Granados Hondares, Yaimara 321
Graß, Alexander 103
Guizzardi, Giancarlo 137

H

Hadad, Moshe 86
Herbaut, Nicolas 78
Hörner, Luca Franziska 286
Horsfield, Martin 70

J

Jalali, Amin 111

K

Kecht, Christoph 37
Khayatbashi, Shahrzad 111
König, Maximilian 189
Körner, Maximilian 189
Kratsch, Wolfgang 37
Kryston, Michele 173
Kulkarni, Vinay 128

L

Laurenzi, Emanuele 181
Lichtenstein, Tom 189
López, Lidia 213

M

Macé-Ramète, Guillaume 145
Marangone, Edoardo 173
Matos Claro, Susel María 305
Meroni, Giovanni 119, 197
Miri, Najmeh 111
Möller, Maximilian 294

N

Nemmi, Eugenio Nerio 173
Nguyen, Guillaume 205
Nikiforova, Anastasija 95
Norta, Alex 197

O

Oriol, Marc 213

P

Palu, Giacomo 20
Pesl, Robin D. 313
Pettinari, Sara 53
Pinoli, Pietro 20
Portell, Xavier 249

R

Rajbhoj, Asha 128
Re, Barbara 53
Röglinger, Maximilian 37
Romanenko, Elena 137
Rossi, Lorenzo 53

S

Sadeghianasl, Sareh 37
Salinesi, Camille 78
Samory, Mattia 173
Sampaolo, Massimiliano 53
Sant, Tanay 128
Sarr, Lala Aïcha 145
Schoonderbeek, Jan 223
Seidel, Anjo 189
Severin, Sefanja 231
Soffer, Pnina 86
Somase, Akanksha 128
Spina, Michele 173
Stirna, Janis 161
Syriani, Eugene 153

T

Tsai, Chen Hsi 161

V

Vale, Sushant 128
Venturi, Daniele 173

W

Weber, Ingo 173
Weske, Mathias 189
Wyffels, Mathis 257
Wynn, Moe T. 37

X

Xu, Huihui 213

Z

Zaheri, MohammadAmin 153
Zdravkovic, Jelena 161

The manufacturer's authorised representative in the EU is Springer Nature Customer Service Centre GmbH, Europaplatz 3, 69115 Heidelberg, Germany. If you have any concerns regarding our products, please contact ProductSafety@springernature.com

Printed and bound by CPI Group (UK) Ltd, Croydon, CR0 4YY

26/03/2026

02078952-0010